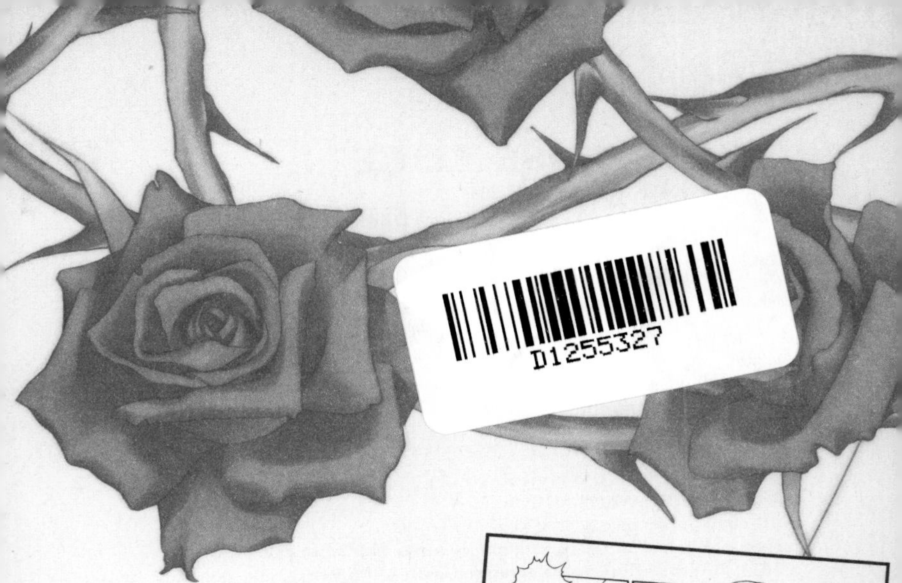

This is the last page.

In keeping with the original Japanese comic format, this book reads from right to left—so action, sound effects, and word balloons are completely reversed. This preserves the orientation of the original artwork—plus, it's fun! Check out the diagram shown here to get the hang of things, and then turn to the other side of the book to get started!

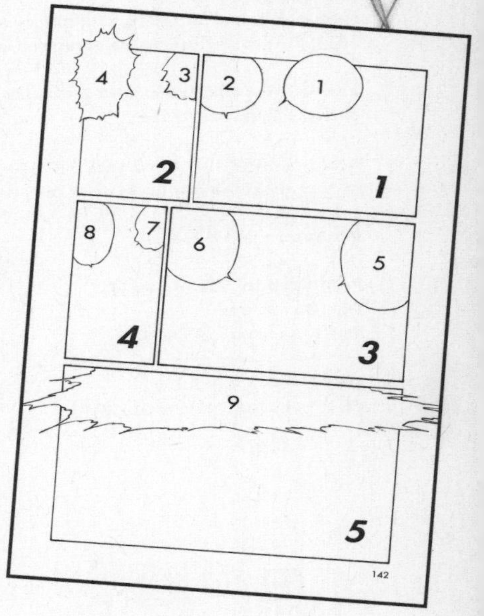
1
2
1
3
4
2
5
6
3
7
8
4
9
5
142

BLACK ROSE ALICE
VOLUME 2
Shojo Beat Edition

STORY AND ART BY
Setona Mizushiro

English Translation & Adaptation/John Werry
Touch-up Art & Lettering/Evan Waldinger
Design/Yukiko Whitley
Editor/Pancha Diaz

BLACK ROSE ALICE Volume 2
© 2009 SETONA MIZUSHIRO
All rights reserved.
First published in Japan in 2009 by Akita Publishing Co., Ltd., Tokyo
English translation rights arranged with Akita Publishing Co., Ltd.

Printed in the U.S.A.

Published by VIZ Media, LLC
P.O. Box 77010
San Francisco, CA 94107

10 9 8 7 6 5 4 3 2 1
First printing, November 2014

www.viz.com

www.shojobeat.com

Black Rose ALICE

Black Rose ALICE

2

Story & Art by
Setona Mizushiro

Characters & Story

Dimitri
A tenor vocalist. After an accident, he became a vampire.

Leo

Kai & Reiji

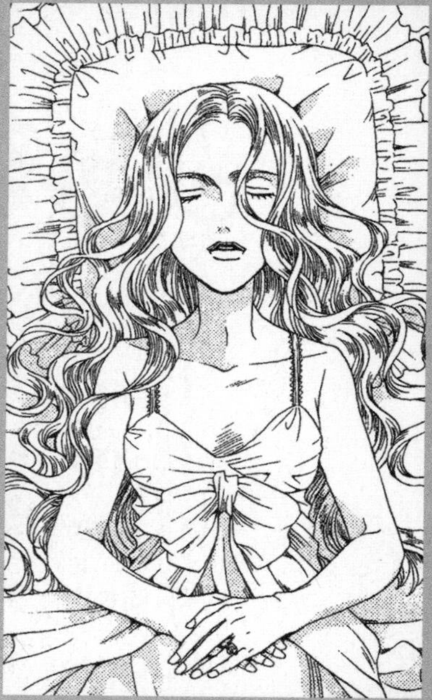

Agnieszka

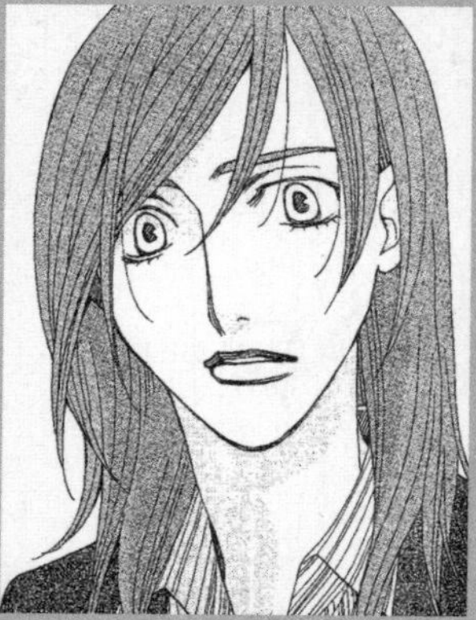

Azusa
Kikukawa

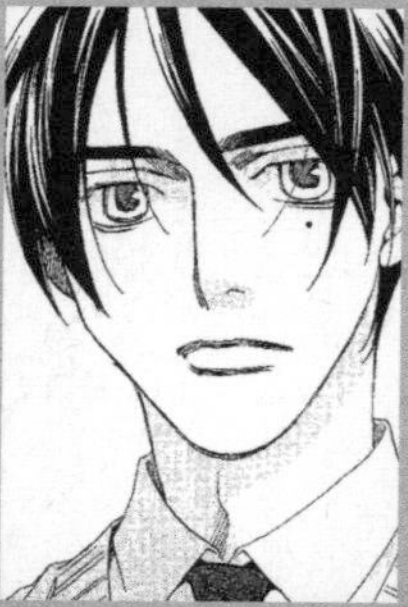

Koya
Ikushima

Vienna, 1908. Tenor vocalist Dimitri has an accident but miraculously survives. Then a man named Maximilian appears and tells him he has become a vampire.

Believing that a vampire dies after propagating, Dimitri tries to force his beloved Agnieszka to sleep with him, but she kills herself. Taking Agnieszka's soulless body with him, Dimitri leaves Vienna.

Tokyo, 2008. High school teacher Azusa is confused by her student Koya's single-minded love for her. When the two are in a car accident, Dimitri appears in Azusa's hospital room and proposes a bargain: he will save Koya if she offers him her soul. Then Azusa's soul enters Agnieszka's body...

CONTENTS

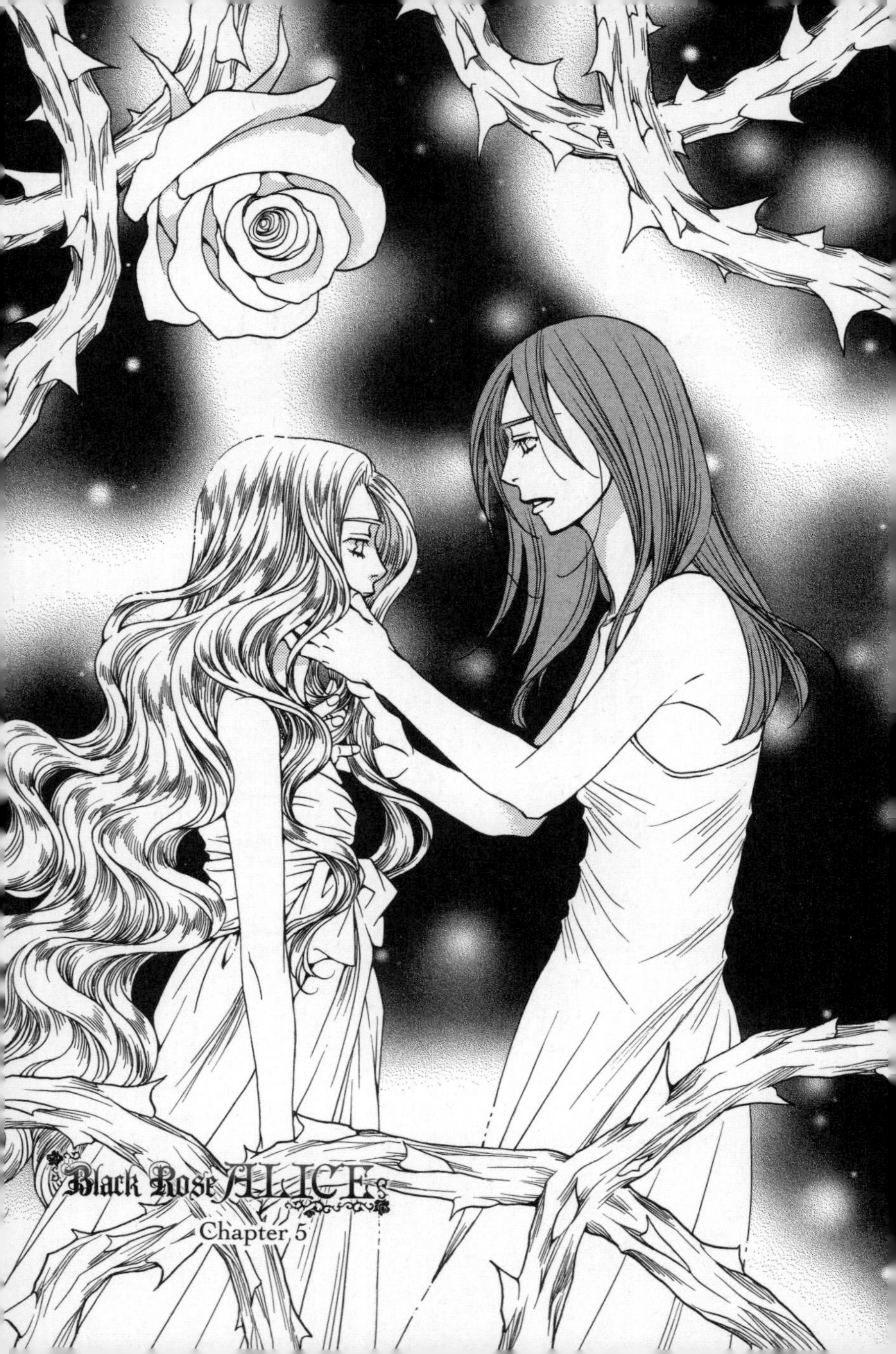
Black Rose Alice
Chapter 5

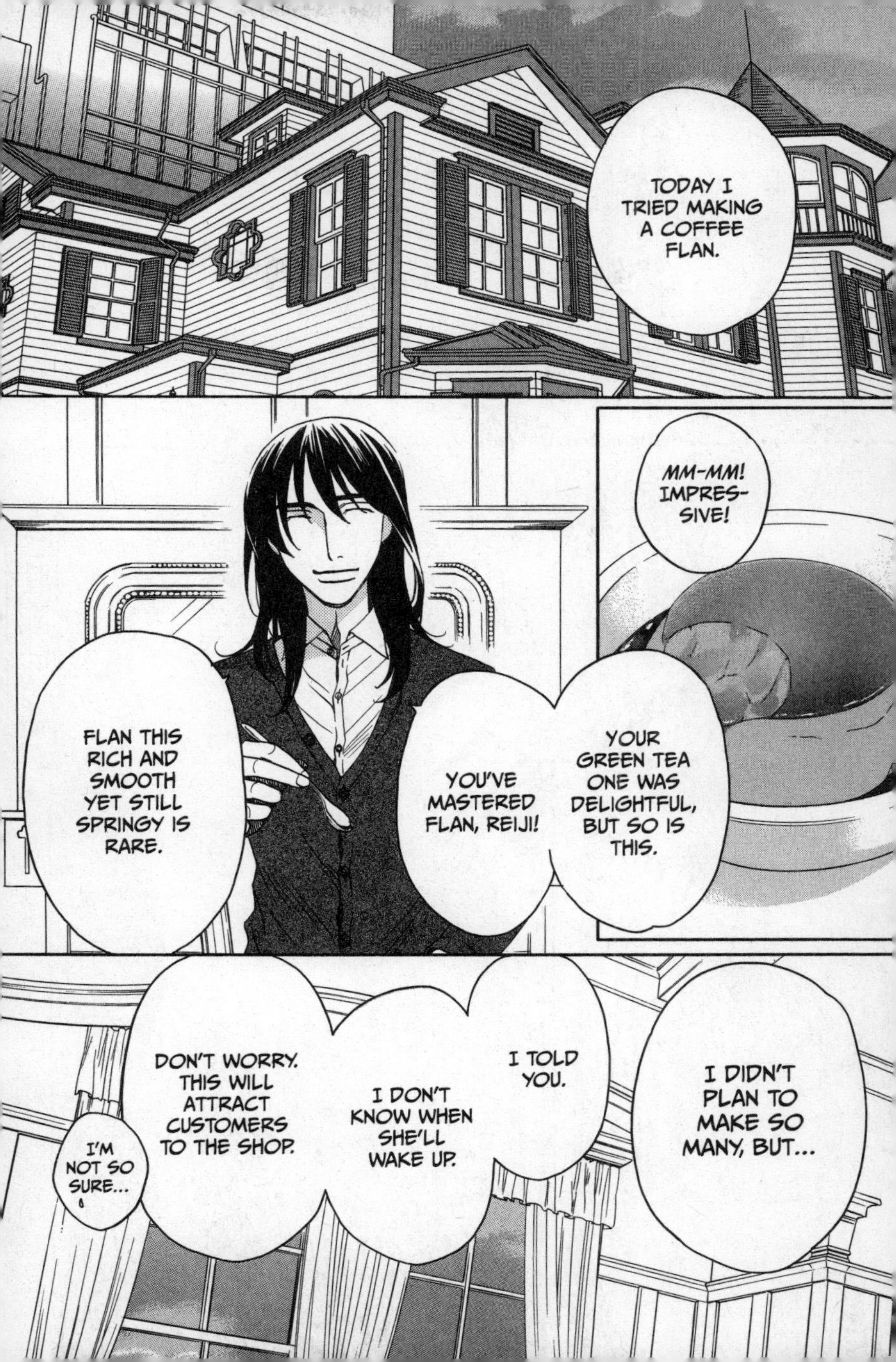
TODAY I TRIED MAKING A COFFEE FLAN.
MM-MM! IMPRES-SIVE!
YOUR GREEN TEA ONE WAS DELIGHTFUL, BUT SO IS THIS.
YOU'VE MASTERED FLAN, REIJI!
FLAN THIS RICH AND SMOOTH YET STILL SPRINGY IS RARE.
I DIDN'T PLAN TO MAKE SO MANY, BUT...
I TOLD YOU.
I DON'T KNOW WHEN SHE'LL WAKE UP.
DON'T WORRY. THIS WILL ATTRACT CUSTOMERS TO THE SHOP.
I'M NOT SO SURE...

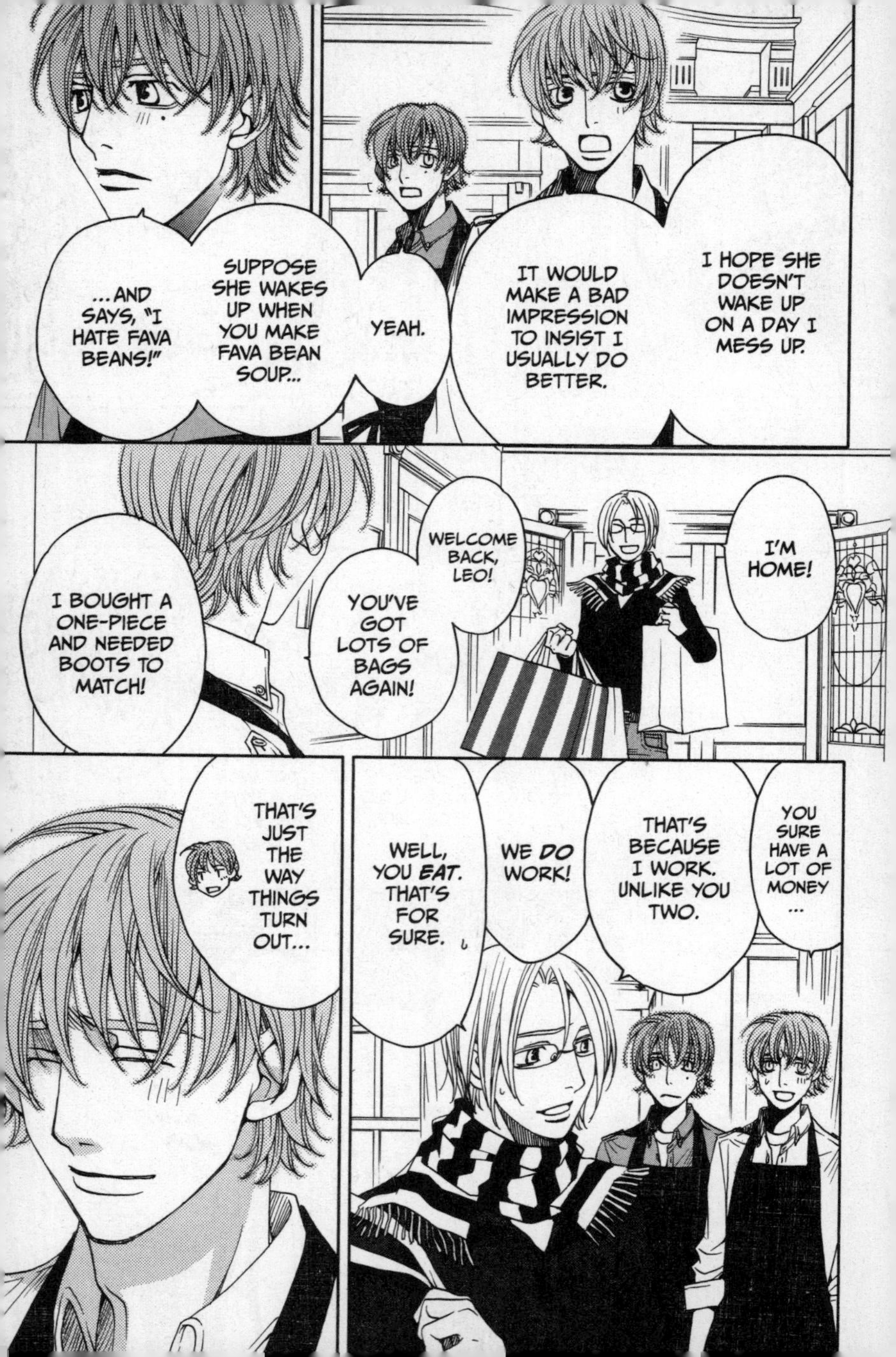
I HOPE SHE DOESN'T WAKE UP ON A DAY I MESS UP.
IT WOULD MAKE A BAD IMPRESSION TO INSIST I USUALLY DO BETTER.
YEAH.
SUPPOSE SHE WAKES UP WHEN YOU MAKE FAVA BEAN SOUP...
...AND SAYS, "I HATE FAVA BEANS!"
I'M HOME!
WELCOME BACK, LEO!
YOU'VE GOT LOTS OF BAGS AGAIN!
I BOUGHT A ONE-PIECE AND NEEDED BOOTS TO MATCH!
YOU SURE HAVE A LOT OF MONEY...
THAT'S BECAUSE I WORK. UNLIKE YOU TWO.
WE *DO* WORK!
WELL, YOU *EAT*. THAT'S FOR SURE.
THAT'S JUST THE WAY THINGS TURN OUT...

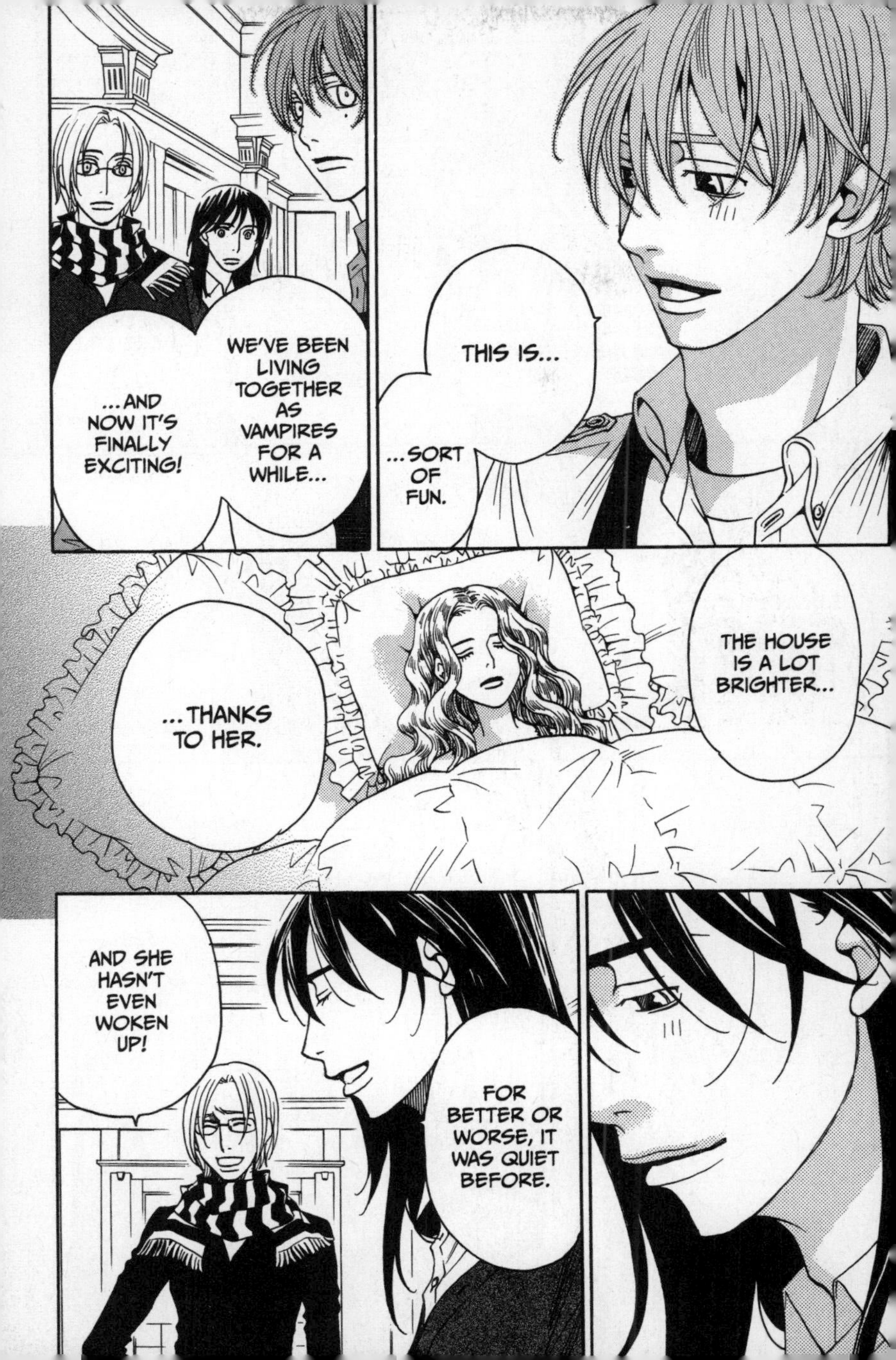
THIS IS...
...SORT OF FUN.
WE'VE BEEN LIVING TOGETHER AS VAMPIRES FOR A WHILE...
...AND NOW IT'S FINALLY EXCITING!
THE HOUSE IS A LOT BRIGHTER...
...THANKS TO HER.
FOR BETTER OR WORSE, IT WAS QUIET BEFORE.
AND SHE HASN'T EVEN WOKEN UP!

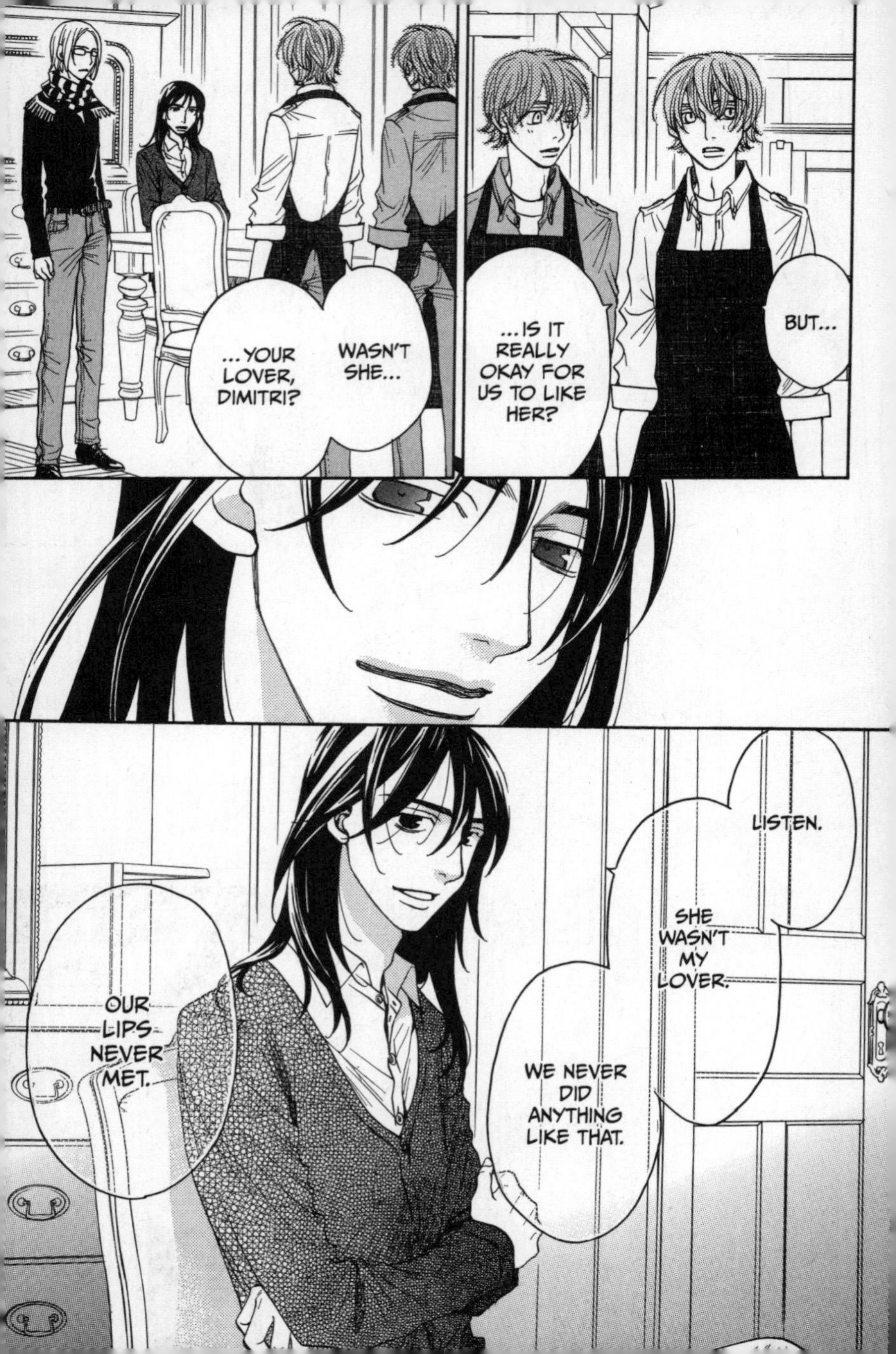
BUT...
...IS IT REALLY OKAY FOR US TO LIKE HER?
WASN'T SHE...
...YOUR LOVER, DIMITRI?
LISTEN.
SHE WASN'T MY LOVER.
WE NEVER DID ANYTHING LIKE THAT.
OUR LIPS NEVER MET.

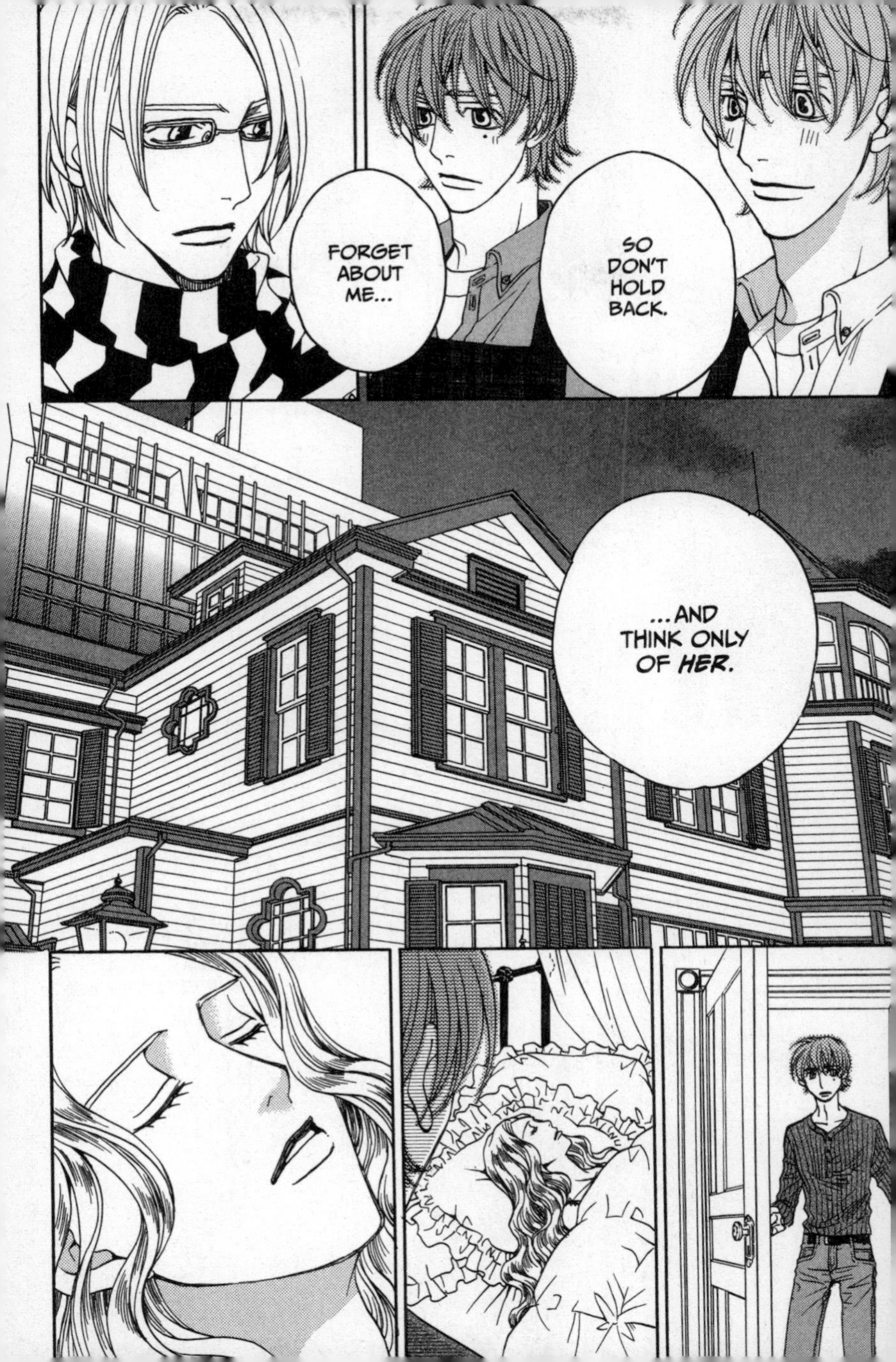
SO DON'T HOLD BACK.
FORGET ABOUT ME...
...AND THINK ONLY OF *HER*.

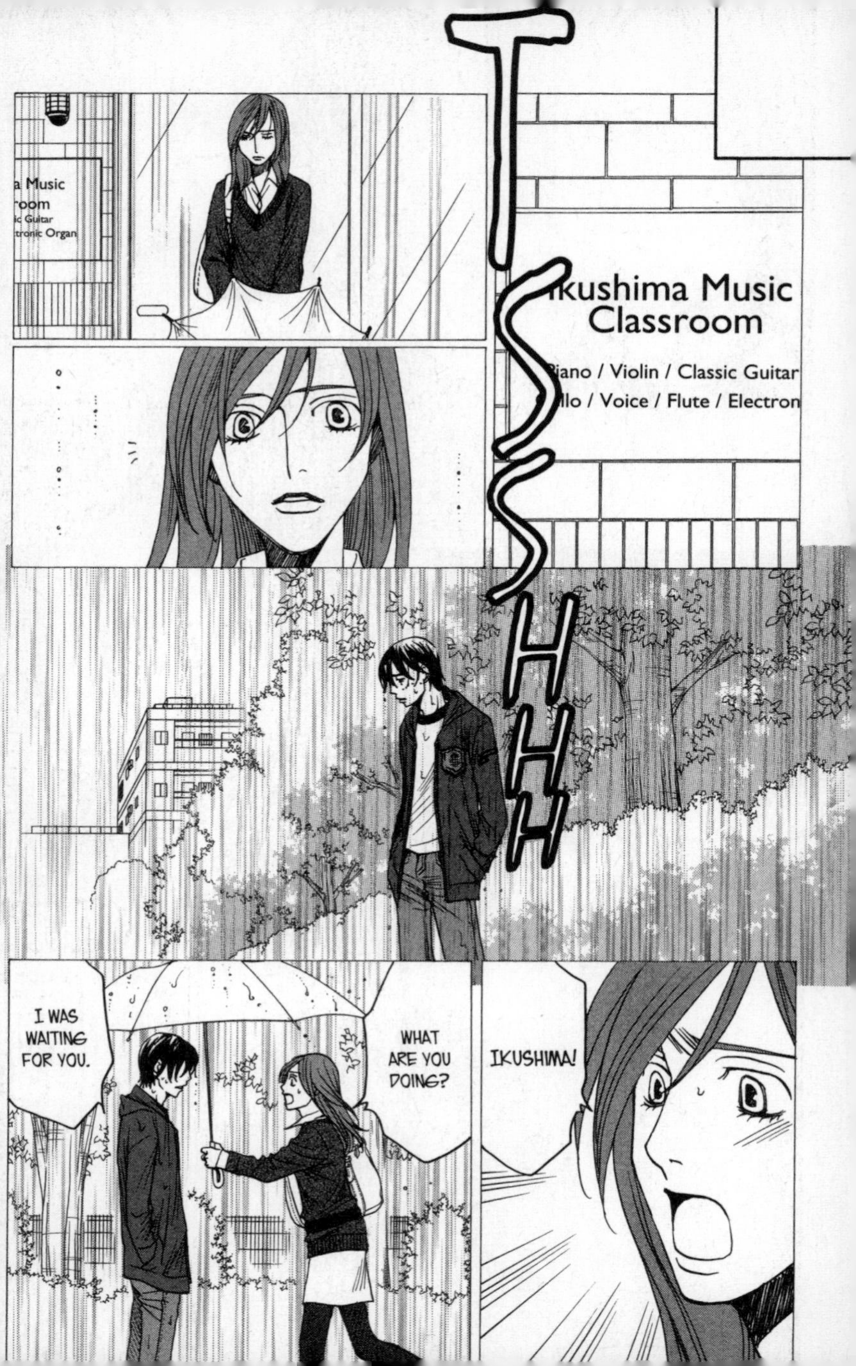
kushima Music
Classroom
Piano / Violin / Classic Guitar
llo / Voice / Flute / Electron
IKUSHIMA!
WHAT ARE YOU DOING?
I WAS WAITING FOR YOU.

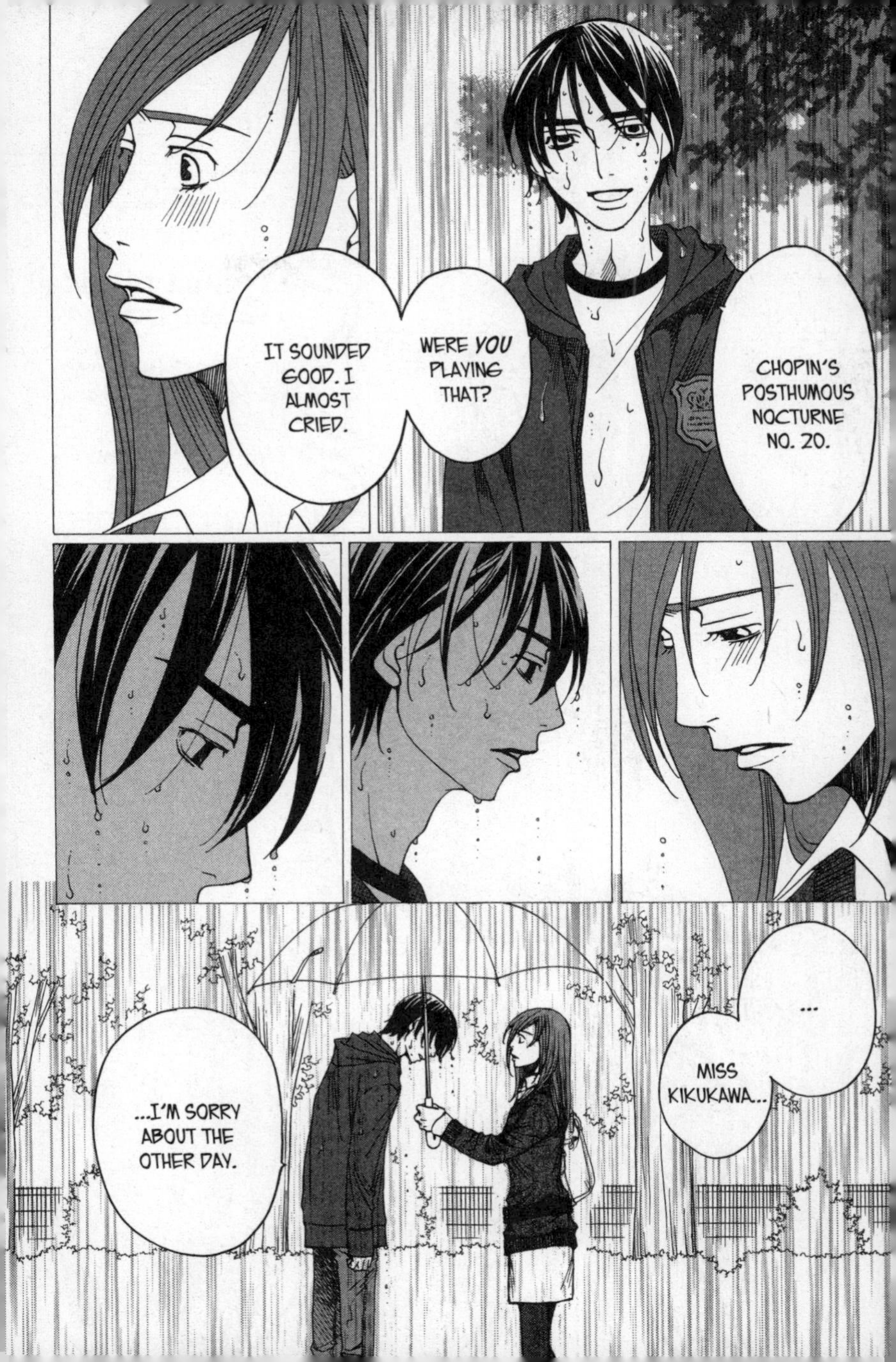
CHOPIN'S POSTHUMOUS NOCTURNE NO. 20.
WERE *YOU* PLAYING THAT?
IT SOUNDED GOOD. I ALMOST CRIED.
...
MISS KIKUKAWA...
...I'M SORRY ABOUT THE OTHER DAY.

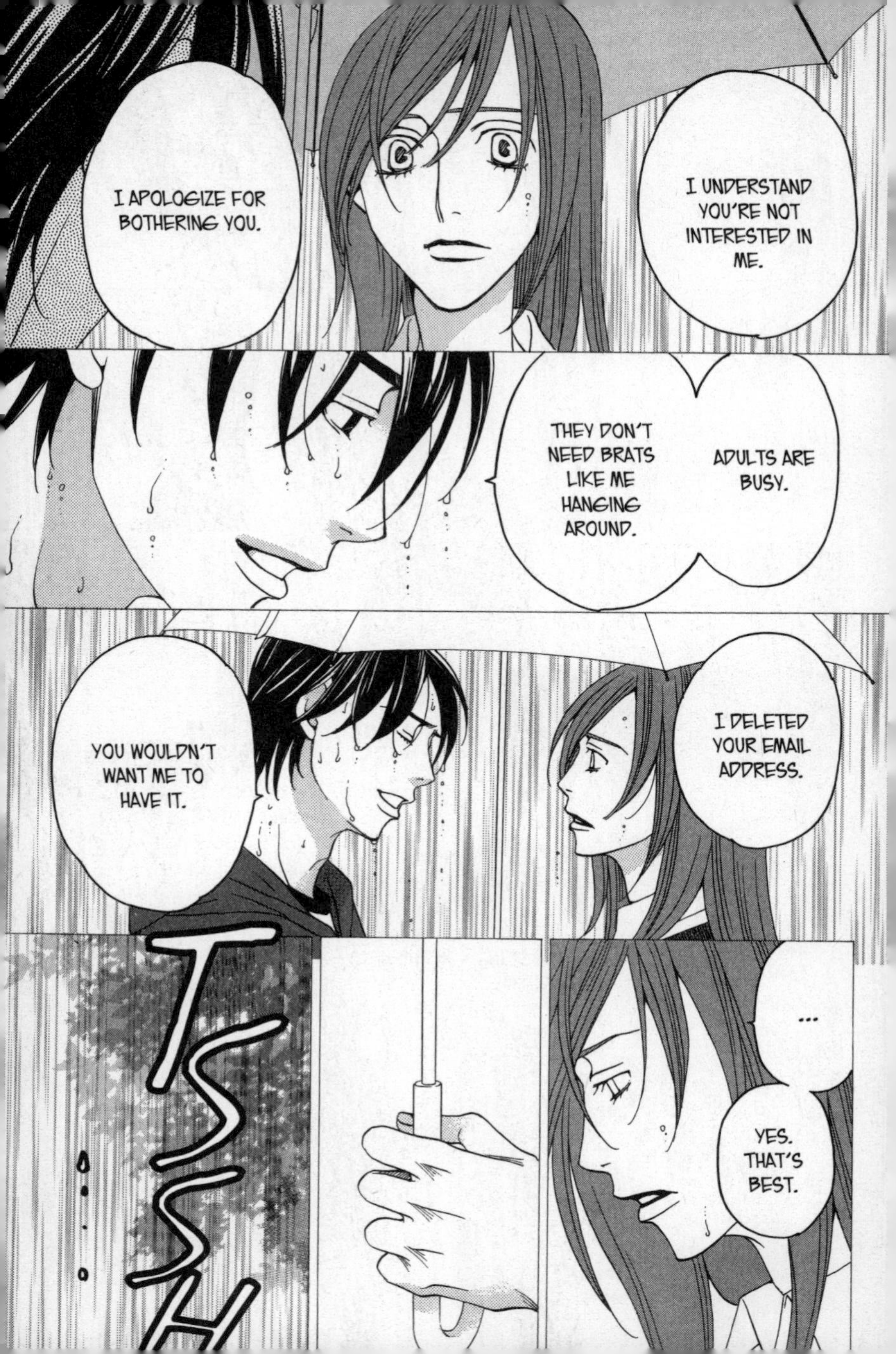
I UNDERSTAND YOU'RE NOT INTERESTED IN ME.
I APOLOGIZE FOR BOTHERING YOU.
ADULTS ARE BUSY.
THEY DON'T NEED BRATS LIKE ME HANGING AROUND.
I DELETED YOUR EMAIL ADDRESS.
YOU WOULDN'T WANT ME TO HAVE IT.
...
YES. THAT'S BEST.
TSSSH

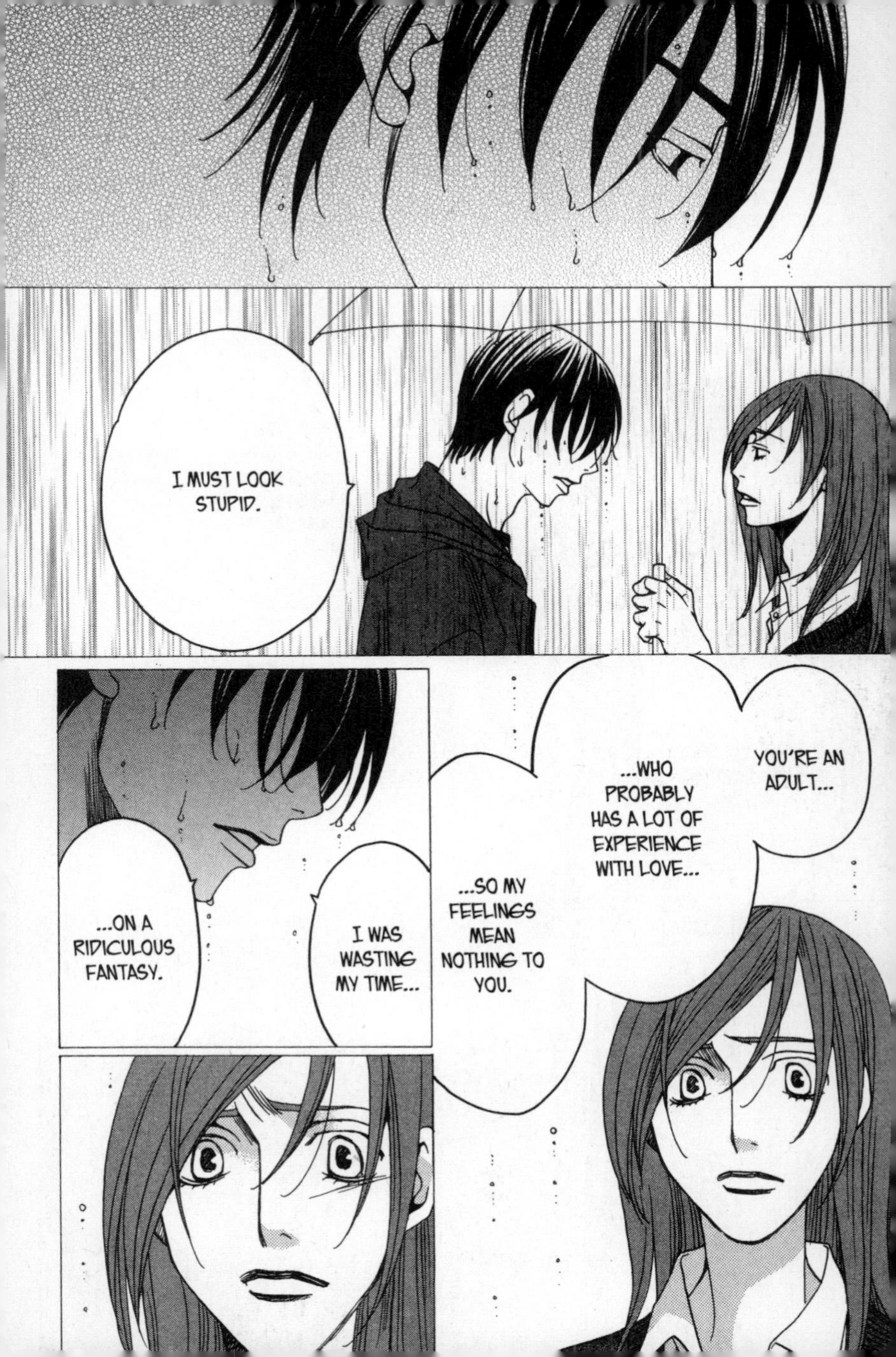
I MUST LOOK STUPID.
YOU'RE AN ADULT...
...WHO PROBABLY HAS A LOT OF EXPERIENCE WITH LOVE...
...SO MY FEELINGS MEAN NOTHING TO YOU.
I WAS WASTING MY TIME...
...ON A RIDICULOUS FANTASY.

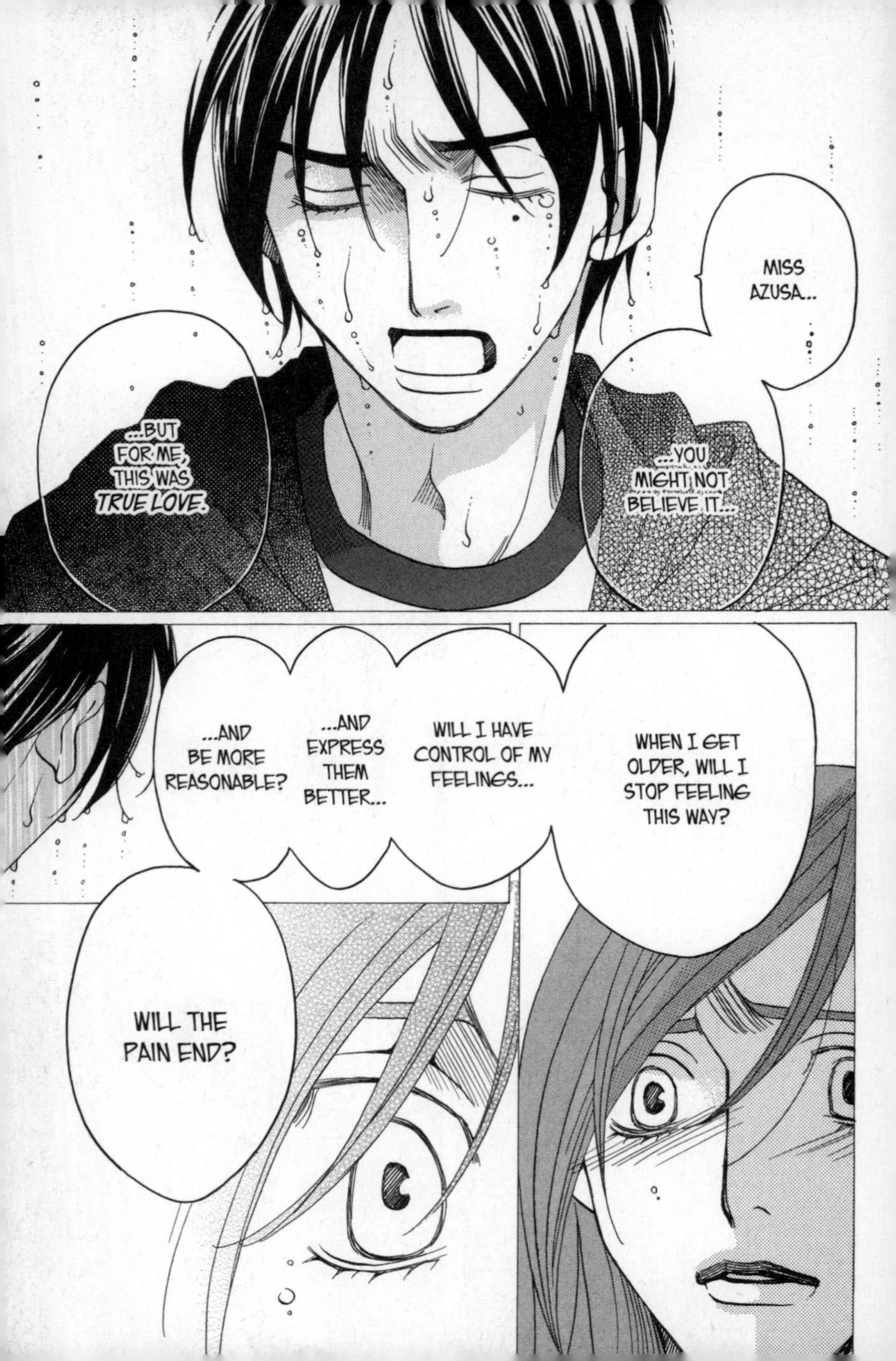
MISS AZUSA...
...YOU MIGHT NOT BELIEVE IT...
...BUT FOR ME, THIS WAS TRUE LOVE.
WHEN I GET OLDER, WILL I STOP FEELING THIS WAY?
WILL I HAVE CONTROL OF MY FEELINGS...
...AND EXPRESS THEM BETTER...
...AND BE MORE REASONABLE?
WILL THE PAIN END?

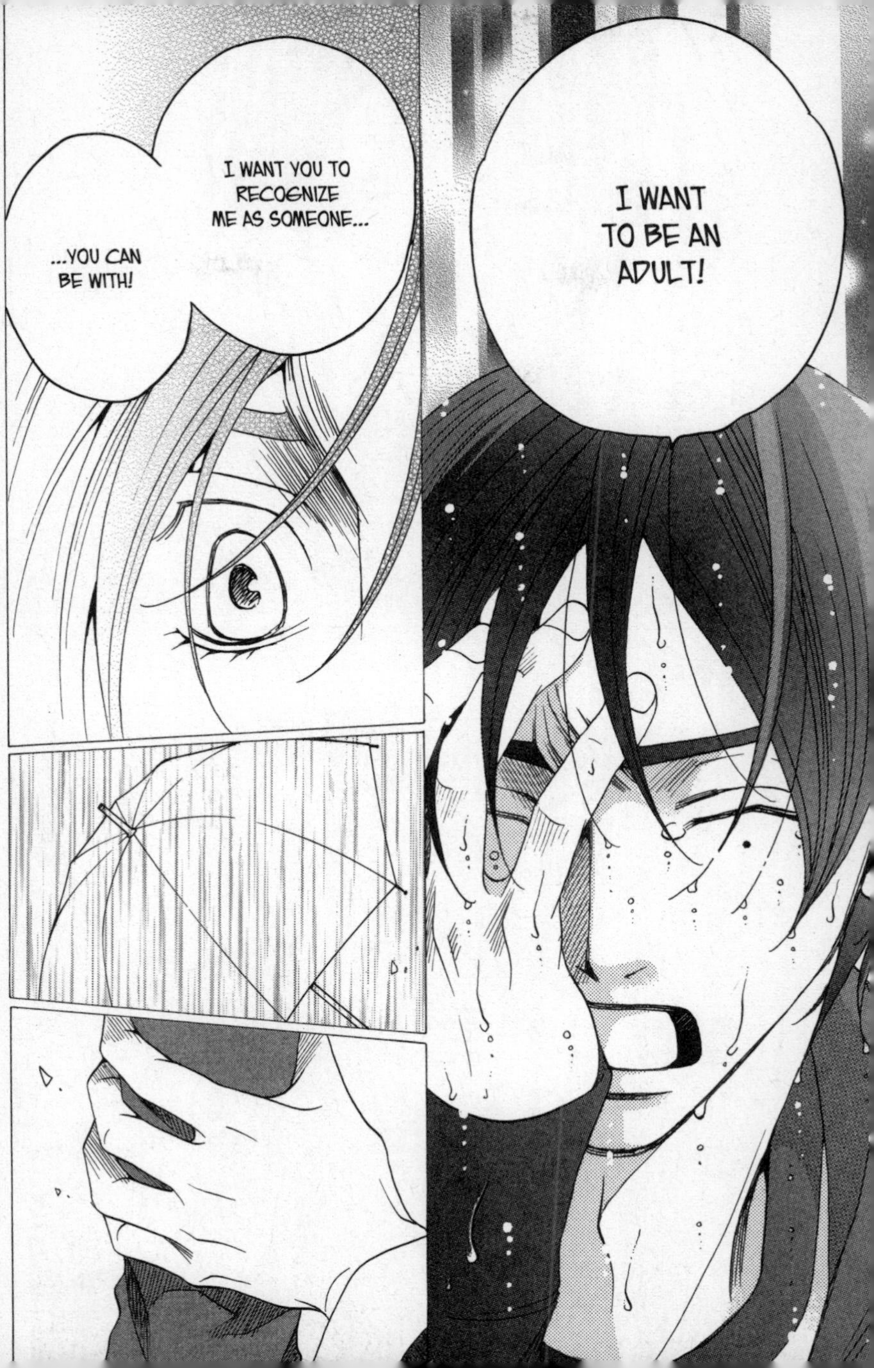
I WANT TO BE AN ADULT!
I WANT YOU TO RECOGNIZE ME AS SOMEONE...
...YOU CAN BE WITH!

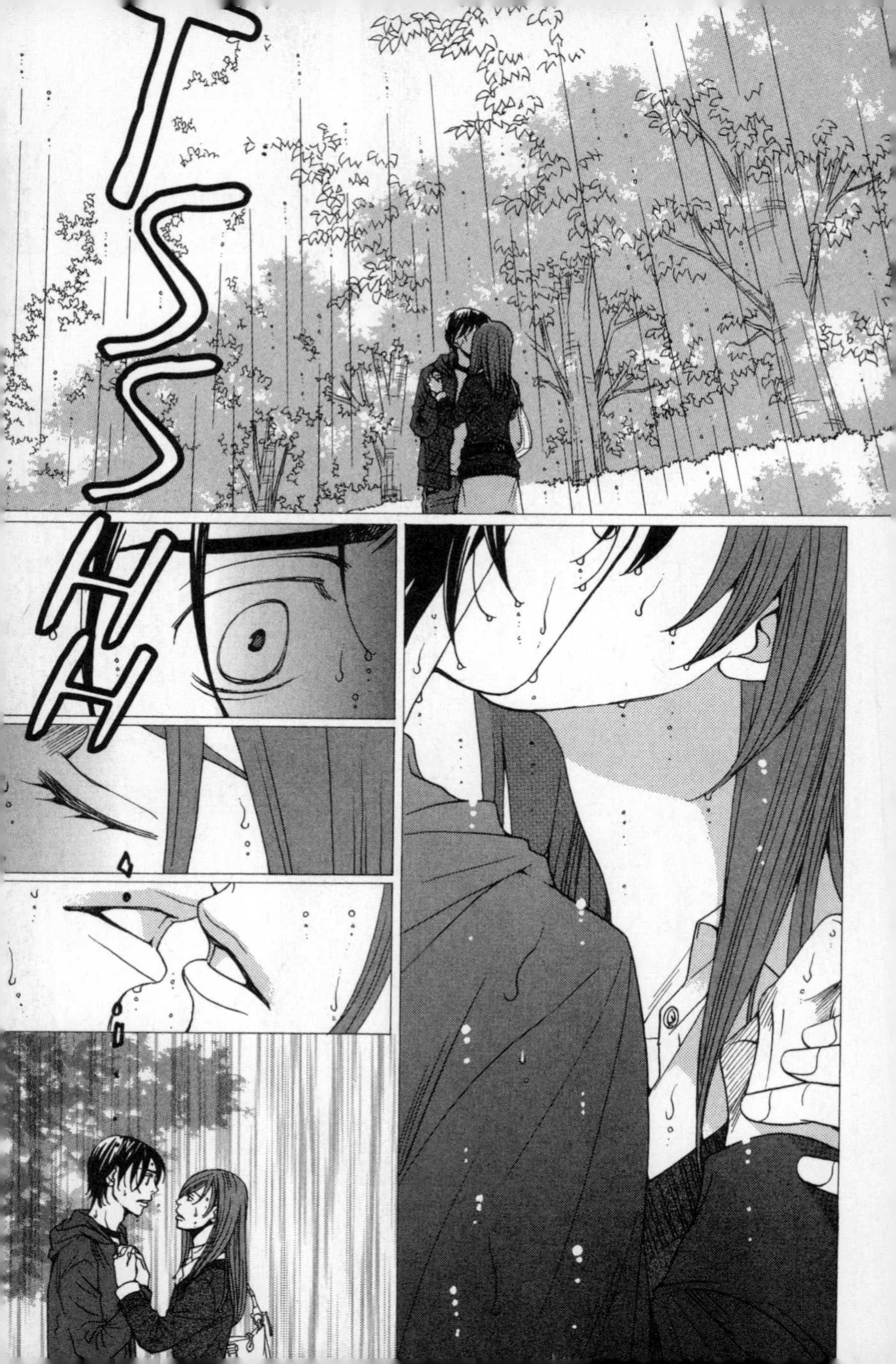
TSSHH

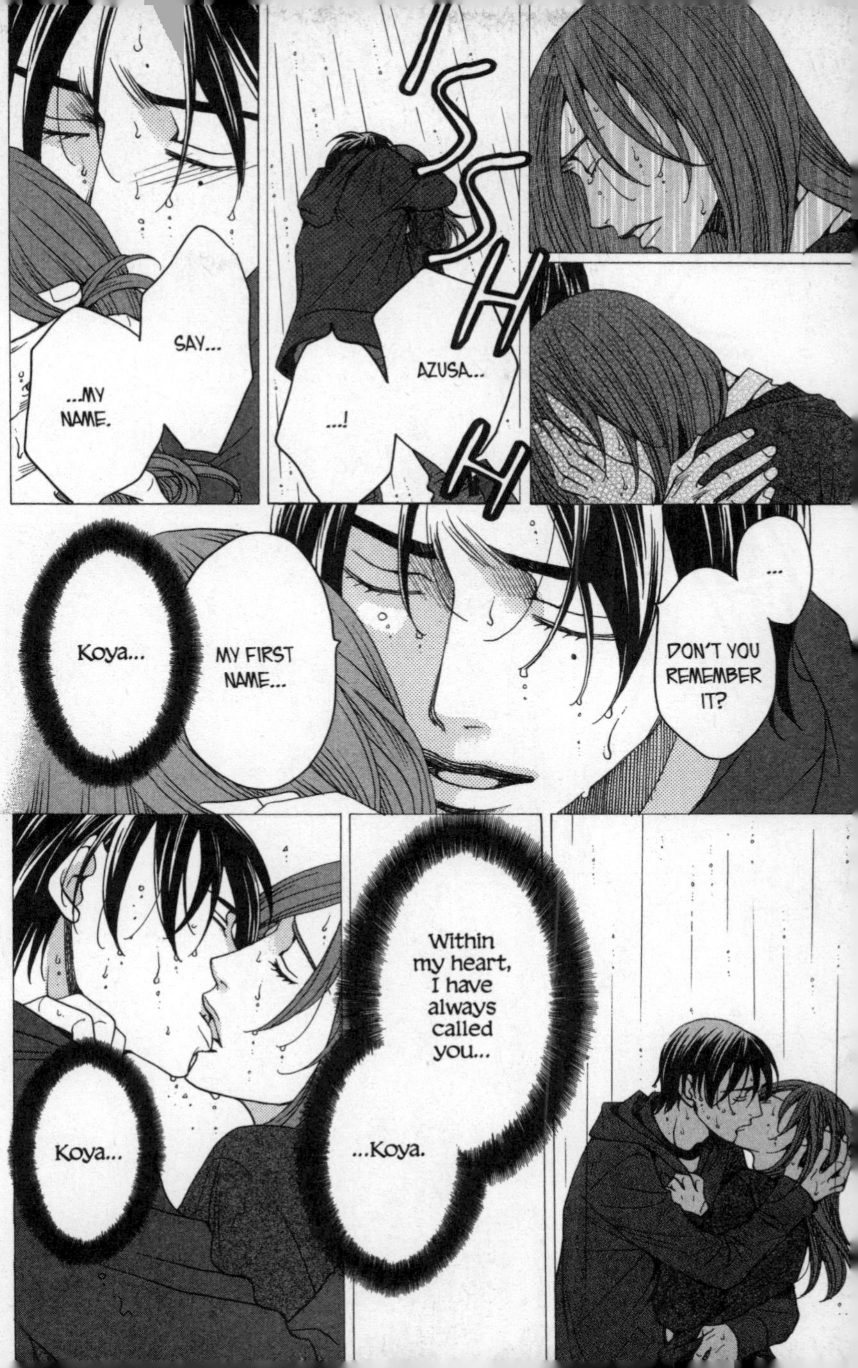
ISSHH
AZUSA...
...!
SAY...
...MY NAME.
...
DON'T YOU REMEMBER IT?
MY FIRST NAME...
Koya...
Within my heart, I have always called you...
...Koya.
Koya...

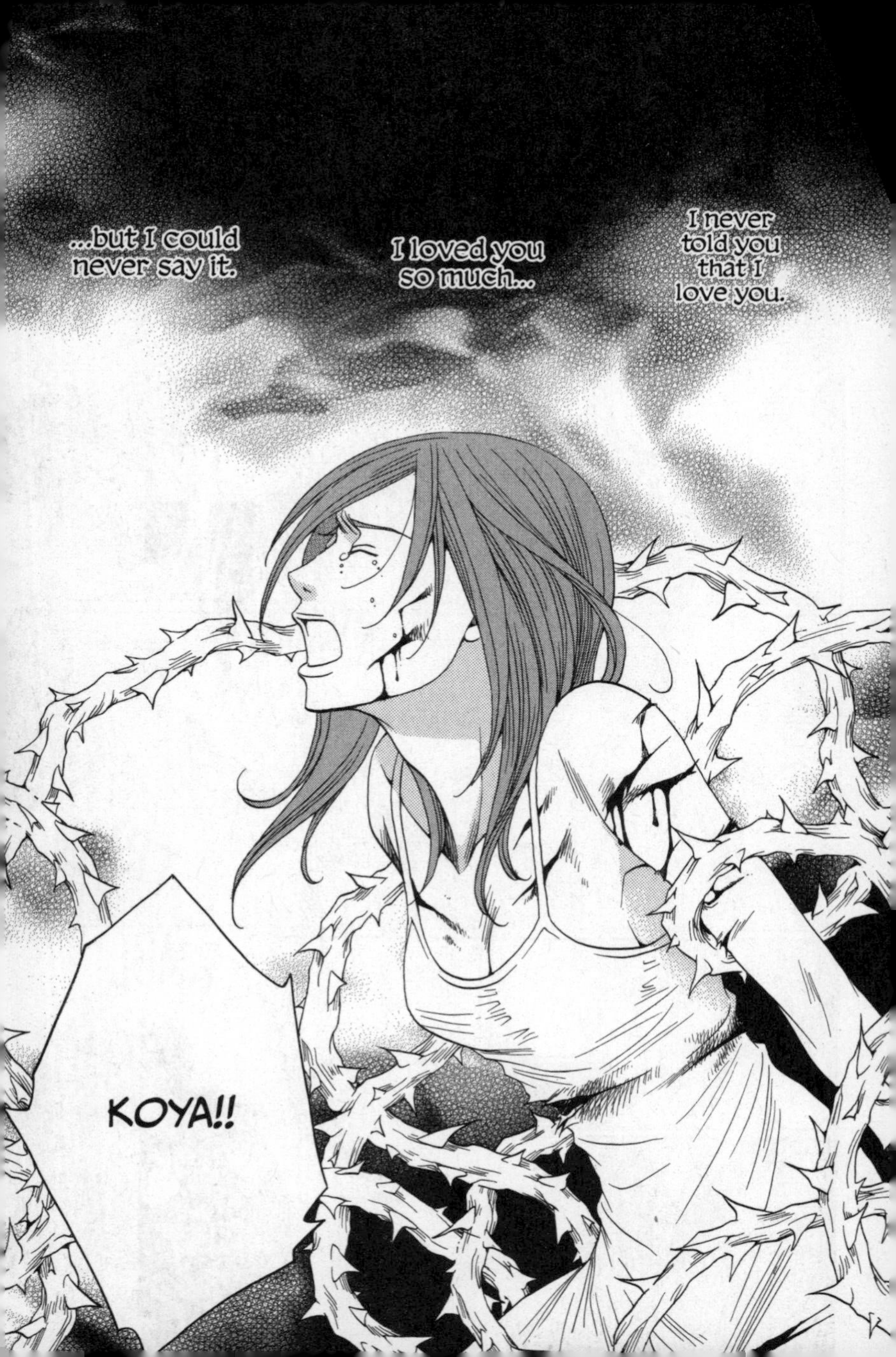
I never told you that I love you.
I loved you so much...
...but I could never say it.
KOYA!!

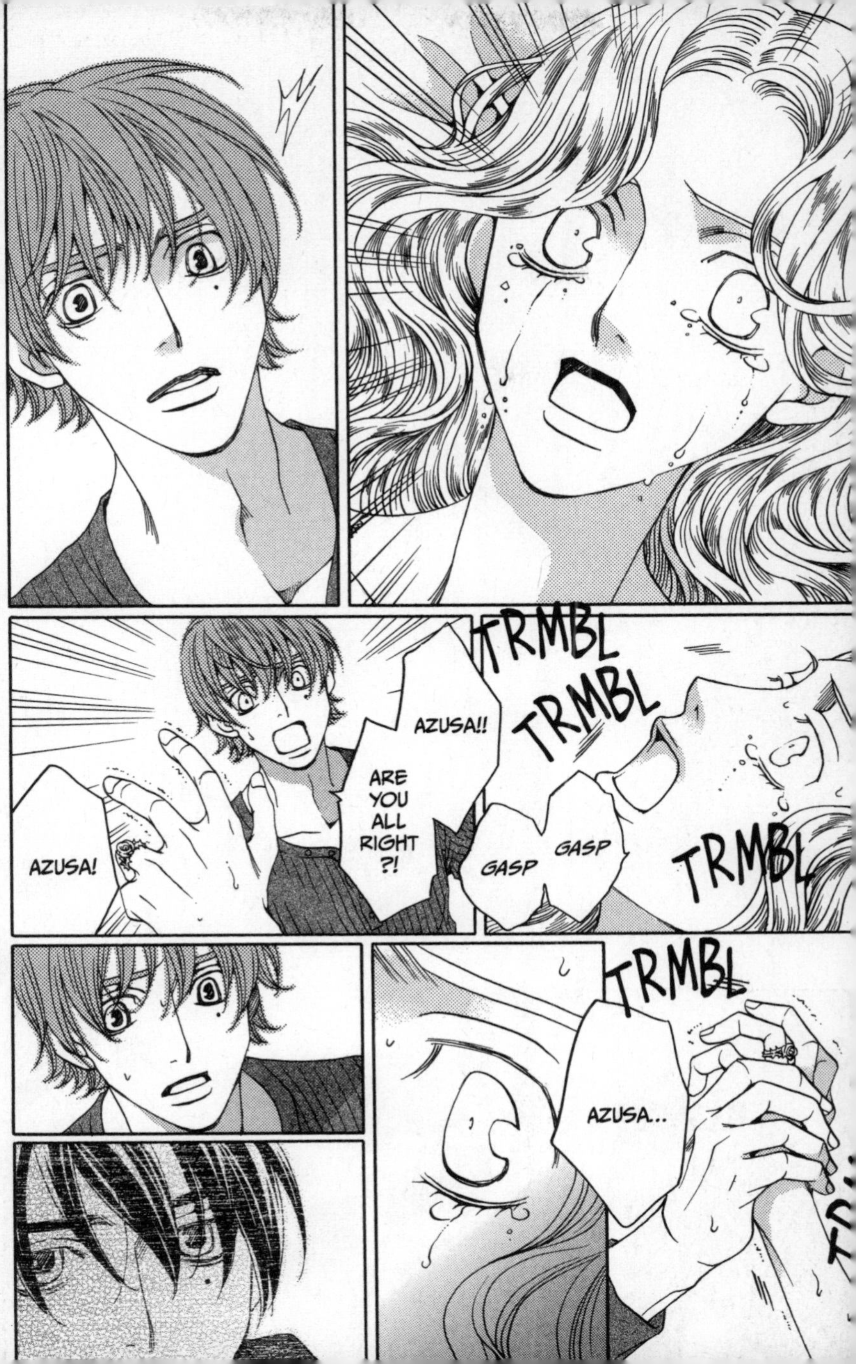
TRMBL
TRMBL
GASP
GASP
TRMBL
AZUSA!!
ARE YOU ALL RIGHT?!
AZUSA!
TRMBL
AZUSA...

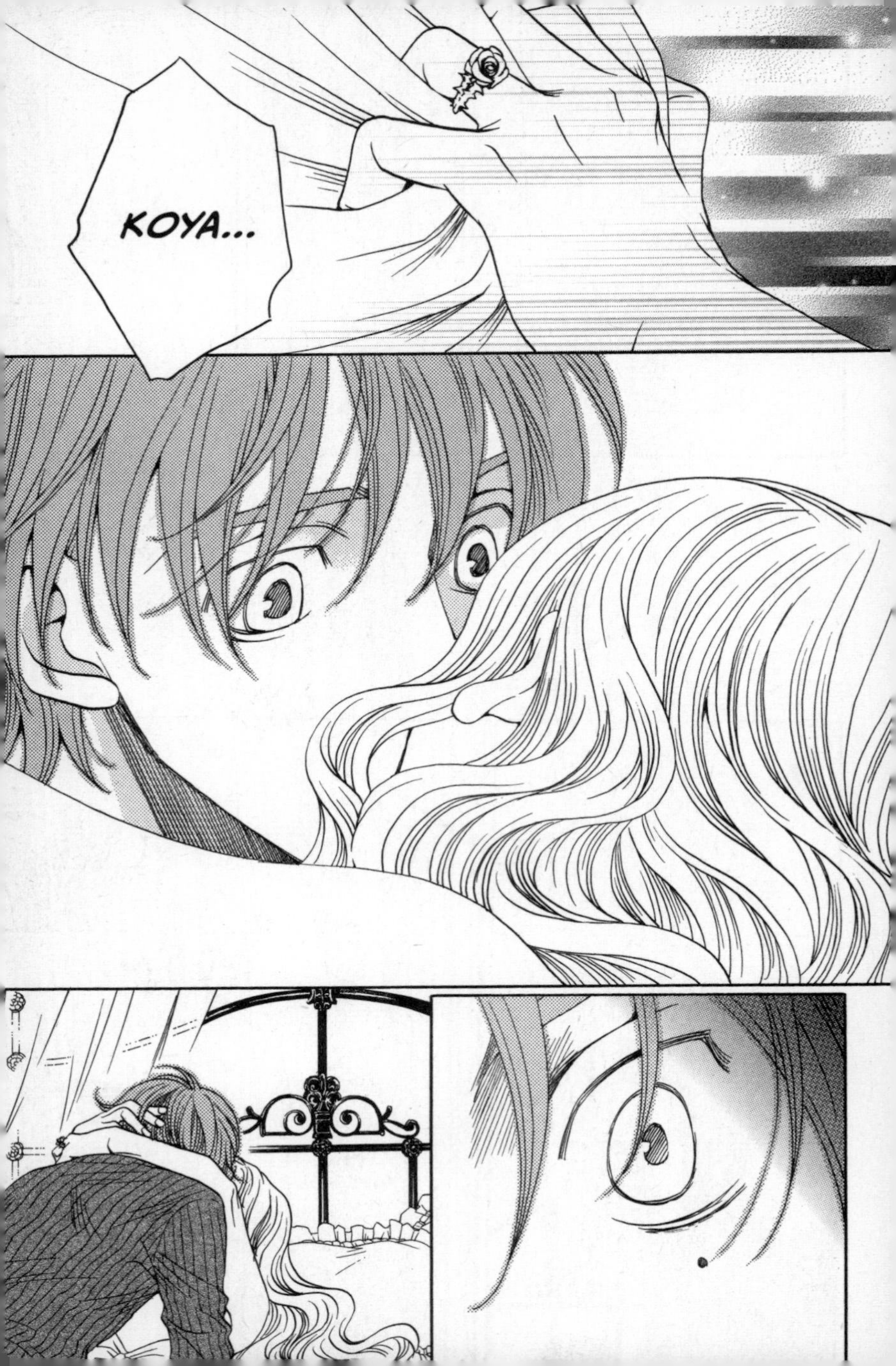
KOYA...

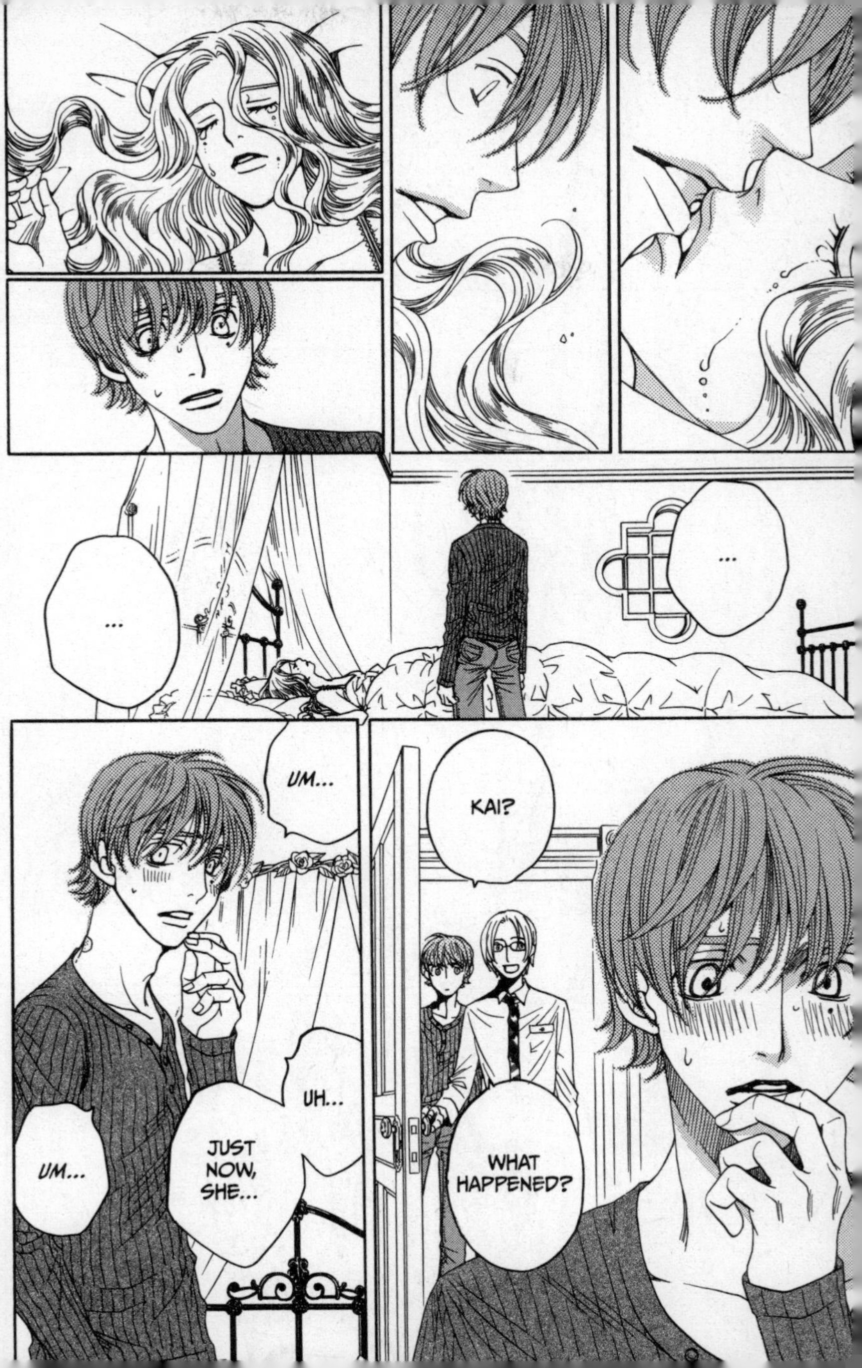
...
...
KAI?
WHAT HAPPENED?
UM...
UH...
JUST NOW, SHE...
UM...

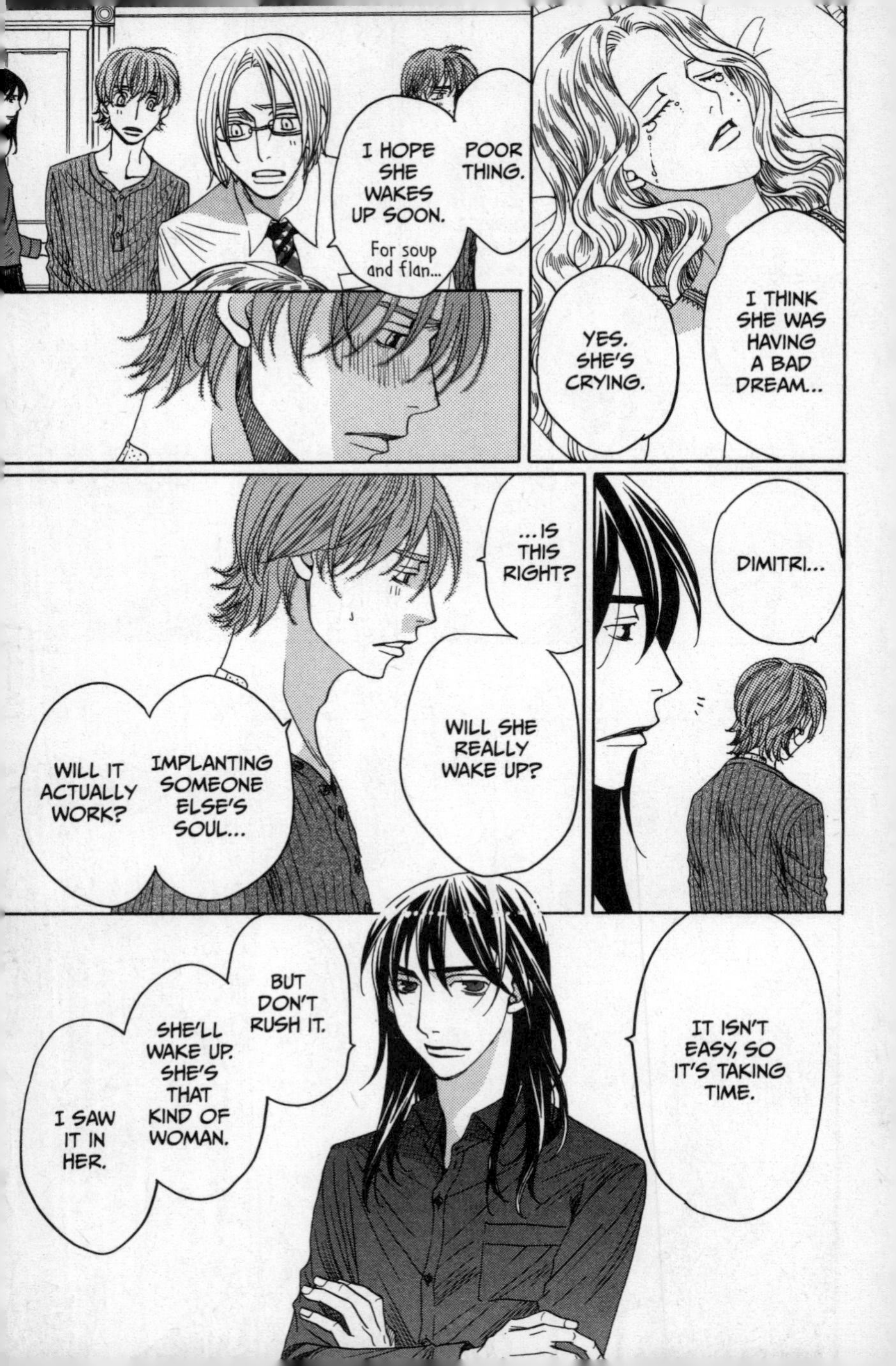
I THINK SHE WAS HAVING A BAD DREAM...
YES. SHE'S CRYING.
POOR THING.
I HOPE SHE WAKES UP SOON.
For soup and flan...
DIMITRI...
...IS THIS RIGHT?
WILL SHE REALLY WAKE UP?
IMPLANTING SOMEONE ELSE'S SOUL...
WILL IT ACTUALLY WORK?
IT ISN'T EASY, SO IT'S TAKING TIME.
BUT DON'T RUSH IT.
SHE'LL WAKE UP. SHE'S THAT KIND OF WOMAN.
I SAW IT IN HER.

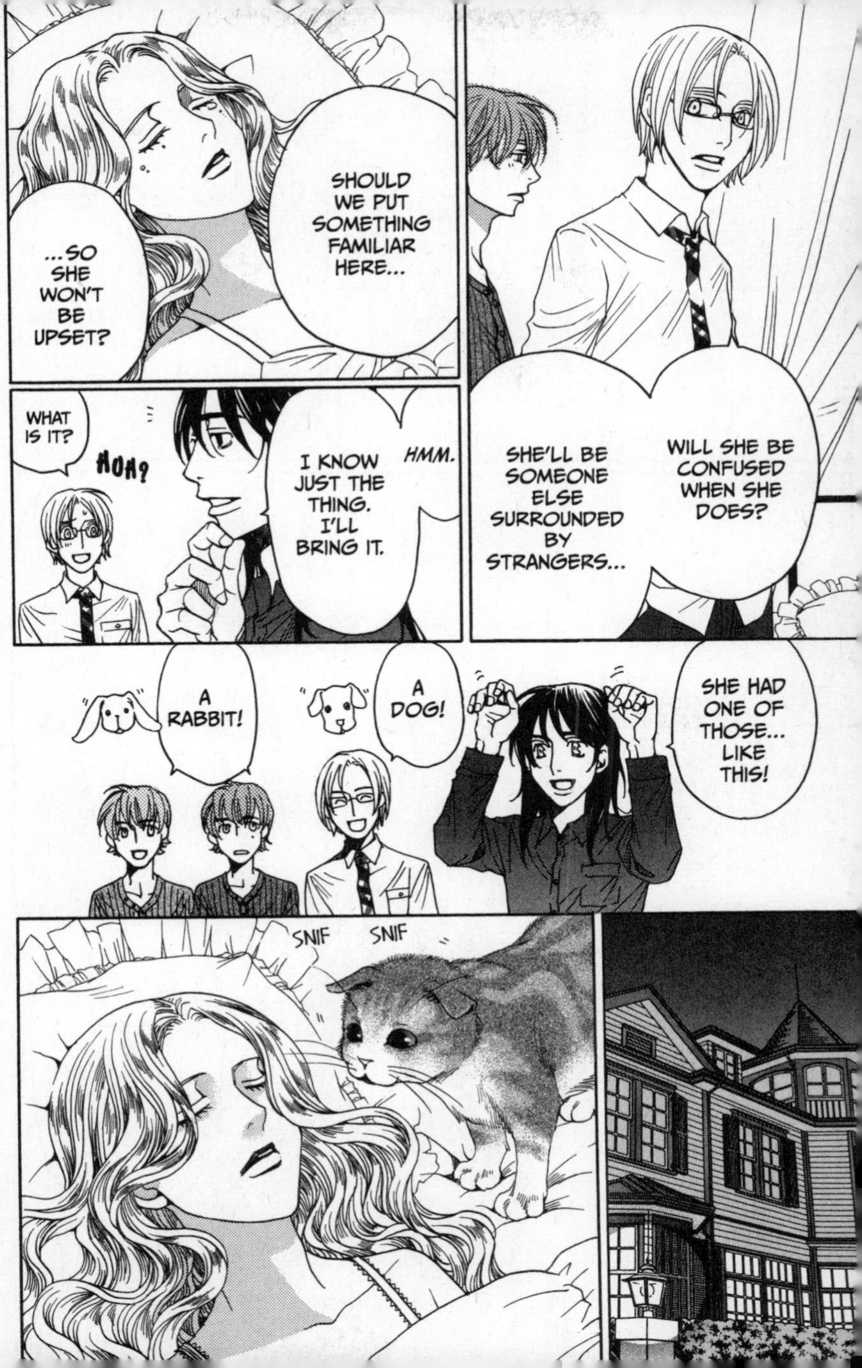
WILL SHE BE CONFUSED WHEN SHE DOES?
SHE'LL BE SOMEONE ELSE SURROUNDED BY STRANGERS...
SHOULD WE PUT SOMETHING FAMILIAR HERE...
...SO SHE WON'T BE UPSET?
HMM.
I KNOW JUST THE THING. I'LL BRING IT.
HUH?
WHAT IS IT?
SHE HAD ONE OF THOSE... LIKE THIS!
A DOG!
A RABBIT!
SNIF SNIF

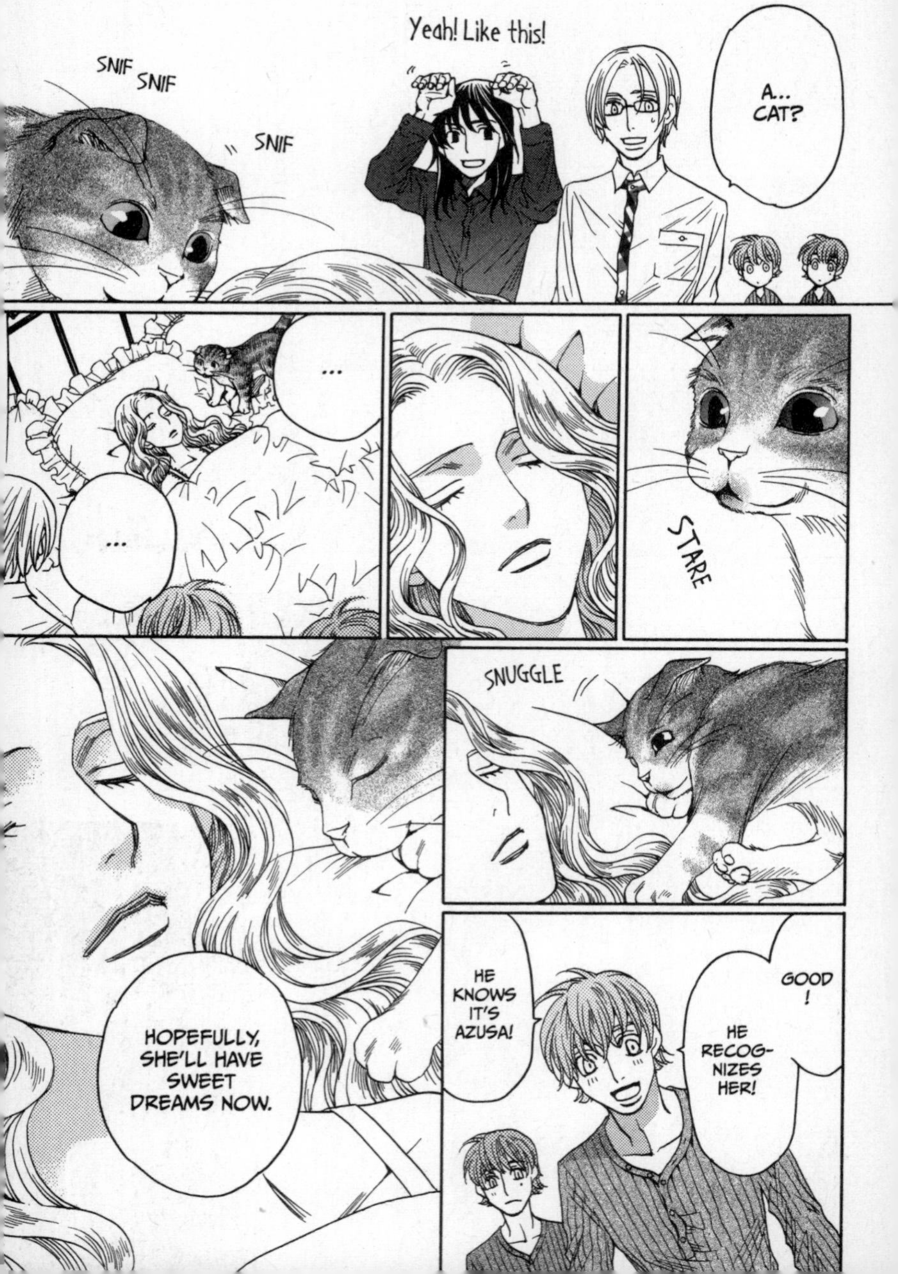
A... CAT?
Yeah! Like this!
SNIF SNIF
SNIF
STARE
...
...
SNUGGLE
GOOD! HE RECOGNIZES HER!
HE KNOWS IT'S AZUSA!
HOPEFULLY, SHE'LL HAVE SWEET DREAMS NOW.

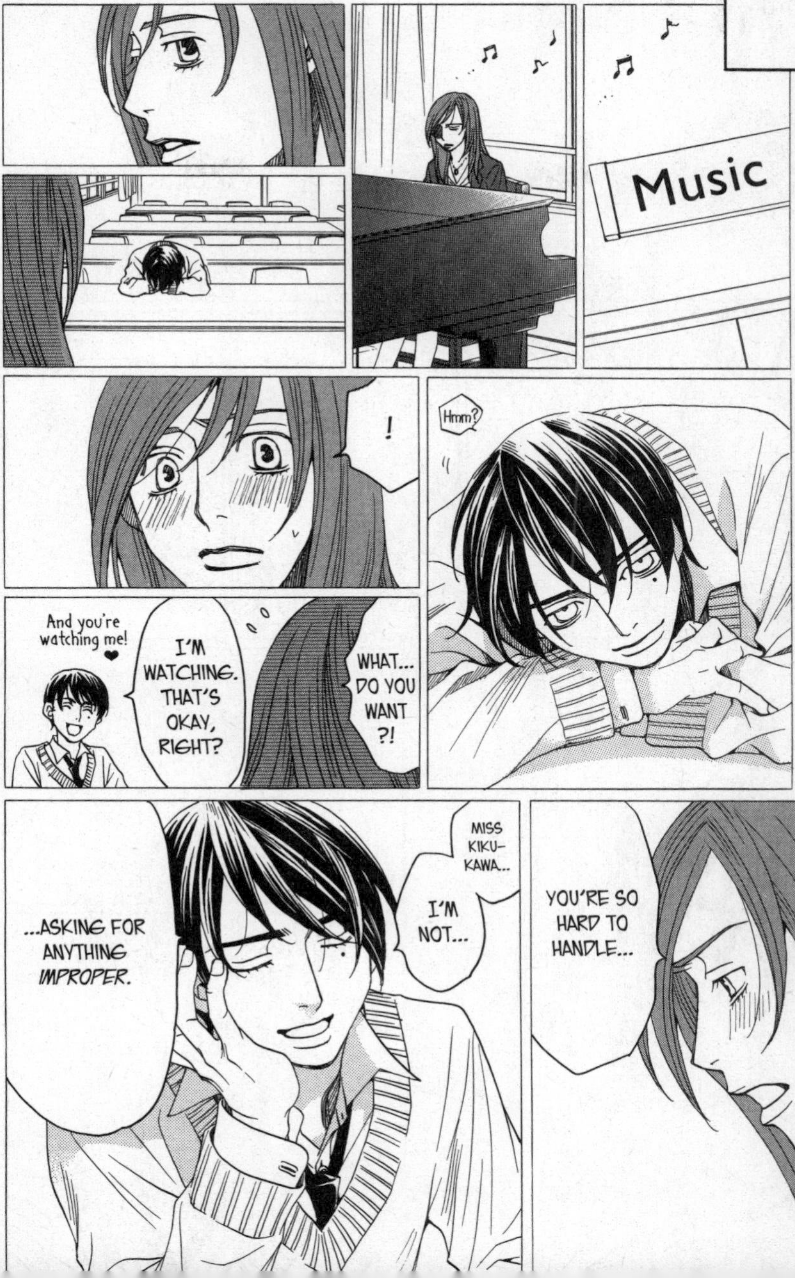
Music
!
Hmm?
WHAT... DO YOU WANT?!
I'M WATCHING. THAT'S OKAY, RIGHT?
And you're watching me! ❤
YOU'RE SO HARD TO HANDLE...
MISS KIKU-KAWA...
I'M NOT...
...ASKING FOR ANYTHING IMPROPER.

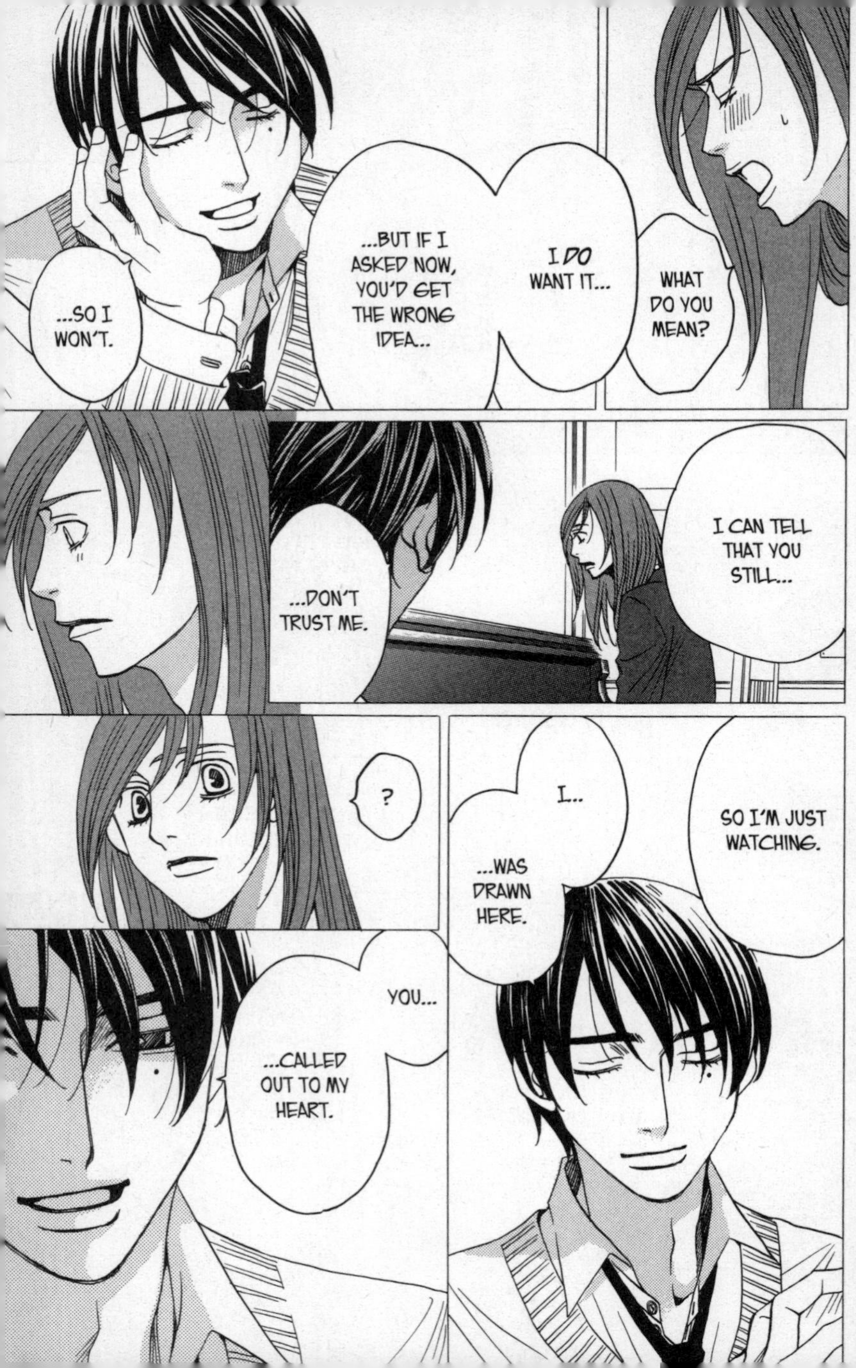
WHAT DO YOU MEAN?
I DO WANT IT...
...BUT IF I ASKED NOW, YOU'D GET THE WRONG IDEA...
...SO I WON'T.
I CAN TELL THAT YOU STILL...
...DON'T TRUST ME.
SO I'M JUST WATCHING.
I...
...WAS DRAWN HERE.
?
YOU...
...CALLED OUT TO MY HEART.

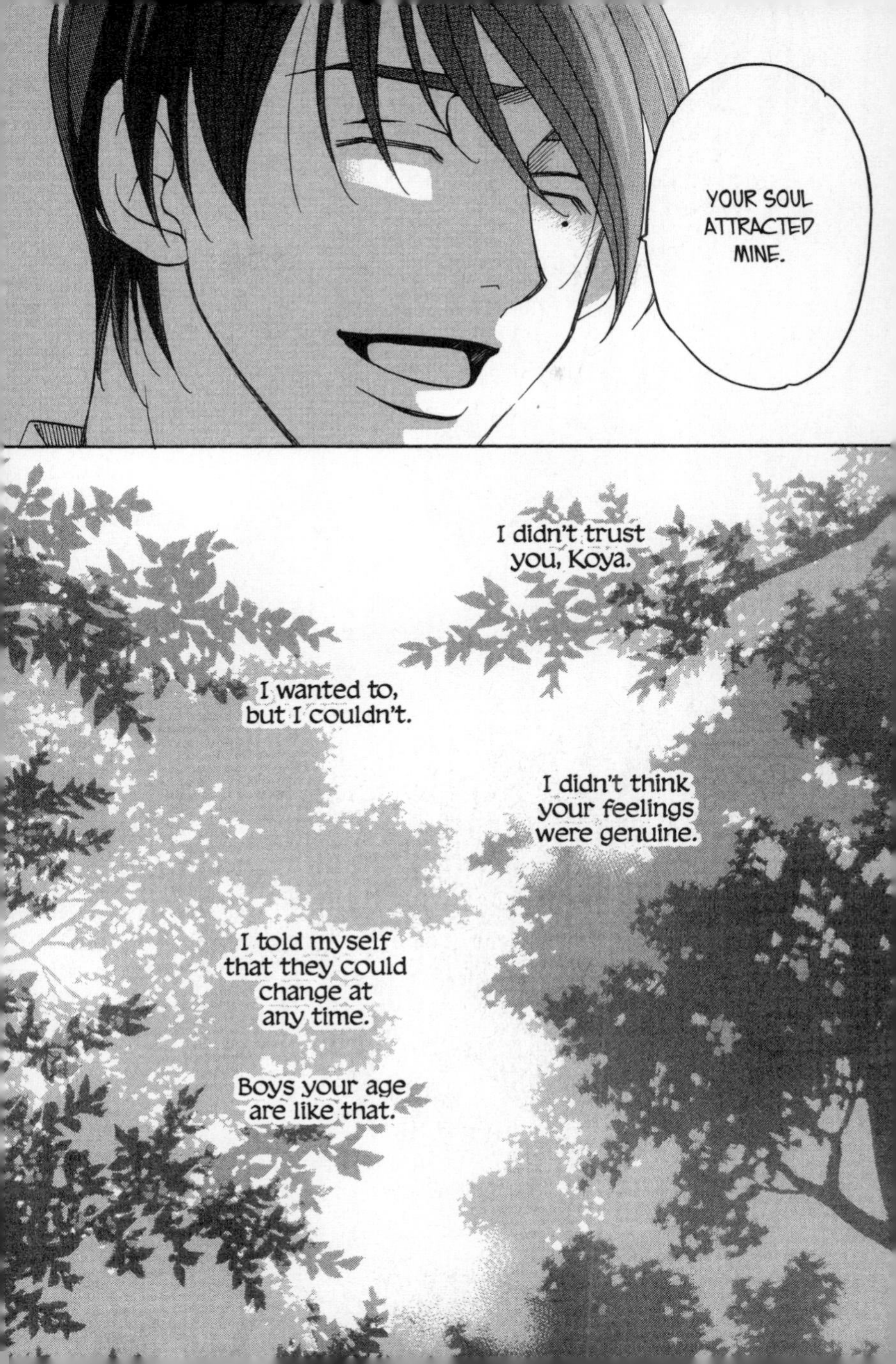
YOUR SOUL ATTRACTED MINE.
I didn't trust you, Koya.
I wanted to, but I couldn't.
I didn't think your feelings were genuine.
I told myself that they could change at any time.
Boys your age are like that.

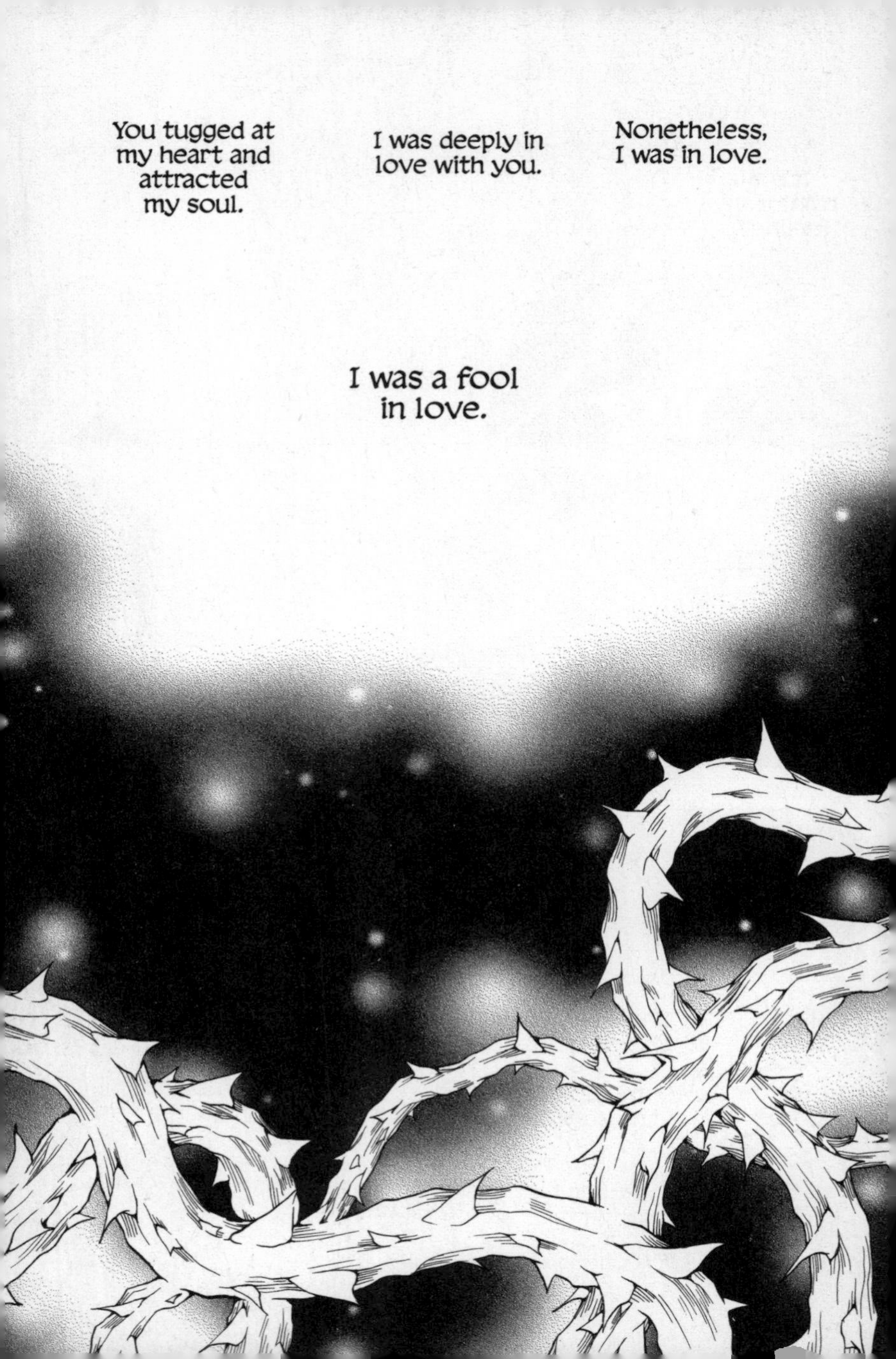
Nonetheless, I was in love.
I was deeply in love with you.
You tugged at my heart and attracted my soul.
I was a fool in love.

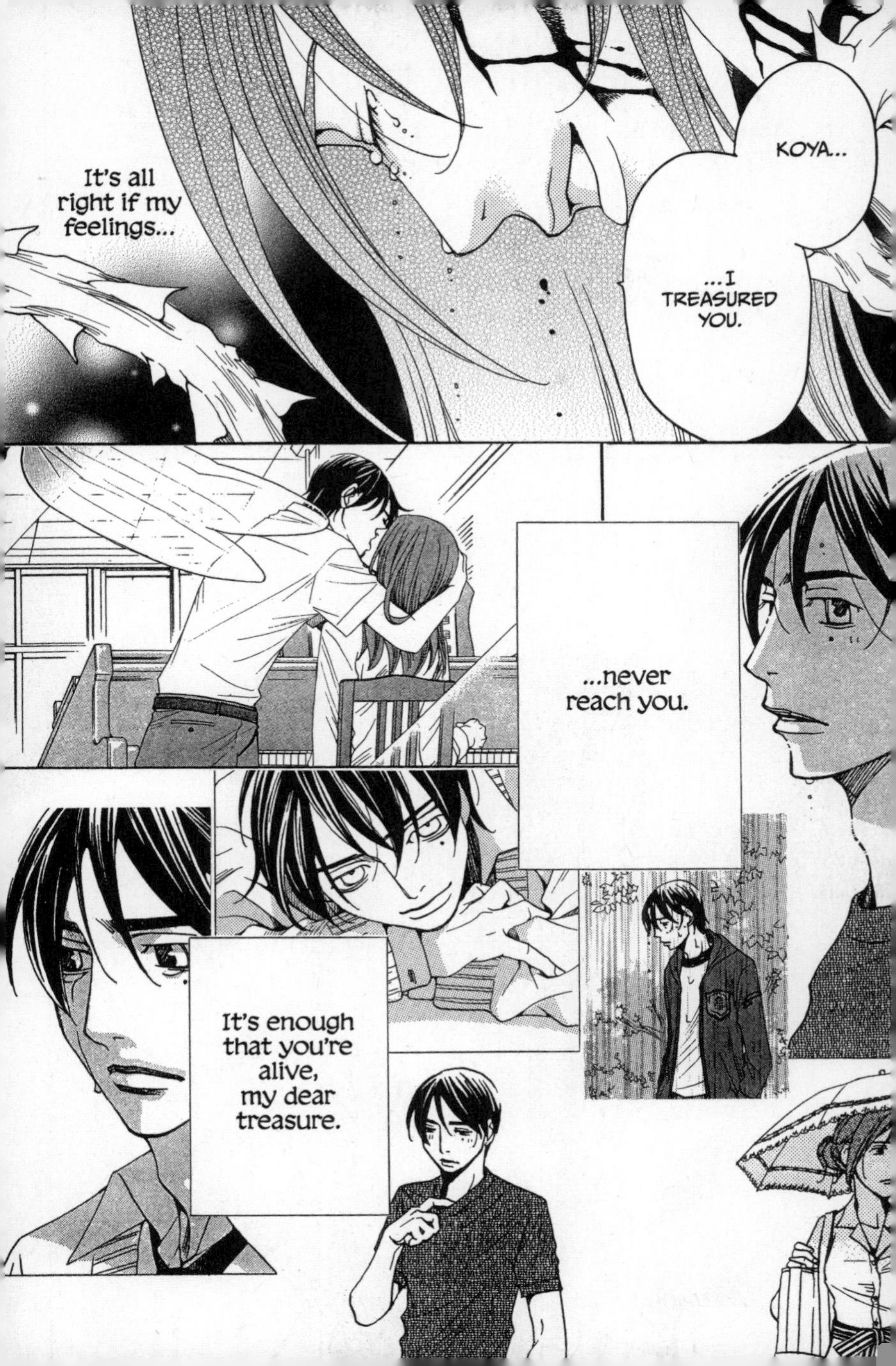
KOYA...
...I TREASURED YOU.
It's all right if my feelings...
...never reach you.
It's enough that you're alive, my dear treasure.

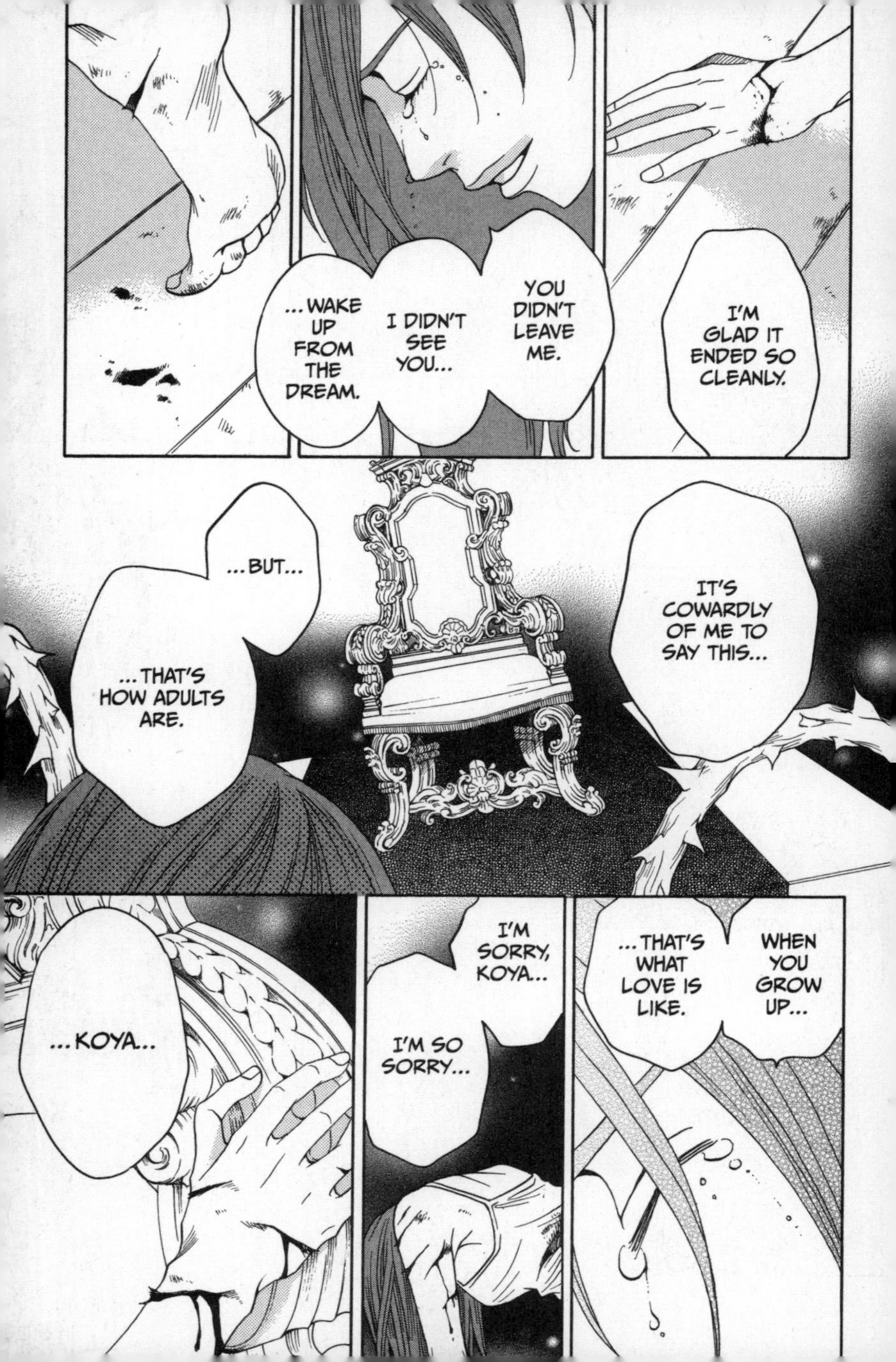
I'M GLAD IT ENDED SO CLEANLY.
YOU DIDN'T LEAVE ME.
I DIDN'T SEE YOU...
...WAKE UP FROM THE DREAM.
IT'S COWARDLY OF ME TO SAY THIS...
...BUT...
...THAT'S HOW ADULTS ARE.
WHEN YOU GROW UP...
...THAT'S WHAT LOVE IS LIKE.
I'M SORRY, KOYA...
I'M SO SORRY...
...KOYA...

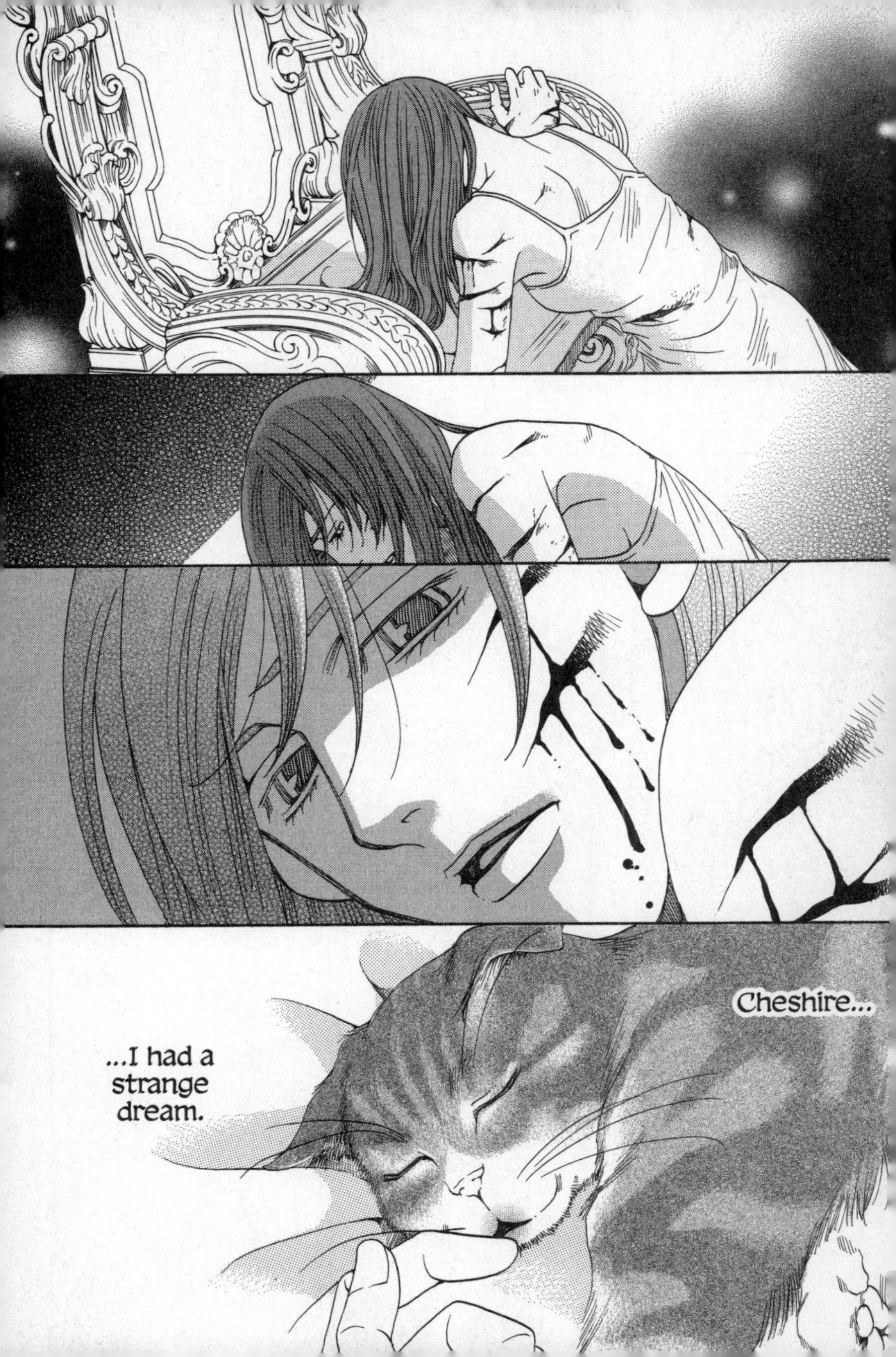
Cheshire...
...I had a strange dream.

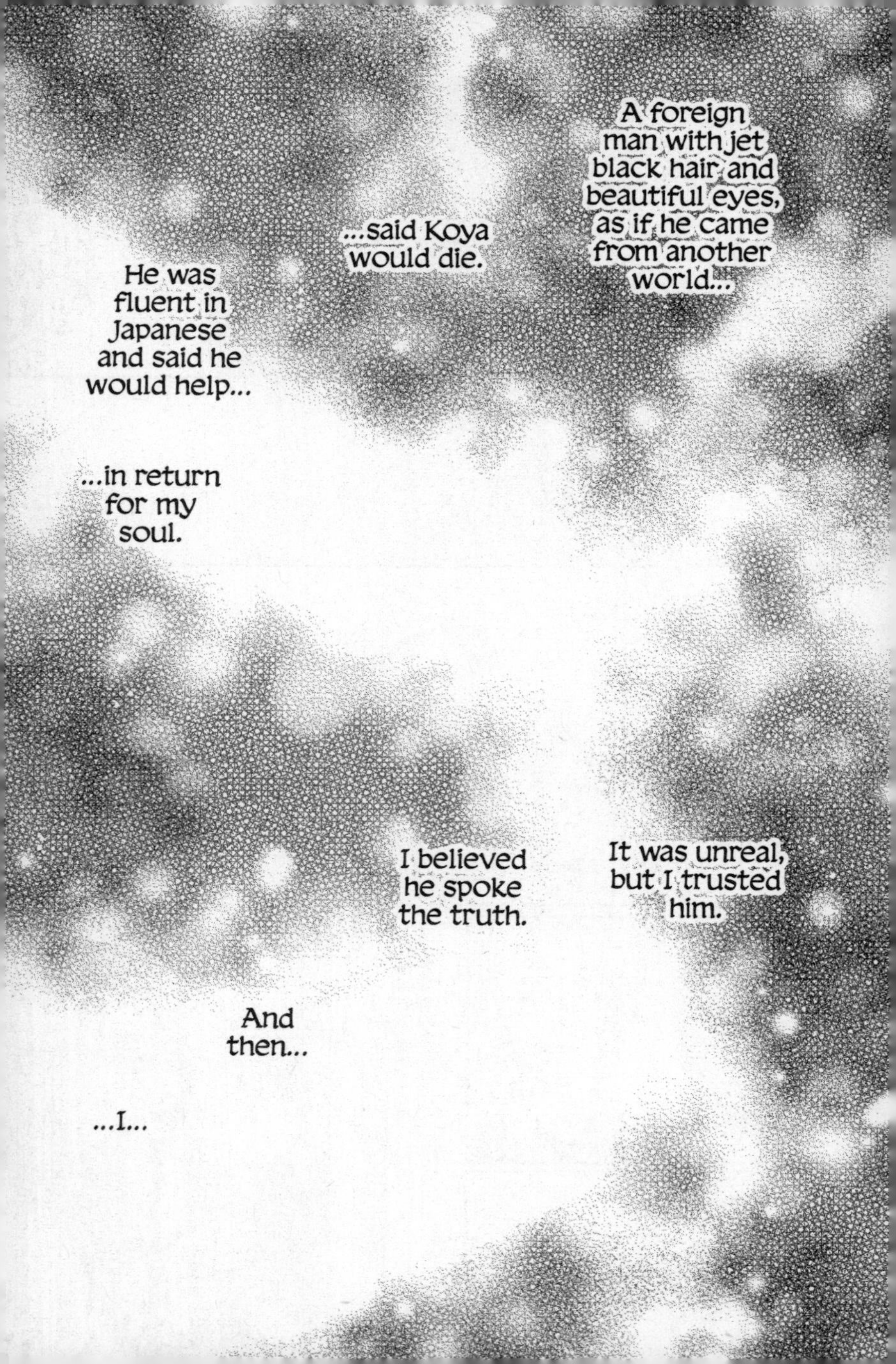
A foreign man with jet black hair and beautiful eyes, as if he came from another world...
...said Koya would die.
He was fluent in Japanese and said he would help...
...in return for my soul.
It was unreal, but I trusted him.
I believed he spoke the truth.
And then...
...I...

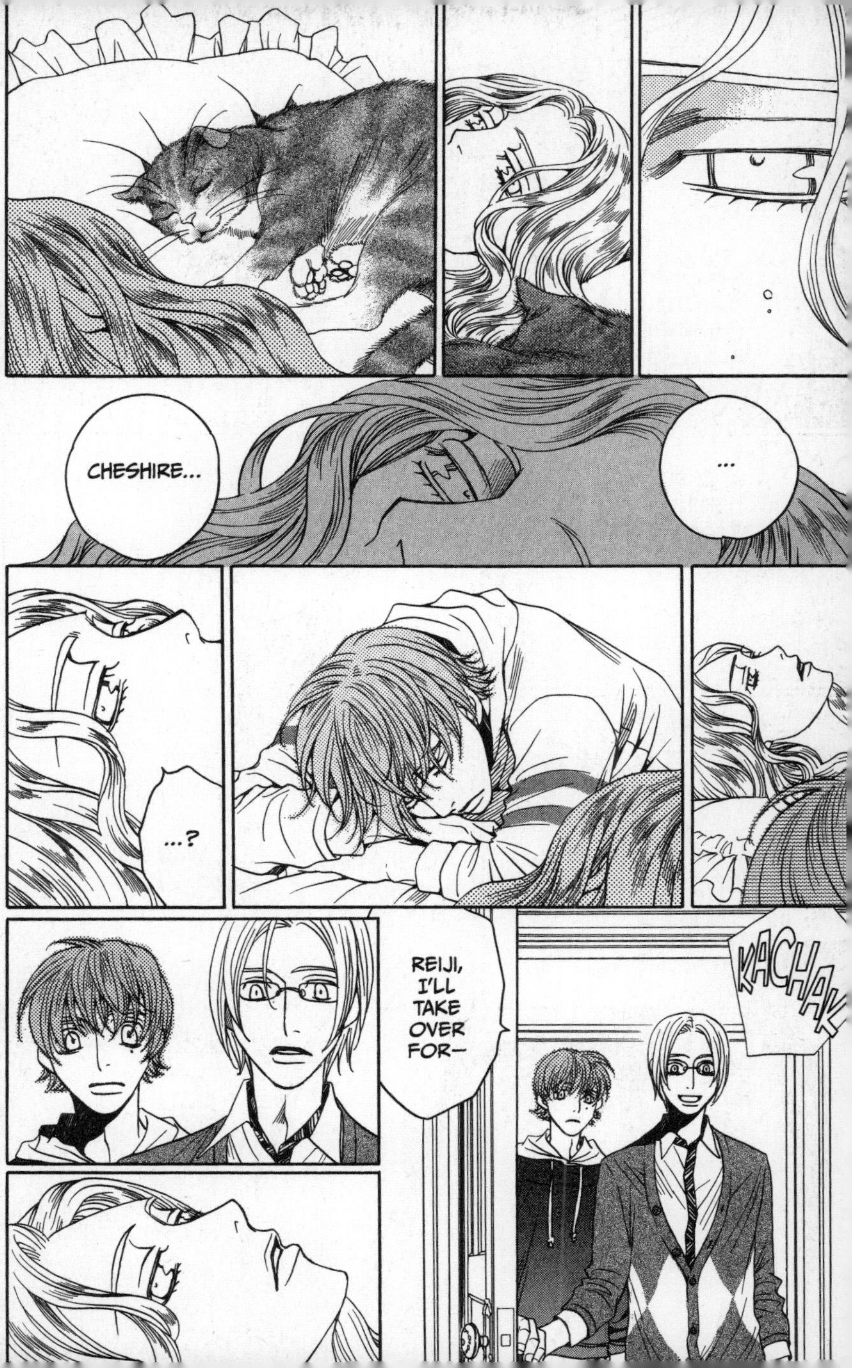
...
CHESHIRE...
...?
KACHAK
REIJI, I'LL TAKE OVER FOR—

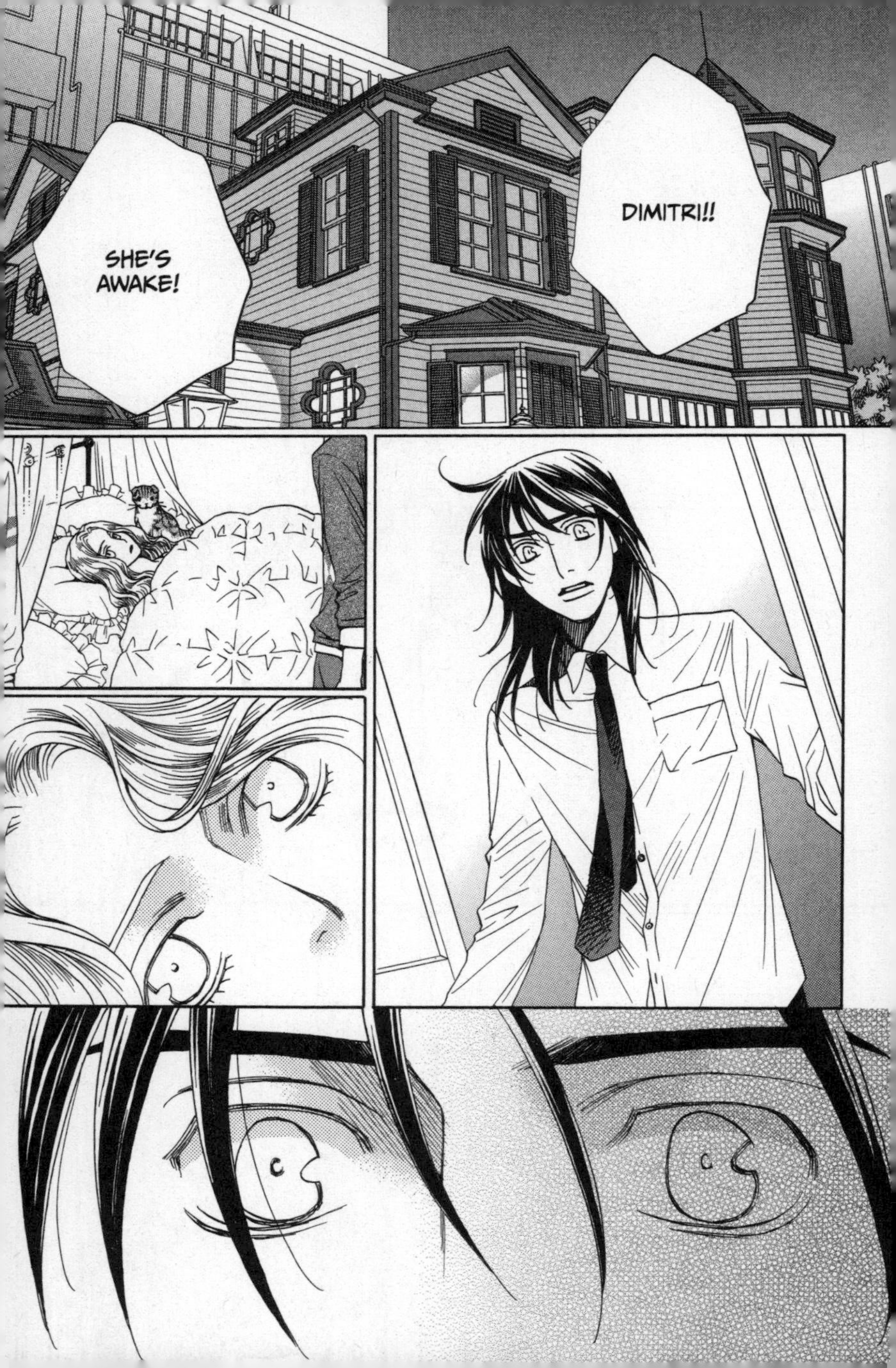
DIMITRI!!
SHE'S AWAKE!

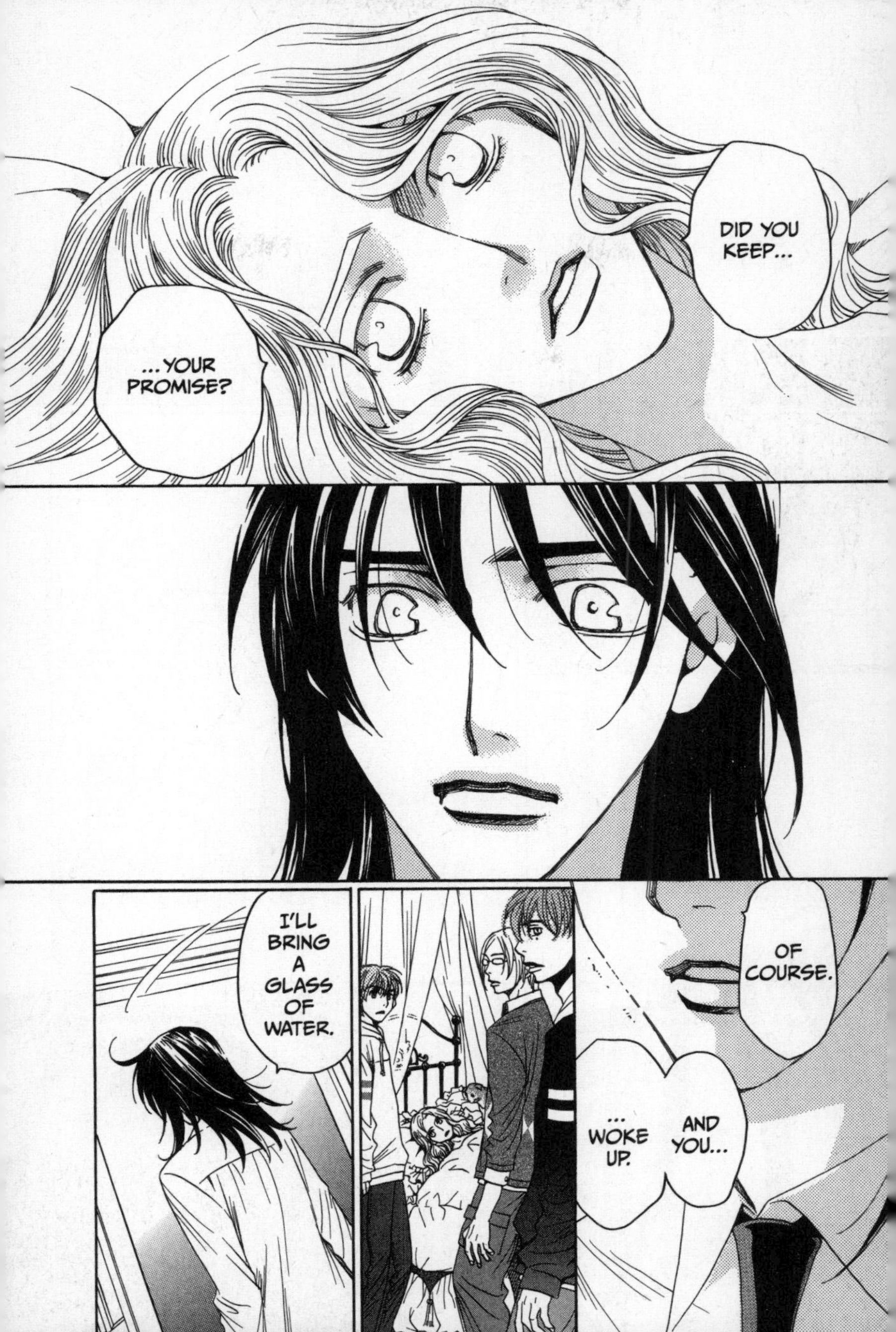
DID YOU KEEP...
...YOUR PROMISE?
OF COURSE.
AND YOU...
...WOKE UP.
I'LL BRING A GLASS OF WATER.

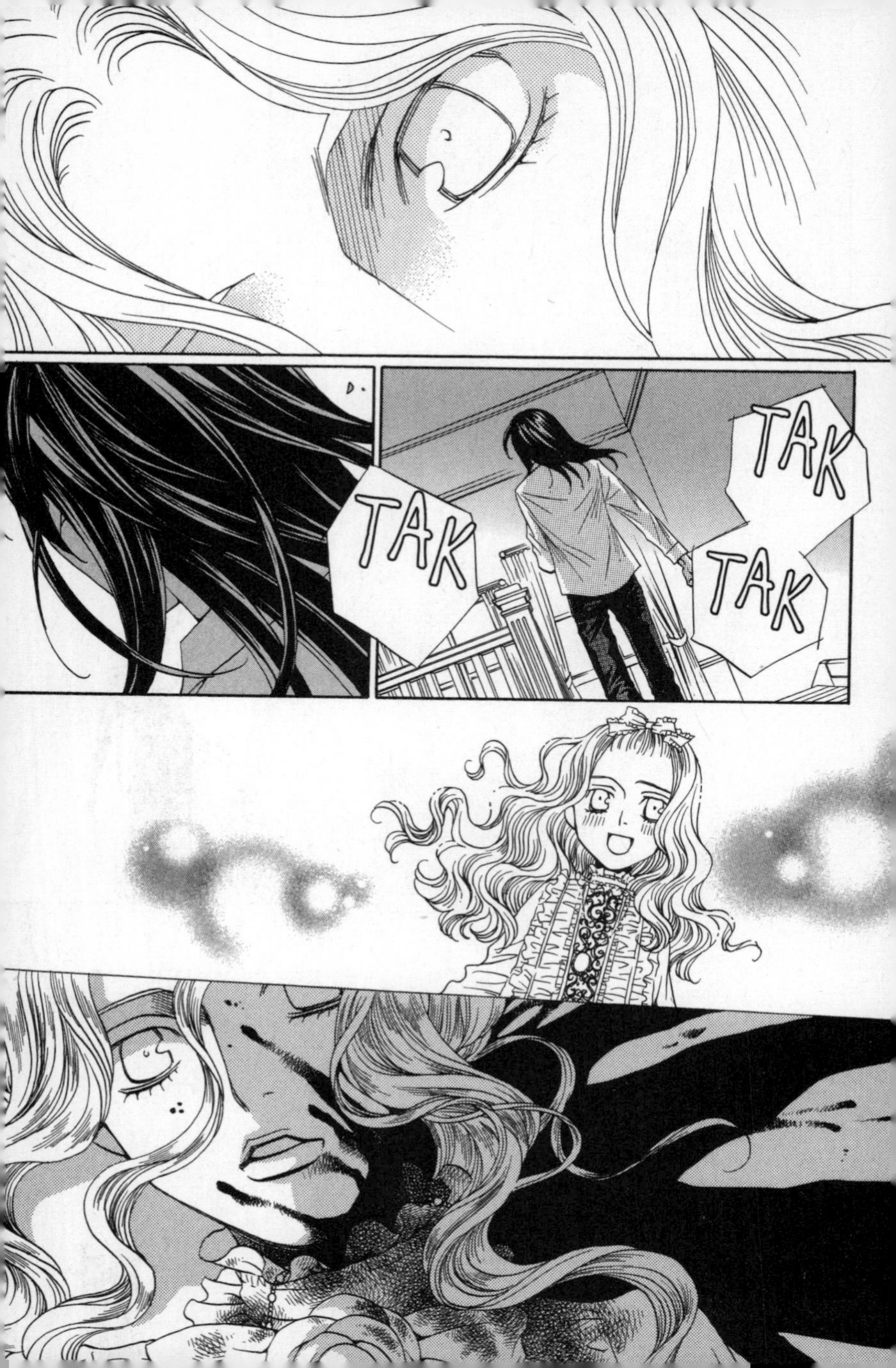
TAK
TAK TAK
TAK

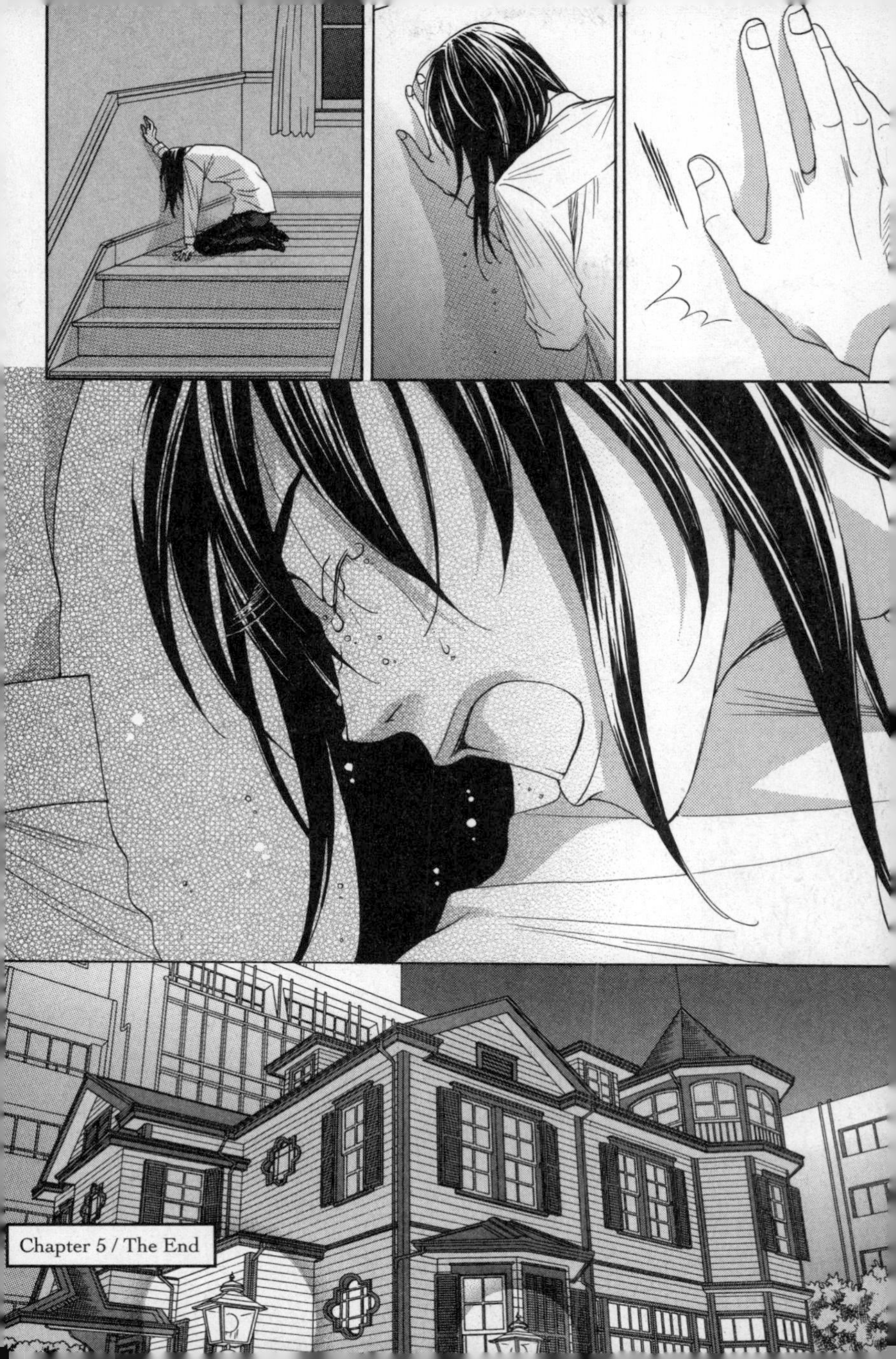
Chapter 5 / The End

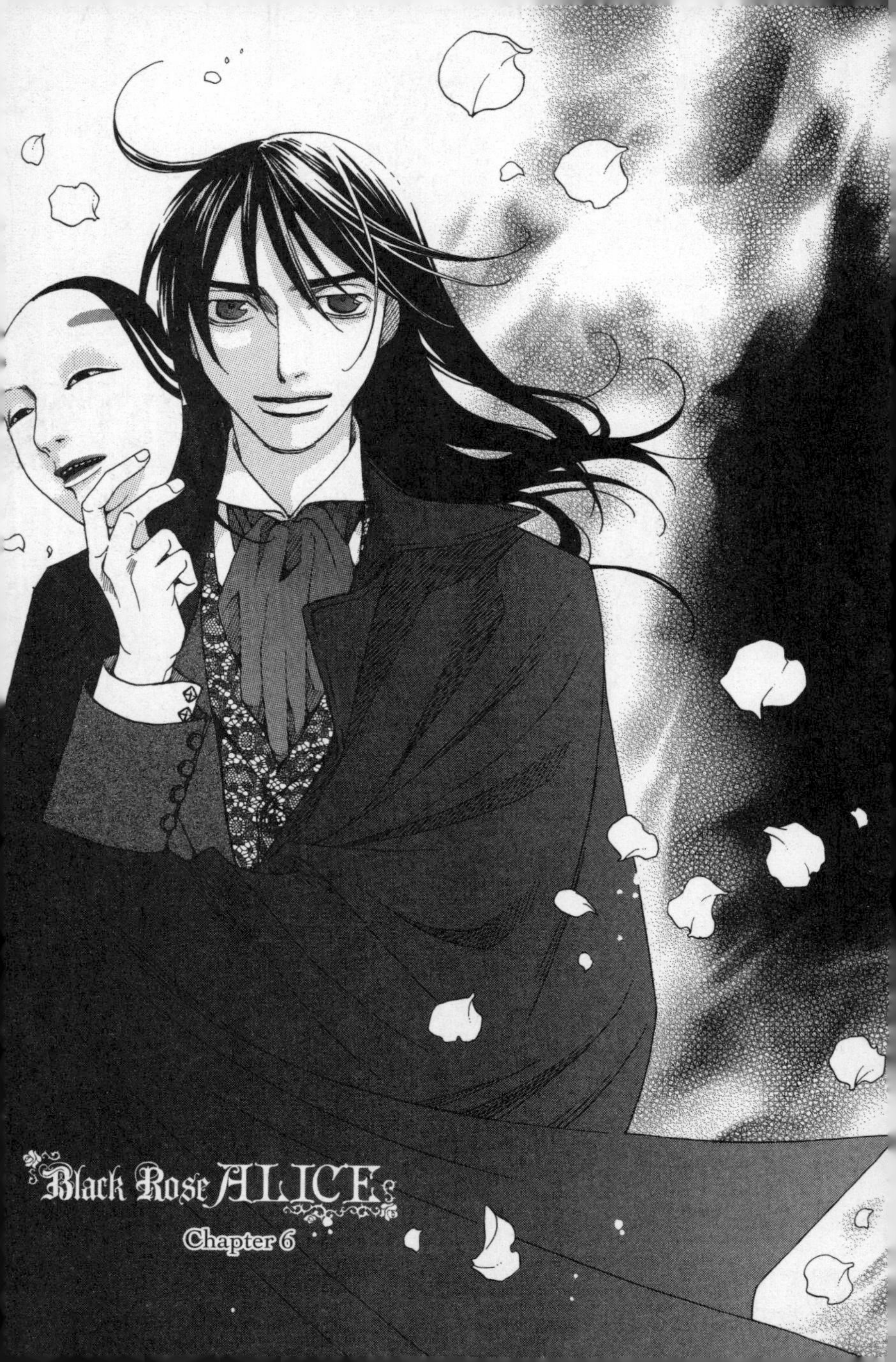
Black Rose ALICE
Chapter 6

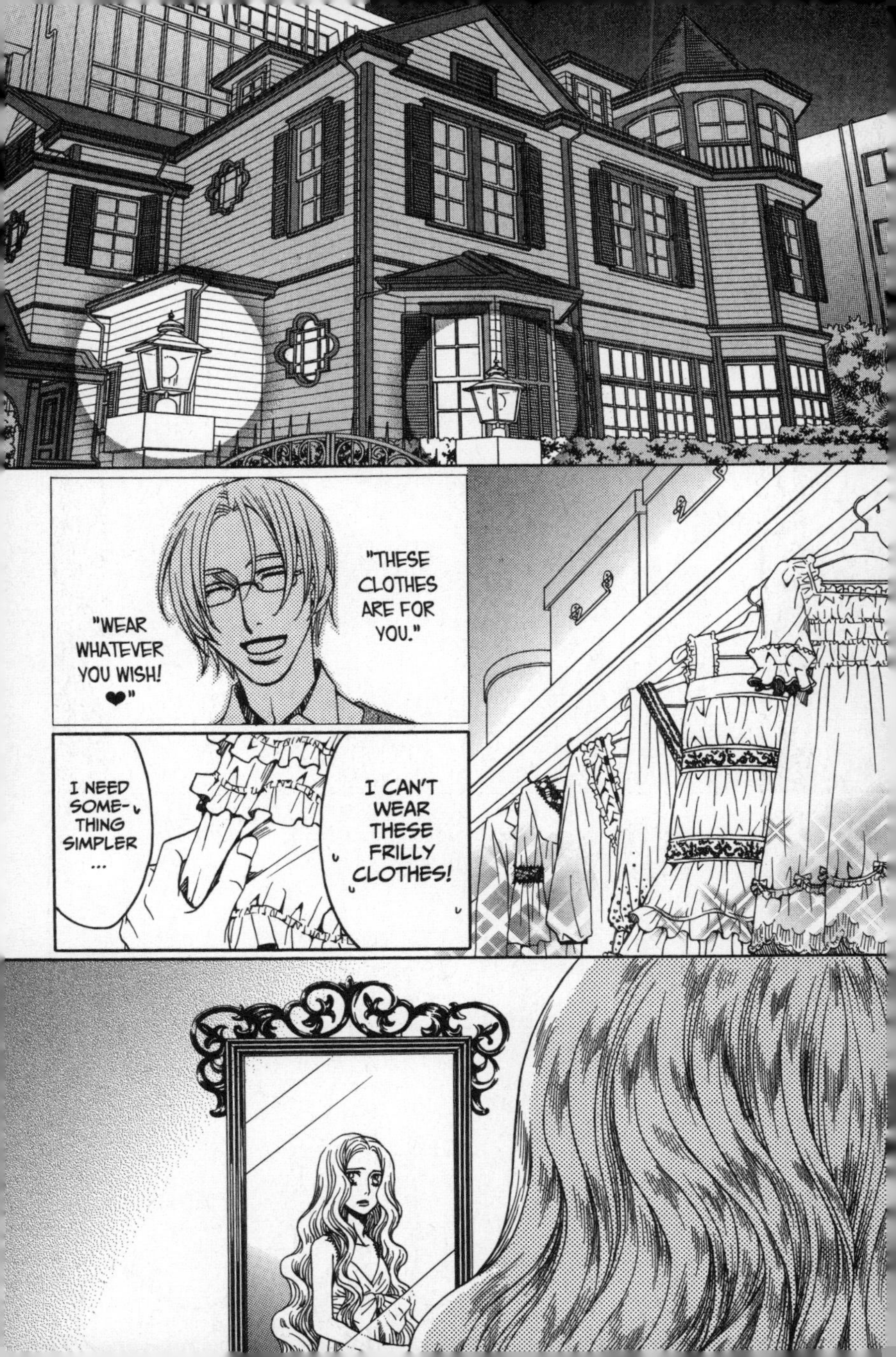
"THESE CLOTHES ARE FOR YOU."
"WEAR WHATEVER YOU WISH! ❤"
I CAN'T WEAR THESE FRILLY CLOTHES!
I NEED SOME-THING SIMPLER ...

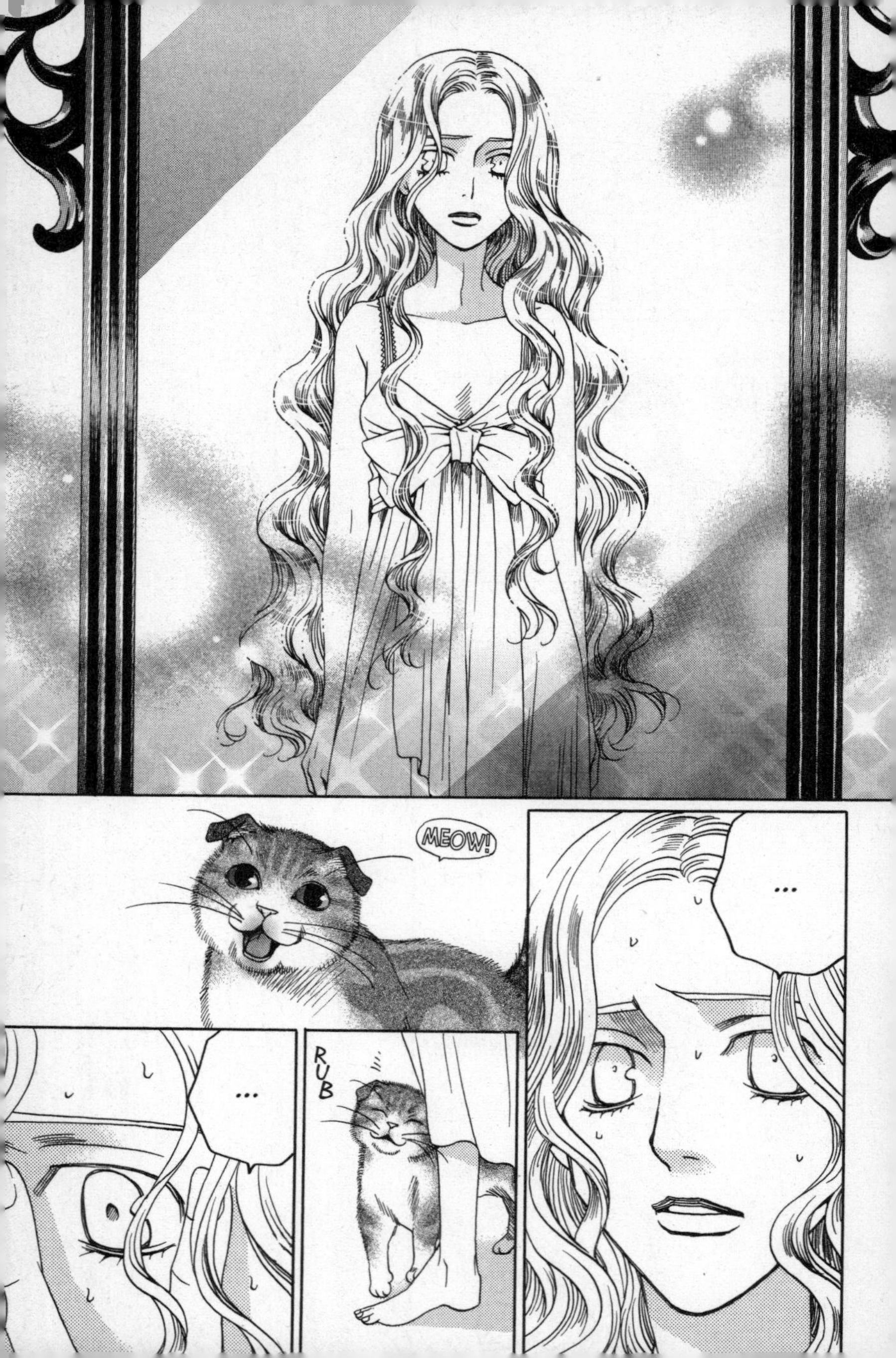
...
MEOW!
RUB
...

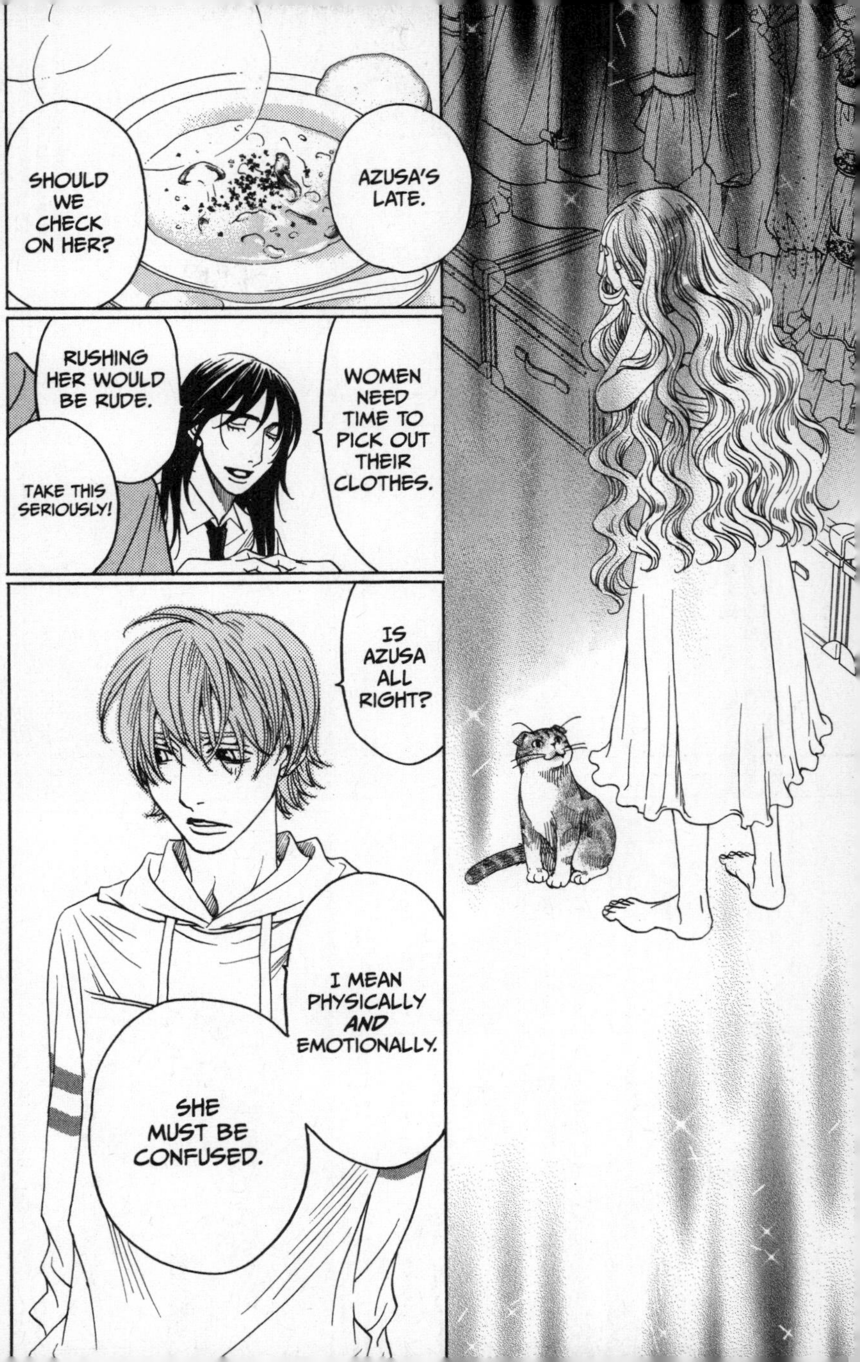
AZUSA'S LATE.
SHOULD WE CHECK ON HER?
WOMEN NEED TIME TO PICK OUT THEIR CLOTHES.
RUSHING HER WOULD BE RUDE.
TAKE THIS SERIOUSLY!
IS AZUSA ALL RIGHT?
I MEAN PHYSICALLY *AND* EMOTIONALLY.
SHE MUST BE CONFUSED.

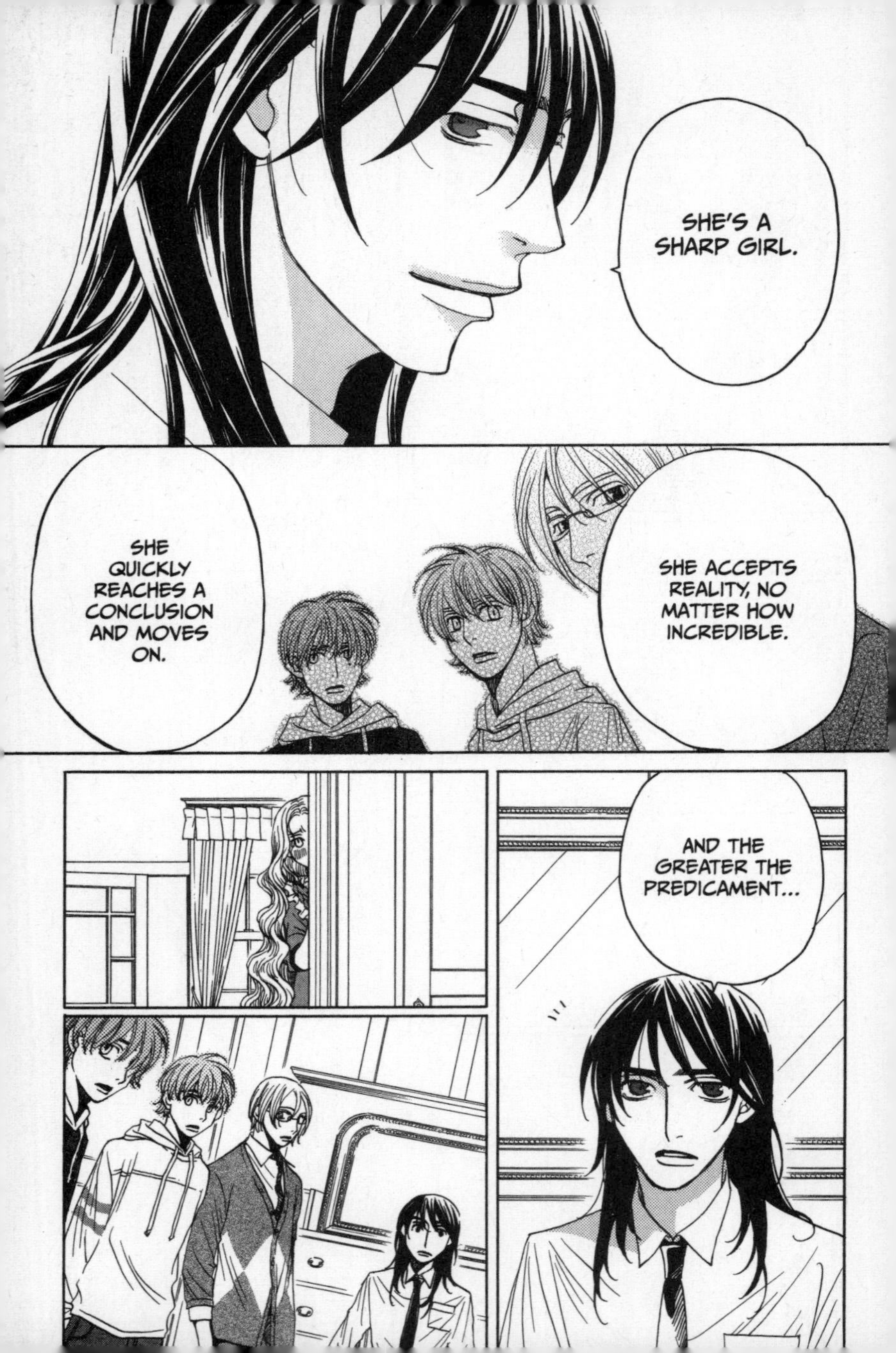
SHE'S A SHARP GIRL.
SHE ACCEPTS REALITY, NO MATTER HOW INCREDIBLE.
SHE QUICKLY REACHES A CONCLUSION AND MOVES ON.
AND THE GREATER THE PREDICAMENT...

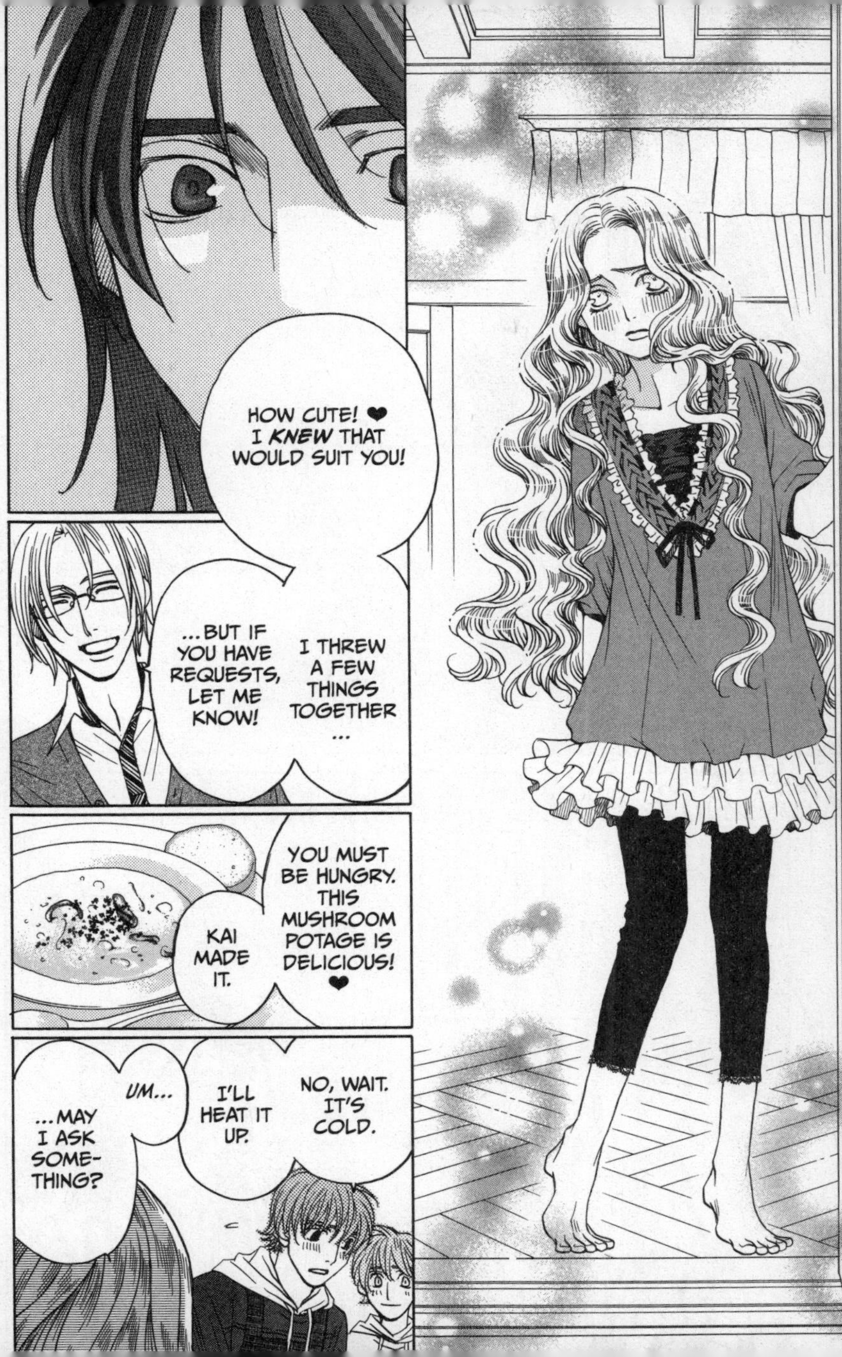
HOW CUTE! ❤ I *KNEW* THAT WOULD SUIT YOU!
I THREW A FEW THINGS TOGETHER...
...BUT IF YOU HAVE REQUESTS, LET ME KNOW!
YOU MUST BE HUNGRY. THIS MUSHROOM POTAGE IS DELICIOUS! ❤
KAI MADE IT.
NO, WAIT. IT'S COLD.
I'LL HEAT IT UP.
UM...
...MAY I ASK SOME-THING?

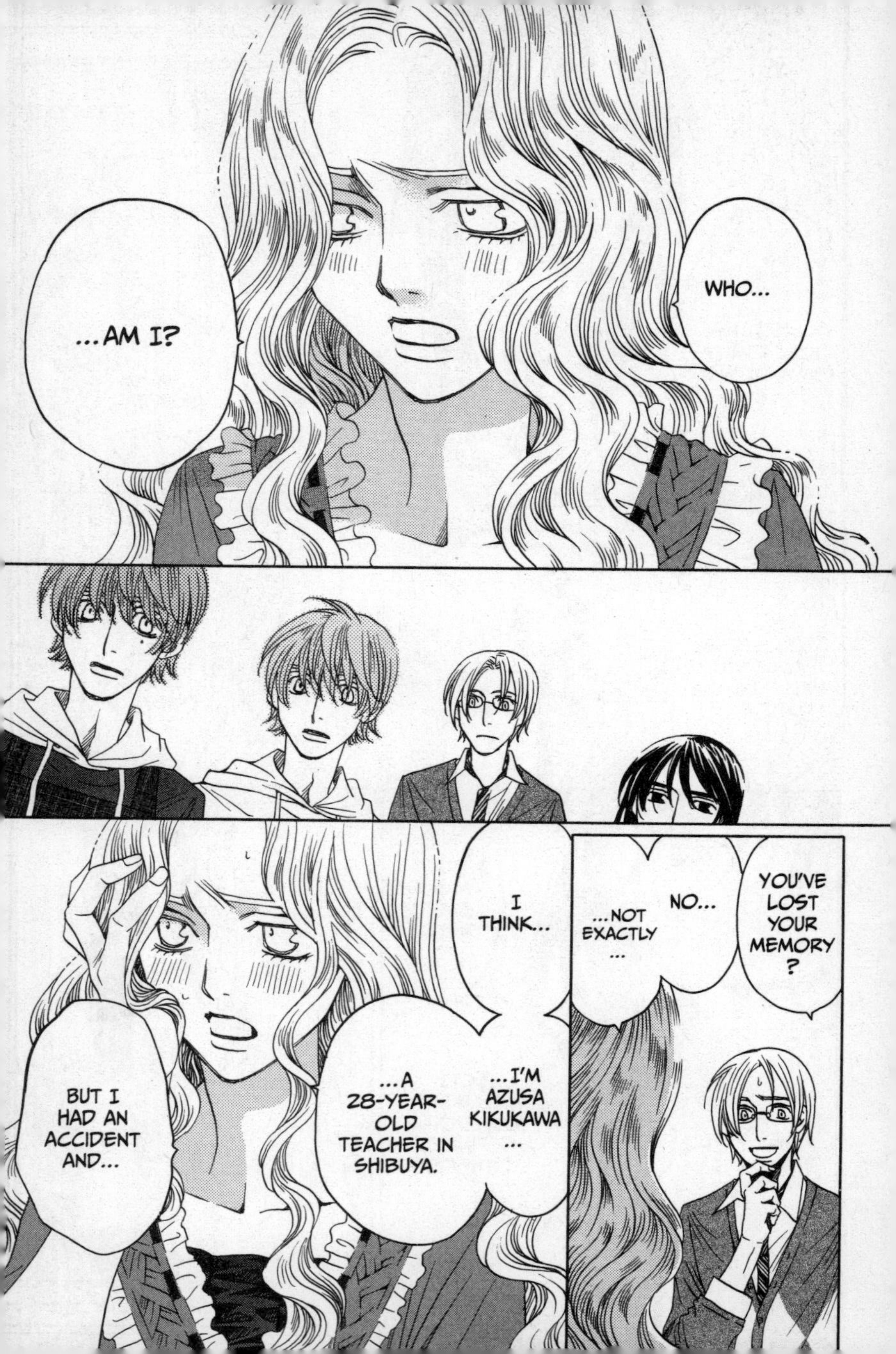
WHO...
...AM I?
YOU'VE LOST YOUR MEMORY?
NO... ...NOT EXACTLY ...
I THINK...
...I'M AZUSA KIKUKAWA ...
...A 28-YEAR-OLD TEACHER IN SHIBUYA.
BUT I HAD AN ACCIDENT AND...

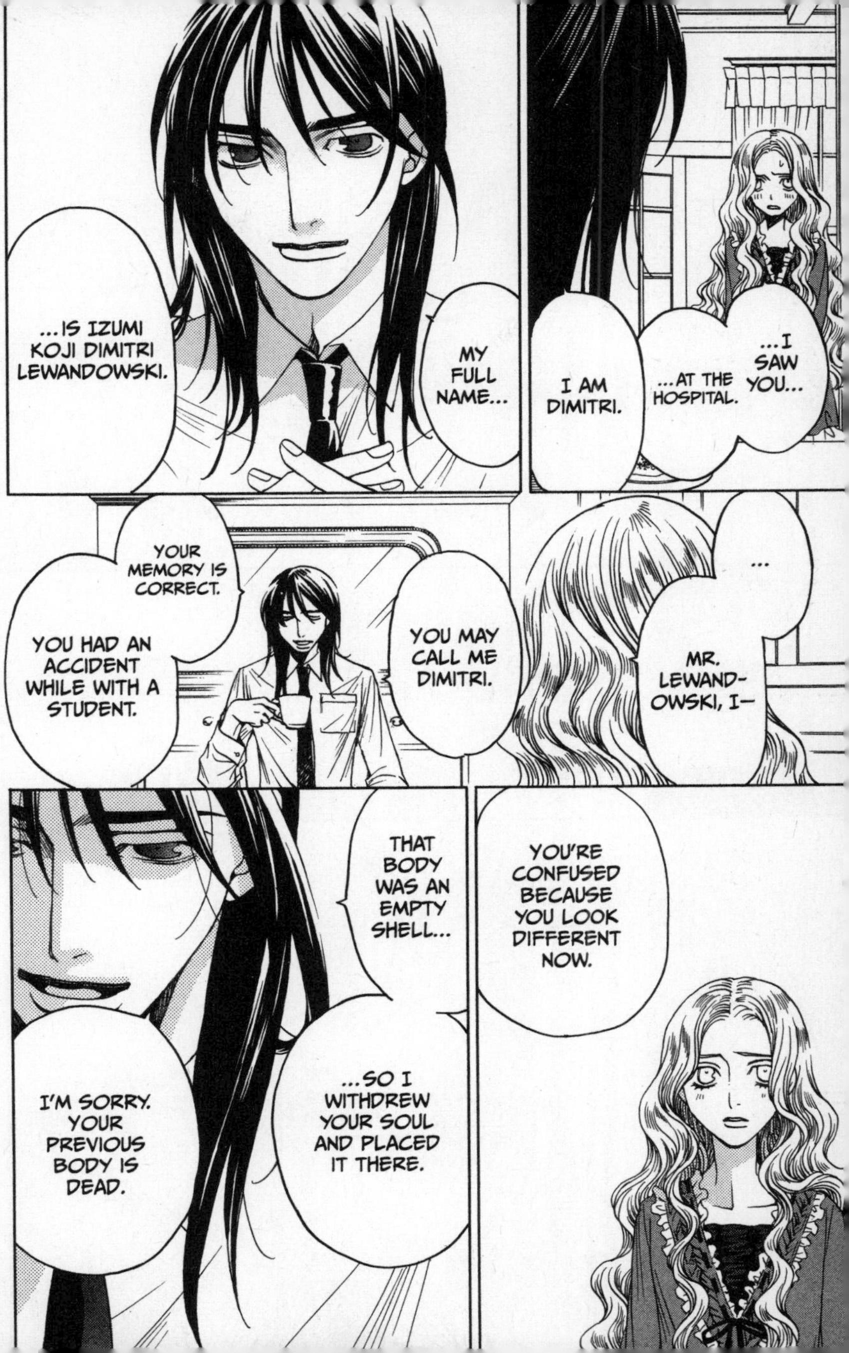
...I SAW YOU...
...AT THE HOSPITAL.
I AM DIMITRI.
MY FULL NAME...
...IS IZUMI KOJI DIMITRI LEWANDOWSKI.
...
MR. LEWANDOWSKI, I—
YOU MAY CALL ME DIMITRI.
YOUR MEMORY IS CORRECT.
YOU HAD AN ACCIDENT WHILE WITH A STUDENT.
YOU'RE CONFUSED BECAUSE YOU LOOK DIFFERENT NOW.
THAT BODY WAS AN EMPTY SHELL...
...SO I WITHDREW YOUR SOUL AND PLACED IT THERE.
I'M SORRY. YOUR PREVIOUS BODY IS DEAD.

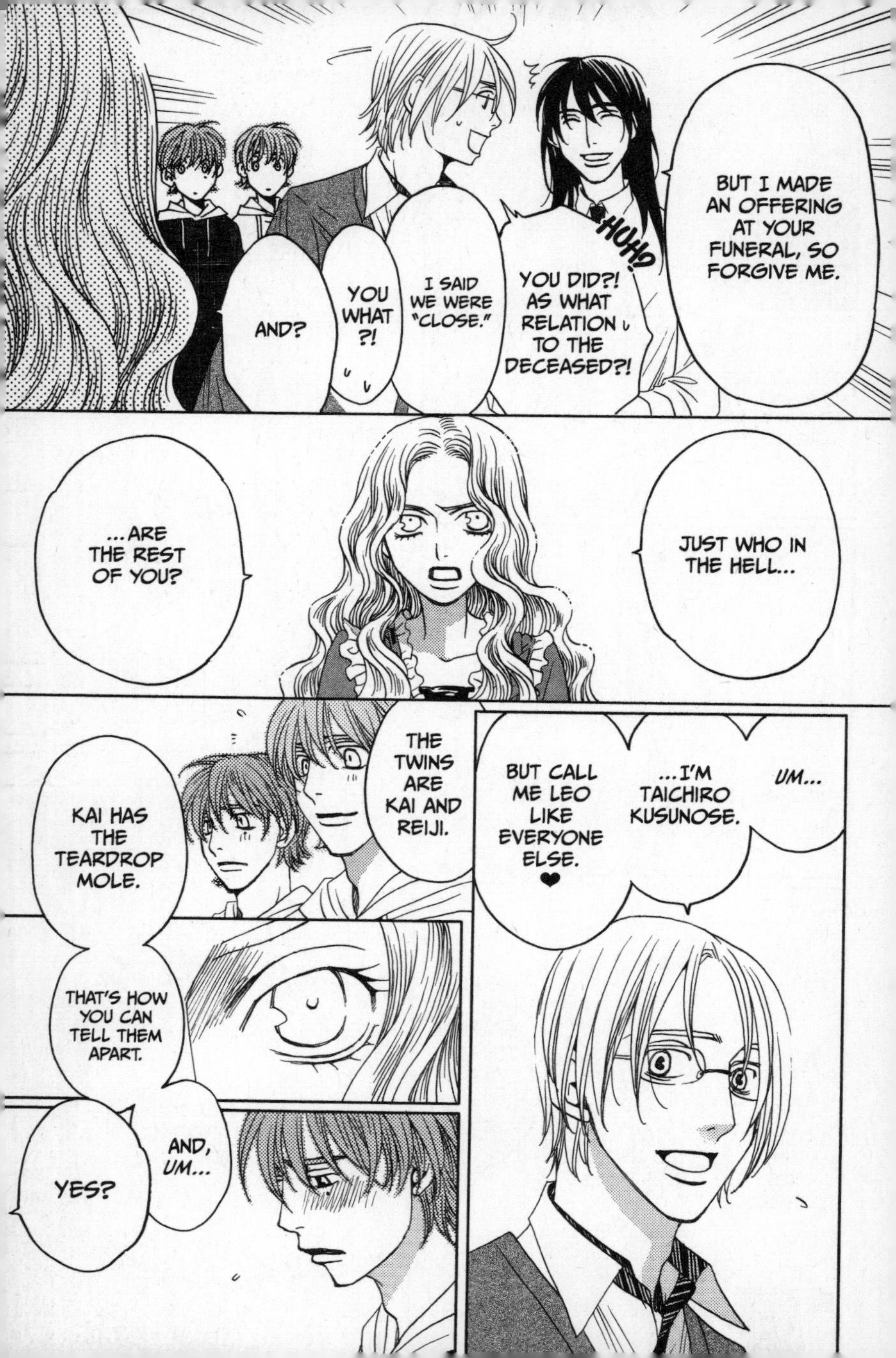
BUT I MADE AN OFFERING AT YOUR FUNERAL, SO FORGIVE ME.
HUH?
YOU DID?! AS WHAT RELATION TO THE DECEASED?!
I SAID WE WERE "CLOSE."
YOU WHAT ?!
AND?
JUST WHO IN THE HELL...
...ARE THE REST OF YOU?
UM...
...I'M TAICHIRO KUSUNOSE.
BUT CALL ME LEO LIKE EVERYONE ELSE. ❤
THE TWINS ARE KAI AND REIJI.
KAI HAS THE TEARDROP MOLE.
THAT'S HOW YOU CAN TELL THEM APART.
AND, UM...
YES?

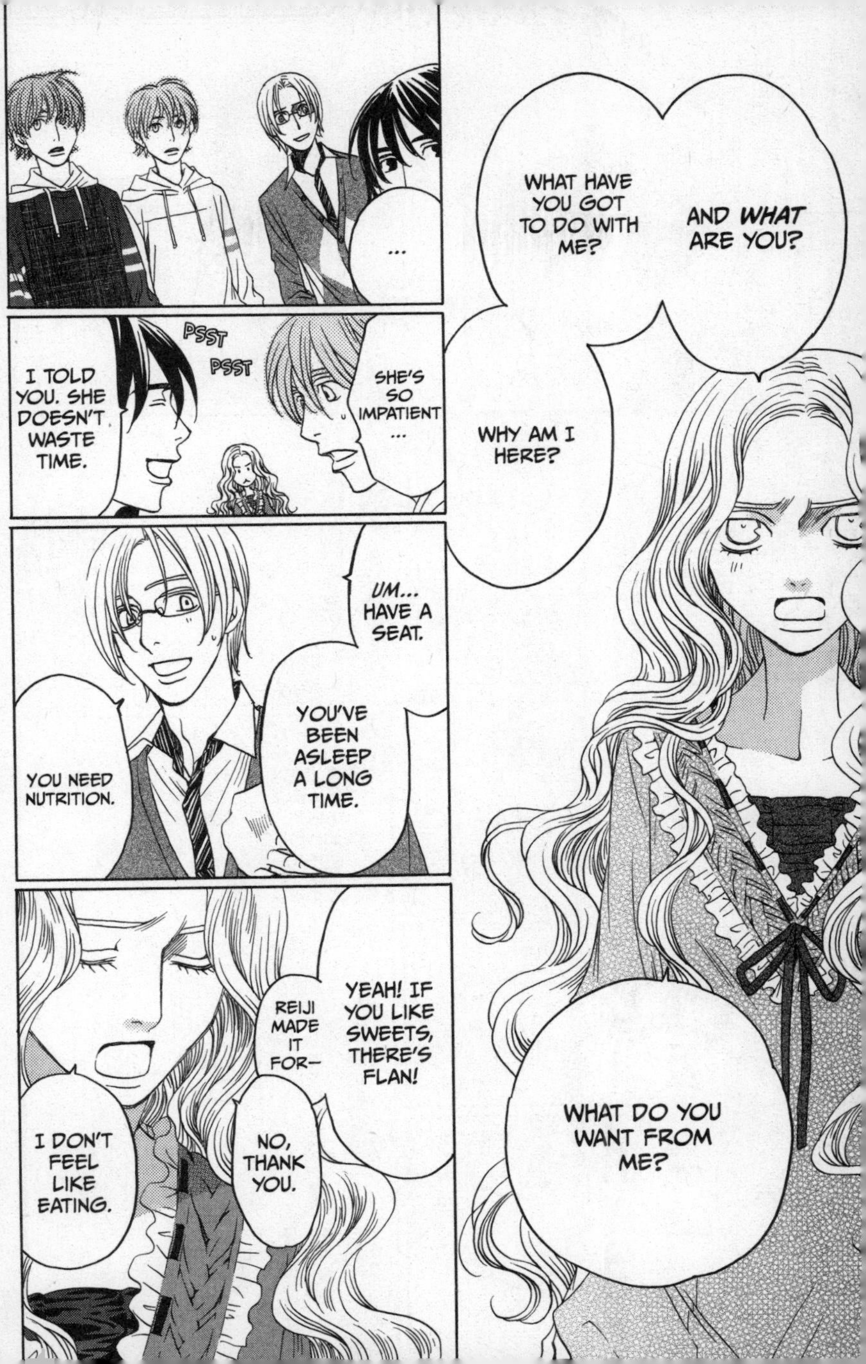
AND *WHAT* ARE YOU?
WHAT HAVE YOU GOT TO DO WITH ME?
WHY AM I HERE?
WHAT DO YOU WANT FROM ME?
...
SHE'S SO IMPATIENT...
PSST
PSST
I TOLD YOU. SHE DOESN'T WASTE TIME.
UM... HAVE A SEAT.
YOU'VE BEEN ASLEEP A LONG TIME.
YOU NEED NUTRITION.
YEAH! IF YOU LIKE SWEETS, THERE'S FLAN!
REIJI MADE IT FOR—
NO, THANK YOU.
I DON'T FEEL LIKE EATING.

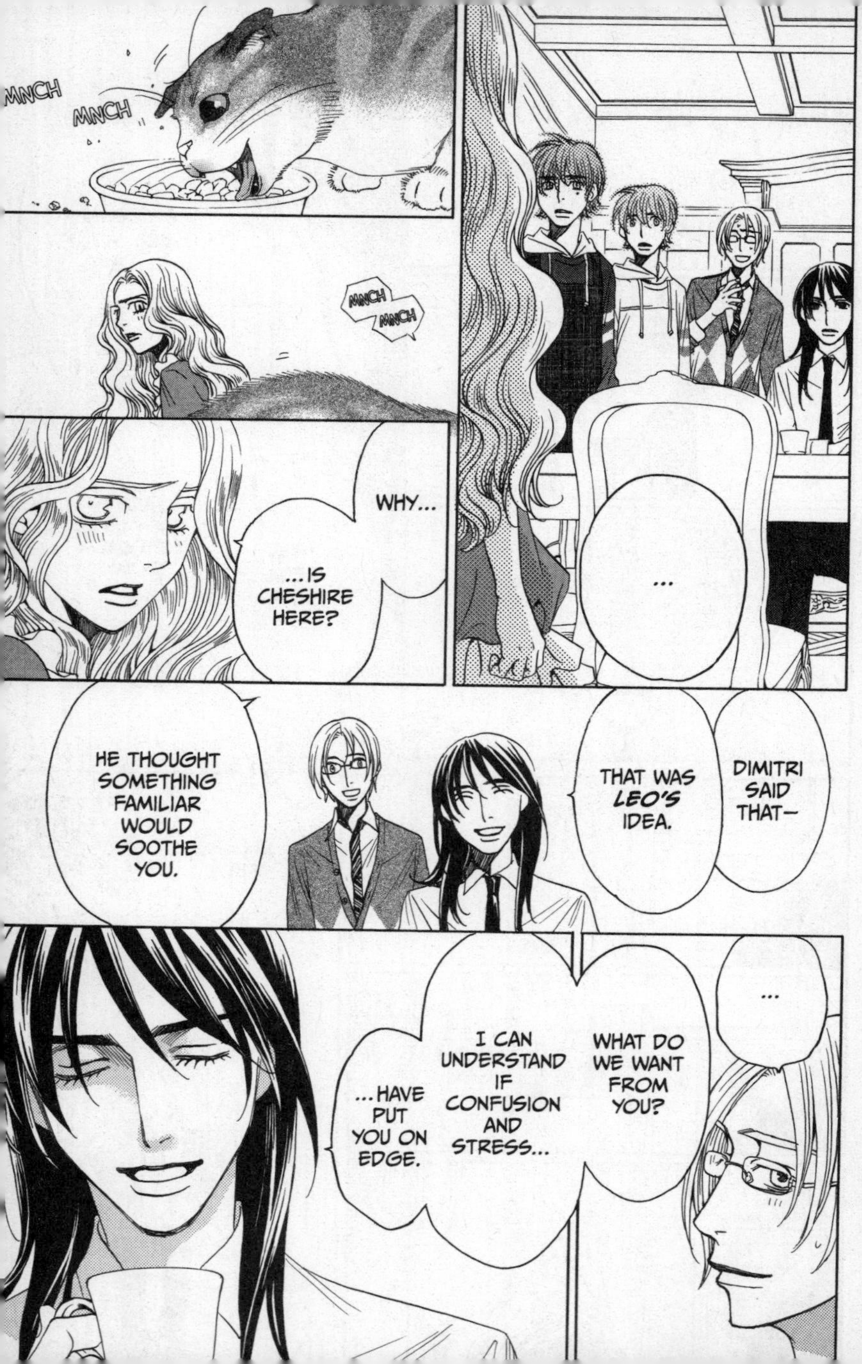
...
MNCH
MNCH
MNCH
MNCH
WHY...
...IS CHESHIRE HERE?
DIMITRI SAID THAT—
THAT WAS *LEO'S* IDEA.
HE THOUGHT SOMETHING FAMILIAR WOULD SOOTHE YOU.
...
WHAT DO WE WANT FROM YOU?
I CAN UNDERSTAND IF CONFUSION AND STRESS...
...HAVE PUT YOU ON EDGE.

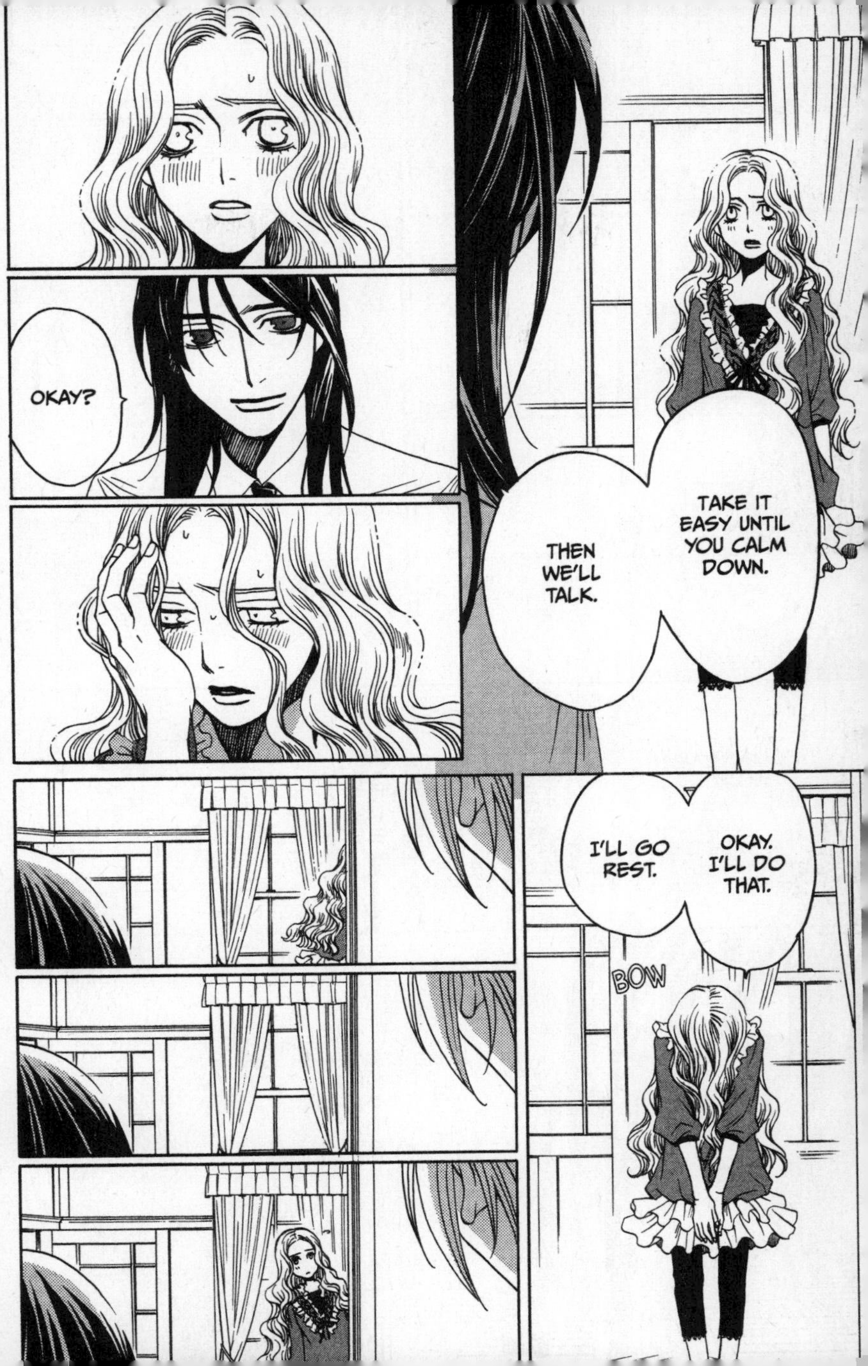
TAKE IT EASY UNTIL YOU CALM DOWN.
THEN WE'LL TALK.
OKAY?
OKAY. I'LL DO THAT.
I'LL GO REST.
BOW

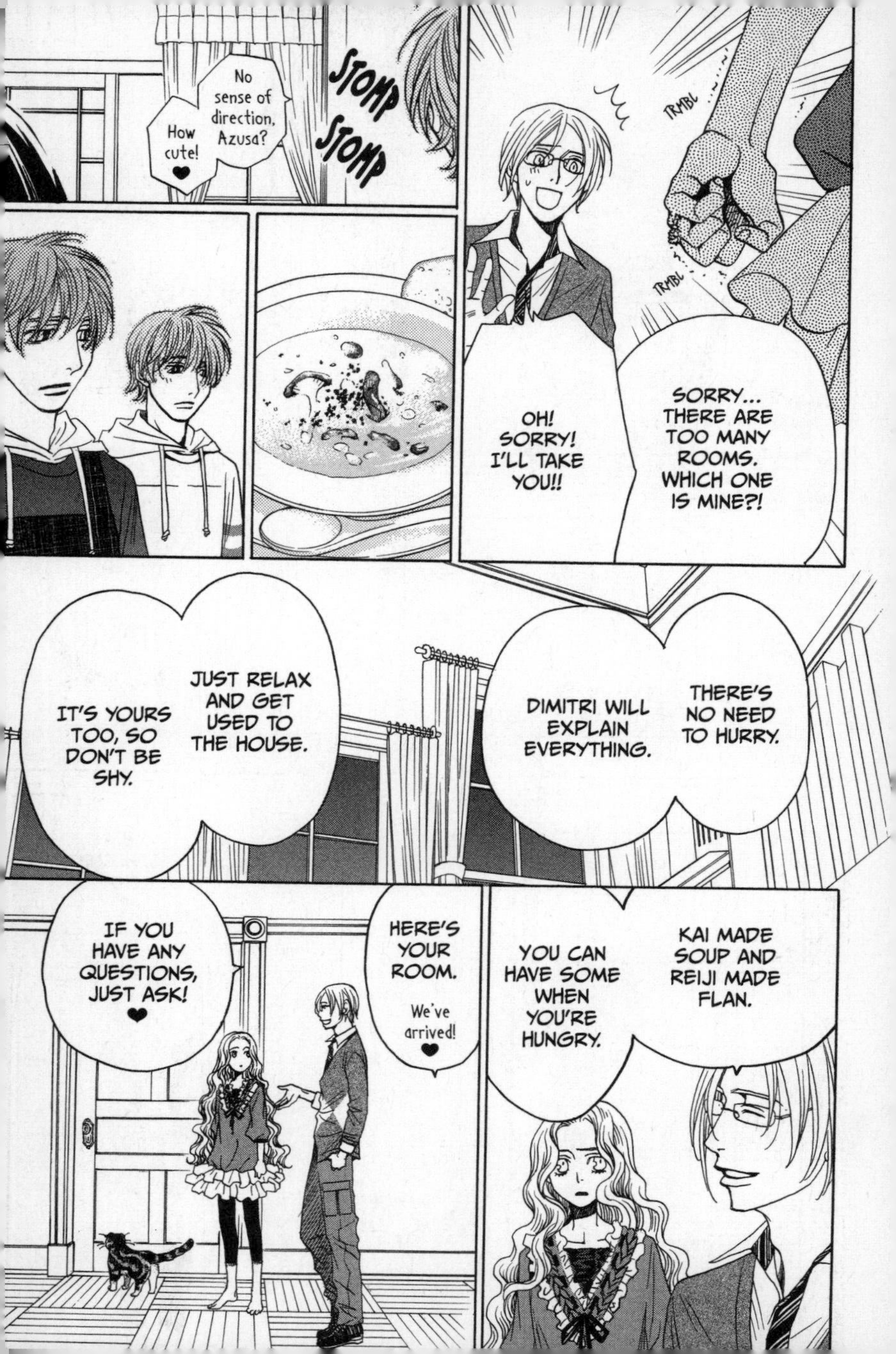
TRMBL
TRMBL
SORRY... THERE ARE TOO MANY ROOMS. WHICH ONE IS MINE?!
OH! SORRY! I'LL TAKE YOU!!
STOMP
STOMP
No sense of direction, Azusa?
How cute!
THERE'S NO NEED TO HURRY.
DIMITRI WILL EXPLAIN EVERYTHING.
JUST RELAX AND GET USED TO THE HOUSE.
IT'S YOURS TOO, SO DON'T BE SHY.
KAI MADE SOUP AND REIJI MADE FLAN.
YOU CAN HAVE SOME WHEN YOU'RE HUNGRY.
HERE'S YOUR ROOM.
We've arrived!
IF YOU HAVE ANY QUESTIONS, JUST ASK!

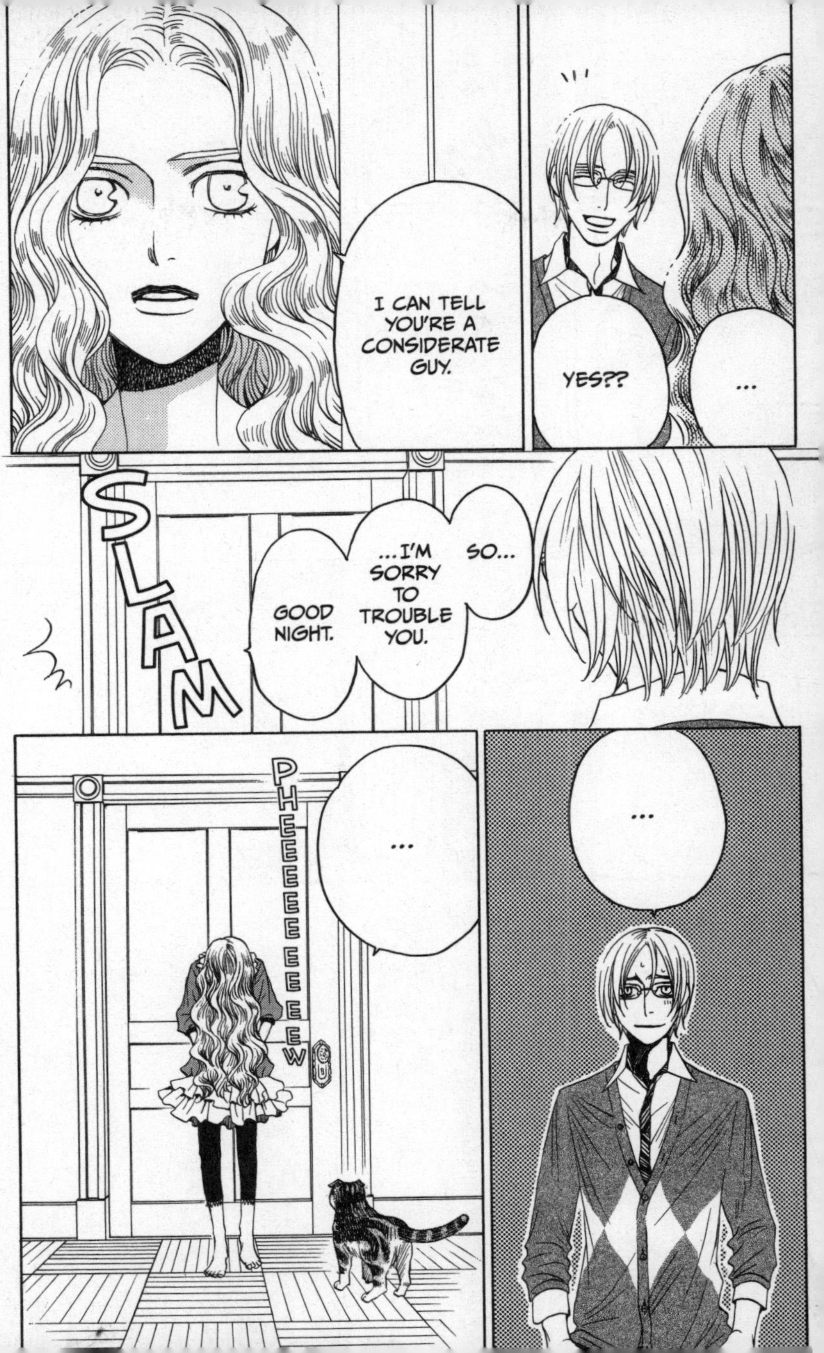
I CAN TELL YOU'RE A CONSIDERATE GUY.
YES??
...
SO...
...I'M SORRY TO TROUBLE YOU.
GOOD NIGHT.
SLAM
...
...
PHEEEEEEEEEEW

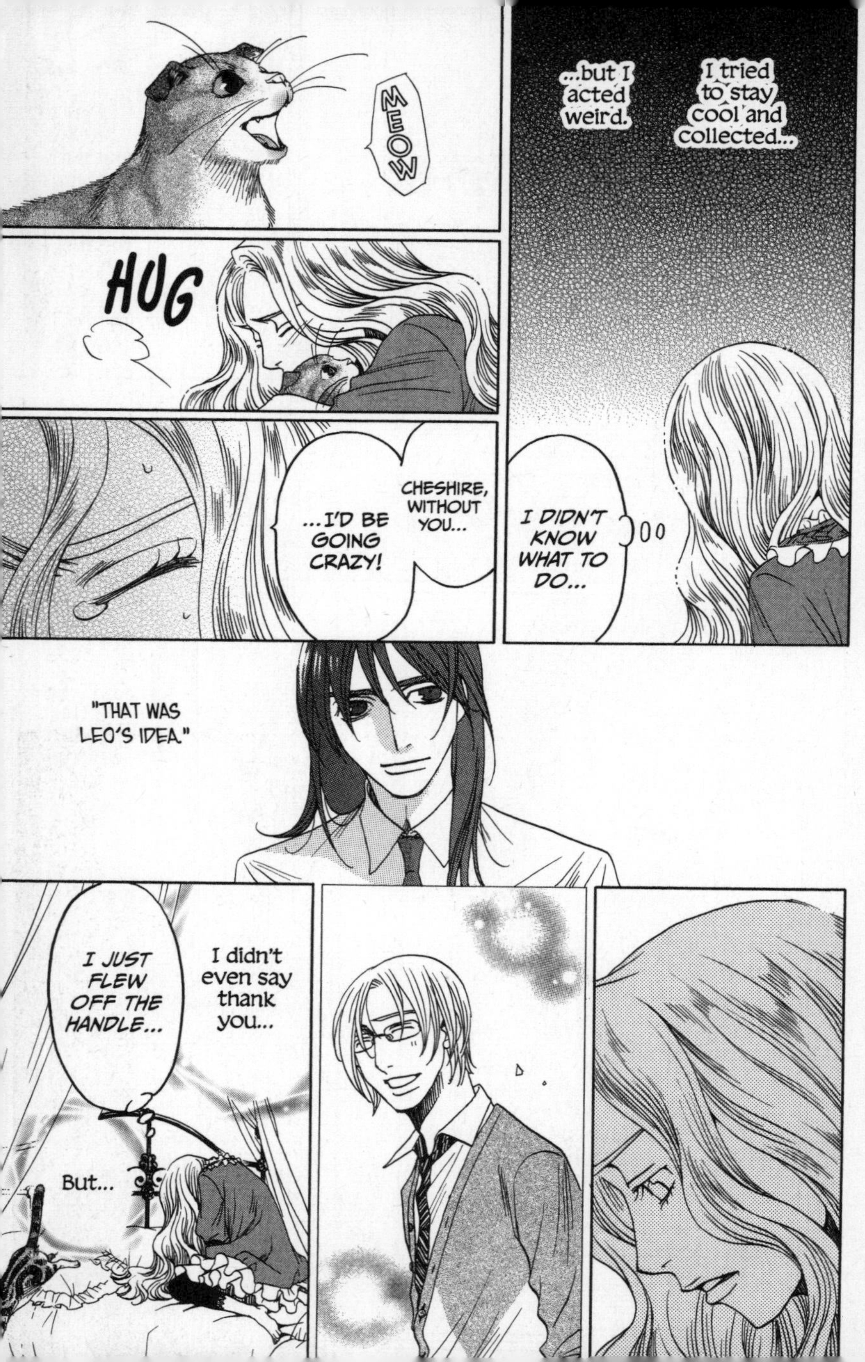
I tried to stay cool and collected...
...but I acted weird.
I DIDN'T KNOW WHAT TO DO...
MEOW
HUG
CHESHIRE, WITHOUT YOU...
...I'D BE GOING CRAZY!
"THAT WAS LEO'S IDEA."
I didn't even say thank you...
I JUST FLEW OFF THE HANDLE...
But...

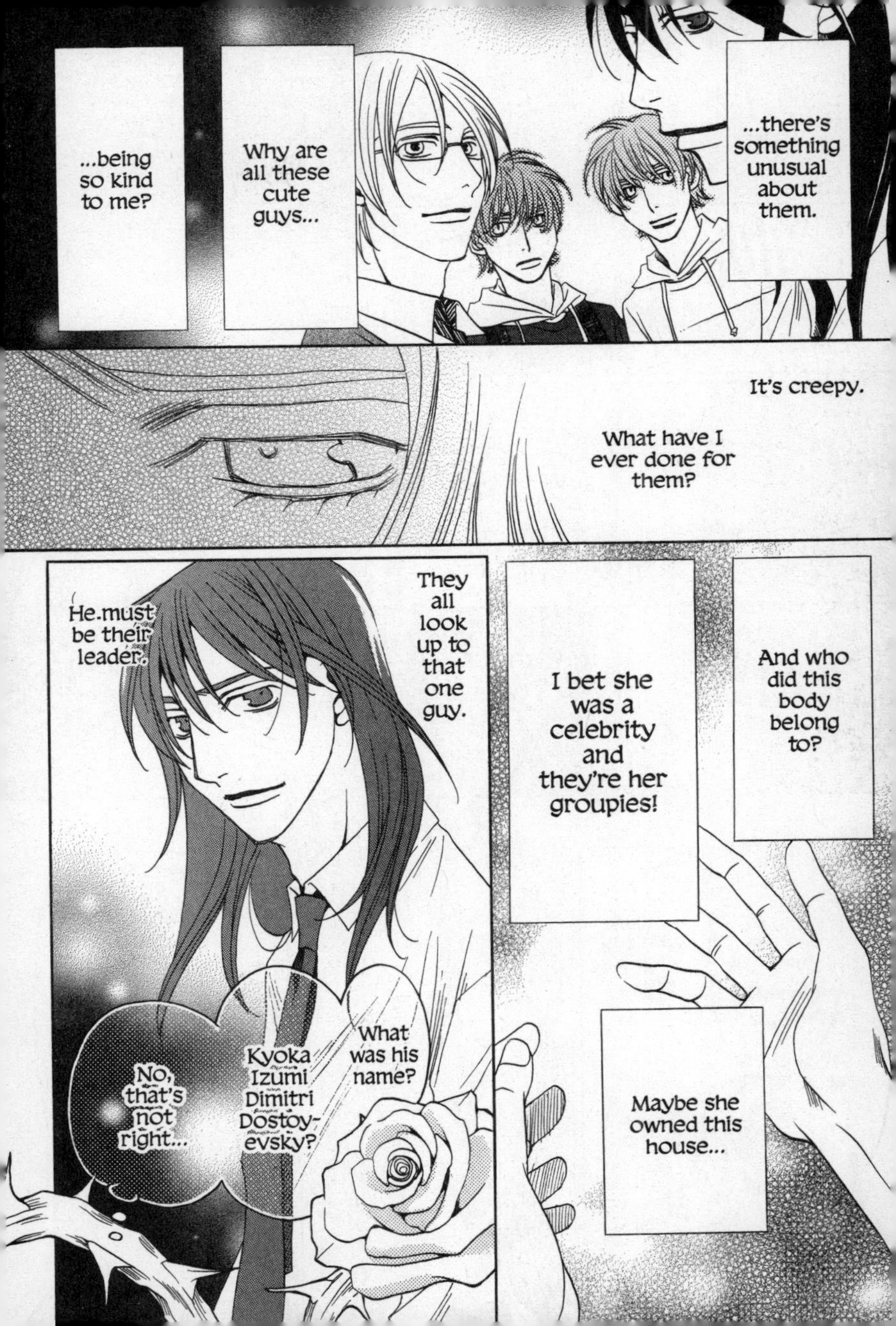
...there's something unusual about them.
Why are all these cute guys...
...being so kind to me?
It's creepy.
What have I ever done for them?
And who did this body belong to?
I bet she was a celebrity and they're her groupies!
Maybe she owned this house...
They all look up to that one guy.
He must be their leader.
What was his name?
Kyoka Izumi Dimitri Dostoy-evsky?
No, that's not right...

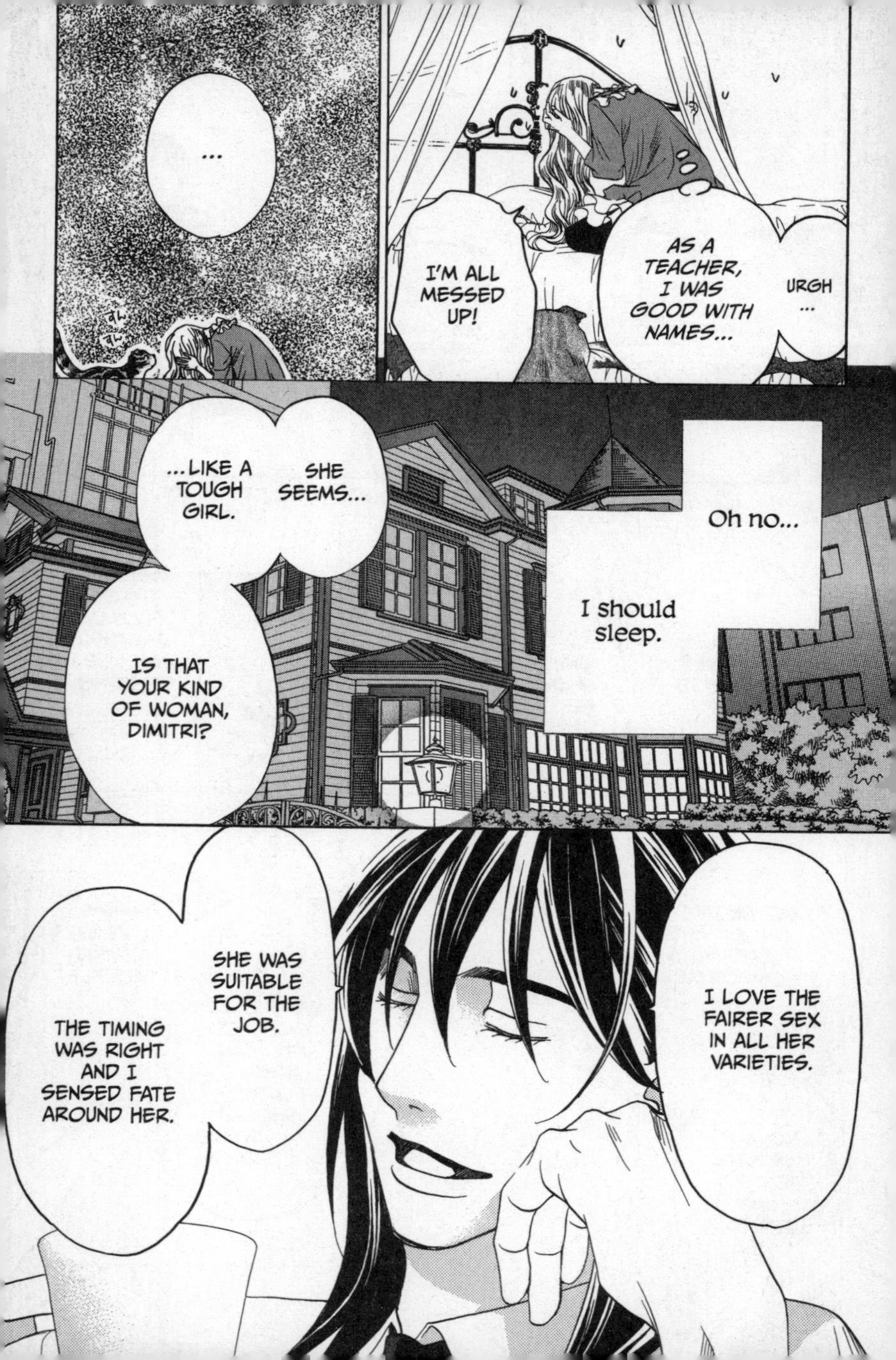
URGH ...
AS A TEACHER, I WAS GOOD WITH NAMES...
I'M ALL MESSED UP!
...
Oh no...
I should sleep.
SHE SEEMS...
...LIKE A TOUGH GIRL.
IS THAT YOUR KIND OF WOMAN, DIMITRI?
I LOVE THE FAIRER SEX IN ALL HER VARIETIES.
SHE WAS SUITABLE FOR THE JOB.
THE TIMING WAS RIGHT AND I SENSED FATE AROUND HER.

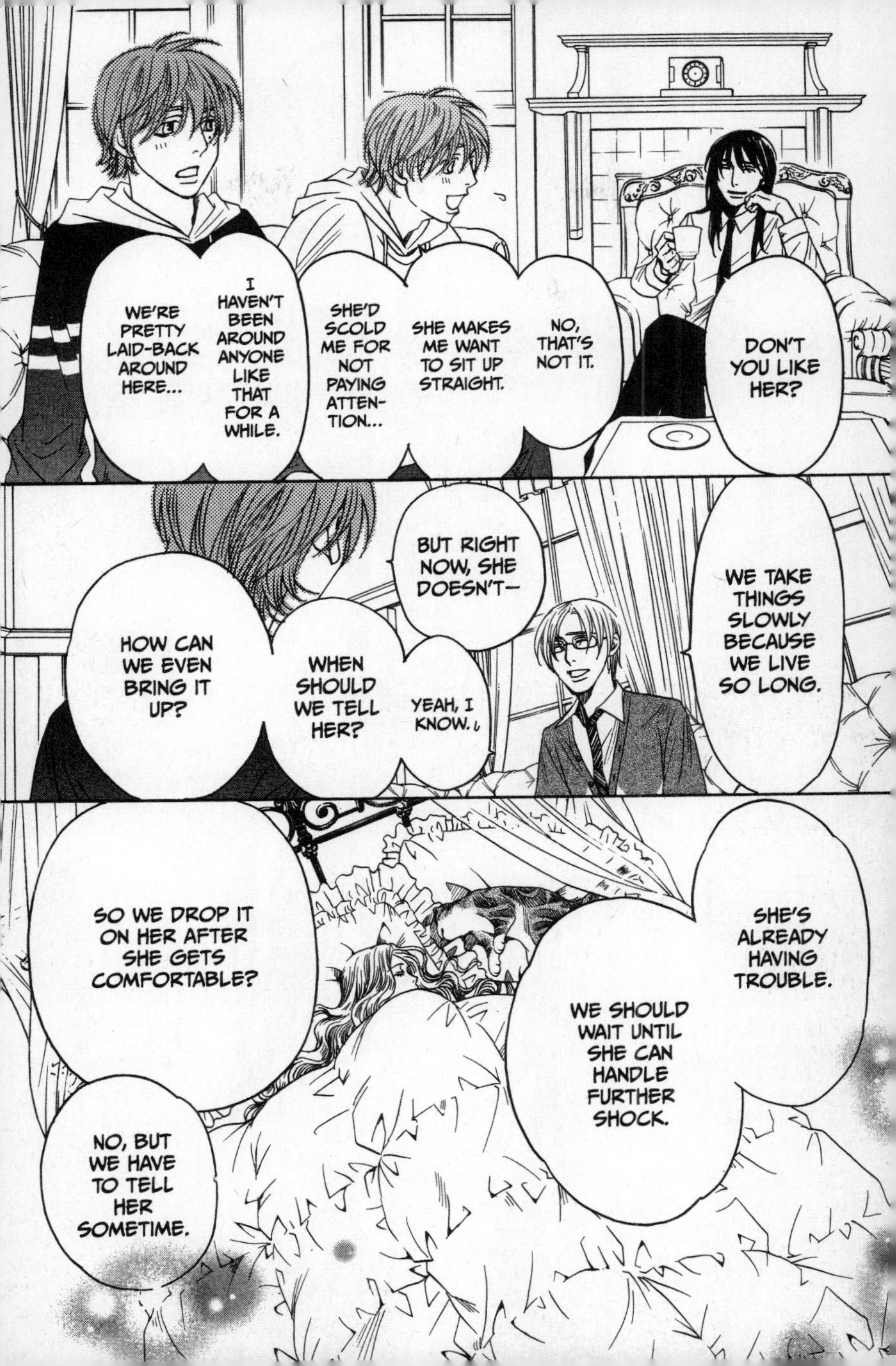
DON'T YOU LIKE HER?
NO, THAT'S NOT IT.
SHE MAKES ME WANT TO SIT UP STRAIGHT.
SHE'D SCOLD ME FOR NOT PAYING ATTEN-TION...
I HAVEN'T BEEN AROUND ANYONE LIKE THAT FOR A WHILE.
WE'RE PRETTY LAID-BACK AROUND HERE...
WE TAKE THINGS SLOWLY BECAUSE WE LIVE SO LONG.
BUT RIGHT NOW, SHE DOESN'T—
YEAH, I KNOW.
WHEN SHOULD WE TELL HER?
HOW CAN WE EVEN BRING IT UP?
SHE'S ALREADY HAVING TROUBLE.
WE SHOULD WAIT UNTIL SHE CAN HANDLE FURTHER SHOCK.
SO WE DROP IT ON HER AFTER SHE GETS COMFORTABLE?
NO, BUT WE HAVE TO TELL HER SOMETIME.

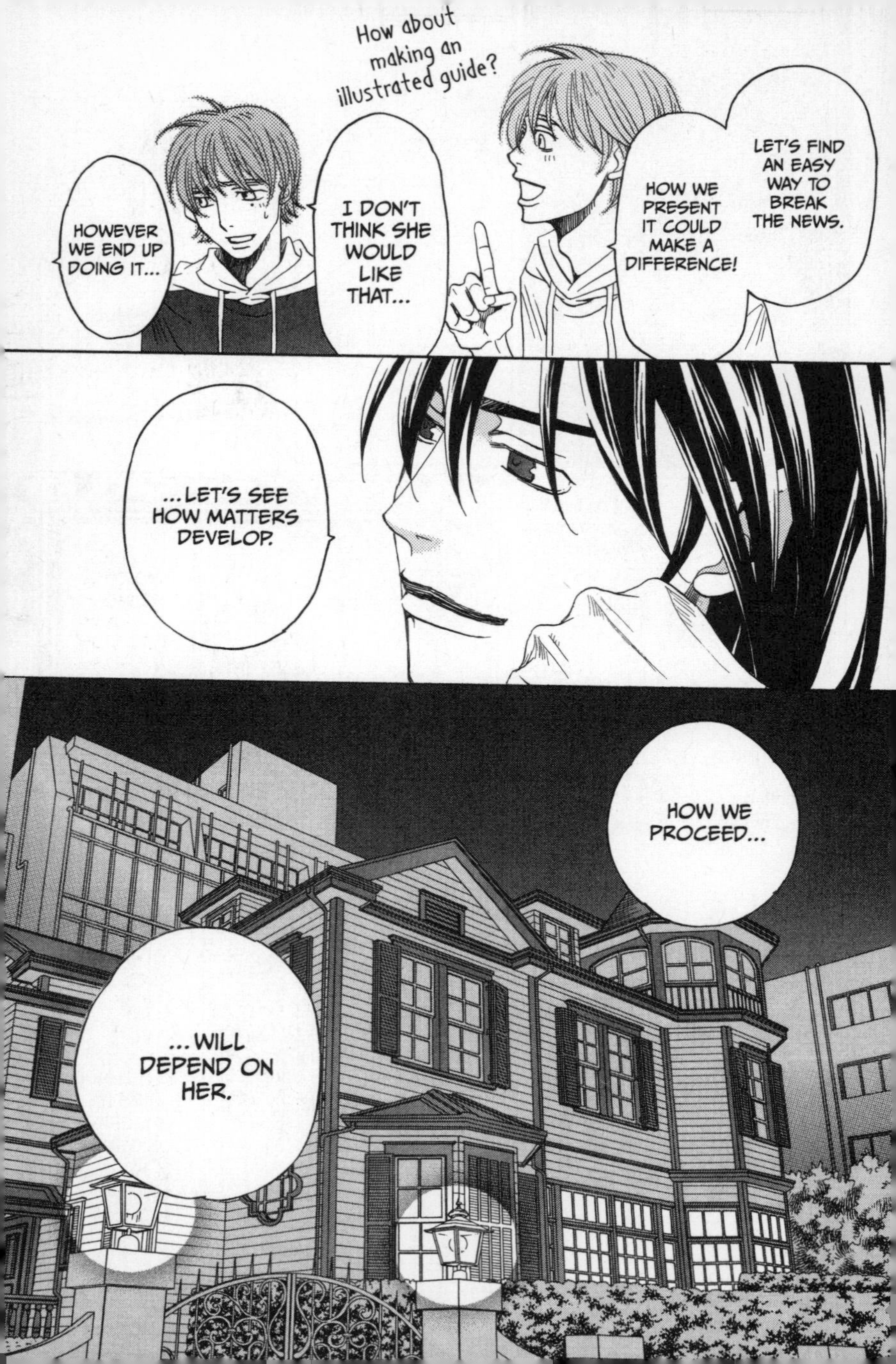
LET'S FIND AN EASY WAY TO BREAK THE NEWS.
HOW WE PRESENT IT COULD MAKE A DIFFERENCE!
How about making an illustrated guide?
I DON'T THINK SHE WOULD LIKE THAT...
HOWEVER WE END UP DOING IT...
...LET'S SEE HOW MATTERS DEVELOP.
HOW WE PROCEED...
...WILL DEPEND ON HER.

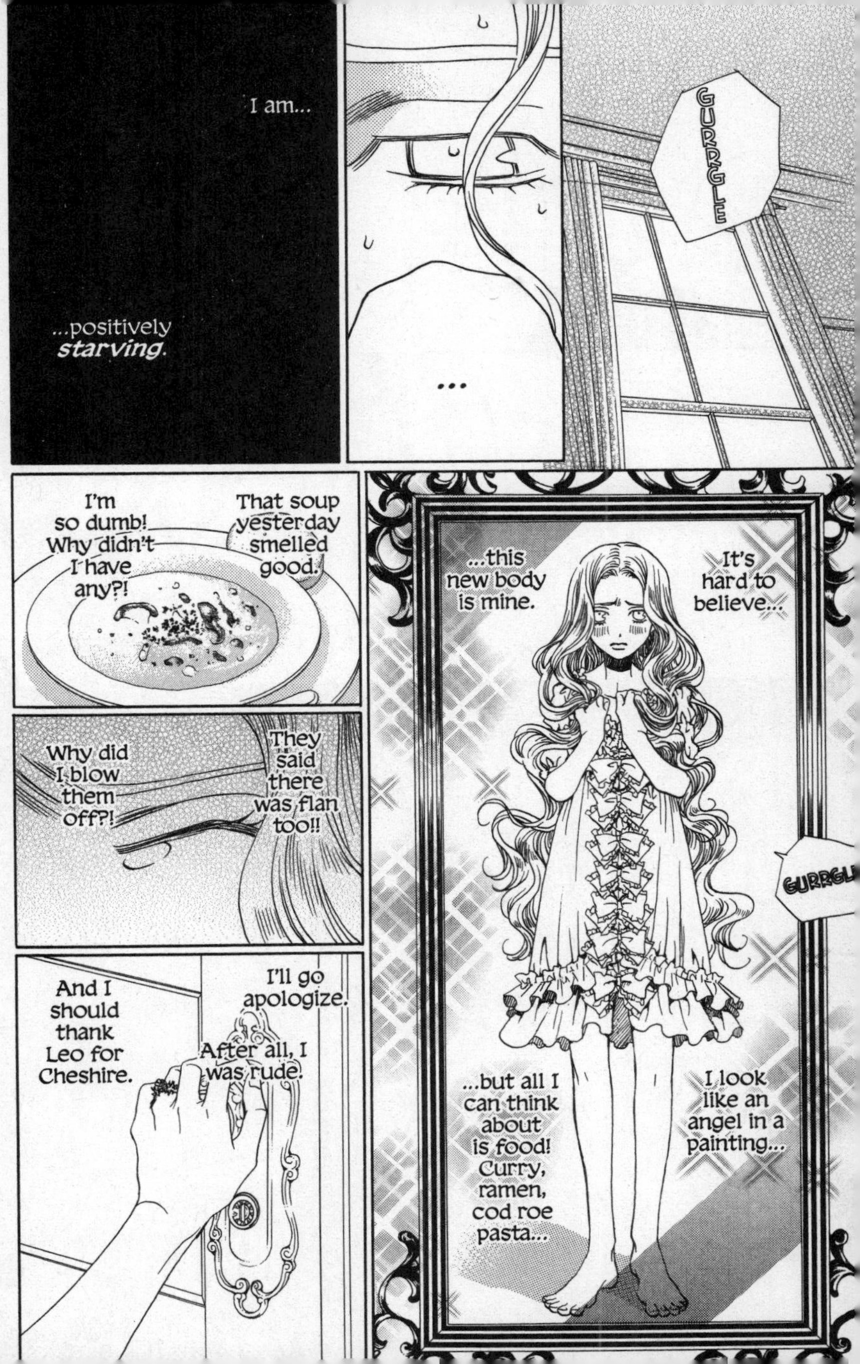

GURRGLE
...
I am...
...positively *starving*.
It's hard to believe...
...this new body is mine.
I look like an angel in a painting...
...but all I can think about is food! Curry, ramen, cod roe pasta...
GURRGL
That soup yesterday smelled good.
I'm so dumb! Why didn't I have any?!
They said there was flan too!!
Why did I blow them off?!
I'll go apologize.
After all, I was rude.
And I should thank Leo for Cheshire.

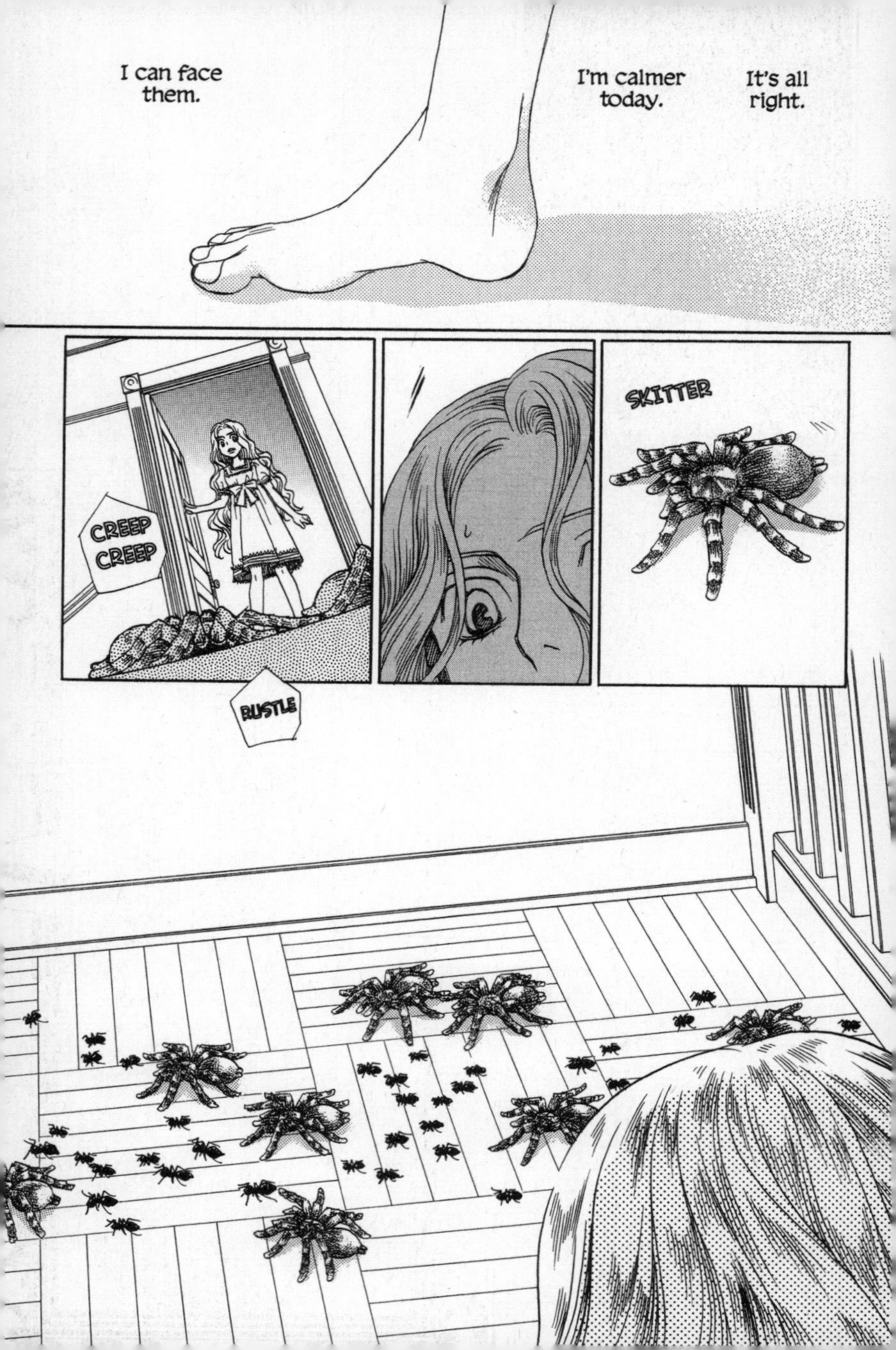
It's all right.
I'm calmer today.
I can face them.
SKITTER
CREEP CREEP
RUSTLE

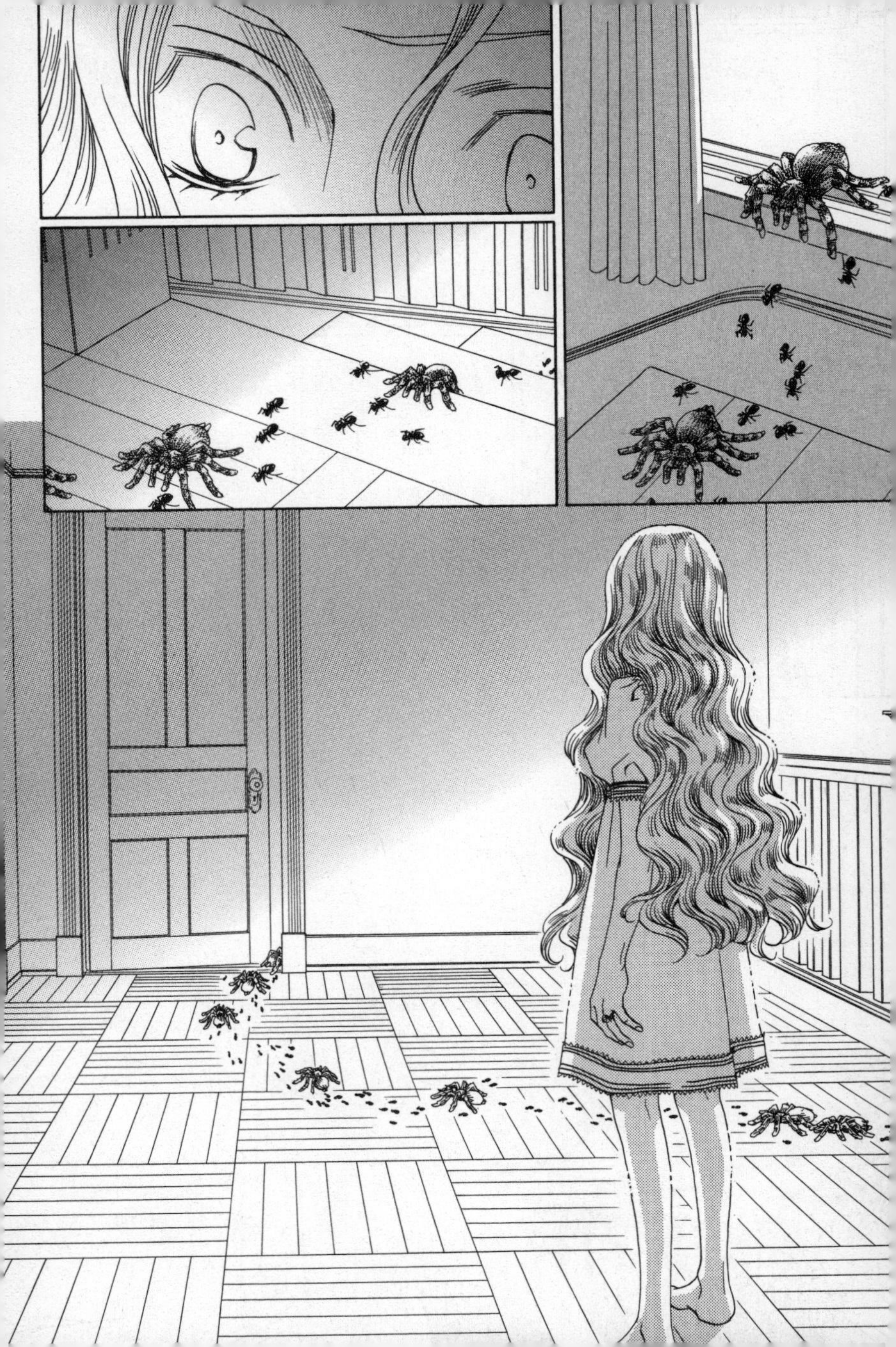

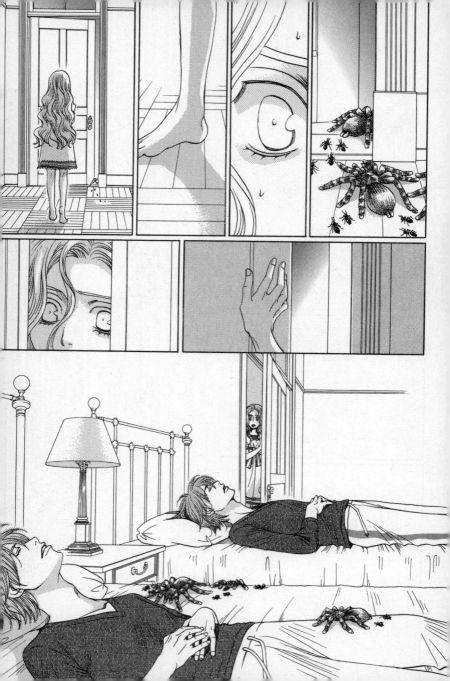

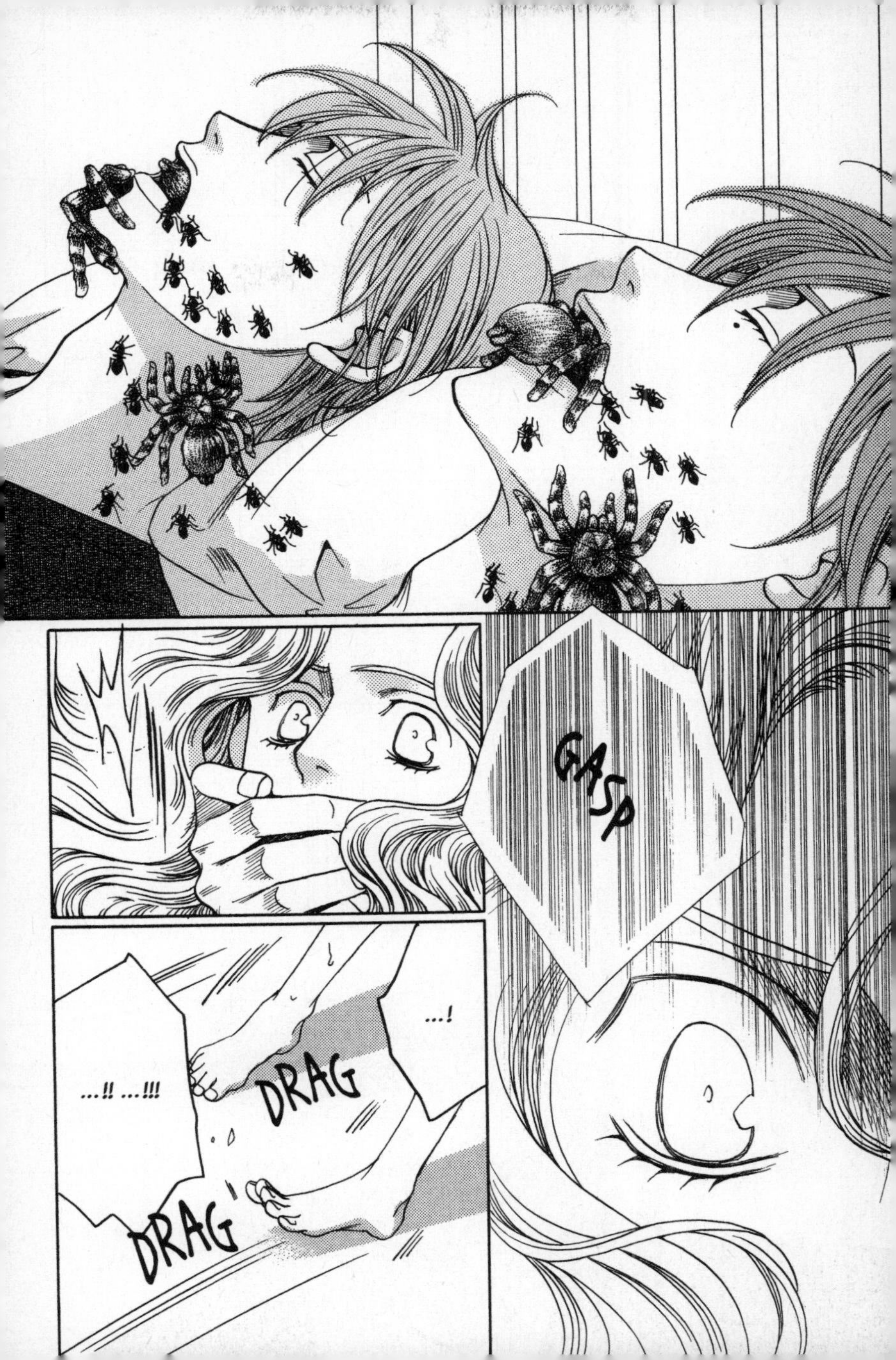
GASP
...!
DRAG
...!! ...!!!
DRAG

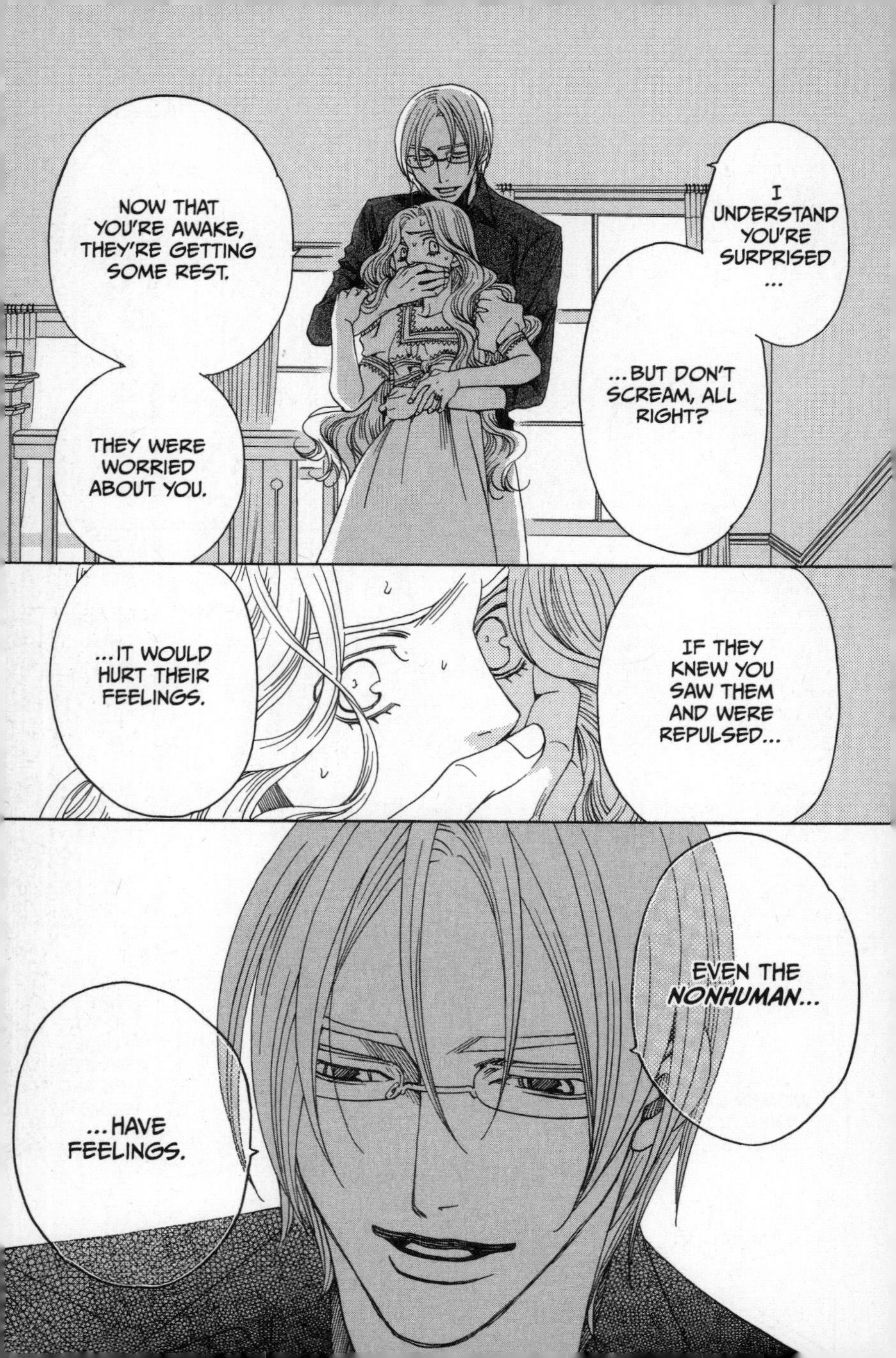
I UNDERSTAND YOU'RE SURPRISED ...
...BUT DON'T SCREAM, ALL RIGHT?
NOW THAT YOU'RE AWAKE, THEY'RE GETTING SOME REST.
THEY WERE WORRIED ABOUT YOU.
IF THEY KNEW YOU SAW THEM AND WERE REPULSED...
...IT WOULD HURT THEIR FEELINGS.
EVEN THE *NONHUMAN*...
...HAVE FEELINGS.

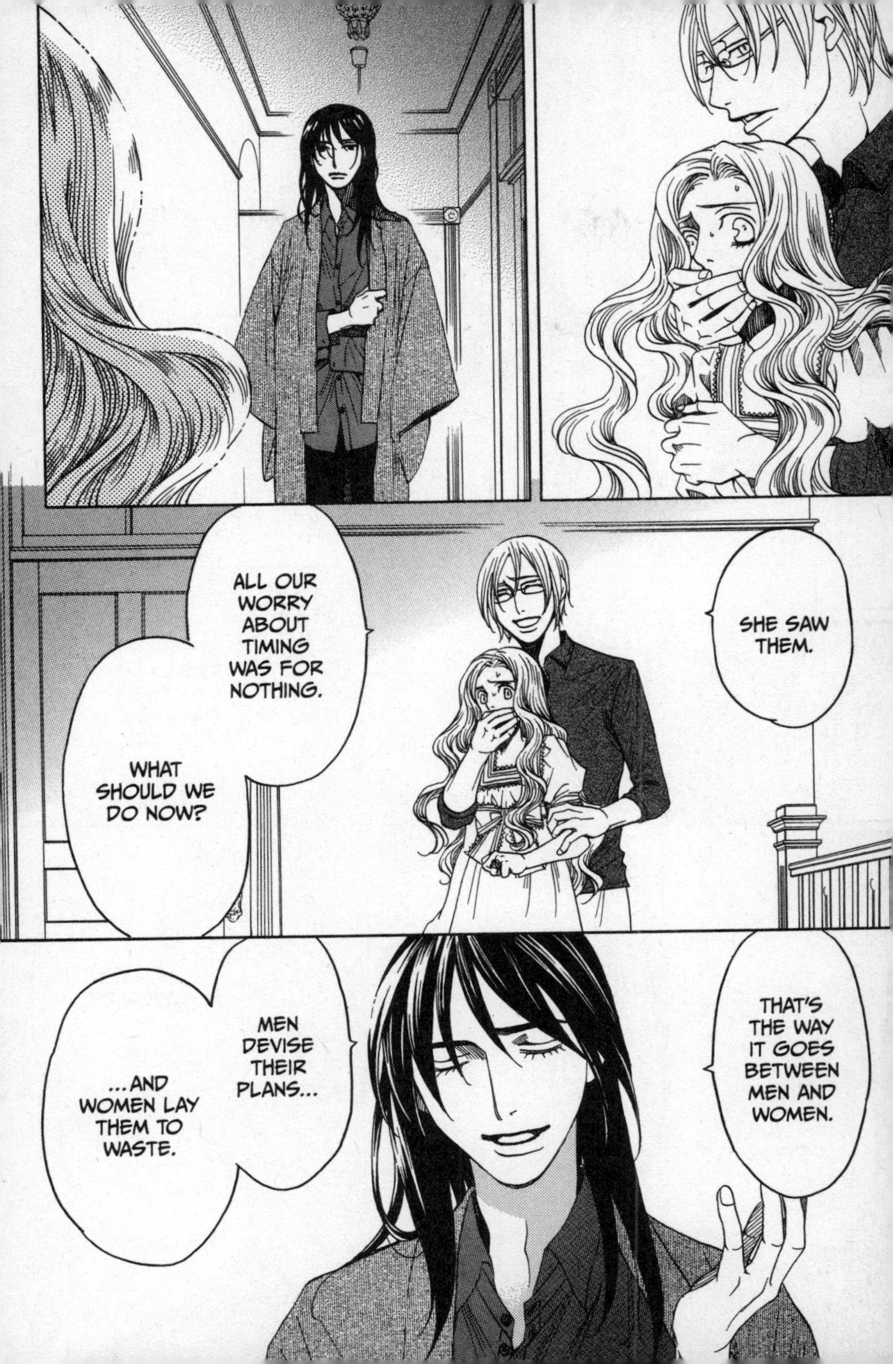
SHE SAW THEM.
ALL OUR WORRY ABOUT TIMING WAS FOR NOTHING.
WHAT SHOULD WE DO NOW?
THAT'S THE WAY IT GOES BETWEEN MEN AND WOMEN.
MEN DEVISE THEIR PLANS...
...AND WOMEN LAY THEM TO WASTE.

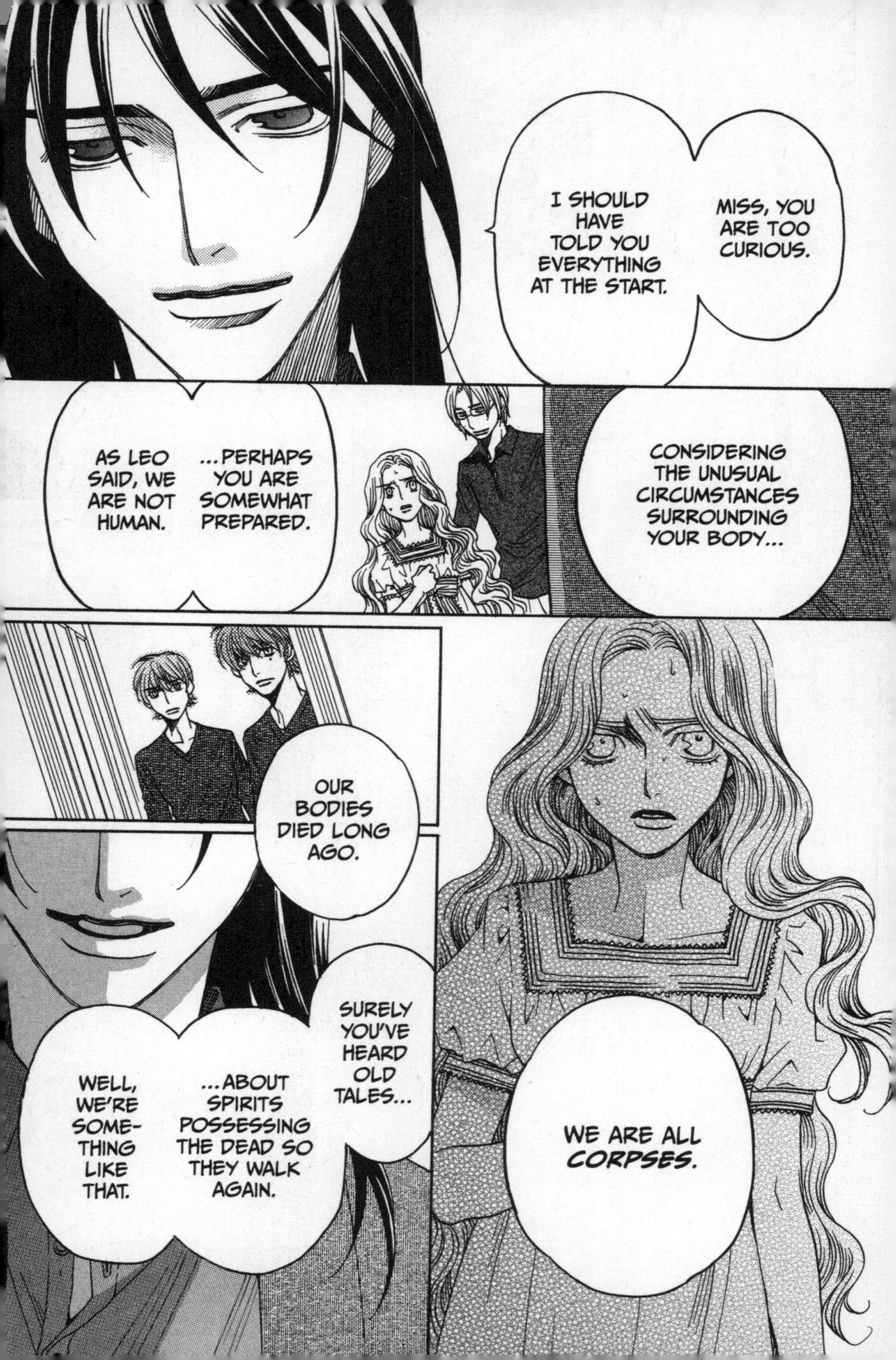
MISS, YOU ARE TOO CURIOUS.
I SHOULD HAVE TOLD YOU EVERYTHING AT THE START.
CONSIDERING THE UNUSUAL CIRCUMSTANCES SURROUNDING YOUR BODY...
...PERHAPS YOU ARE SOMEWHAT PREPARED.
AS LEO SAID, WE ARE NOT HUMAN.
WE ARE ALL *CORPSES*.
OUR BODIES DIED LONG AGO.
SURELY YOU'VE HEARD OLD TALES...
...ABOUT SPIRITS POSSESSING THE DEAD SO THEY WALK AGAIN.
WELL, WE'RE SOME-THING LIKE THAT.

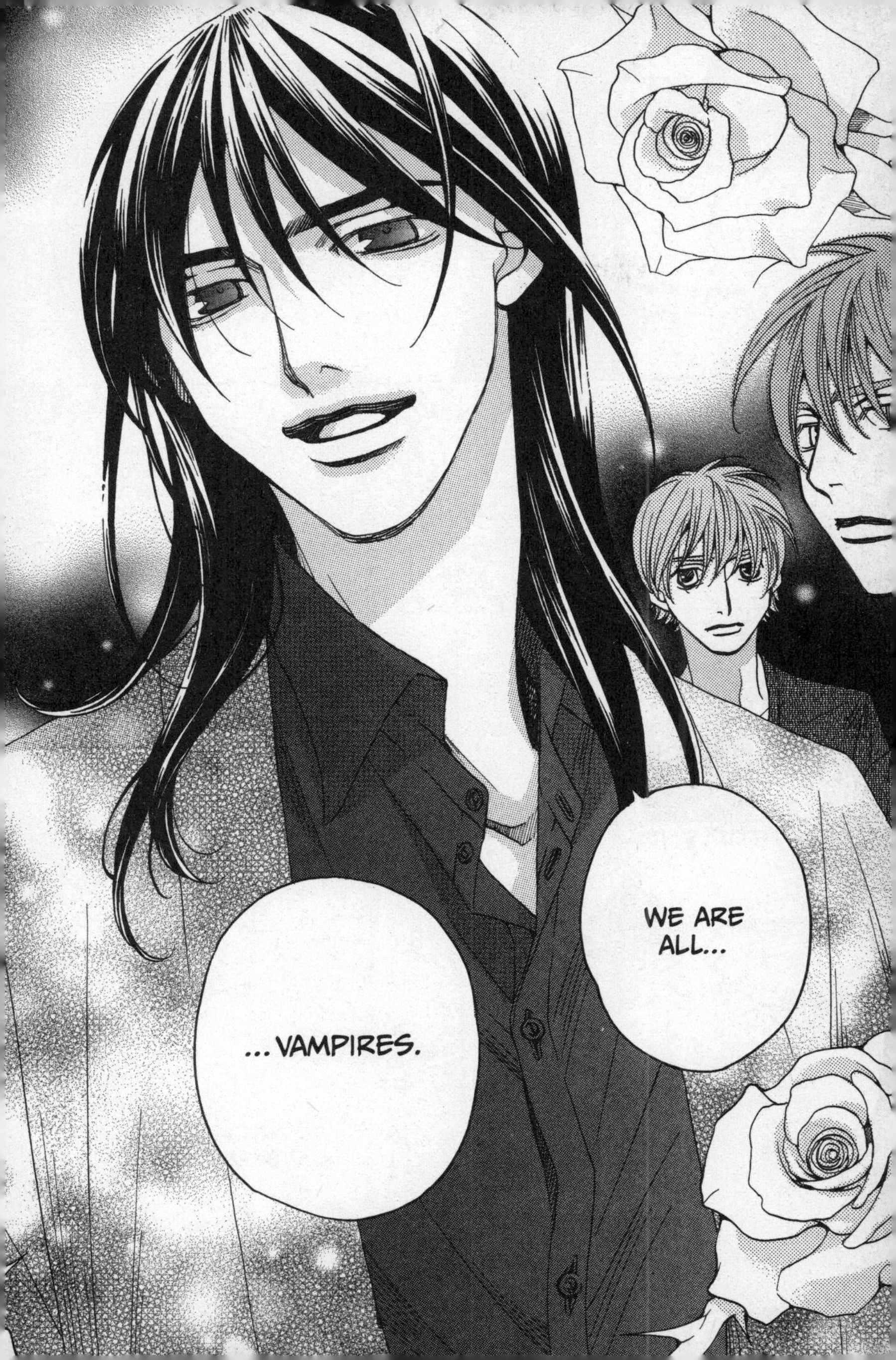
WE ARE ALL...
...VAMPIRES.

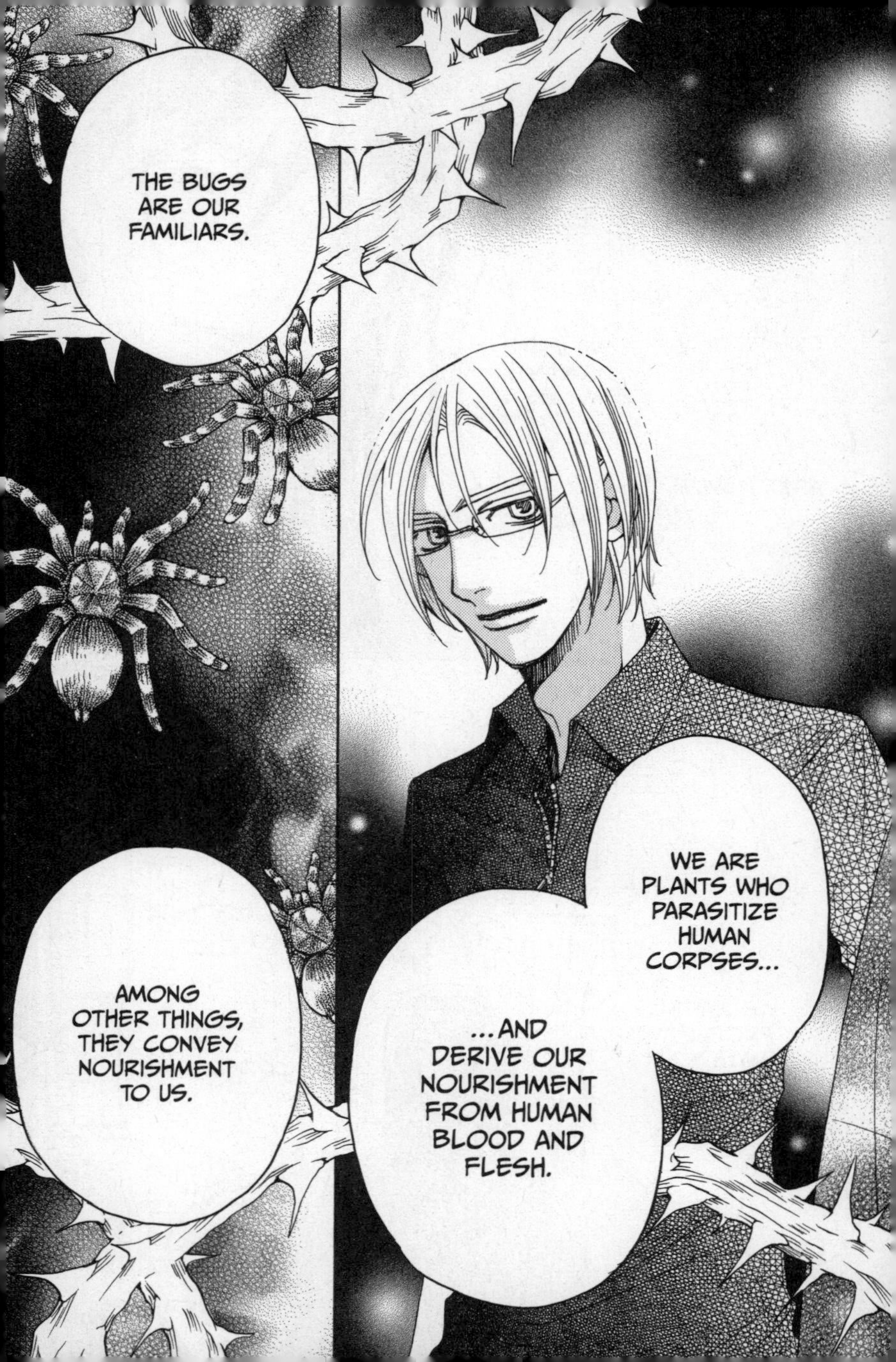
WE ARE PLANTS WHO PARASITIZE HUMAN CORPSES...
...AND DERIVE OUR NOURISHMENT FROM HUMAN BLOOD AND FLESH.
THE BUGS ARE OUR FAMILIARS.
AMONG OTHER THINGS, THEY CONVEY NOURISHMENT TO US.

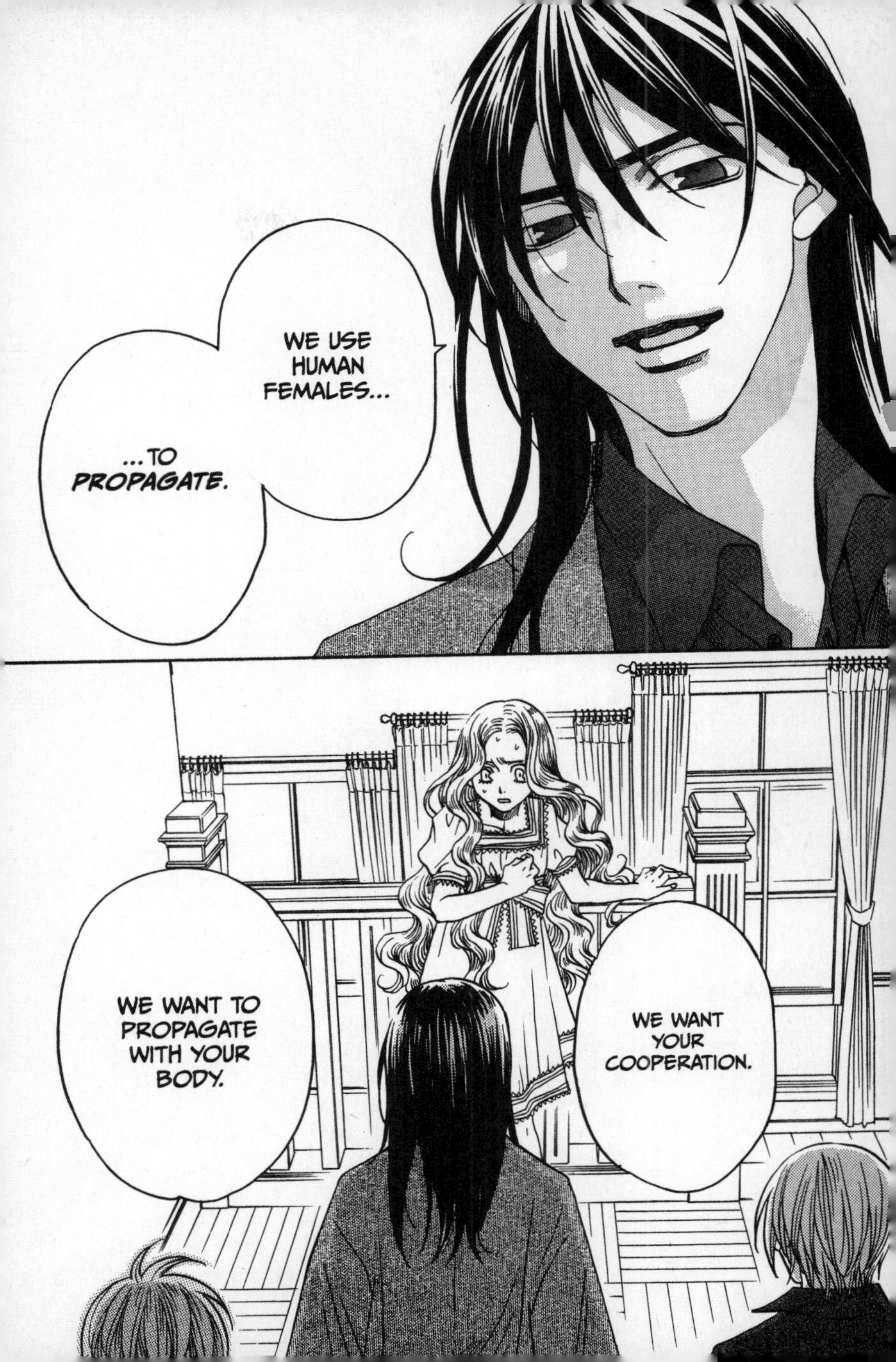
WE USE HUMAN FEMALES...
...TO *PROPAGATE.*
WE WANT YOUR COOPERATION.
WE WANT TO PROPAGATE WITH YOUR BODY.

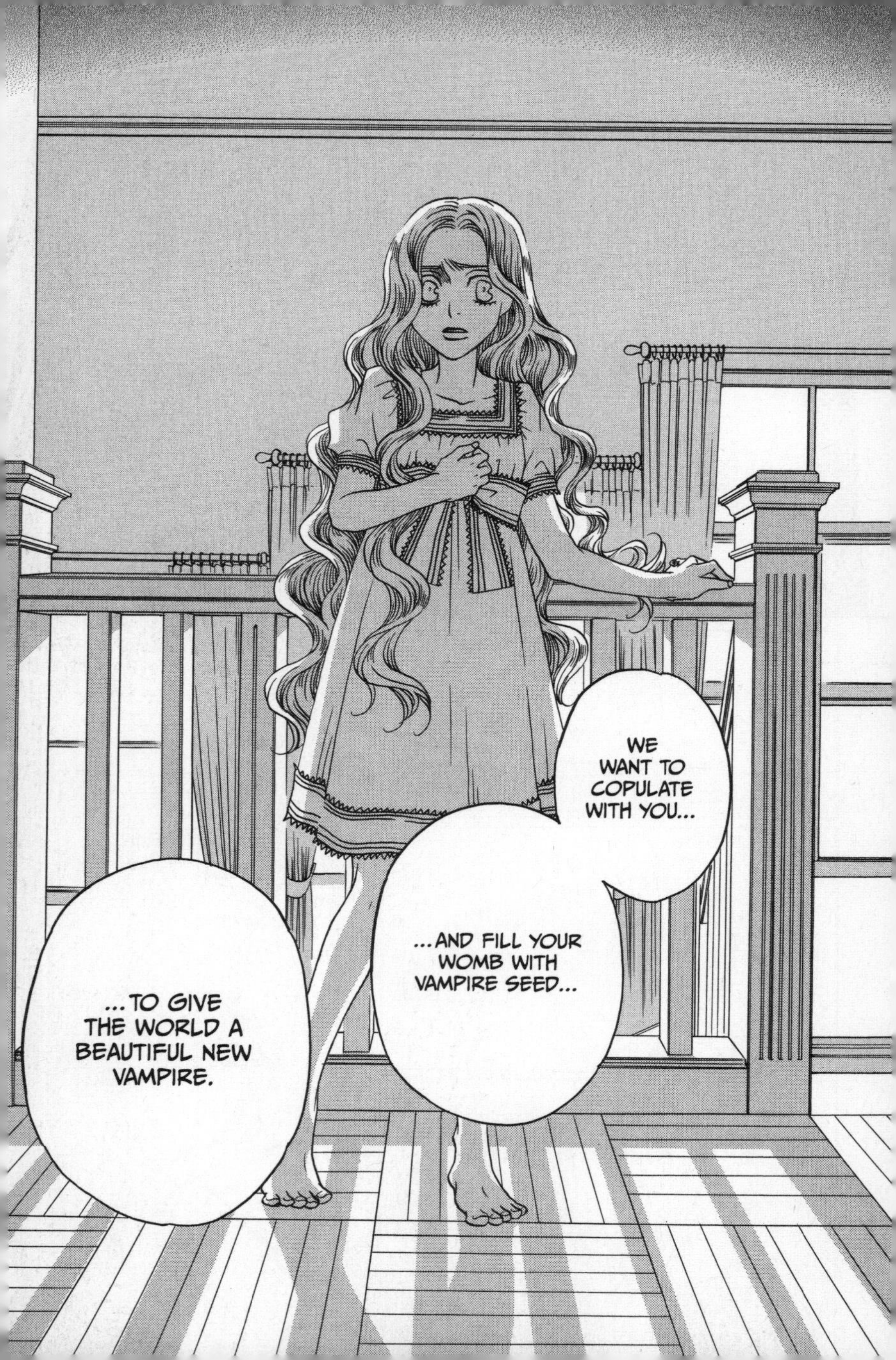
WE WANT TO COPULATE WITH YOU...
...AND FILL YOUR WOMB WITH VAMPIRE SEED...
...TO GIVE THE WORLD A BEAUTIFUL NEW VAMPIRE.

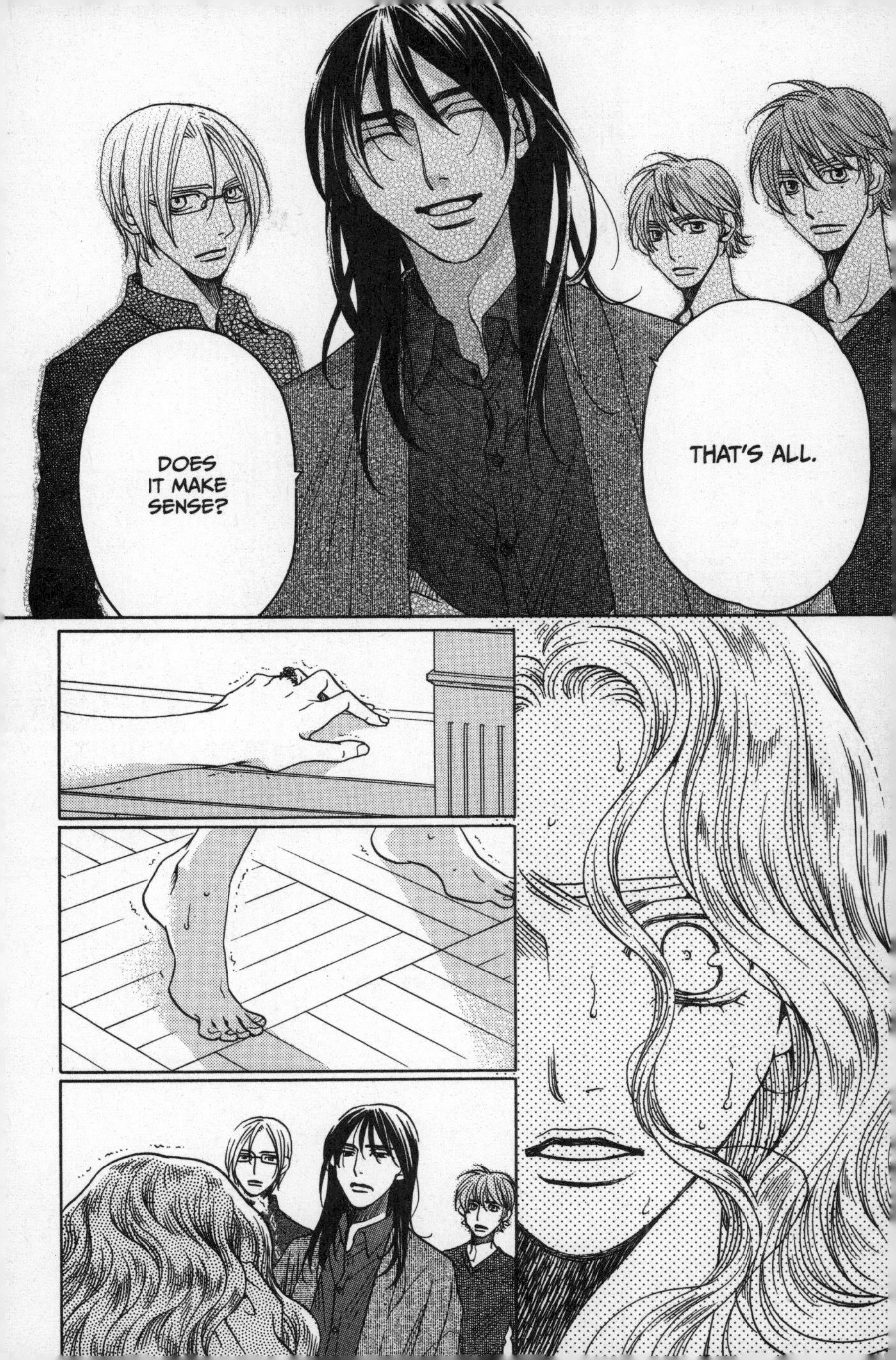
THAT'S ALL.
DOES IT MAKE SENSE?

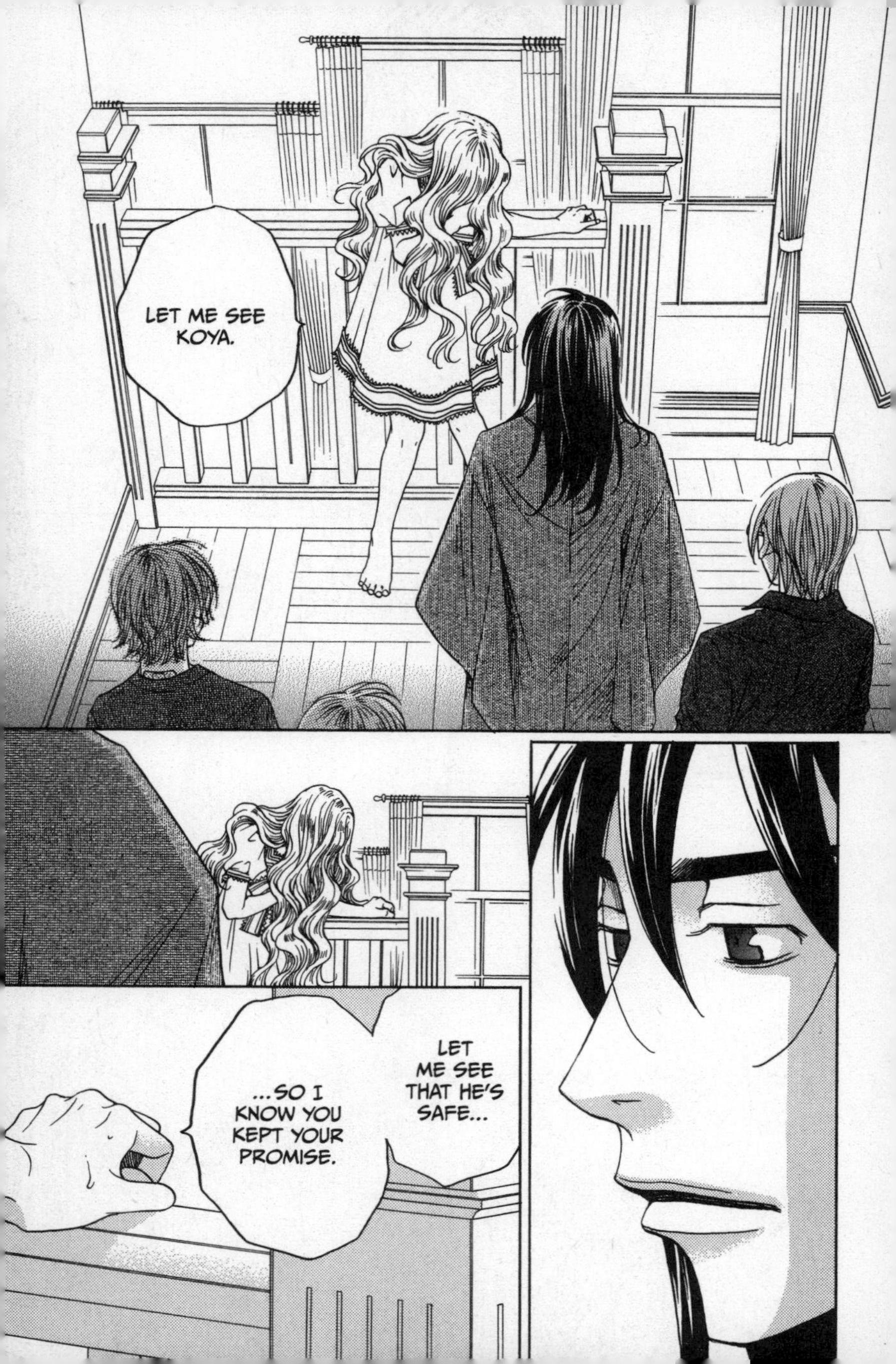
LET ME SEE KOYA.
LET ME SEE THAT HE'S SAFE...
...SO I KNOW YOU KEPT YOUR PROMISE.

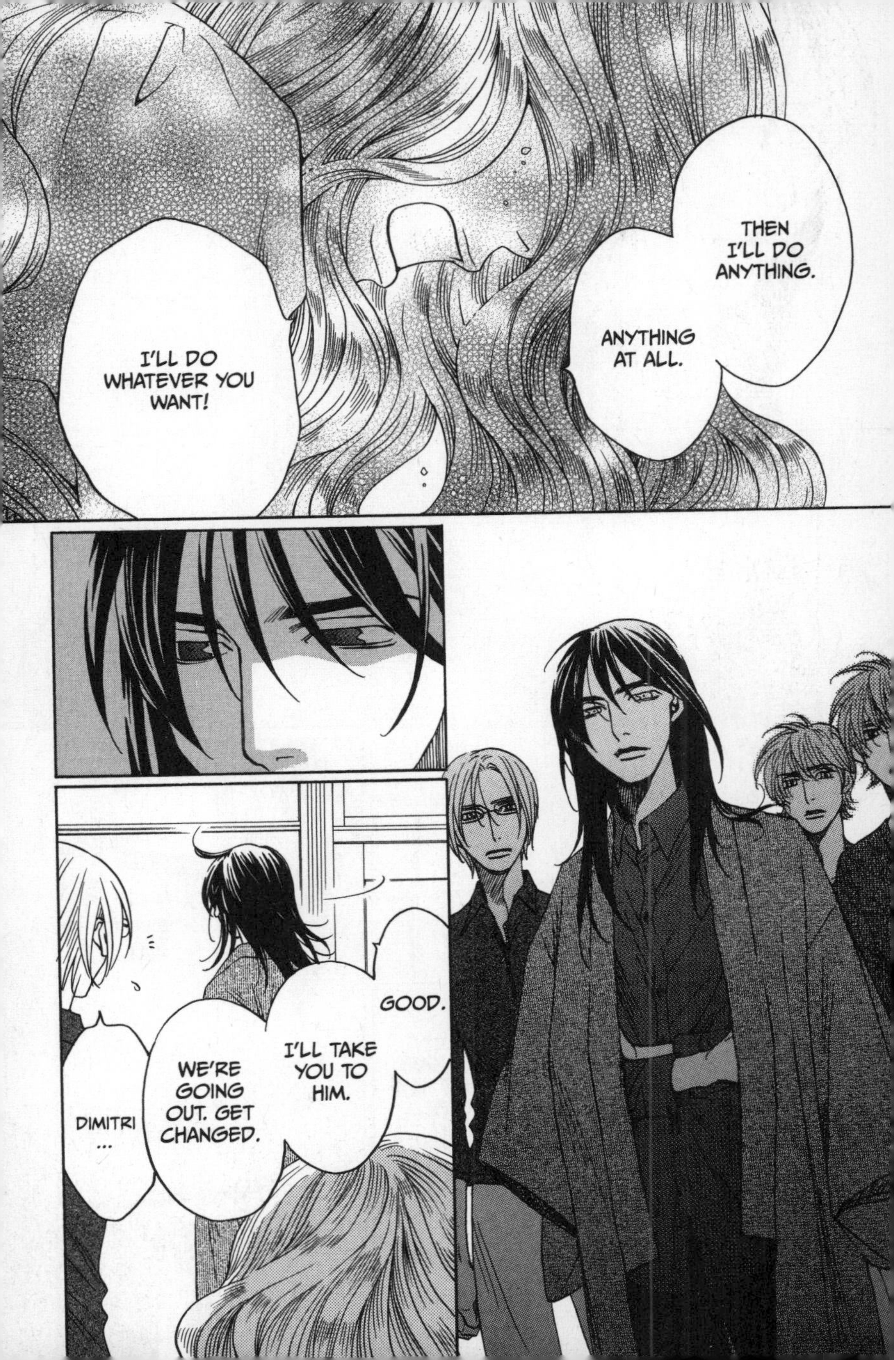
THEN I'LL DO ANYTHING.
ANYTHING AT ALL.
I'LL DO WHATEVER YOU WANT!
GOOD.
I'LL TAKE YOU TO HIM.
WE'RE GOING OUT. GET CHANGED.
DIMITRI ...

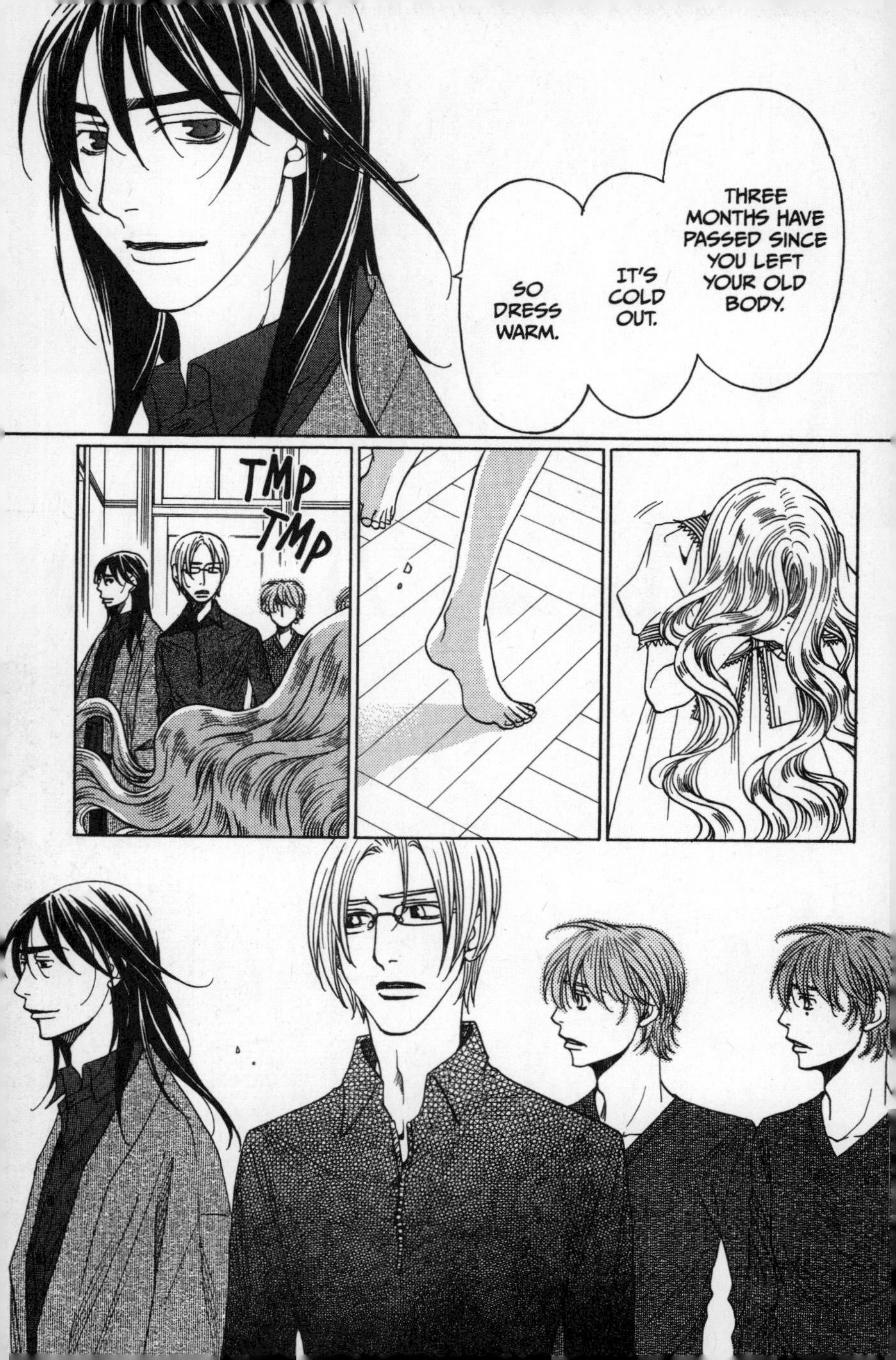
THREE MONTHS HAVE PASSED SINCE YOU LEFT YOUR OLD BODY.
IT'S COLD OUT.
SO DRESS WARM.
TMP TMP

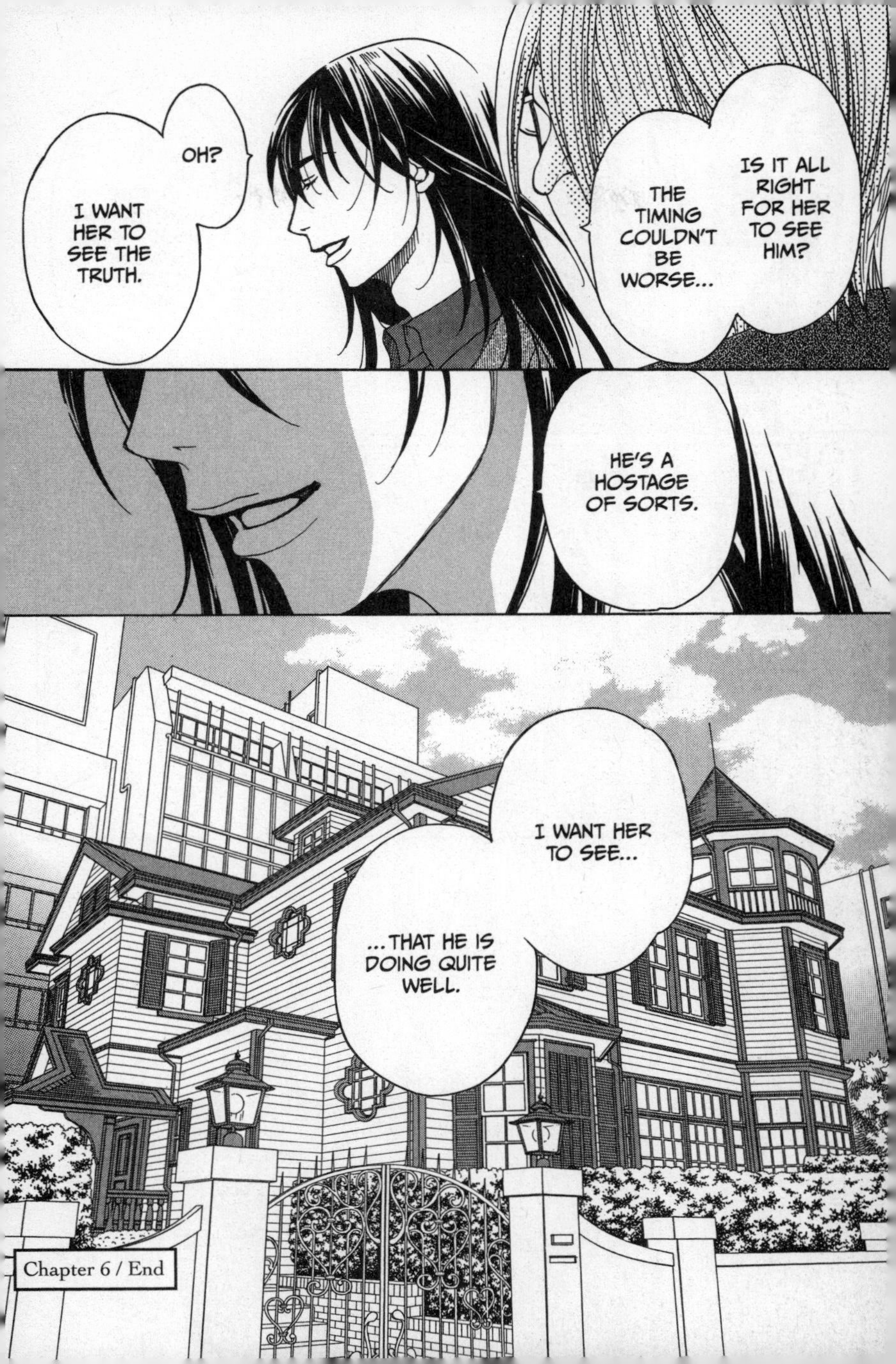
IS IT ALL RIGHT FOR HER TO SEE HIM?
THE TIMING COULDN'T BE WORSE...
OH?
I WANT HER TO SEE THE TRUTH.
HE'S A HOSTAGE OF SORTS.
I WANT HER TO SEE...
...THAT HE IS DOING QUITE WELL.
Chapter 6 / End

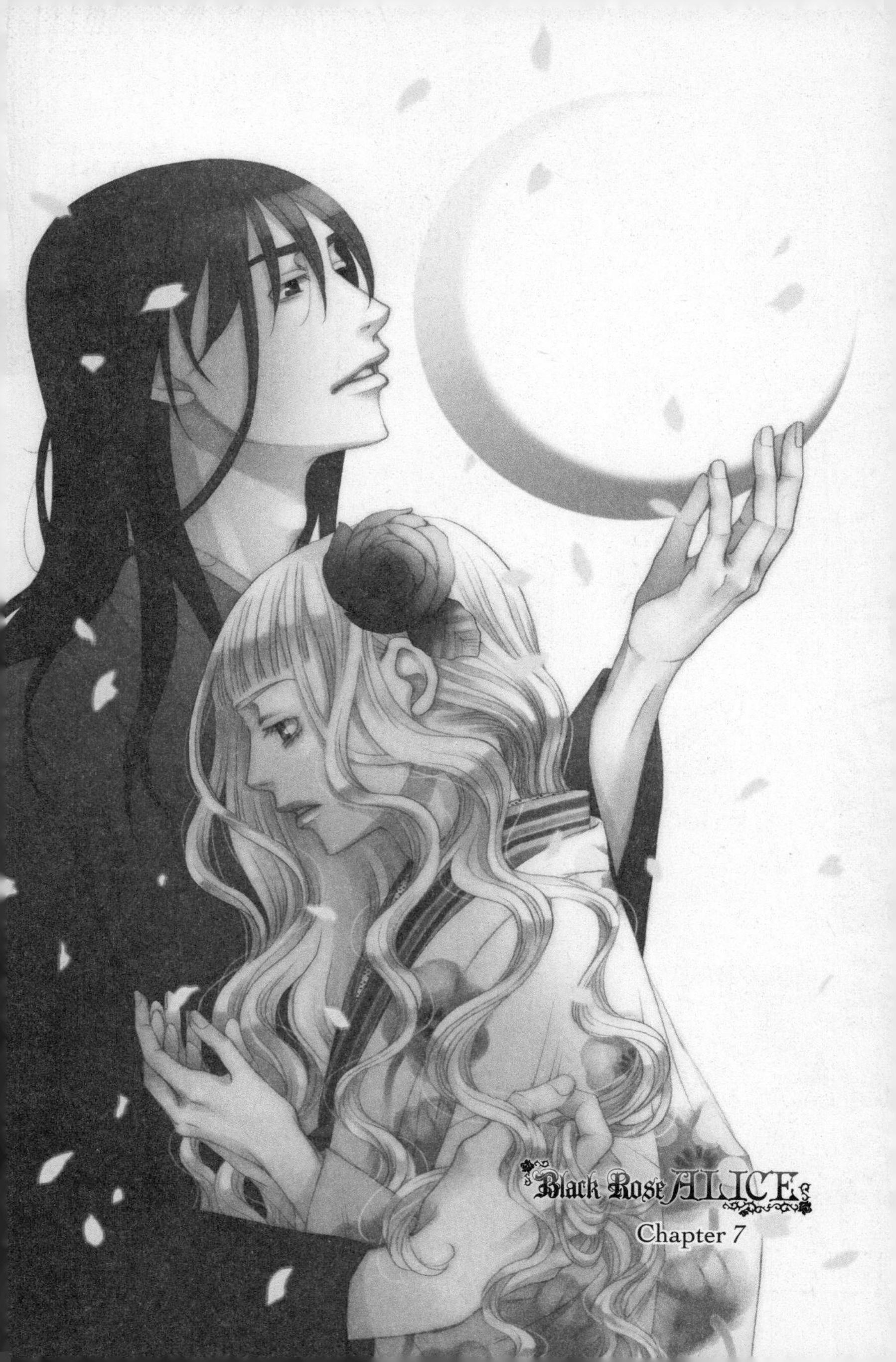
Black Rose ALICE
Chapter 7

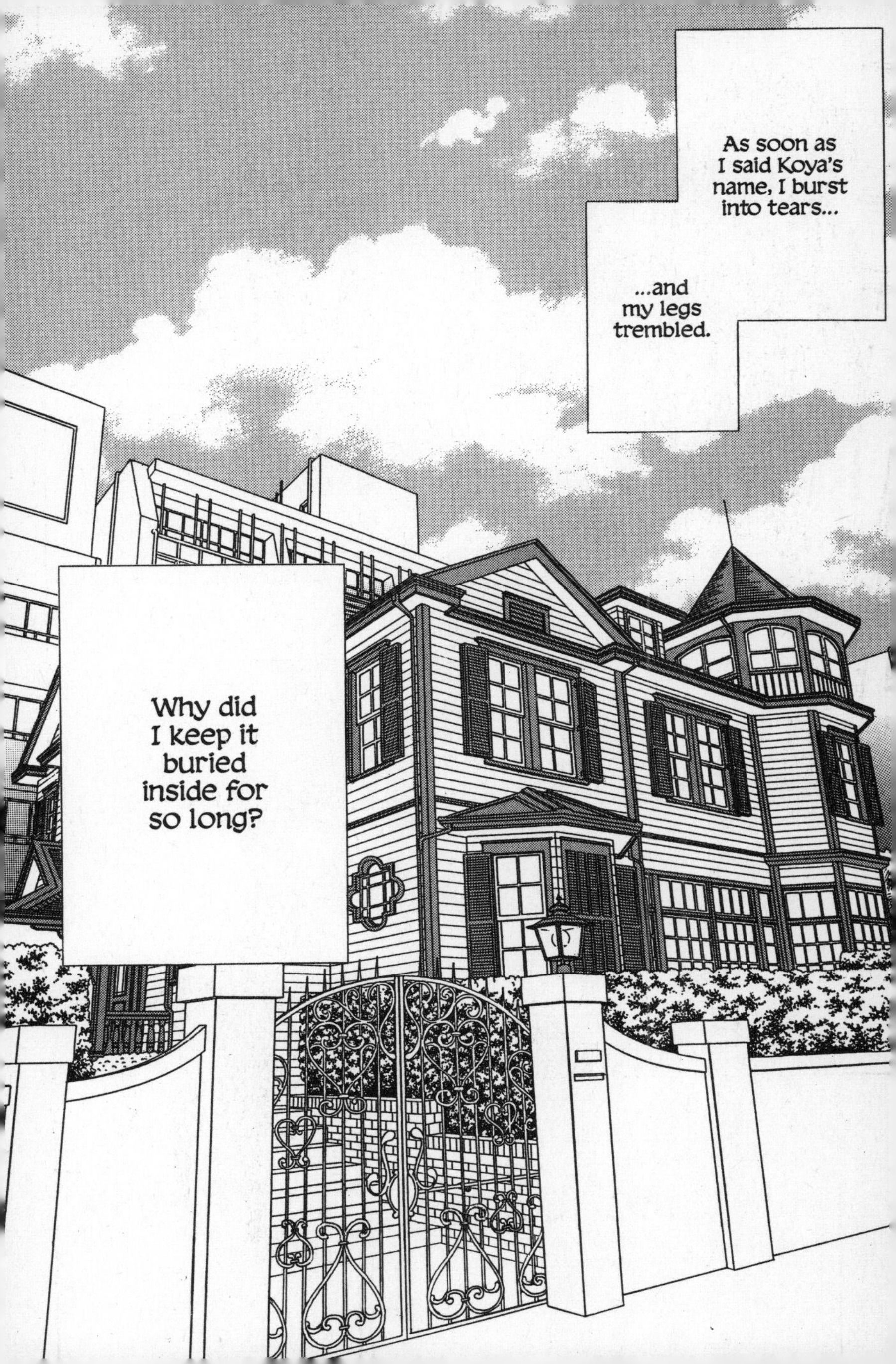
As soon as I said Koya's name, I burst into tears...
...and my legs trembled.
Why did I keep it buried inside for so long?

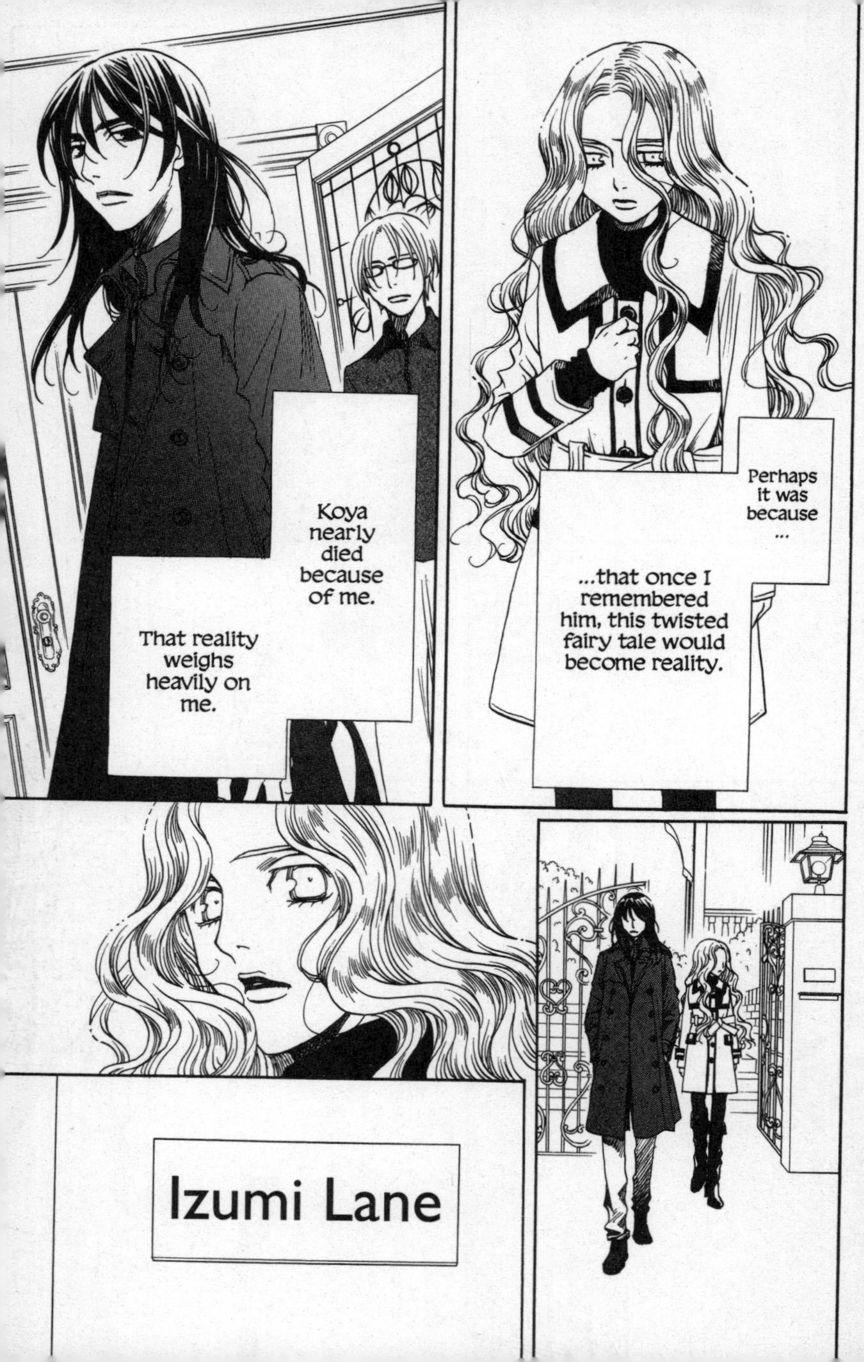
Perhaps it was because ...
...that once I remembered him, this twisted fairy tale would become reality.
Koya nearly died because of me.
That reality weighs heavily on me.
Izumi Lane

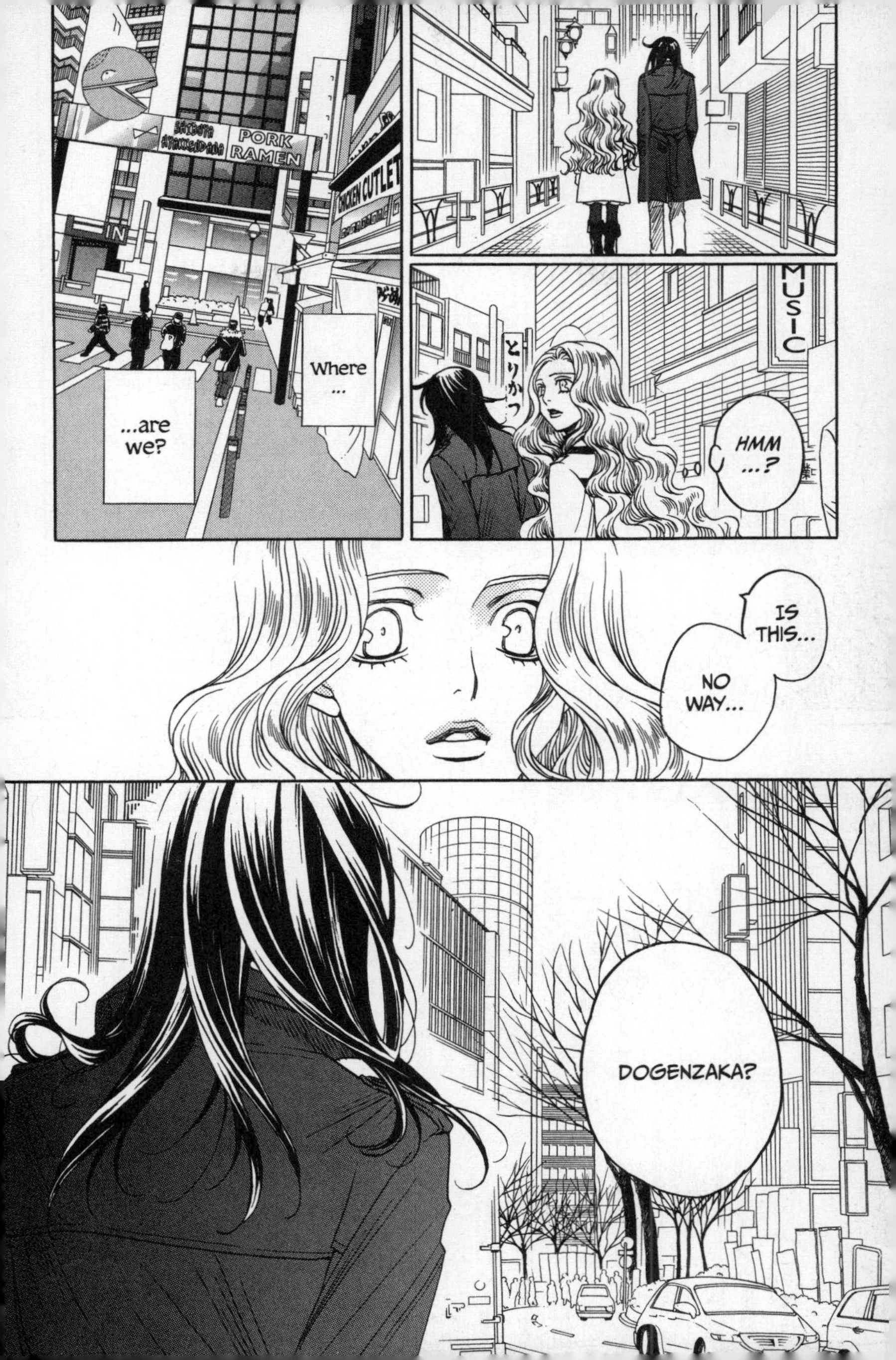
MUSIC
とりかつ
HMM ...?
PORK RAMEN
CHICKEN CUTLET
IN
Where ...
...are we?
IS THIS...
NO WAY...
DOGENZAKA?

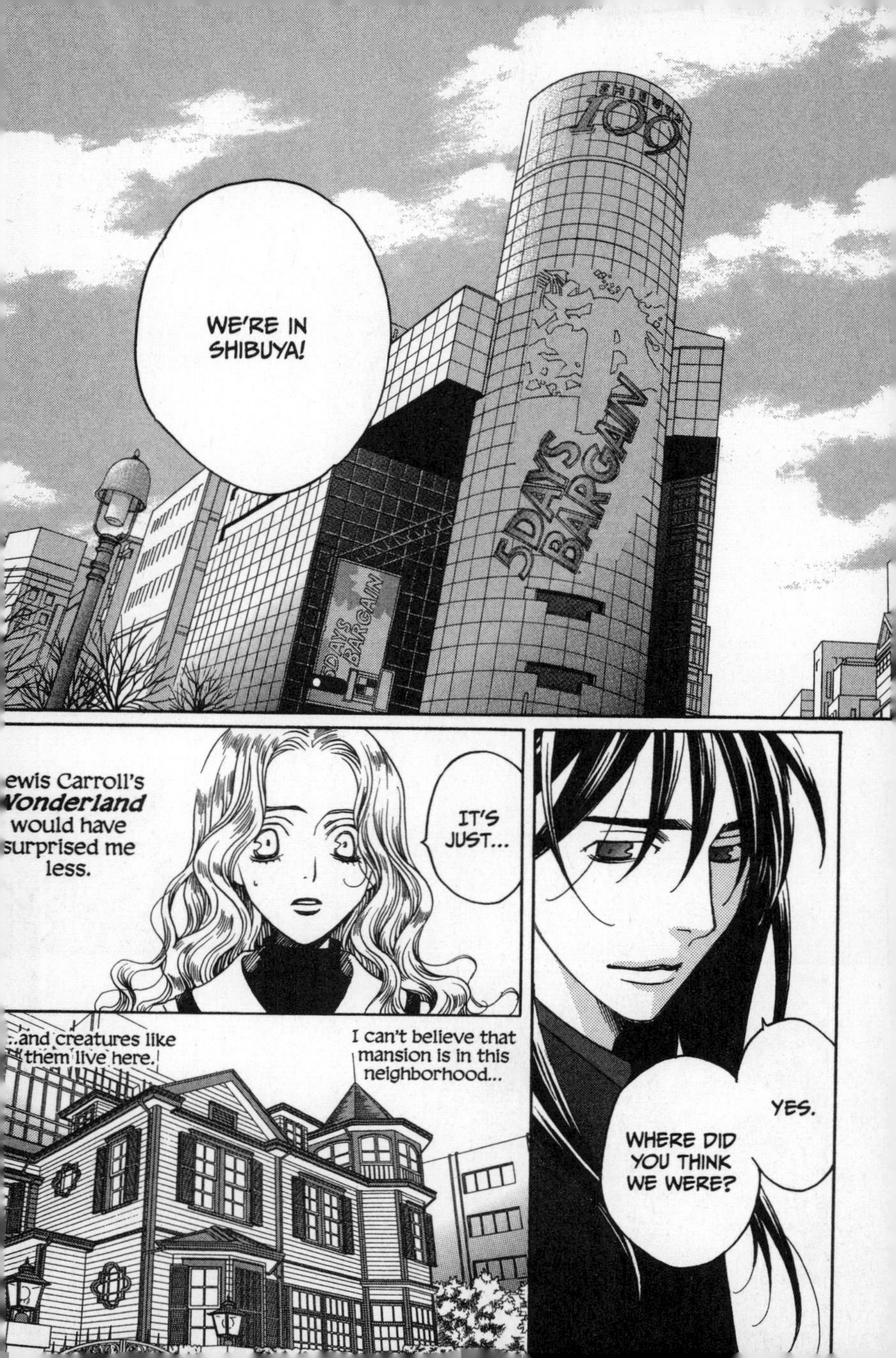
SHIBUYA 109
WE'RE IN SHIBUYA!
5DAYS BARGAIN
5DAYS BARGAIN
YES.
WHERE DID YOU THINK WE WERE?
IT'S JUST...
ewis Carroll's *Wonderland* would have surprised me less.
I can't believe that mansion is in this neighborhood...
...and creatures like them live here.

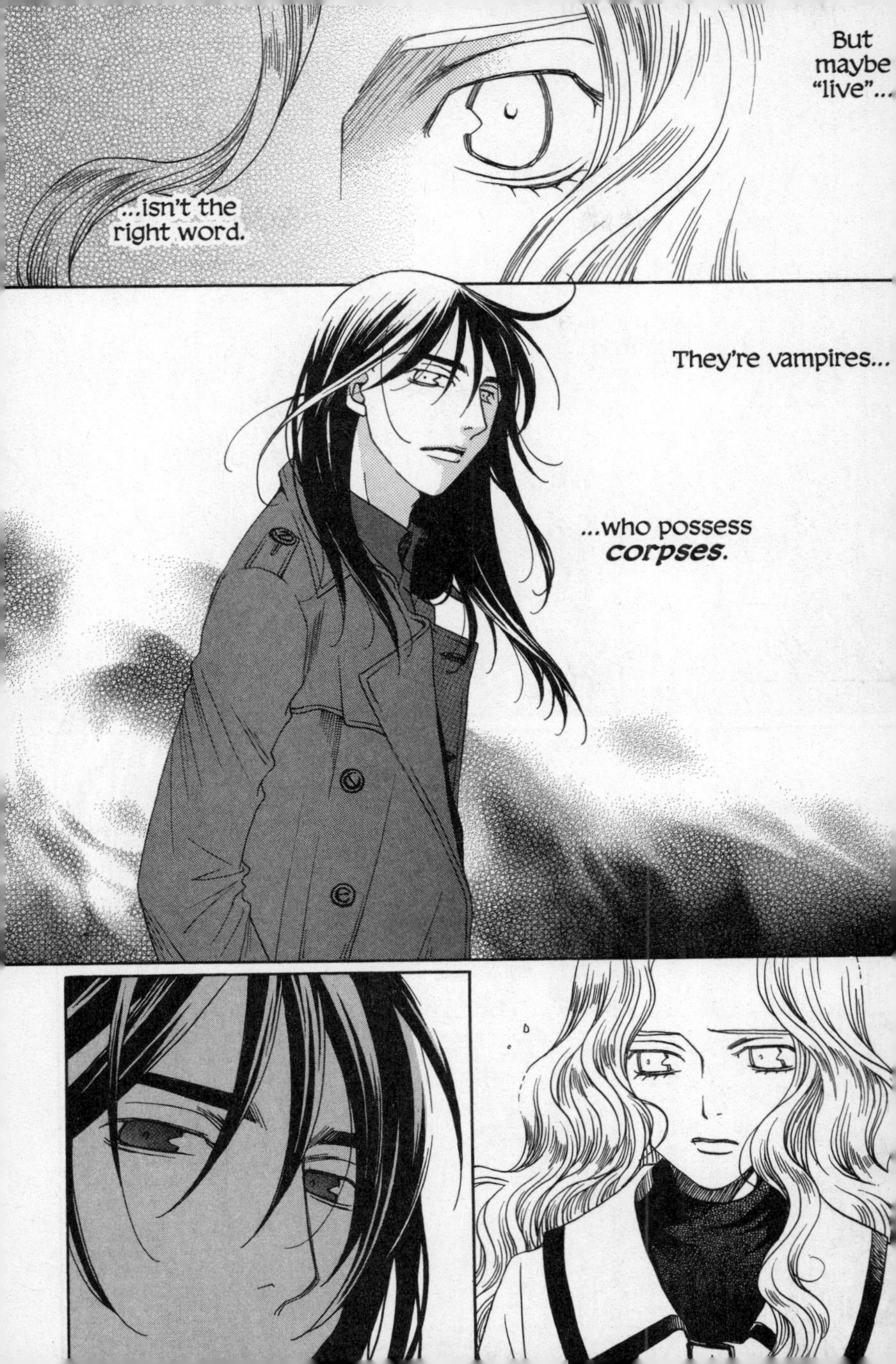
But maybe "live"...
...isn't the right word.
They're vampires...
...who possess *corpses*.

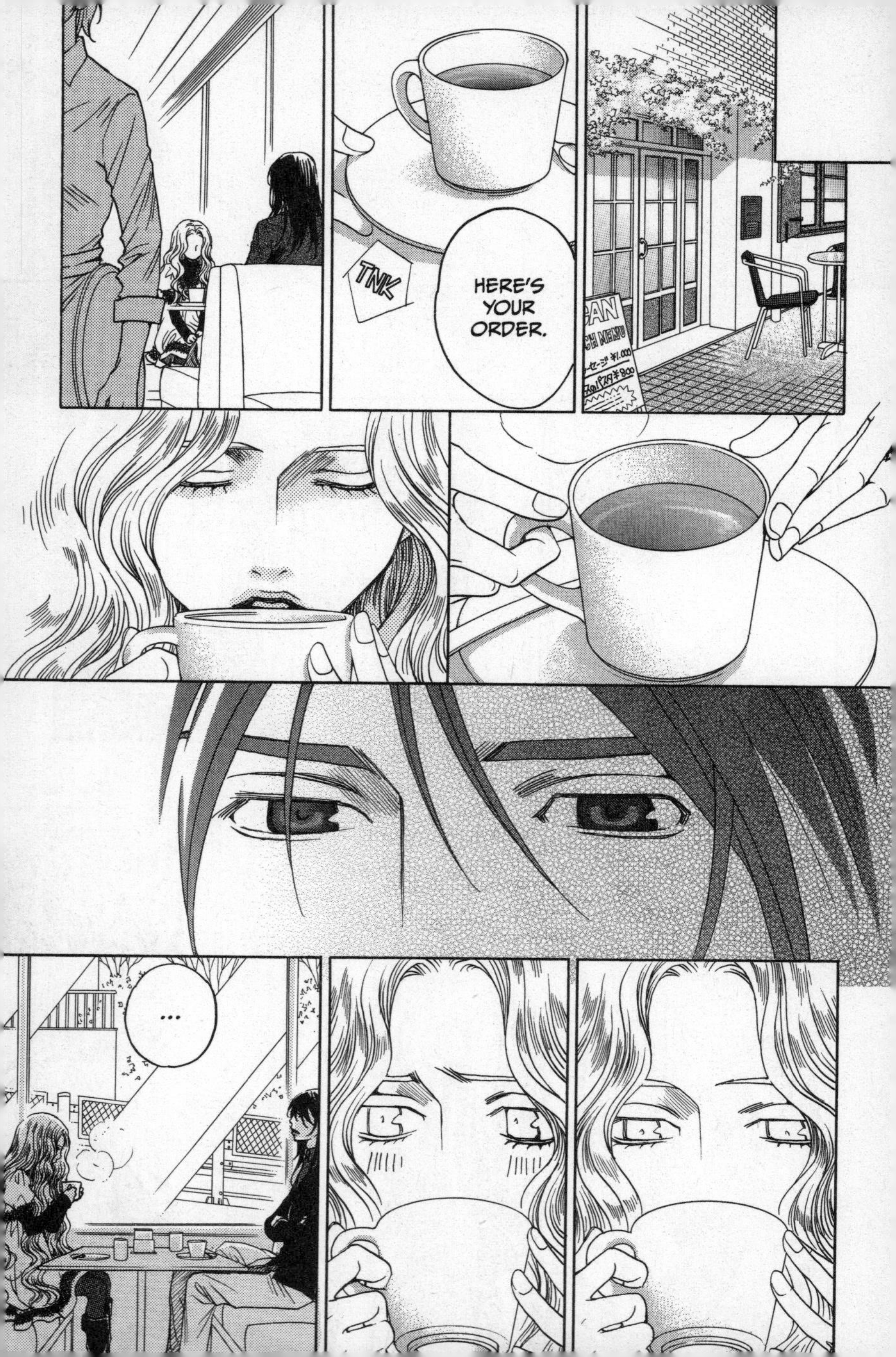
TNK
HERE'S YOUR ORDER.
...

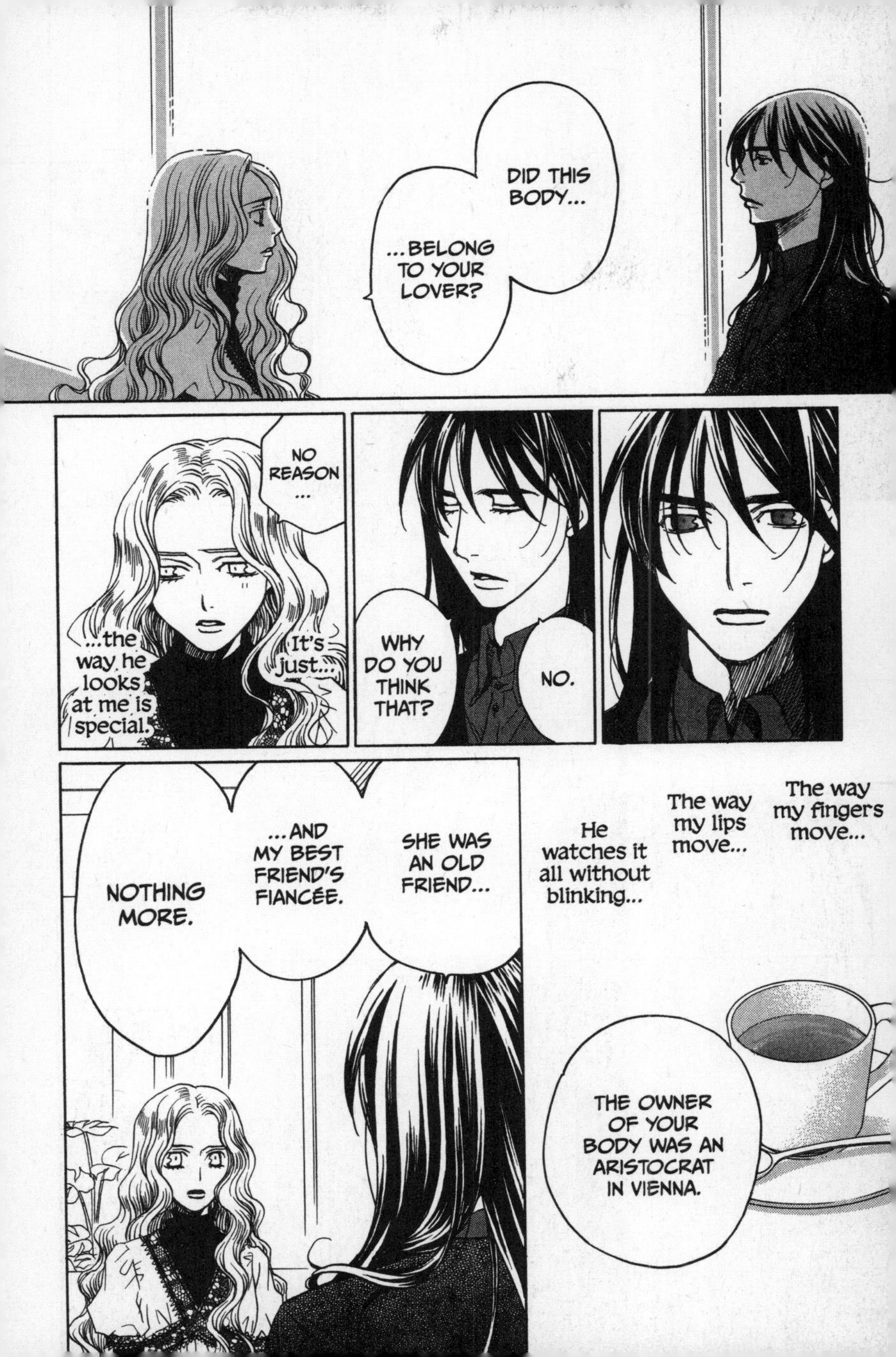
DID THIS BODY...
...BELONG TO YOUR LOVER?
NO.
WHY DO YOU THINK THAT?
NO REASON ...
It's just...
...the way he looks at me is special.
The way my fingers move...
The way my lips move...
He watches it all without blinking...
SHE WAS AN OLD FRIEND...
...AND MY BEST FRIEND'S FIANCÉE.
NOTHING MORE.
THE OWNER OF YOUR BODY WAS AN ARISTOCRAT IN VIENNA.

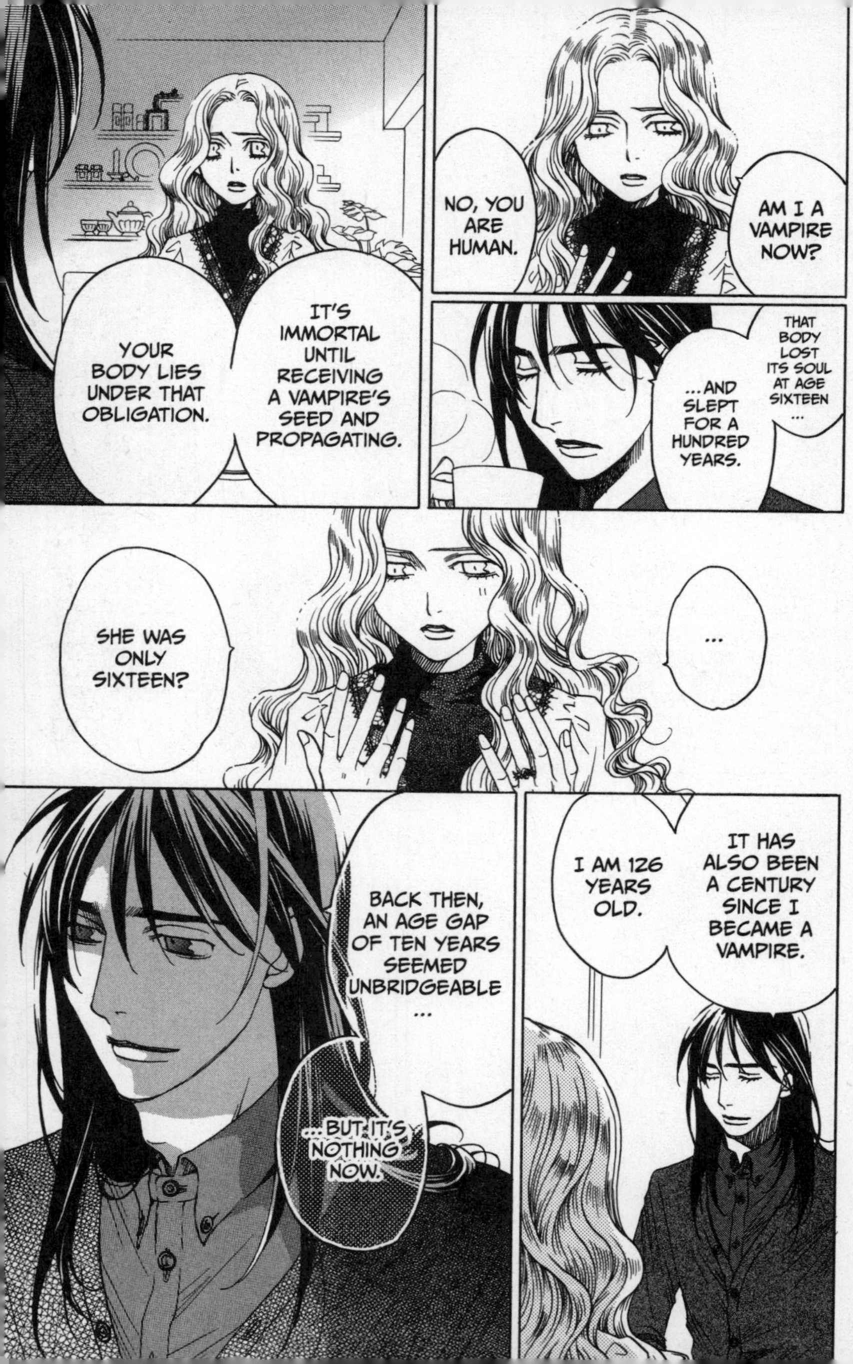
AM I A VAMPIRE NOW?
NO, YOU ARE HUMAN.
THAT BODY LOST ITS SOUL AT AGE SIXTEEN...
...AND SLEPT FOR A HUNDRED YEARS.
IT'S IMMORTAL UNTIL RECEIVING A VAMPIRE'S SEED AND PROPAGATING.
YOUR BODY LIES UNDER THAT OBLIGATION.
...
SHE WAS ONLY SIXTEEN?
IT HAS ALSO BEEN A CENTURY SINCE I BECAME A VAMPIRE.
I AM 126 YEARS OLD.
BACK THEN, AN AGE GAP OF TEN YEARS SEEMED UNBRIDGEABLE...
...BUT IT'S NOTHING NOW.

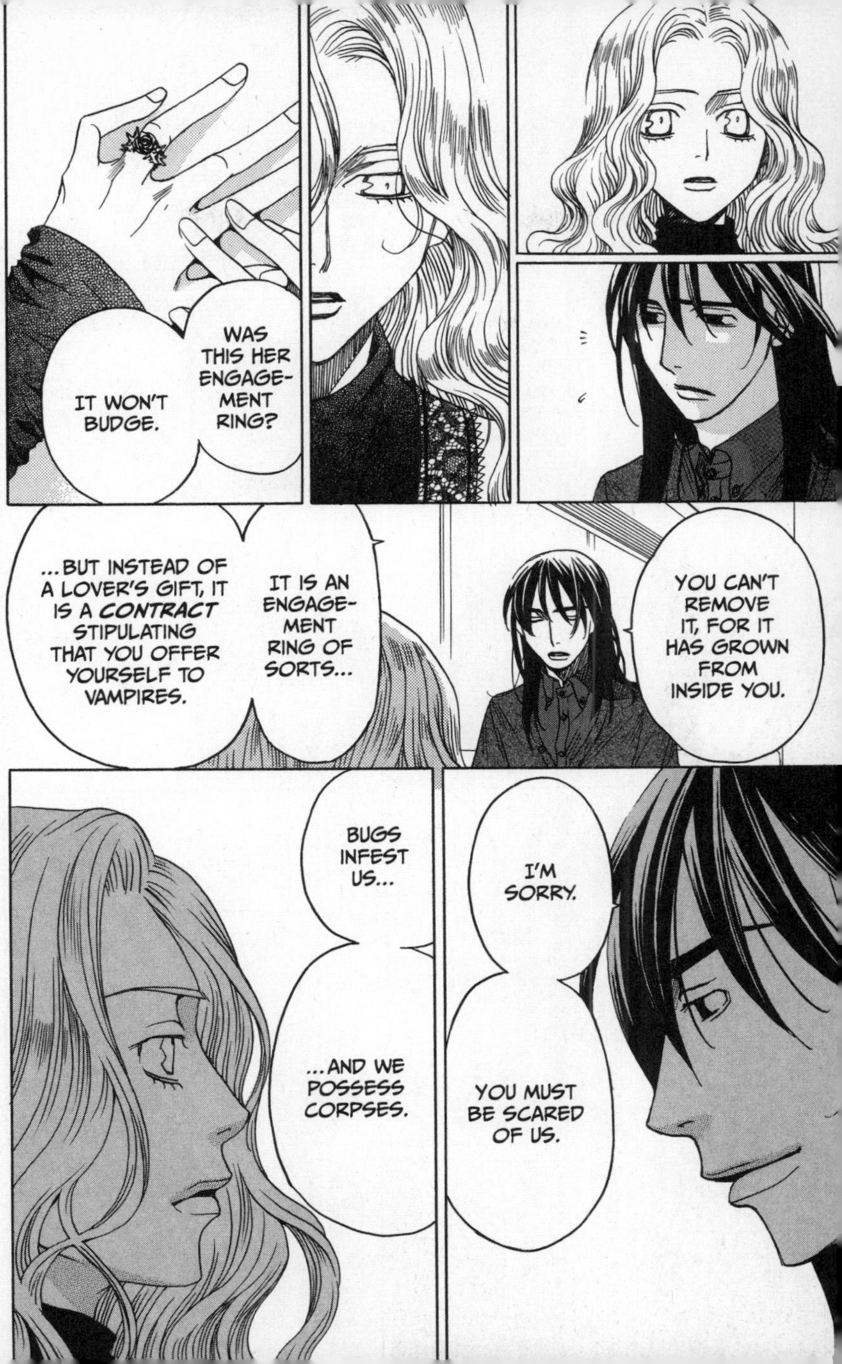
WAS THIS HER ENGAGEMENT RING?
IT WON'T BUDGE.
YOU CAN'T REMOVE IT, FOR IT HAS GROWN FROM INSIDE YOU.
IT IS AN ENGAGEMENT RING OF SORTS...
...BUT INSTEAD OF A LOVER'S GIFT, IT IS A *CONTRACT* STIPULATING THAT YOU OFFER YOURSELF TO VAMPIRES.
I'M SORRY.
YOU MUST BE SCARED OF US.
BUGS INFEST US...
...AND WE POSSESS CORPSES.

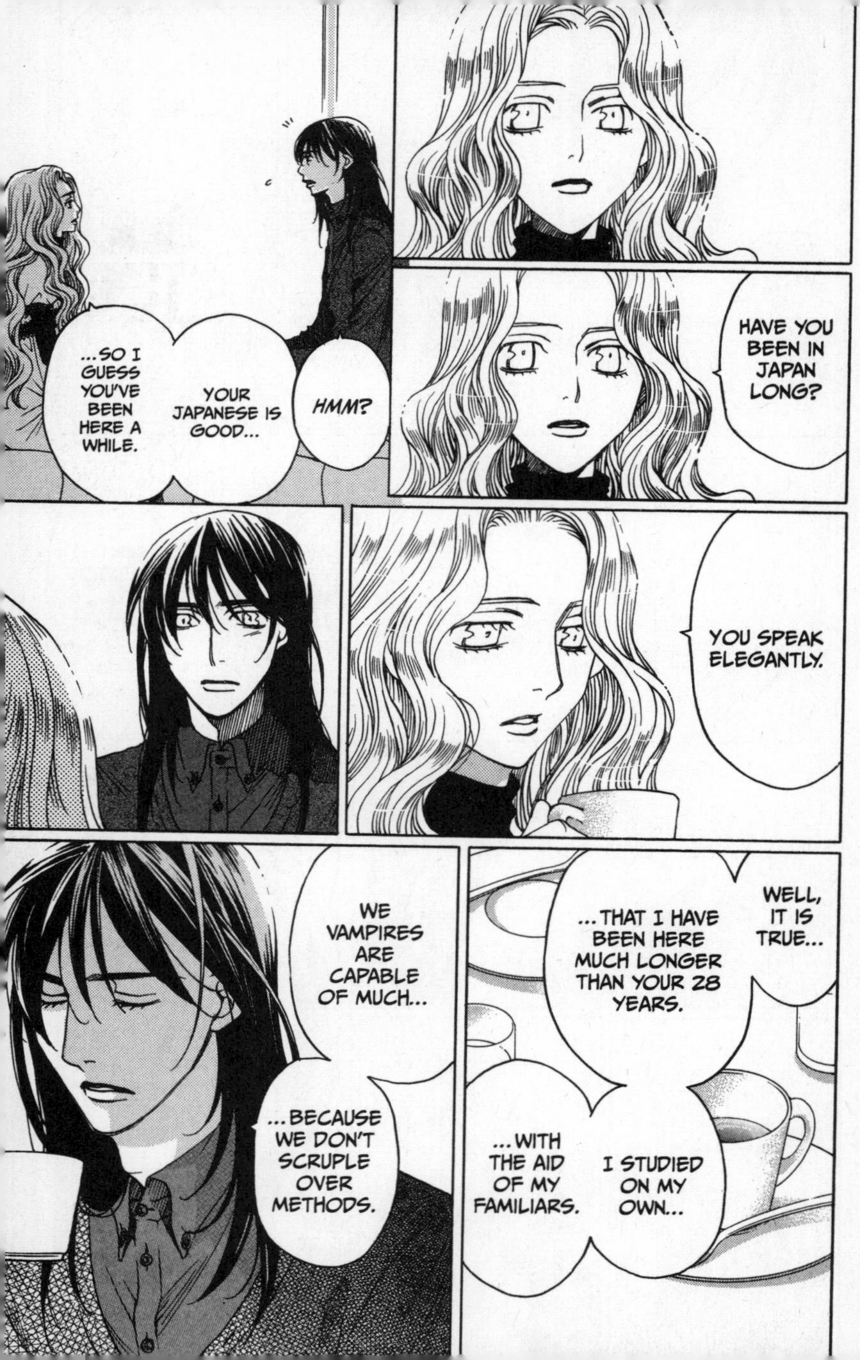
HAVE YOU BEEN IN JAPAN LONG?
HMM?
YOUR JAPANESE IS GOOD...
...SO I GUESS YOU'VE BEEN HERE A WHILE.
YOU SPEAK ELEGANTLY.
WELL, IT IS TRUE...
...THAT I HAVE BEEN HERE MUCH LONGER THAN YOUR 28 YEARS.
I STUDIED ON MY OWN...
...WITH THE AID OF MY FAMILIARS.
WE VAMPIRES ARE CAPABLE OF MUCH...
...BECAUSE WE DON'T SCRUPLE OVER METHODS.

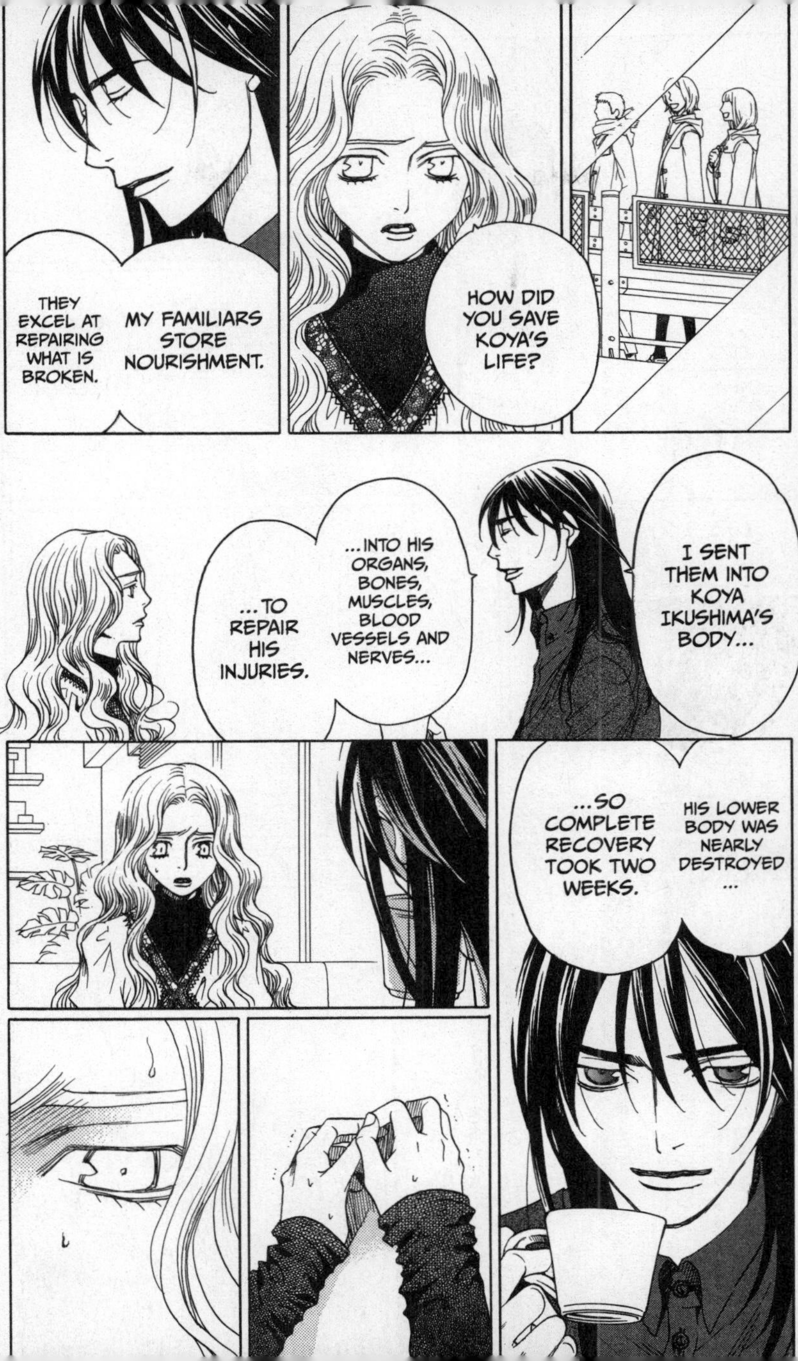
HOW DID YOU SAVE KOYA'S LIFE?
MY FAMILIARS STORE NOURISHMENT.
THEY EXCEL AT REPAIRING WHAT IS BROKEN.
I SENT THEM INTO KOYA IKUSHIMA'S BODY...
...INTO HIS ORGANS, BONES, MUSCLES, BLOOD VESSELS AND NERVES...
...TO REPAIR HIS INJURIES.
HIS LOWER BODY WAS NEARLY DESTROYED ...
...SO COMPLETE RECOVERY TOOK TWO WEEKS.

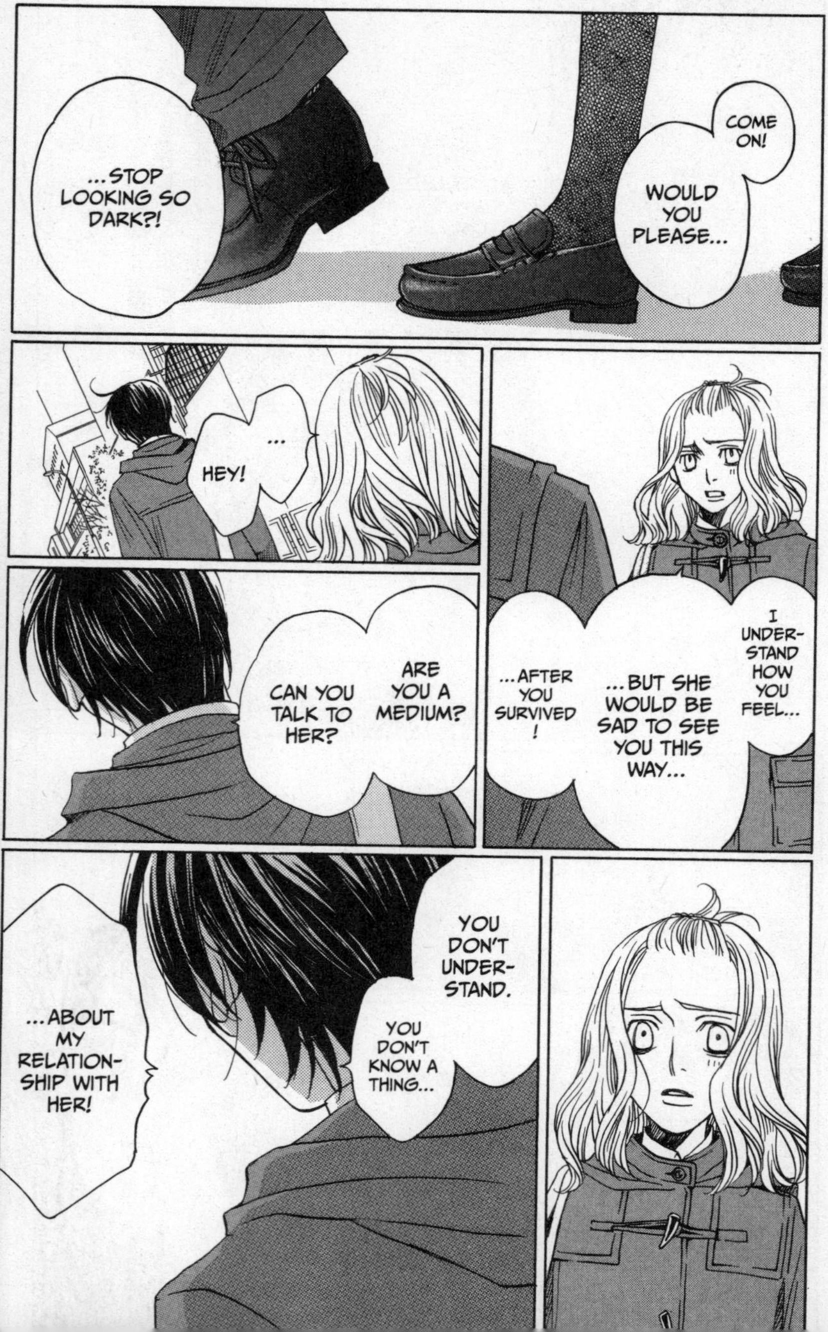
COME ON!
WOULD YOU PLEASE...
...STOP LOOKING SO DARK?!
I UNDER-STAND HOW YOU FEEL...
...BUT SHE WOULD BE SAD TO SEE YOU THIS WAY...
...AFTER YOU SURVIVED!
...
HEY!
ARE YOU A MEDIUM?
CAN YOU TALK TO HER?
YOU DON'T UNDER-STAND.
YOU DON'T KNOW A THING...
...ABOUT MY RELATION-SHIP WITH HER!

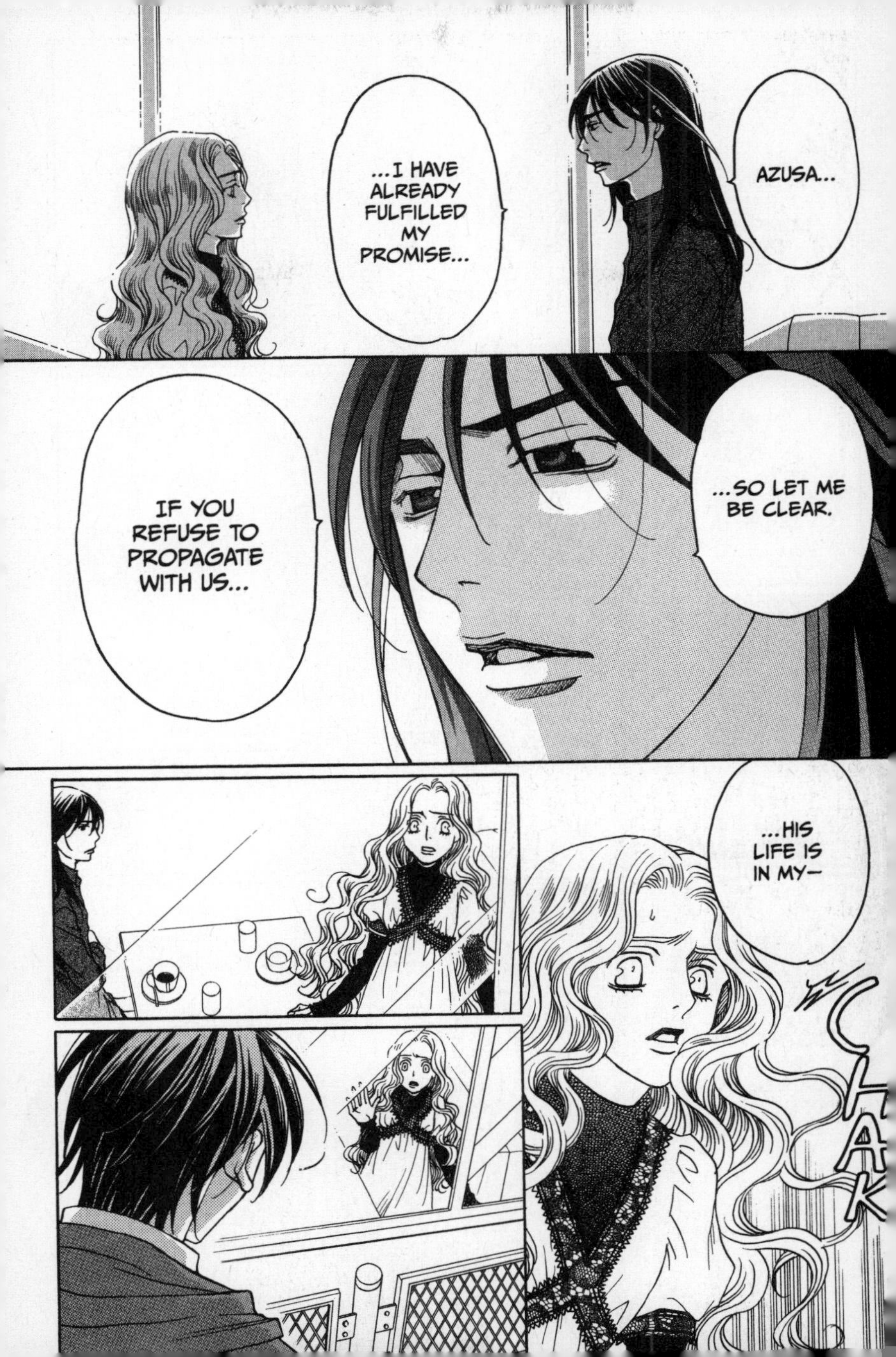
AZUSA...
...I HAVE ALREADY FULFILLED MY PROMISE...
...SO LET ME BE CLEAR.
IF YOU REFUSE TO PROPAGATE WITH US...
...HIS LIFE IS IN MY—
CHAK

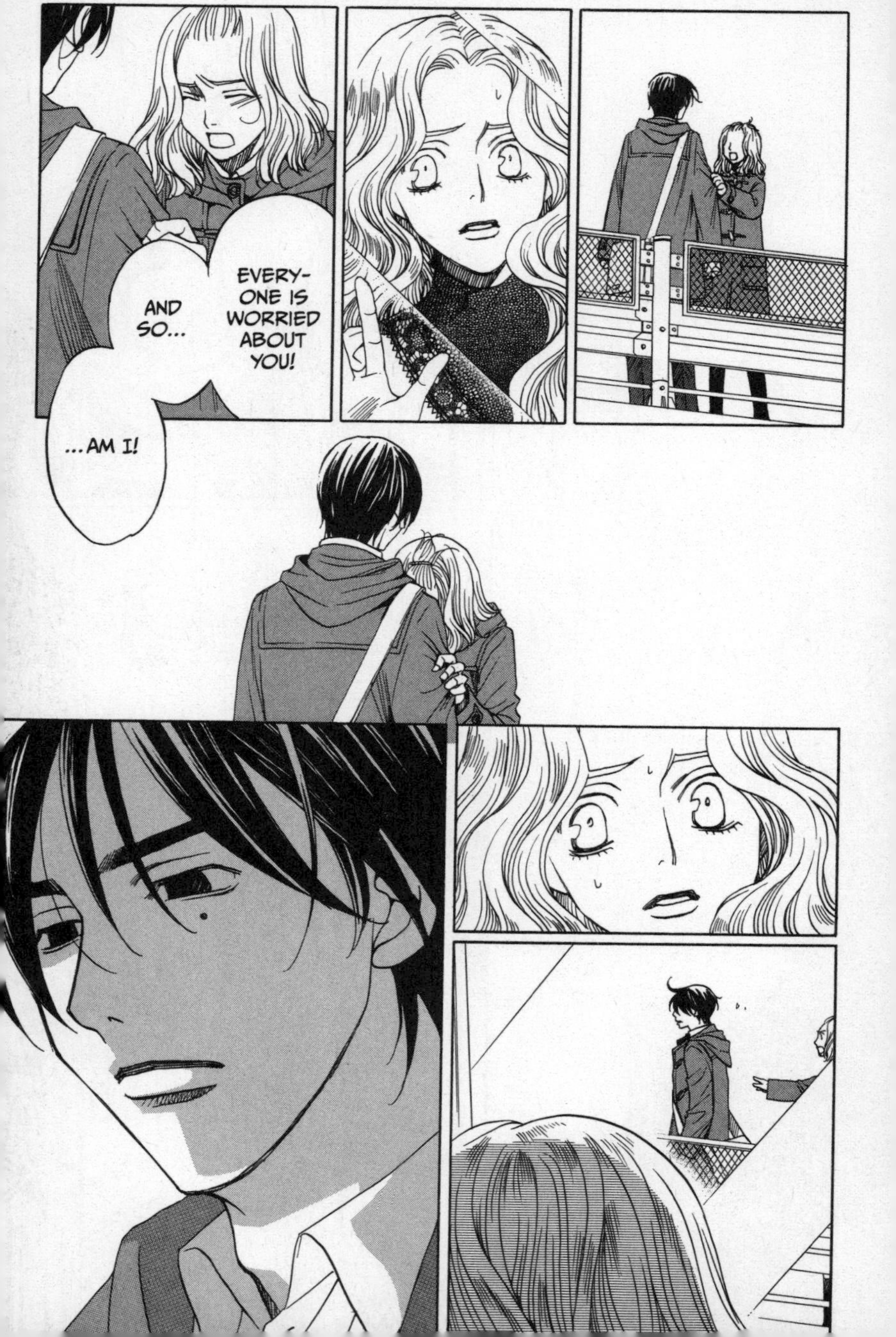
EVERY-ONE IS WORRIED ABOUT YOU!
AND SO...
...AM I!

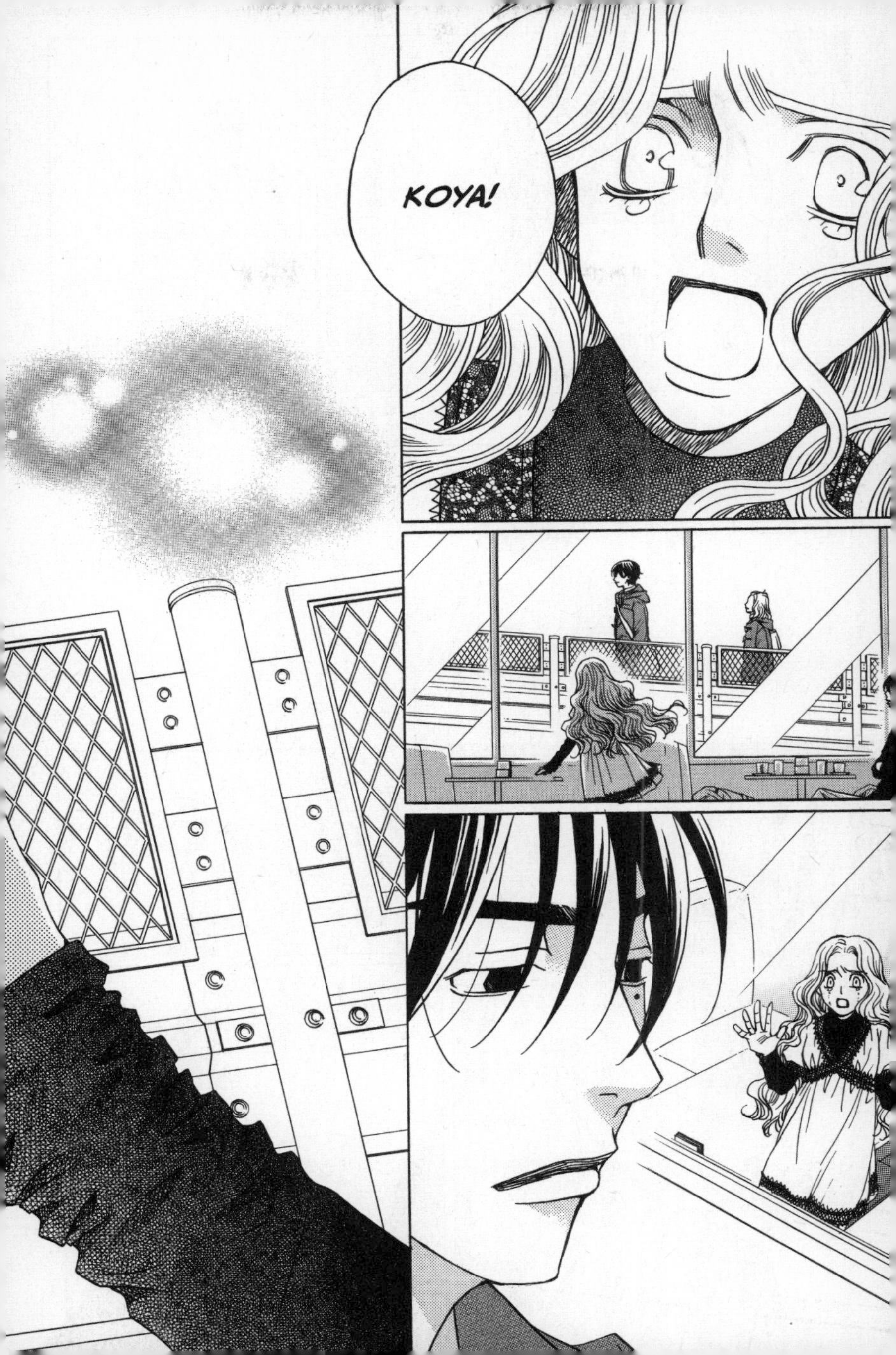
KOYA!

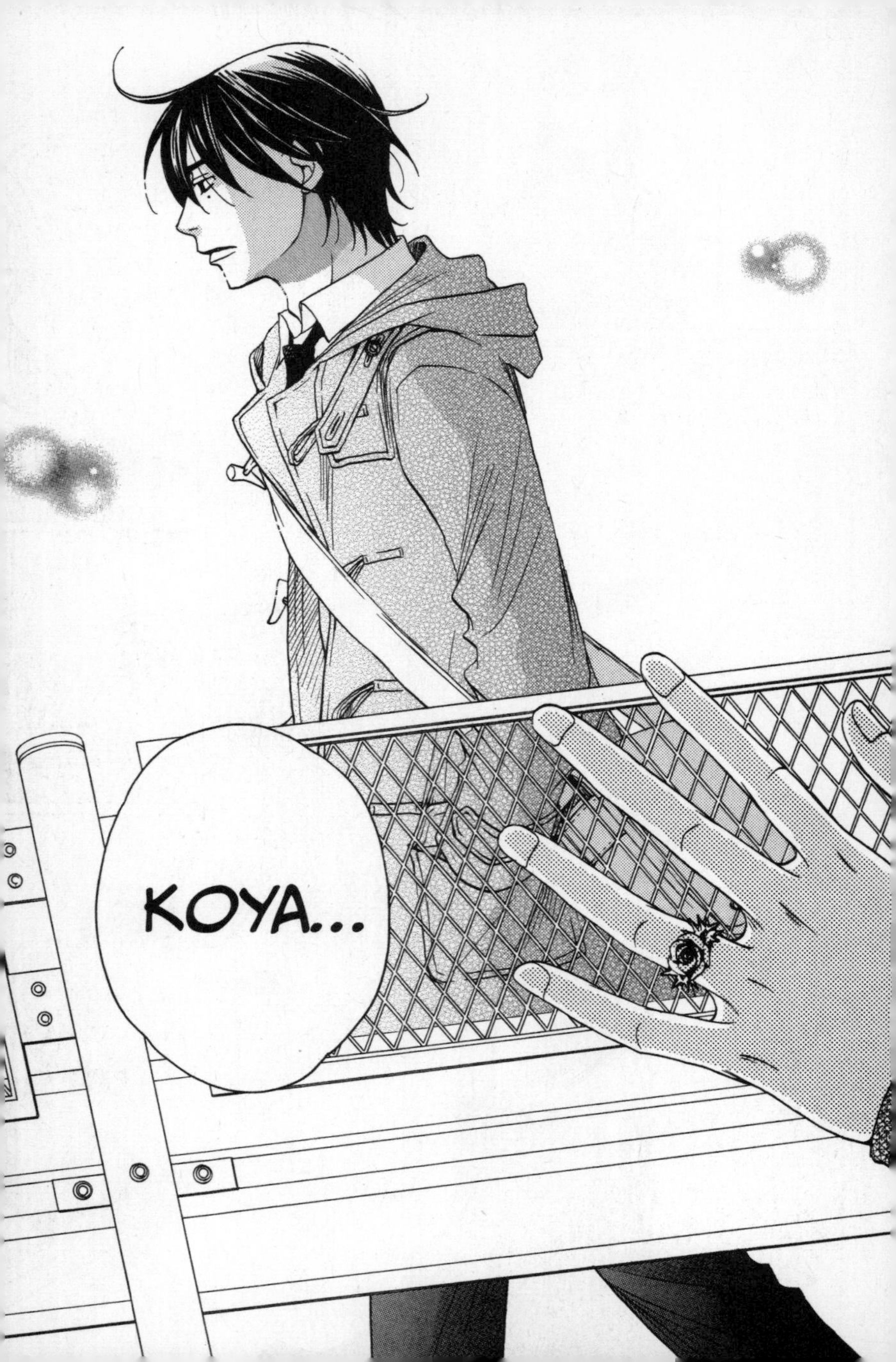
KOYA...

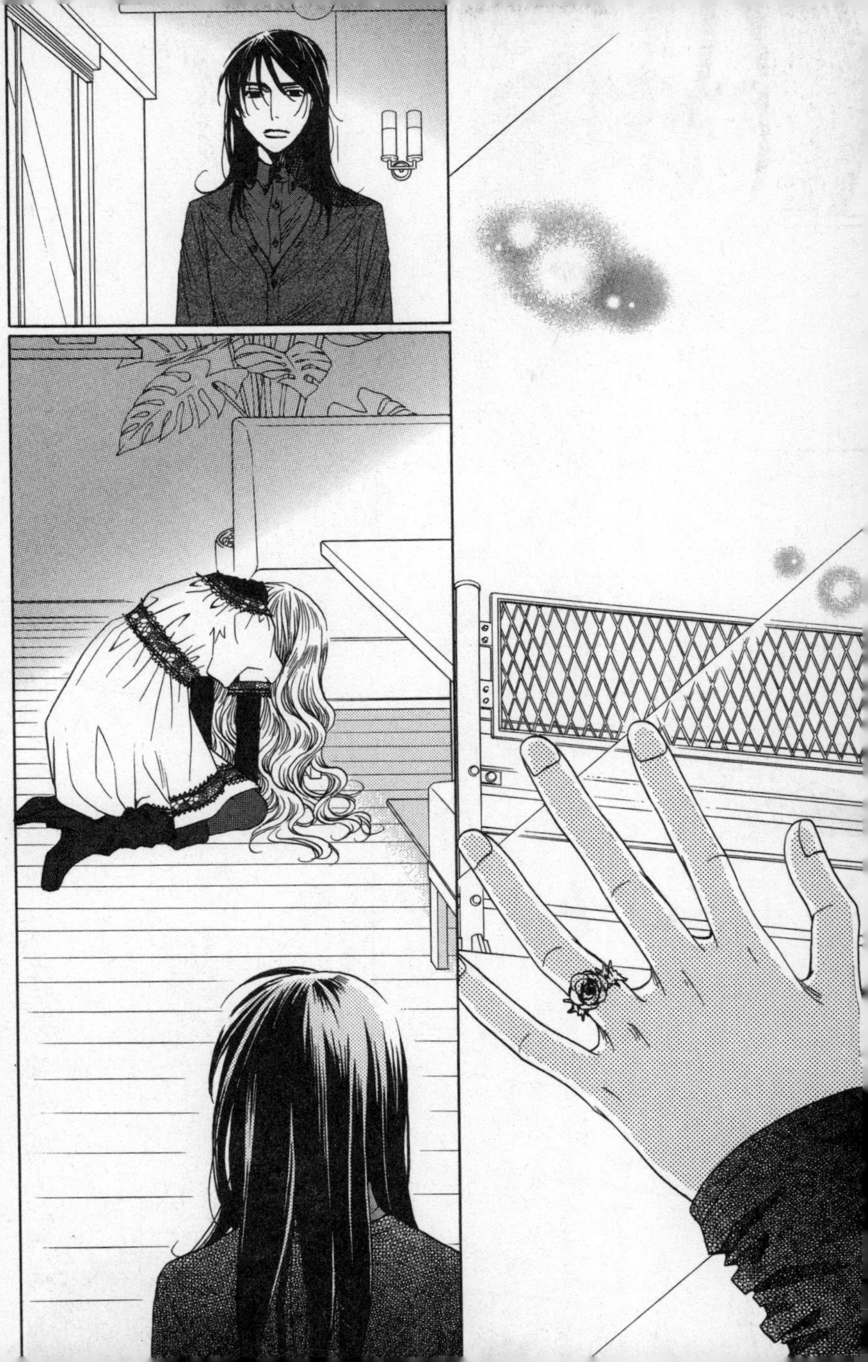

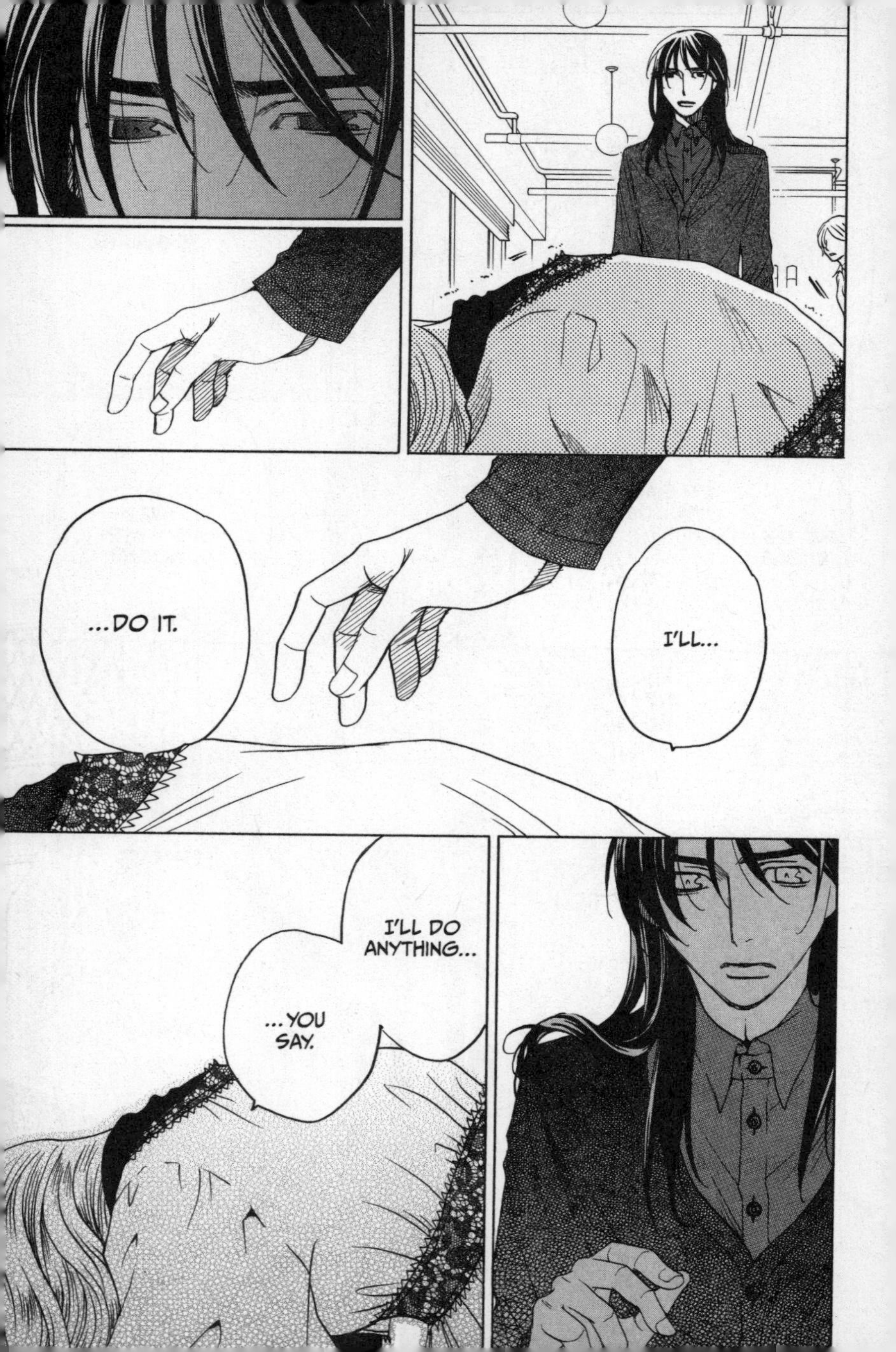
I'LL...
...DO IT.
I'LL DO ANYTHING...
...YOU SAY.

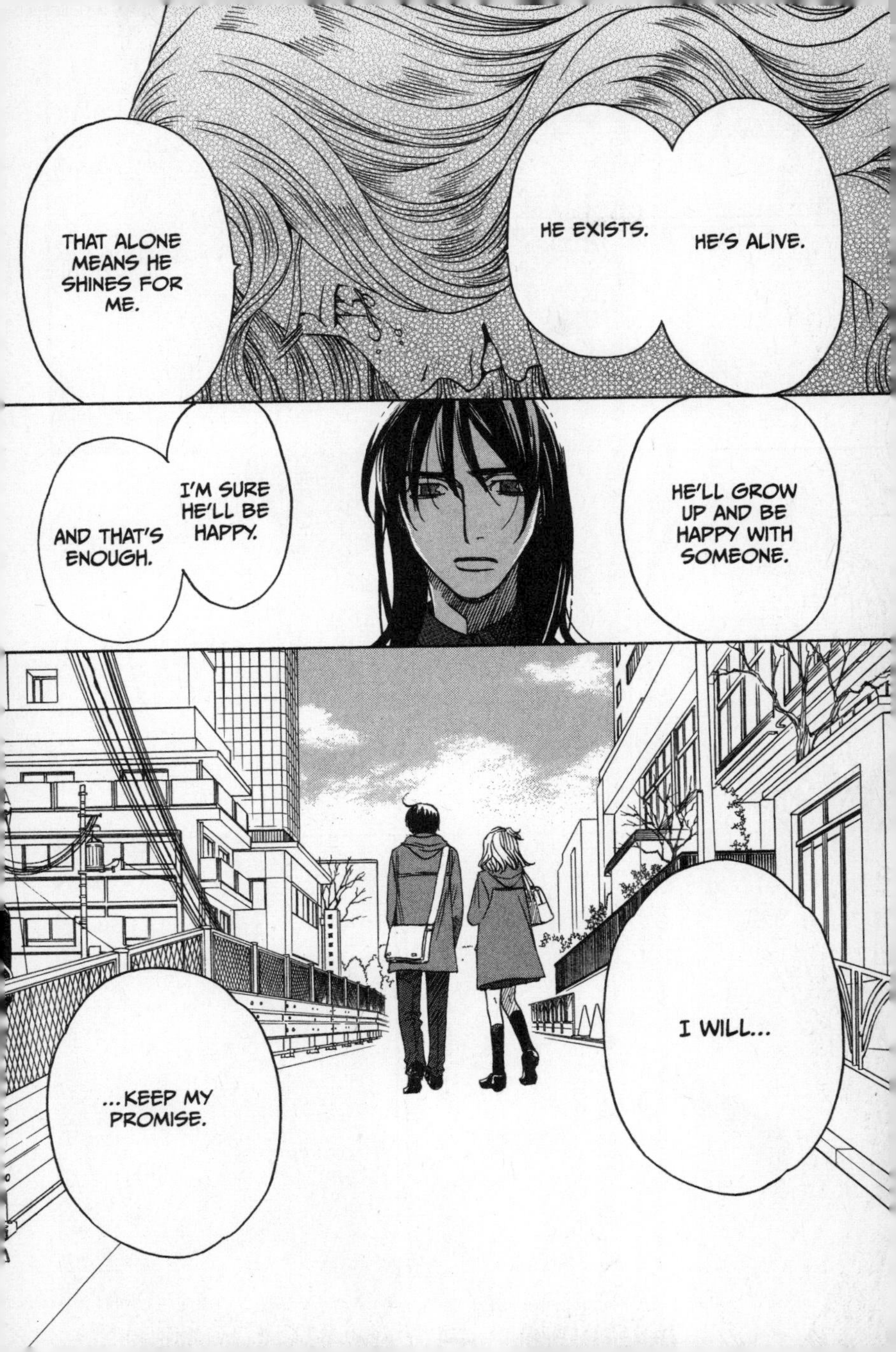
HE'S ALIVE.
HE EXISTS.
THAT ALONE MEANS HE SHINES FOR ME.
HE'LL GROW UP AND BE HAPPY WITH SOMEONE.
I'M SURE HE'LL BE HAPPY.
AND THAT'S ENOUGH.
I WILL...
...KEEP MY PROMISE.

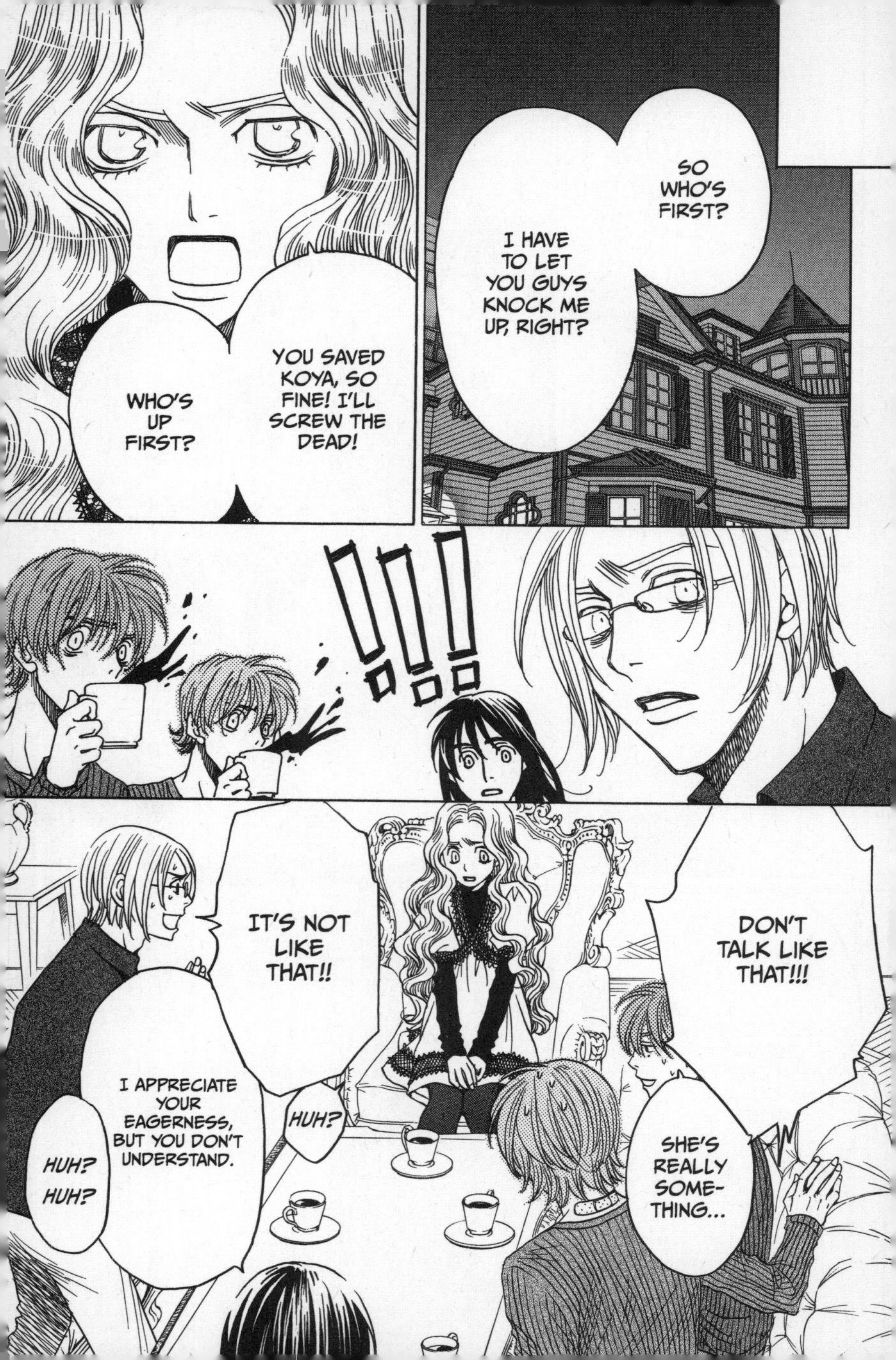
SO WHO'S FIRST?
I HAVE TO LET YOU GUYS KNOCK ME UP, RIGHT?
YOU SAVED KOYA, SO FINE! I'LL SCREW THE DEAD!
WHO'S UP FIRST?
!!!
DON'T TALK LIKE THAT!!!
SHE'S REALLY SOME-THING...
IT'S NOT LIKE THAT!!
HUH?
I APPRECIATE YOUR EAGERNESS, BUT YOU DON'T UNDERSTAND.
HUH? HUH?

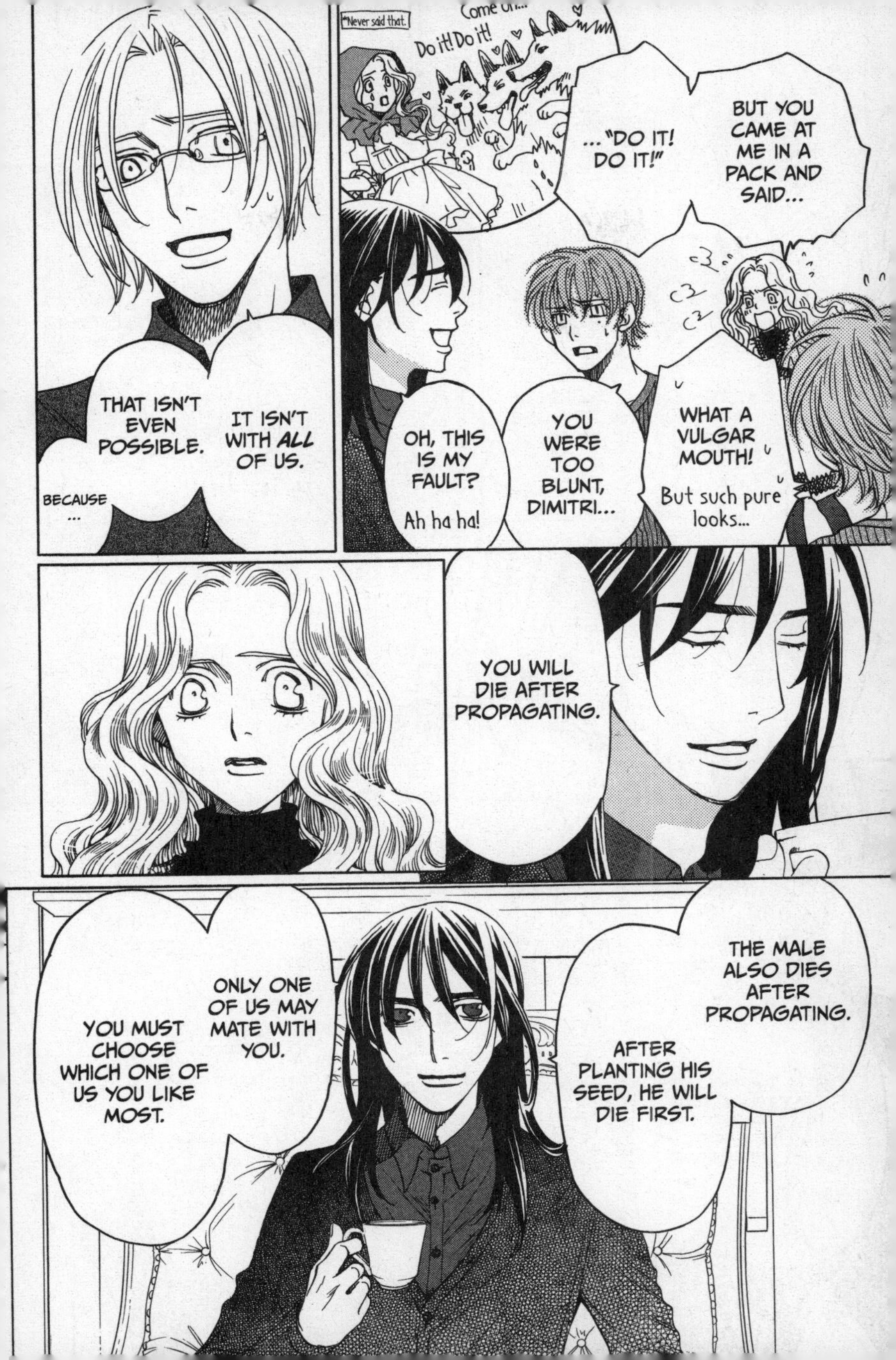
BUT YOU CAME AT ME IN A PACK AND SAID...
..."DO IT! DO IT!"
*Never said that.
Come on...
Do it! Do it!
WHAT A VULGAR MOUTH!
But such pure looks...
YOU WERE TOO BLUNT, DIMITRI...
OH, THIS IS MY FAULT?
Ah ha ha!
IT ISN'T WITH ALL OF US.
THAT ISN'T EVEN POSSIBLE.
BECAUSE ...
YOU WILL DIE AFTER PROPAGATING.
THE MALE ALSO DIES AFTER PROPAGATING.
AFTER PLANTING HIS SEED, HE WILL DIE FIRST.
ONLY ONE OF US MAY MATE WITH YOU.
YOU MUST CHOOSE WHICH ONE OF US YOU LIKE MOST.

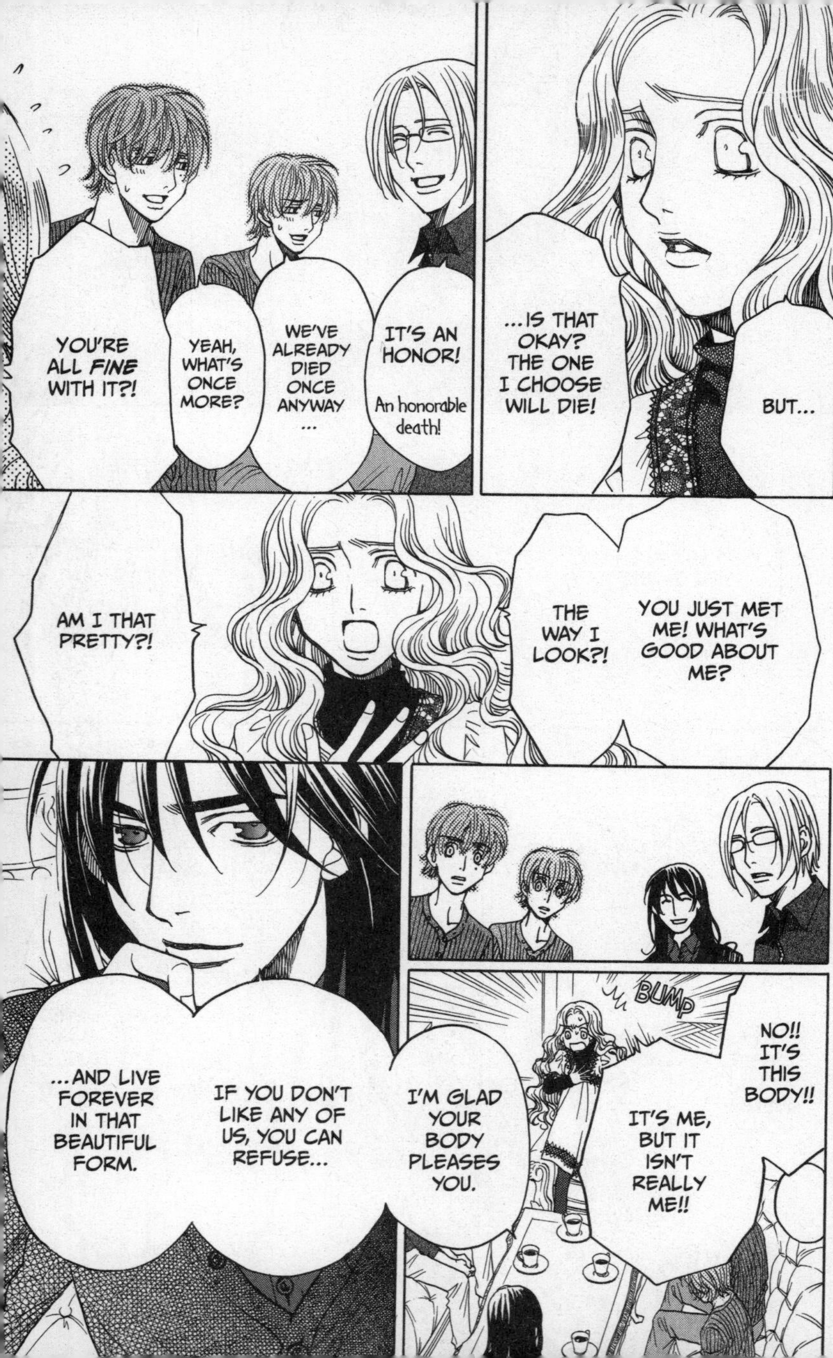
BUT...
...IS THAT OKAY? THE ONE I CHOOSE WILL DIE!
IT'S AN HONOR!
An honorable death!
WE'VE ALREADY DIED ONCE ANYWAY...
YEAH, WHAT'S ONCE MORE?
YOU'RE ALL *FINE* WITH IT?!
YOU JUST MET ME! WHAT'S GOOD ABOUT ME?
THE WAY I LOOK?!
AM I THAT PRETTY?!
BUMP
NO!! IT'S THIS BODY!!
IT'S ME, BUT IT ISN'T REALLY ME!!
I'M GLAD YOUR BODY PLEASES YOU.
IF YOU DON'T LIKE ANY OF US, YOU CAN REFUSE...
...AND LIVE FOREVER IN THAT BEAUTIFUL FORM.

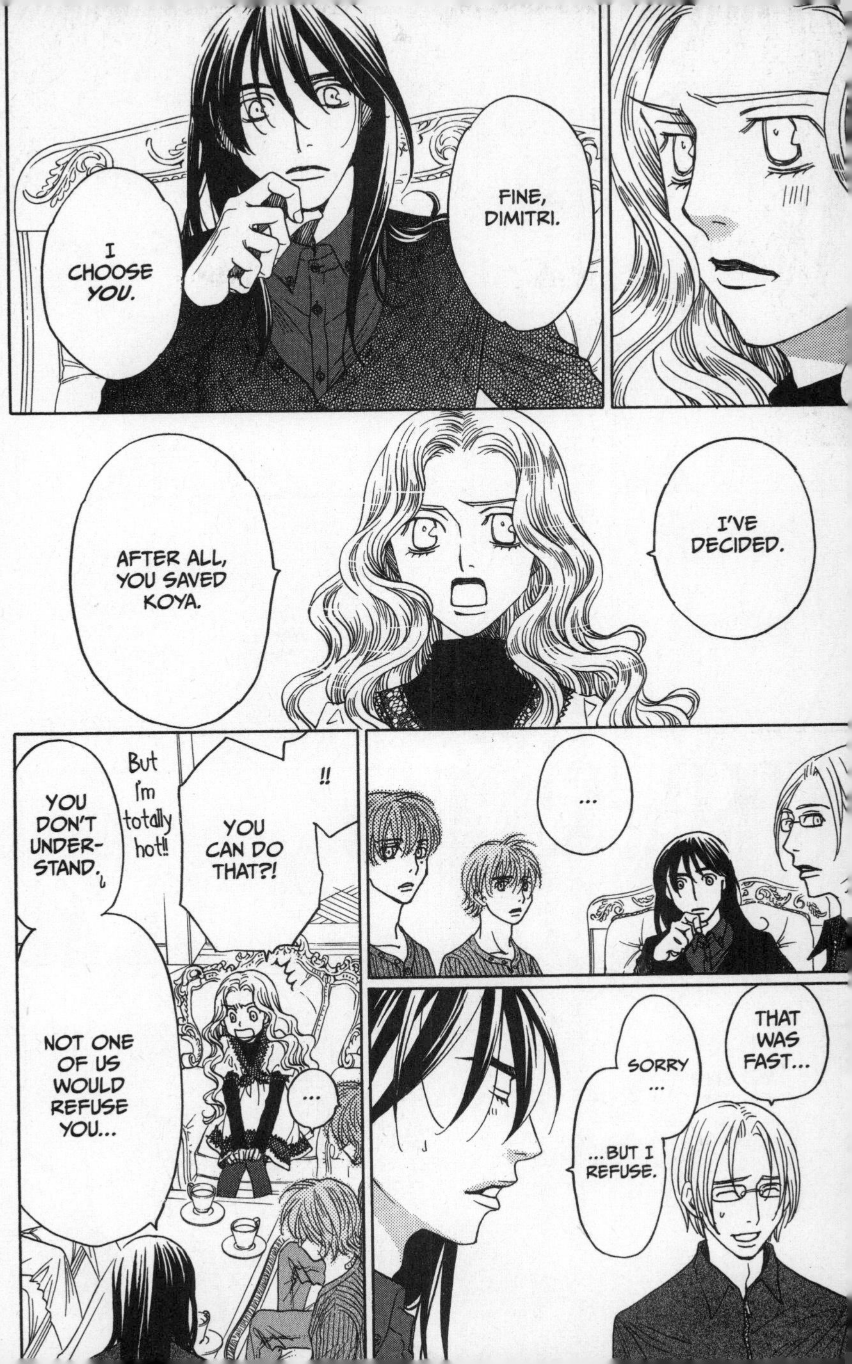
FINE, DIMITRI.
I CHOOSE YOU.
I'VE DECIDED.
AFTER ALL, YOU SAVED KOYA.
...
THAT WAS FAST...
SORRY ...
...BUT I REFUSE.
!!
YOU CAN DO THAT?!
But I'm totally hot!!
YOU DON'T UNDER-STAND.
NOT ONE OF US WOULD REFUSE YOU...
...

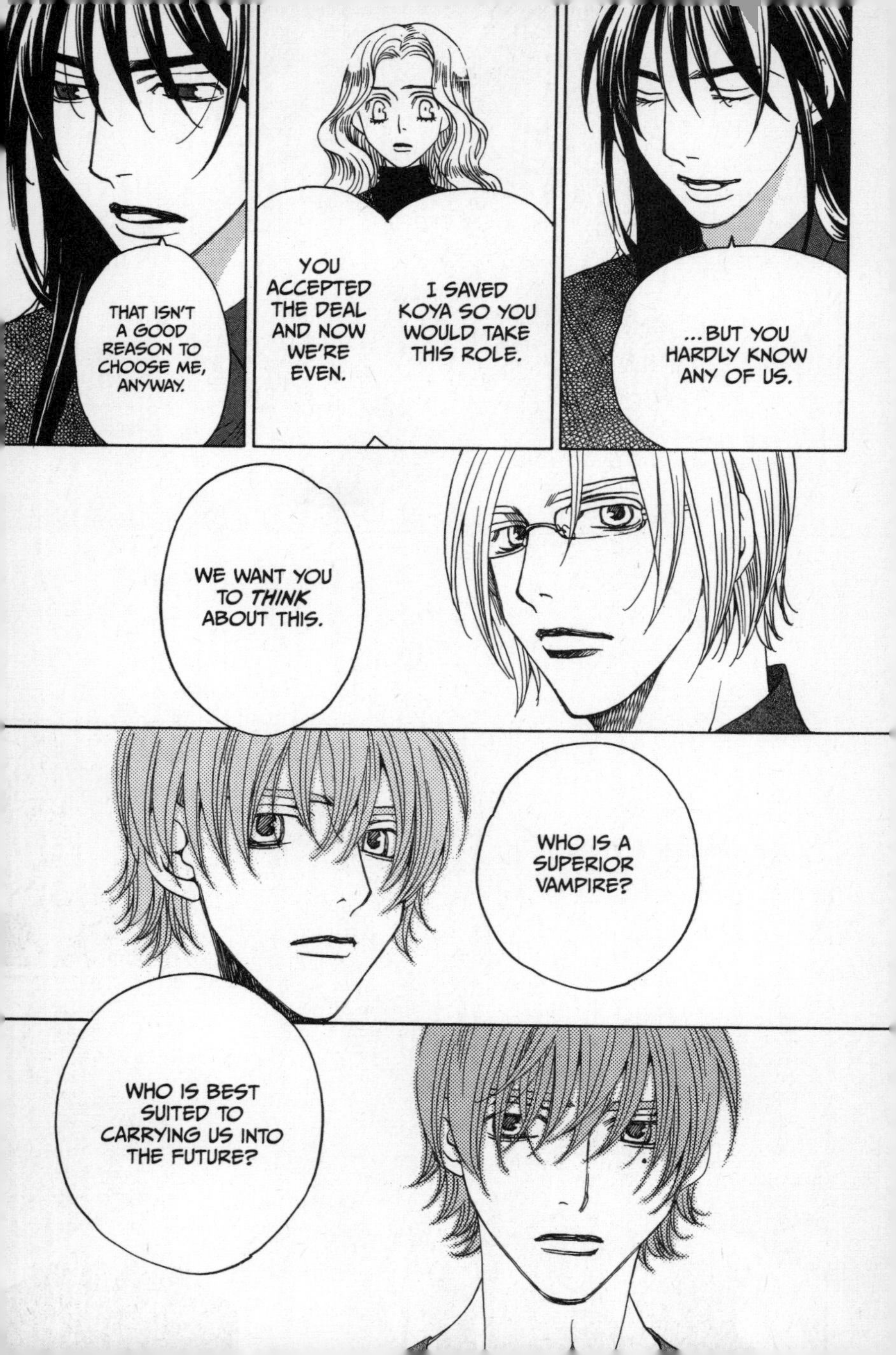
...BUT YOU HARDLY KNOW ANY OF US.
I SAVED KOYA SO YOU WOULD TAKE THIS ROLE.
YOU ACCEPTED THE DEAL AND NOW WE'RE EVEN.
THAT ISN'T A GOOD REASON TO CHOOSE ME, ANYWAY.
WE WANT YOU TO *THINK* ABOUT THIS.
WHO IS A SUPERIOR VAMPIRE?
WHO IS BEST SUITED TO CARRYING US INTO THE FUTURE?

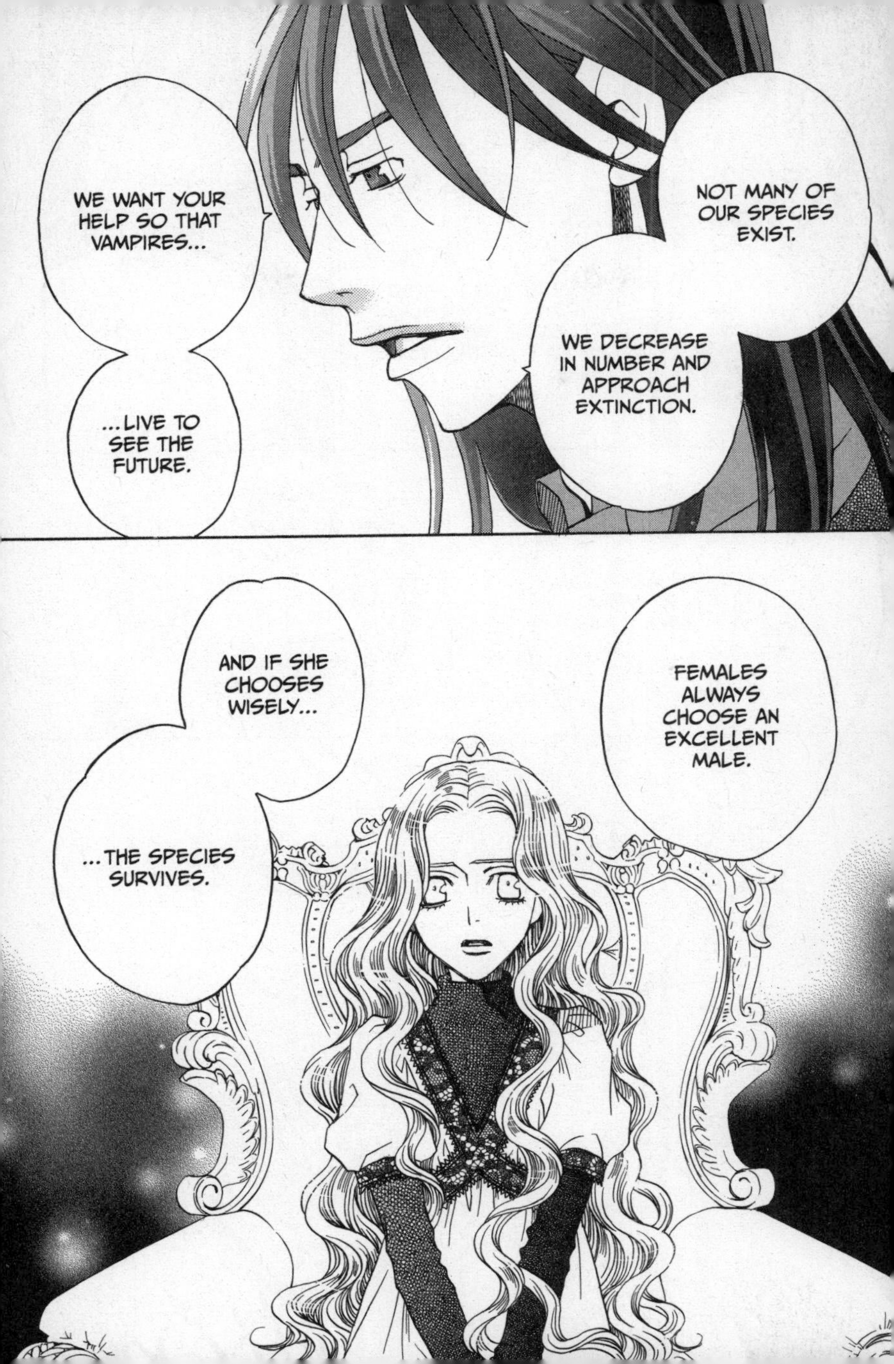
NOT MANY OF OUR SPECIES EXIST.
WE DECREASE IN NUMBER AND APPROACH EXTINCTION.
WE WANT YOUR HELP SO THAT VAMPIRES...
...LIVE TO SEE THE FUTURE.
FEMALES ALWAYS CHOOSE AN EXCELLENT MALE.
AND IF SHE CHOOSES WISELY...
...THE SPECIES SURVIVES.

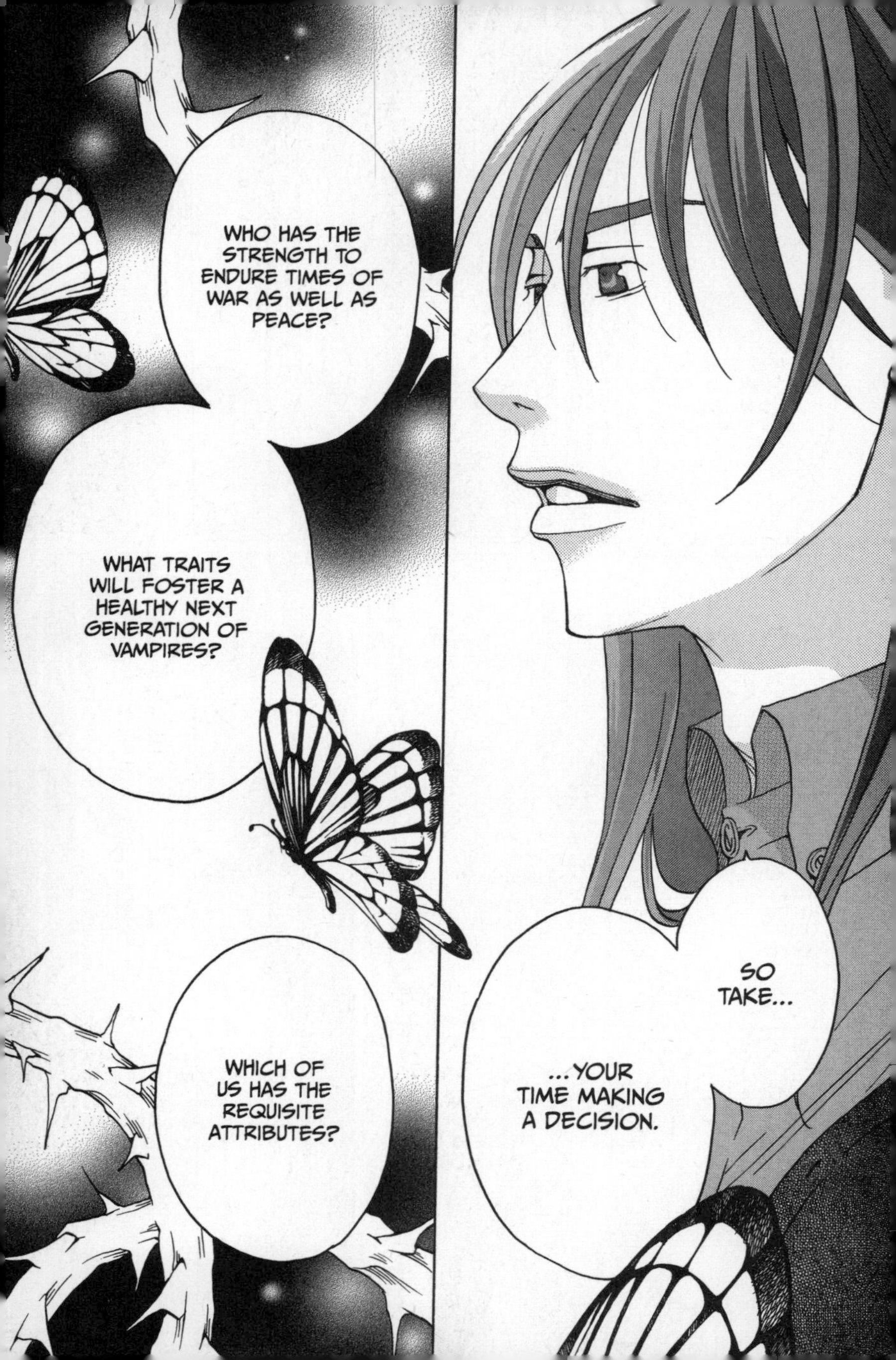
SO TAKE...
...YOUR TIME MAKING A DECISION.
WHO HAS THE STRENGTH TO ENDURE TIMES OF WAR AS WELL AS PEACE?
WHAT TRAITS WILL FOSTER A HEALTHY NEXT GENERATION OF VAMPIRES?
WHICH OF US HAS THE REQUISITE ATTRIBUTES?

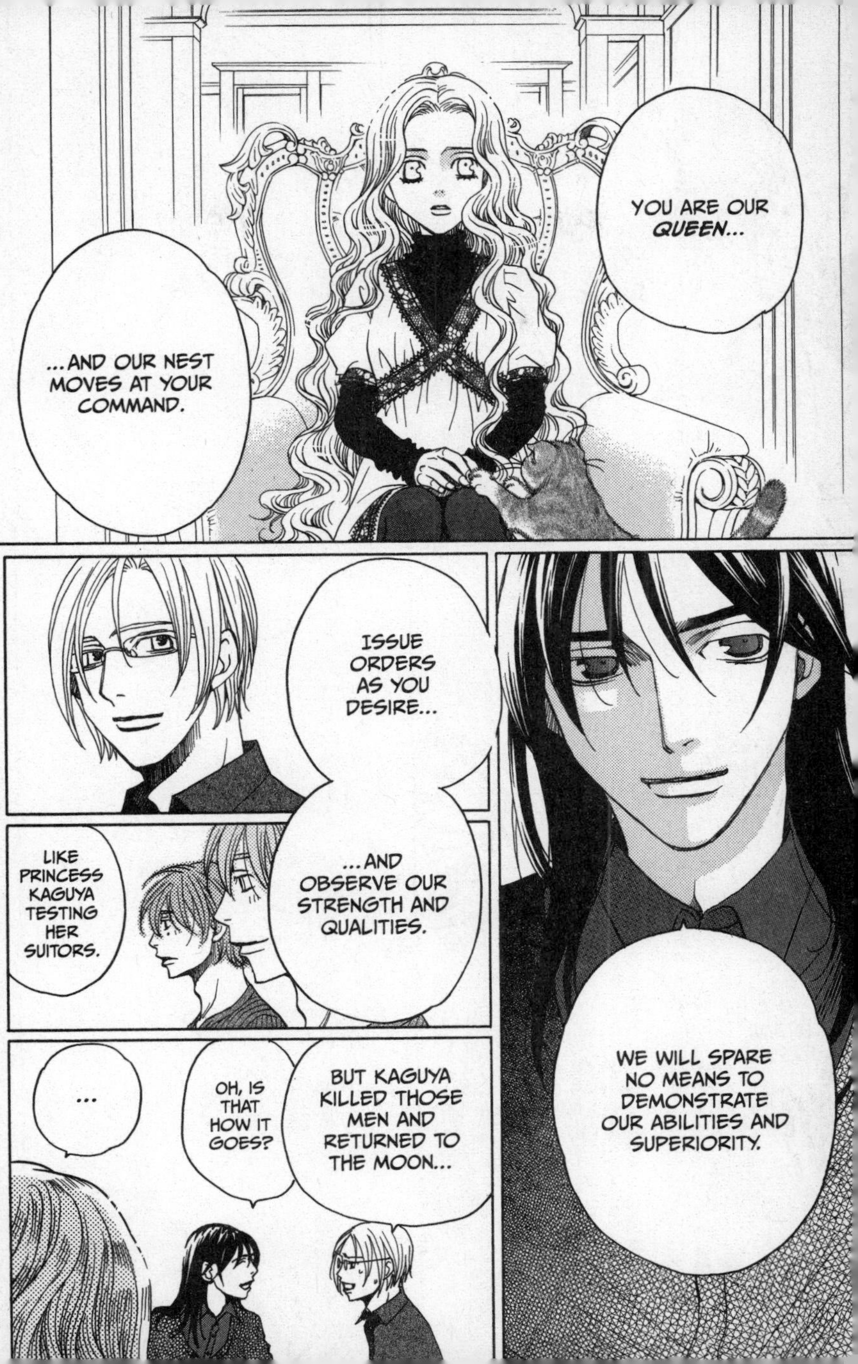

YOU ARE OUR *QUEEN...*
...AND OUR NEST MOVES AT YOUR COMMAND.
ISSUE ORDERS AS YOU DESIRE...
...AND OBSERVE OUR STRENGTH AND QUALITIES.
WE WILL SPARE NO MEANS TO DEMONSTRATE OUR ABILITIES AND SUPERIORITY.
LIKE PRINCESS KAGUYA TESTING HER SUITORS.
BUT KAGUYA KILLED THOSE MEN AND RETURNED TO THE MOON...
OH, IS THAT HOW IT GOES?
...

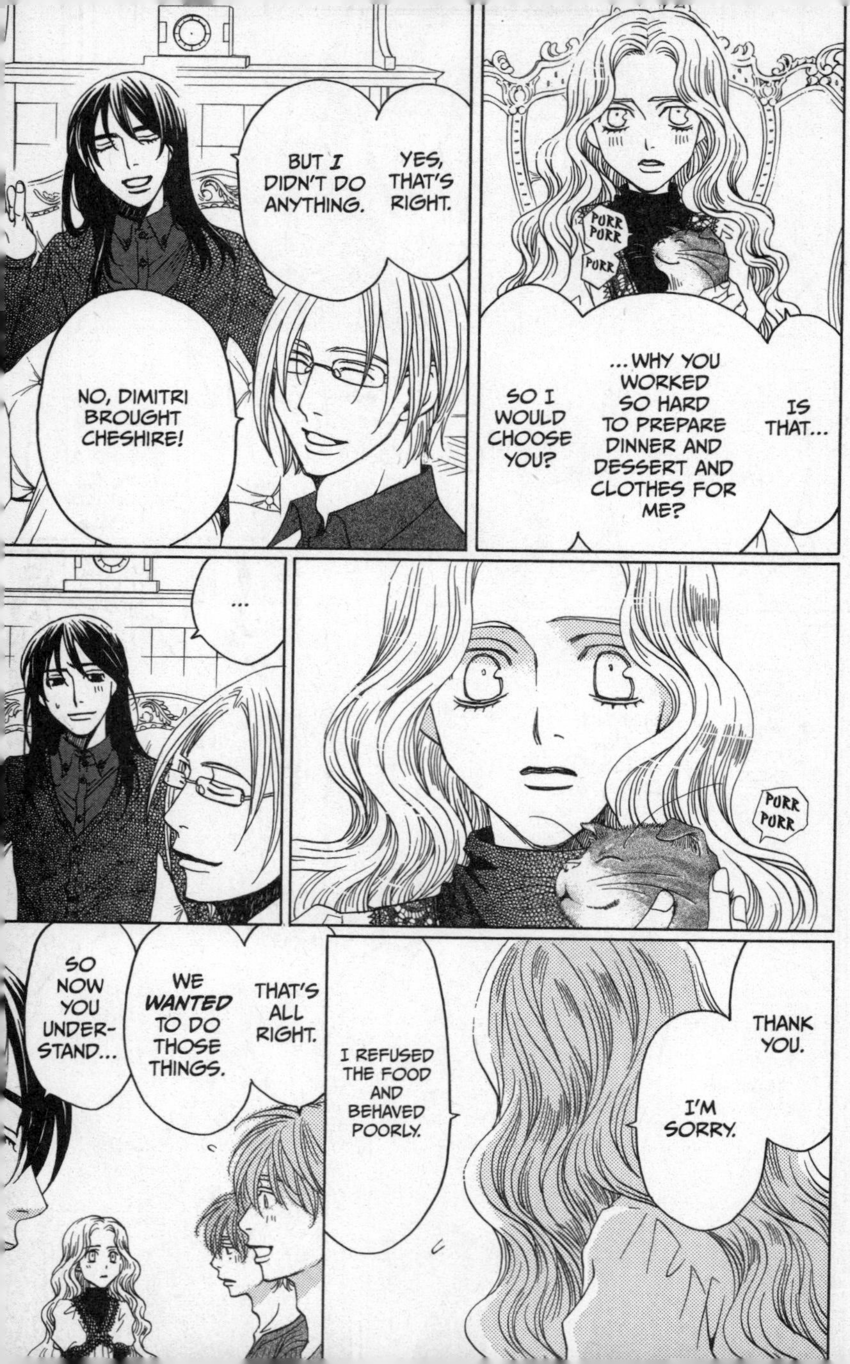
PURR PURR
PURR
IS THAT...
...WHY YOU WORKED SO HARD TO PREPARE DINNER AND DESSERT AND CLOTHES FOR ME?
SO I WOULD CHOOSE YOU?
YES, THAT'S RIGHT.
BUT *I* DIDN'T DO ANYTHING.
NO, DIMITRI BROUGHT CHESHIRE!
PURR PURR
...
THANK YOU.
I'M SORRY.
I REFUSED THE FOOD AND BEHAVED POORLY.
THAT'S ALL RIGHT.
WE *WANTED* TO DO THOSE THINGS.
SO NOW YOU UNDER-STAND...

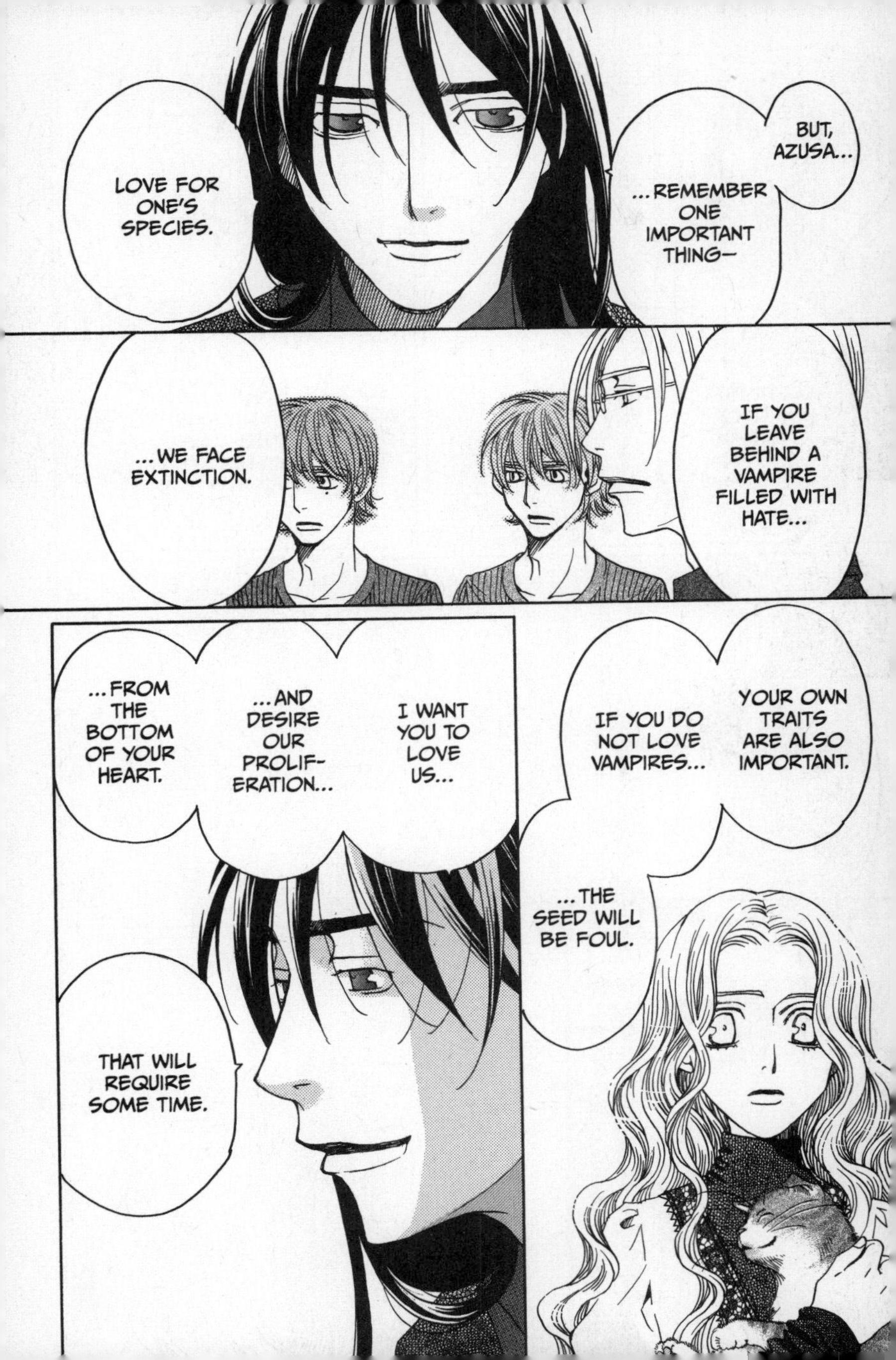
BUT, AZUSA...
...REMEMBER ONE IMPORTANT THING—
LOVE FOR ONE'S SPECIES.
IF YOU LEAVE BEHIND A VAMPIRE FILLED WITH HATE...
...WE FACE EXTINCTION.
YOUR OWN TRAITS ARE ALSO IMPORTANT.
IF YOU DO NOT LOVE VAMPIRES...
...THE SEED WILL BE FOUL.
I WANT YOU TO LOVE US...
...AND DESIRE OUR PROLIF-ERATION...
...FROM THE BOTTOM OF YOUR HEART.
THAT WILL REQUIRE SOME TIME.

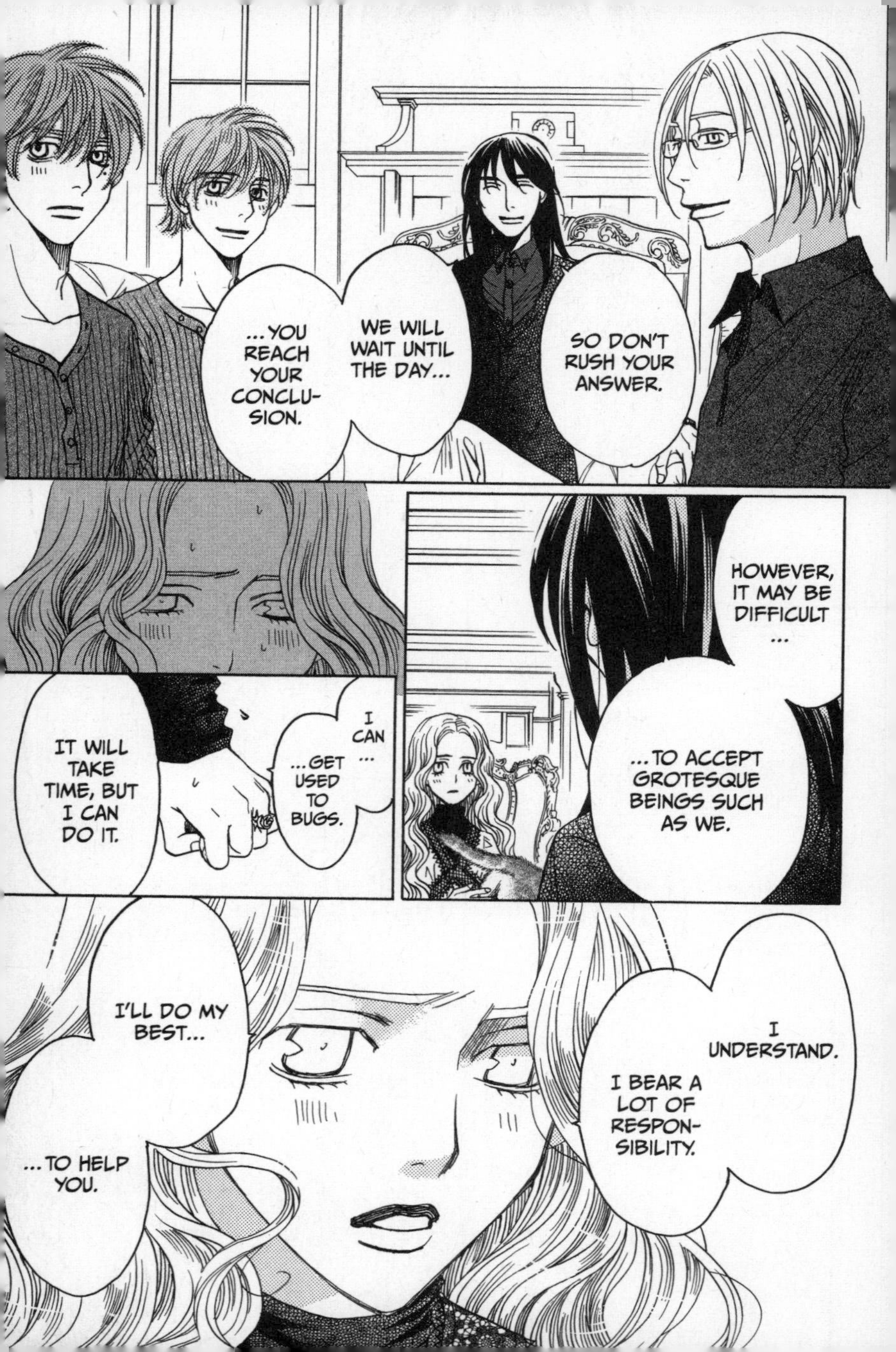
SO DON'T RUSH YOUR ANSWER.
WE WILL WAIT UNTIL THE DAY...
...YOU REACH YOUR CONCLUSION.
HOWEVER, IT MAY BE DIFFICULT ...
...TO ACCEPT GROTESQUE BEINGS SUCH AS WE.
I CAN ...
...GET USED TO BUGS.
IT WILL TAKE TIME, BUT I CAN DO IT.
I UNDERSTAND.
I BEAR A LOT OF RESPONSIBILITY.
I'LL DO MY BEST...
...TO HELP YOU.

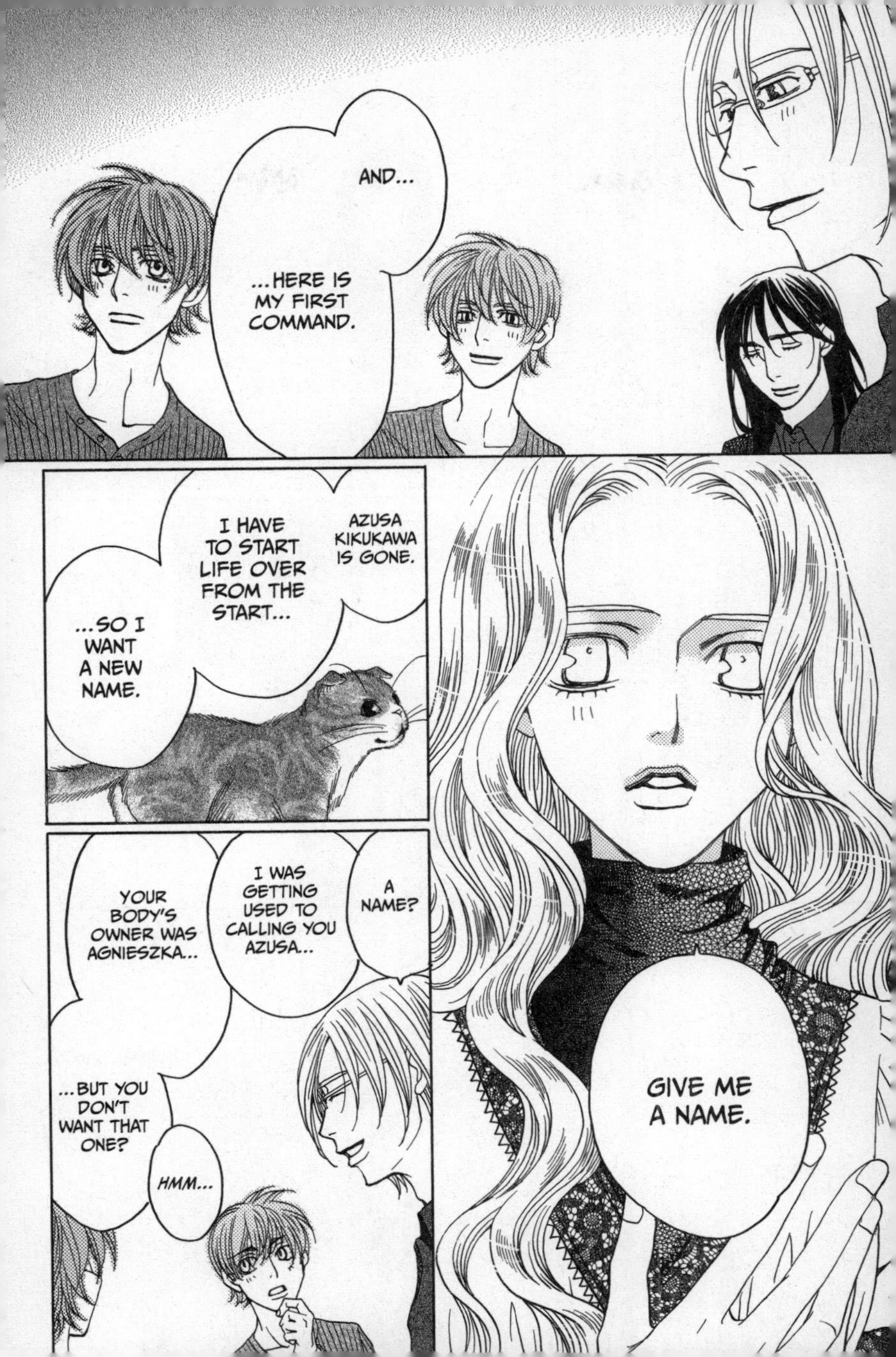
AND...
...HERE IS MY FIRST COMMAND.
GIVE ME A NAME.
AZUSA KIKUKAWA IS GONE.
I HAVE TO START LIFE OVER FROM THE START...
...SO I WANT A NEW NAME.
A NAME?
I WAS GETTING USED TO CALLING YOU AZUSA...
YOUR BODY'S OWNER WAS AGNIESZKA...
...BUT YOU DON'T WANT THAT ONE?
HMM...

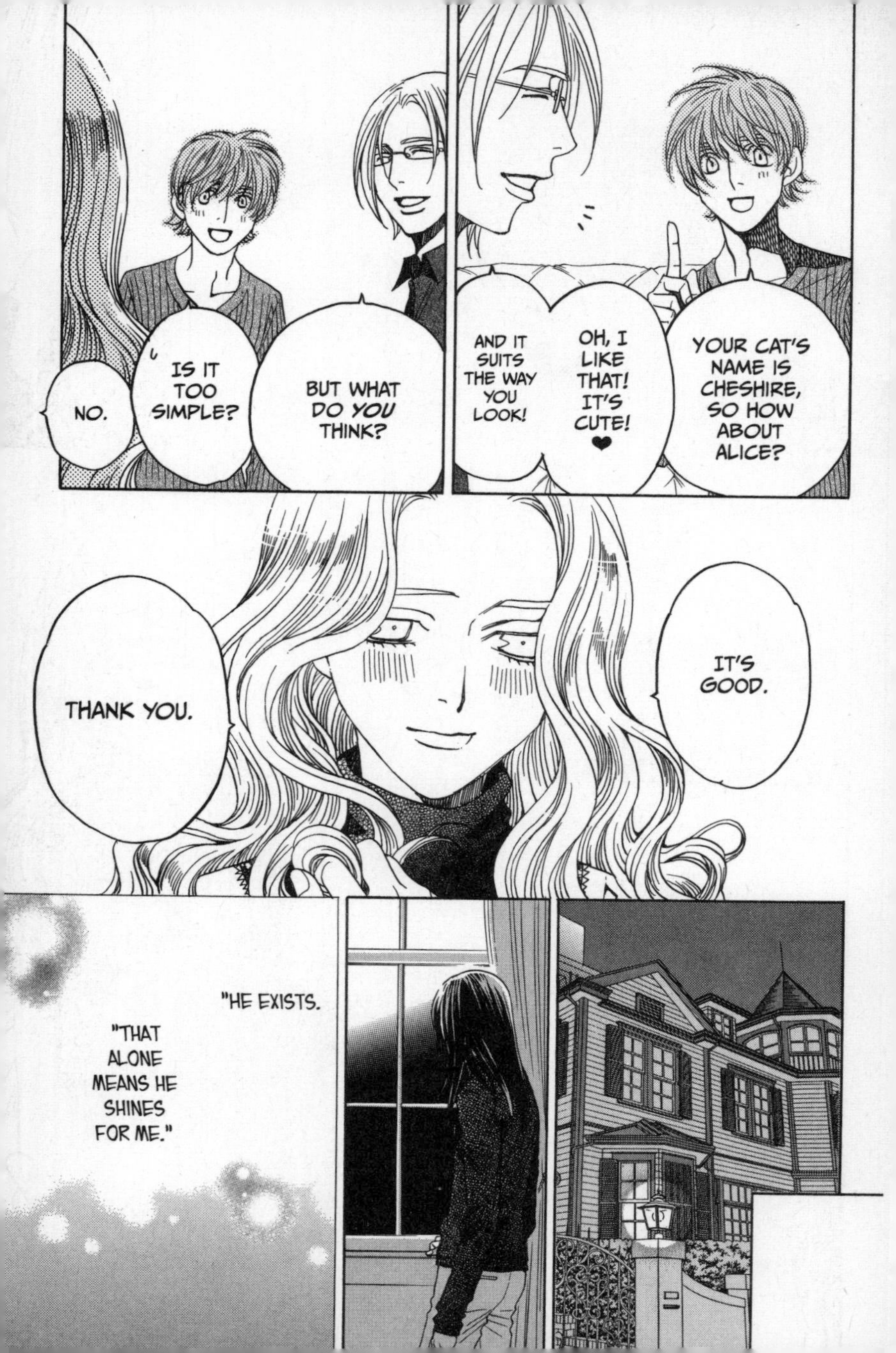
YOUR CAT'S NAME IS CHESHIRE, SO HOW ABOUT ALICE?
OH, I LIKE THAT! IT'S CUTE! ❤
AND IT SUITS THE WAY YOU LOOK!
BUT WHAT DO *YOU* THINK?
IS IT TOO SIMPLE?
NO.
IT'S GOOD.
THANK YOU.
"HE EXISTS.
"THAT ALONE MEANS HE SHINES FOR ME."

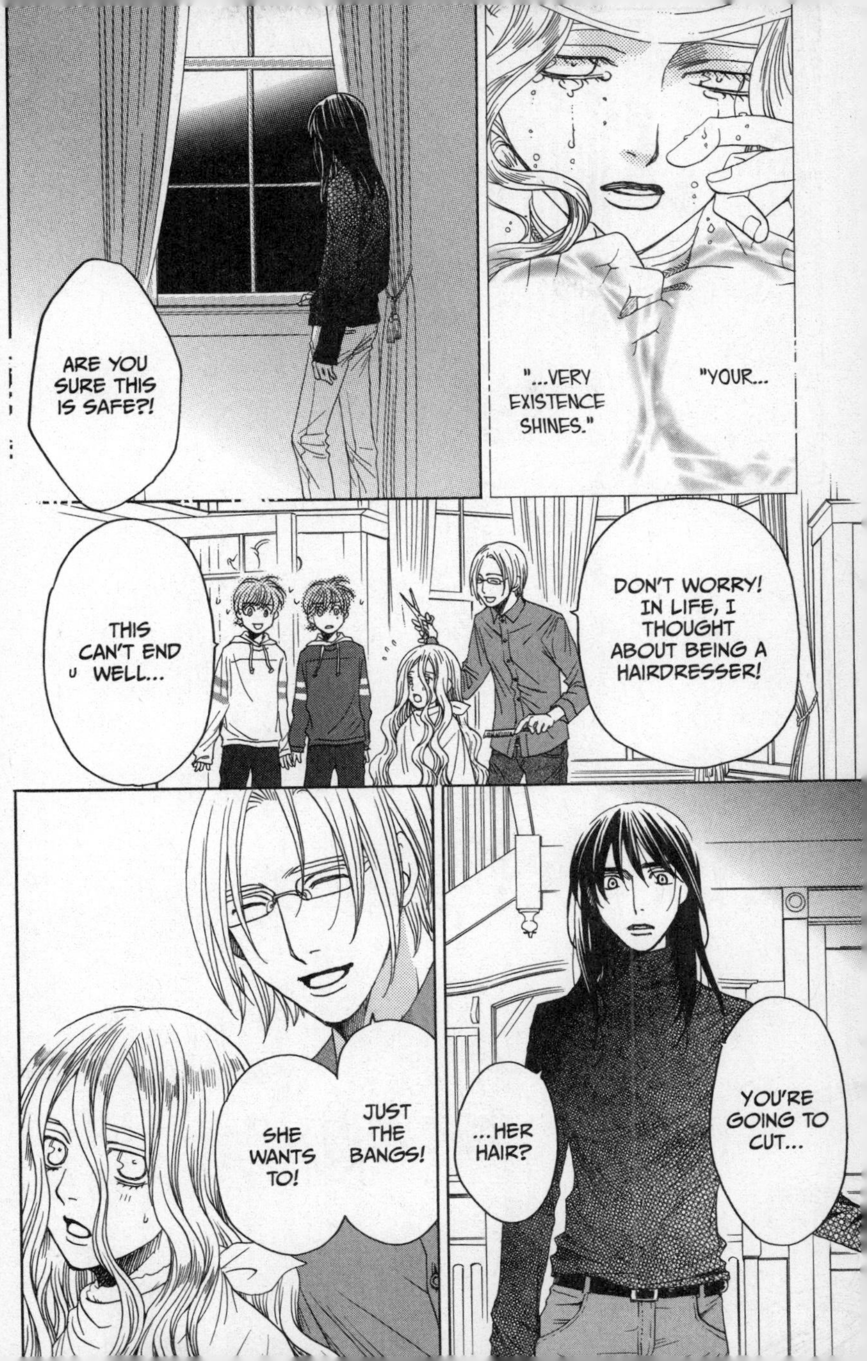
"YOUR...
"...VERY EXISTENCE SHINES."
ARE YOU SURE THIS IS SAFE?!
DON'T WORRY! IN LIFE, I THOUGHT ABOUT BEING A HAIRDRESSER!
THIS CAN'T END WELL...
YOU'RE GOING TO CUT...
...HER HAIR?
JUST THE BANGS!
SHE WANTS TO!

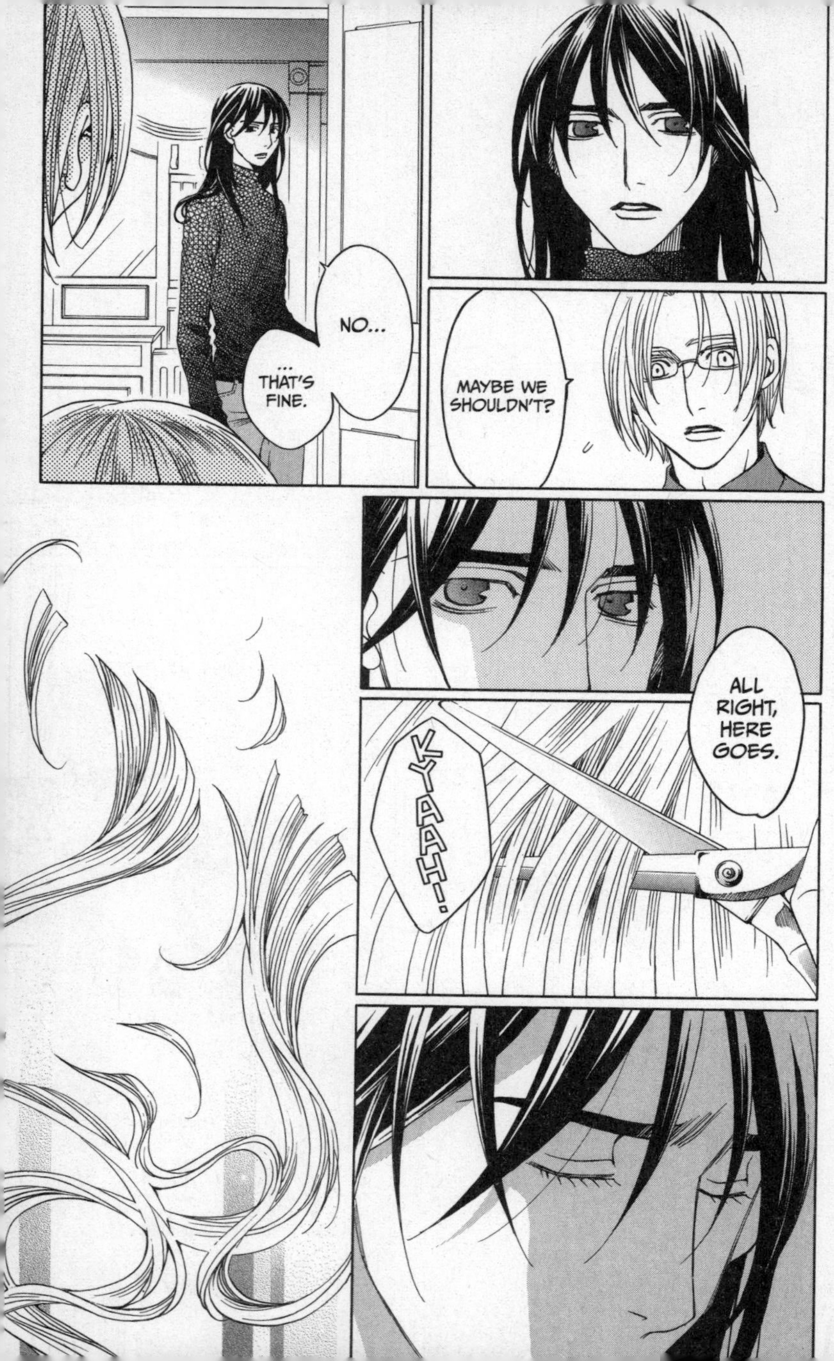
MAYBE WE SHOULDN'T?
NO...
...THAT'S FINE.
ALL RIGHT, HERE GOES.
KYAAAH!

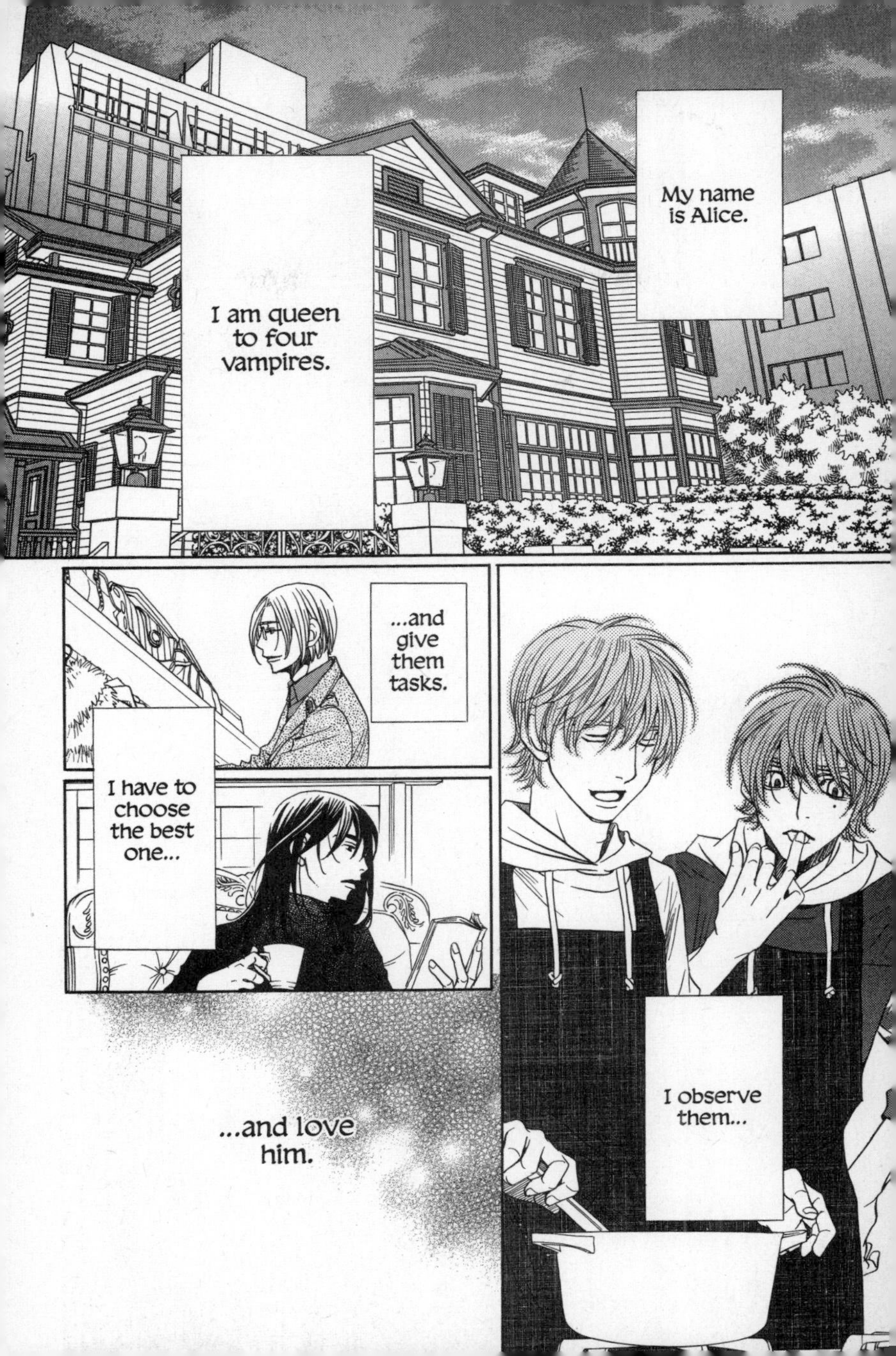
My name is Alice.
I am queen to four vampires.
I observe them...
...and give them tasks.
I have to choose the best one...
...and love him.

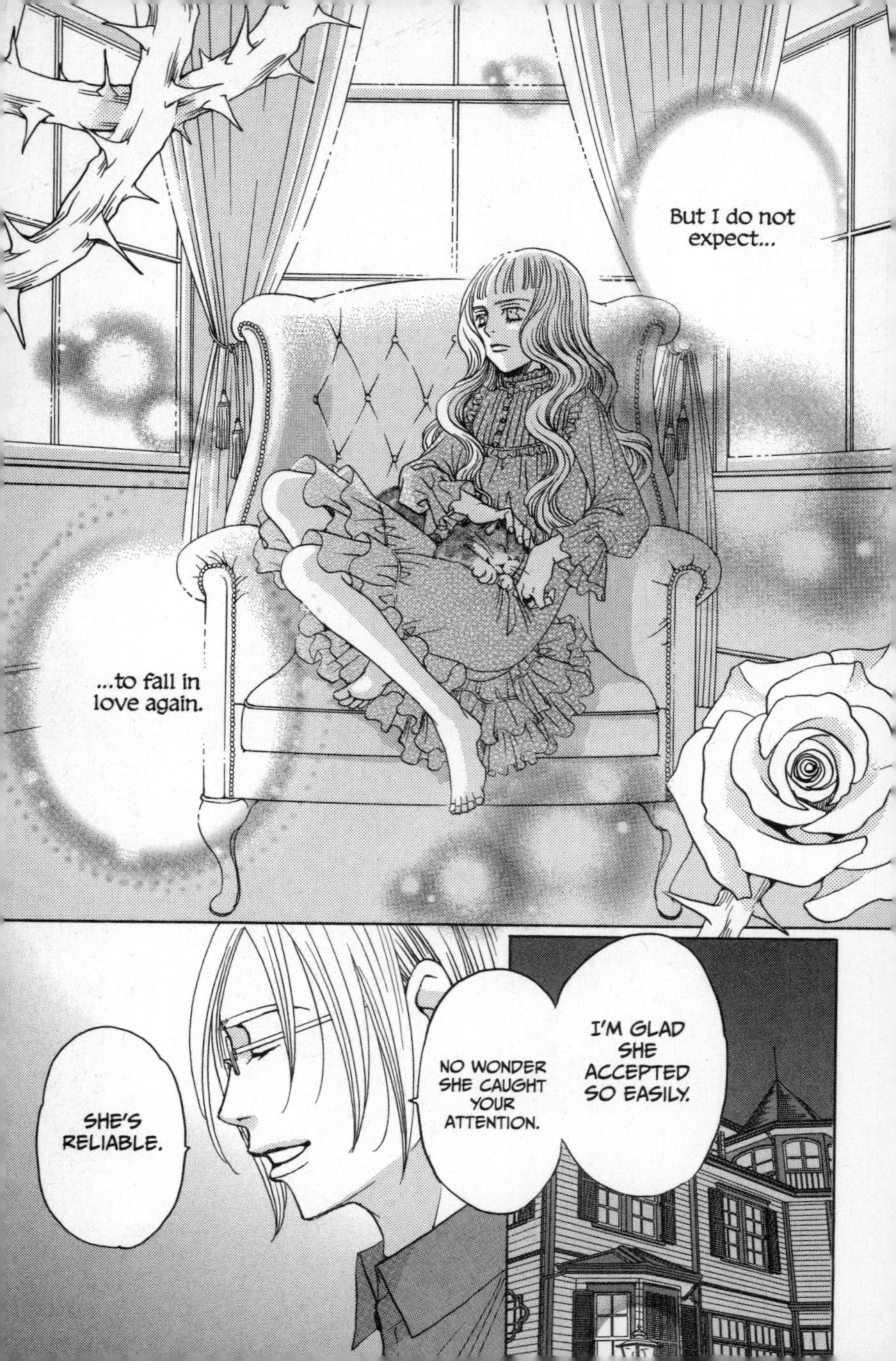
But I do not expect...
...to fall in love again.
I'M GLAD SHE ACCEPTED SO EASILY.
NO WONDER SHE CAUGHT YOUR ATTENTION.
SHE'S RELIABLE.

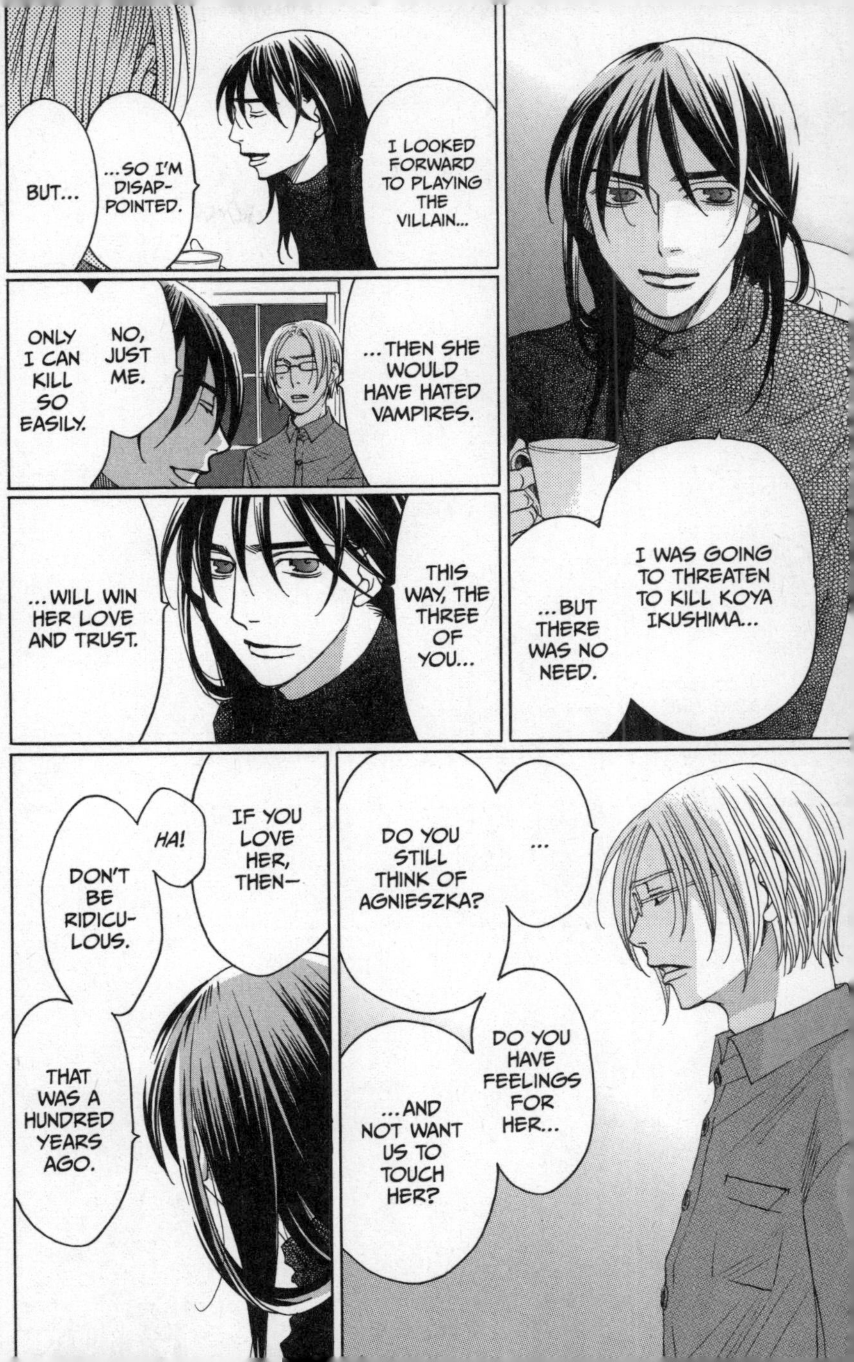
I WAS GOING TO THREATEN TO KILL KOYA IKUSHIMA...
...BUT THERE WAS NO NEED.
I LOOKED FORWARD TO PLAYING THE VILLAIN...
...SO I'M DISAP-POINTED.
BUT...
...THEN SHE WOULD HAVE HATED VAMPIRES.
NO, JUST ME.
ONLY I CAN KILL SO EASILY.
THIS WAY, THE THREE OF YOU...
...WILL WIN HER LOVE AND TRUST.
...
DO YOU STILL THINK OF AGNIESZKA?
DO YOU HAVE FEELINGS FOR HER...
...AND NOT WANT US TO TOUCH HER?
IF YOU LOVE HER, THEN—
HA!
DON'T BE RIDICU-LOUS.
THAT WAS A HUNDRED YEARS AGO.

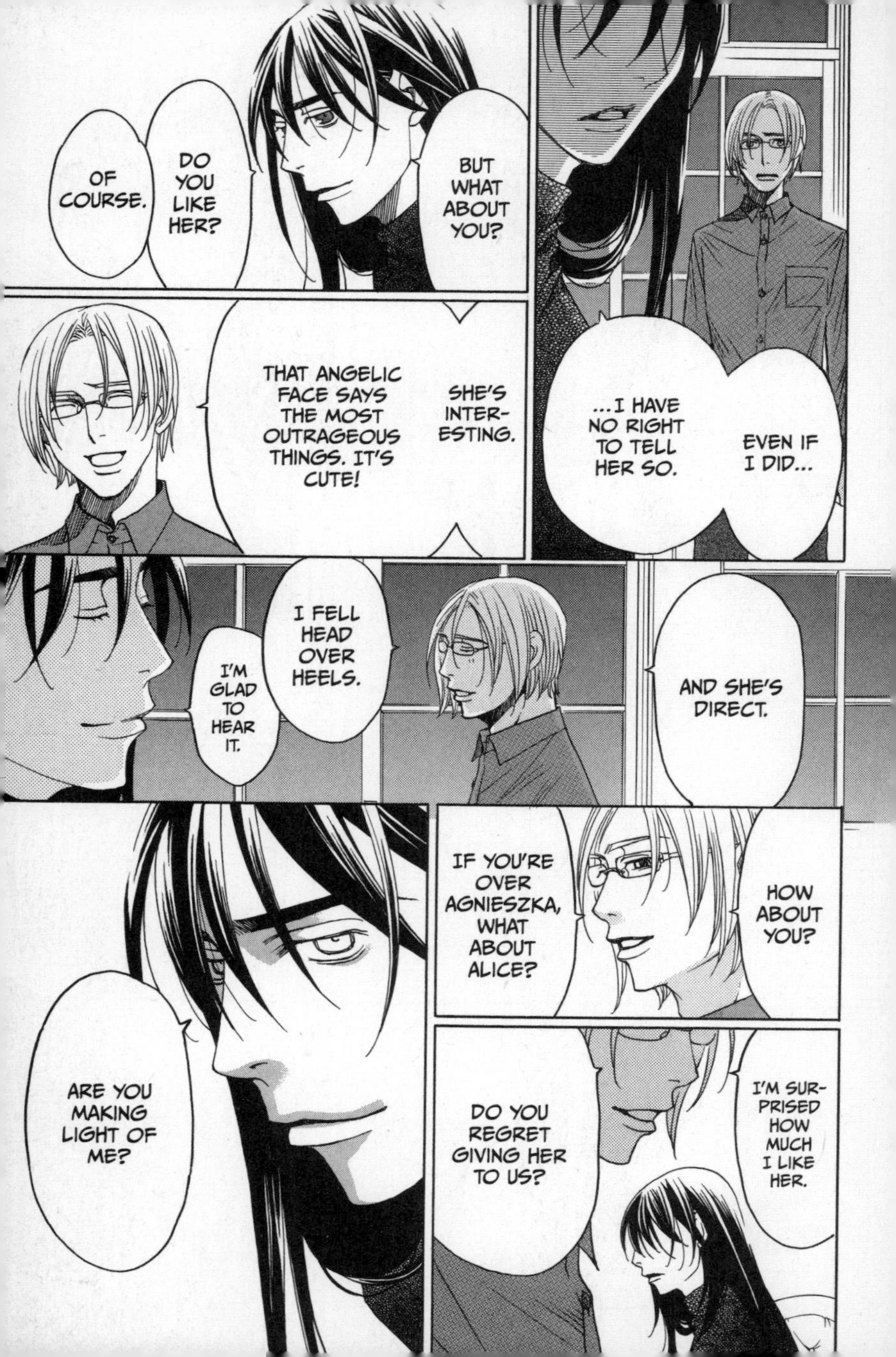
EVEN IF I DID...
...I HAVE NO RIGHT TO TELL HER SO.
BUT WHAT ABOUT YOU?
DO YOU LIKE HER?
OF COURSE.
SHE'S INTERESTING.
THAT ANGELIC FACE SAYS THE MOST OUTRAGEOUS THINGS. IT'S CUTE!
AND SHE'S DIRECT.
I FELL HEAD OVER HEELS.
I'M GLAD TO HEAR IT.
HOW ABOUT YOU?
IF YOU'RE OVER AGNIESZKA, WHAT ABOUT ALICE?
I'M SURPRISED HOW MUCH I LIKE HER.
DO YOU REGRET GIVING HER TO US?
ARE YOU MAKING LIGHT OF ME?

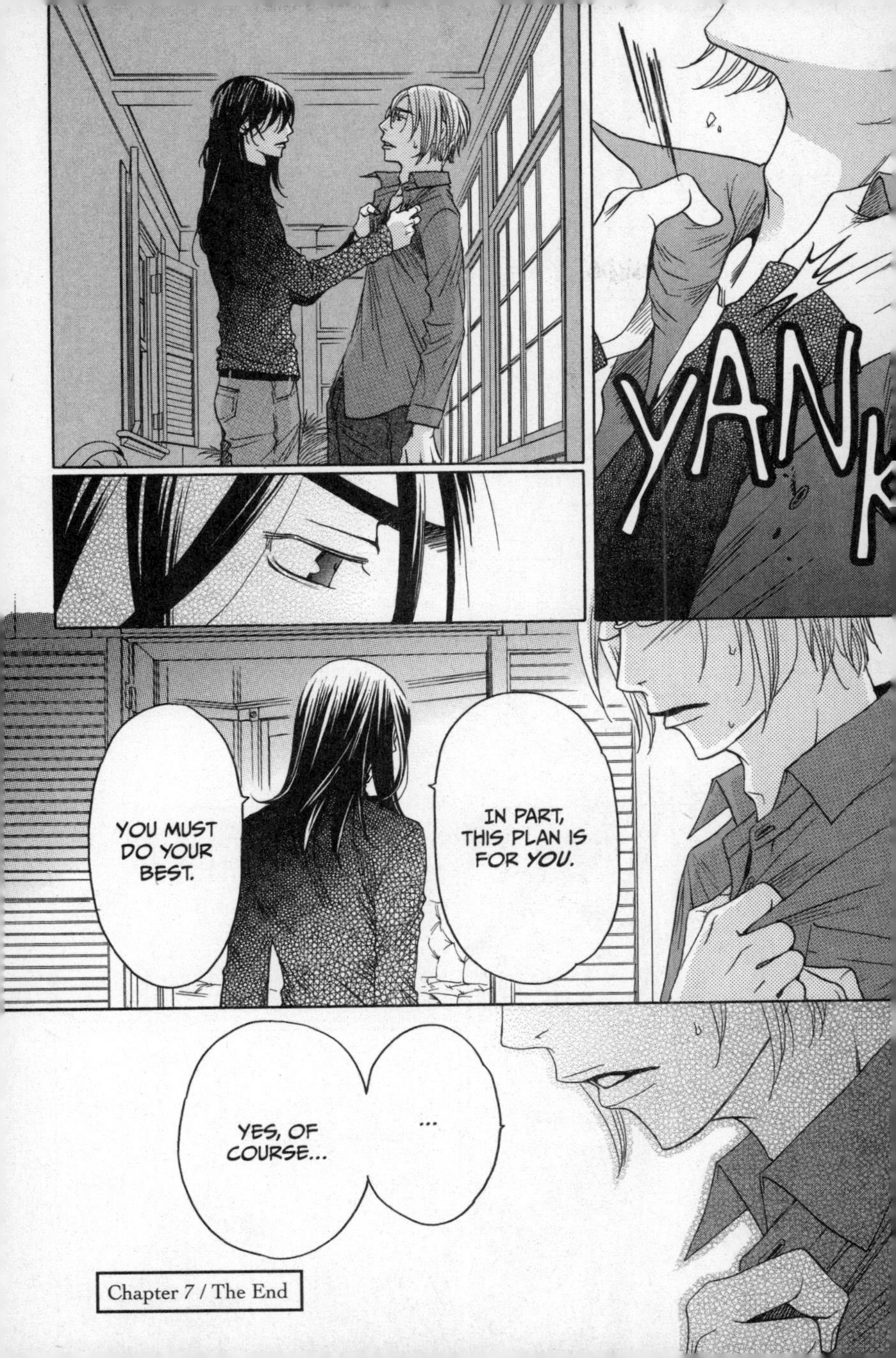
YANK
IN PART, THIS PLAN IS FOR *YOU.*
YOU MUST DO YOUR BEST.
...
YES, OF COURSE...

Chapter 7 / The End

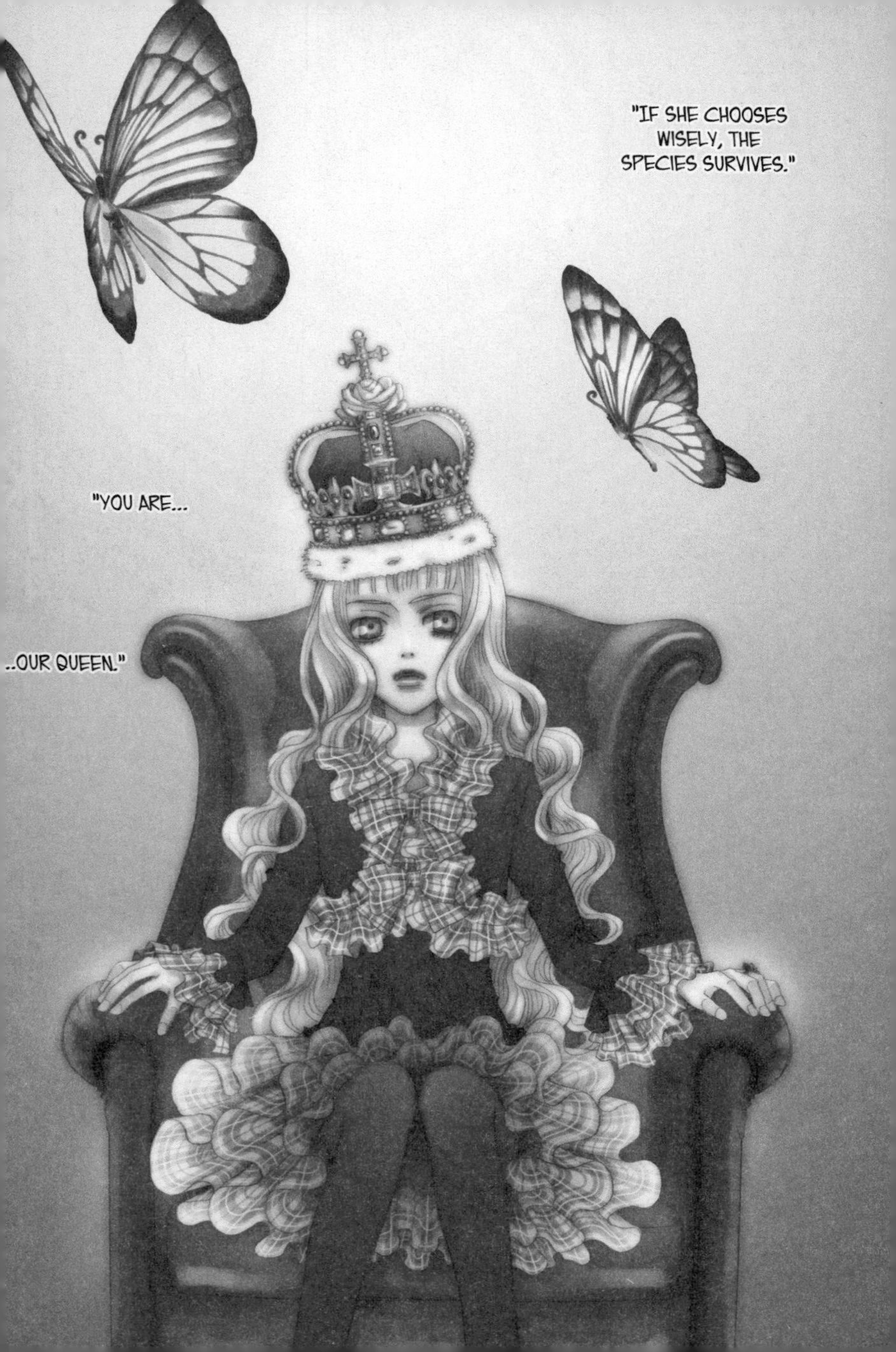
"IF SHE CHOOSES WISELY, THE SPECIES SURVIVES."
"YOU ARE...
..OUR QUEEN."

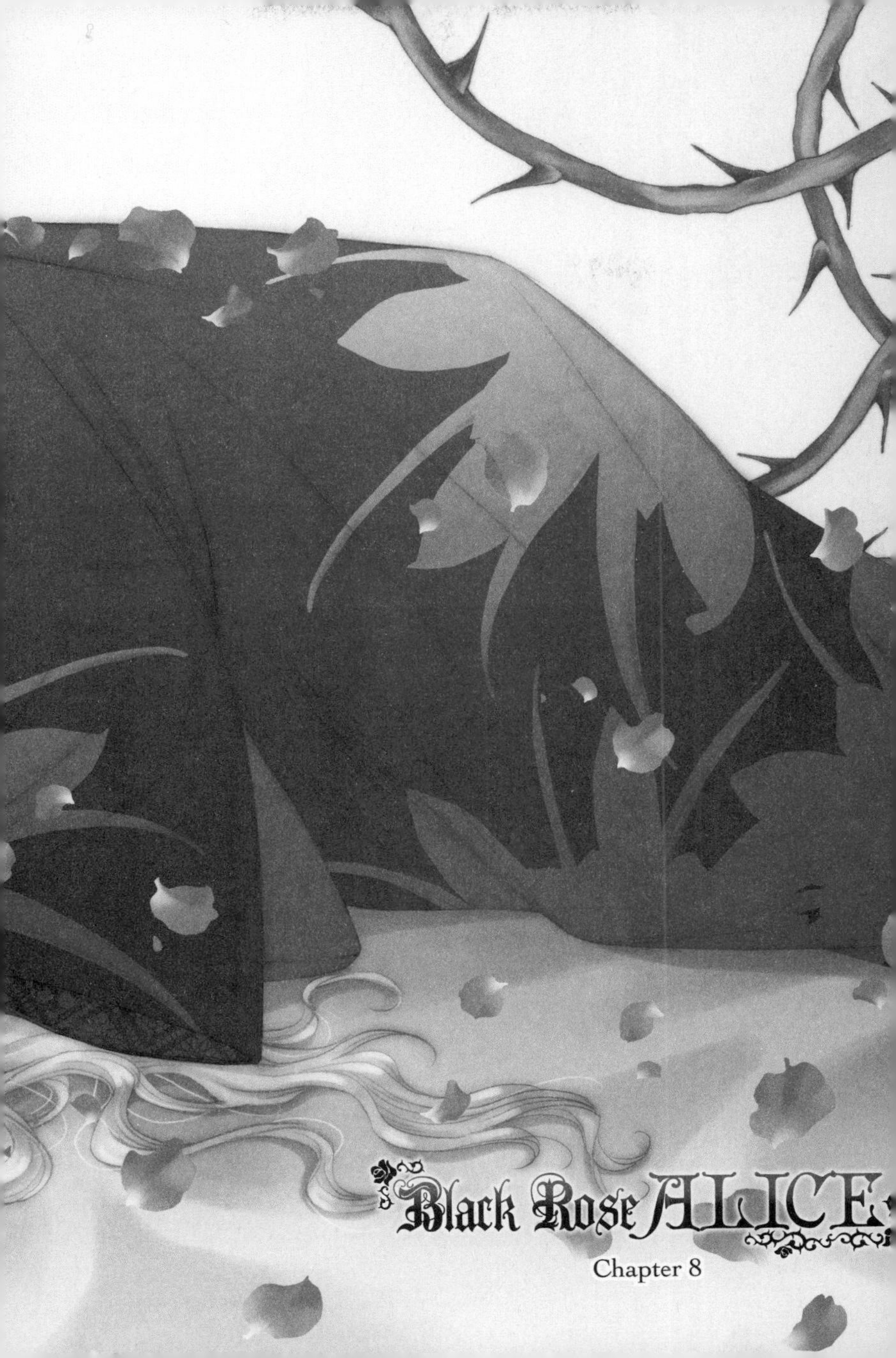
Black Rose ALICE
Chapter 8

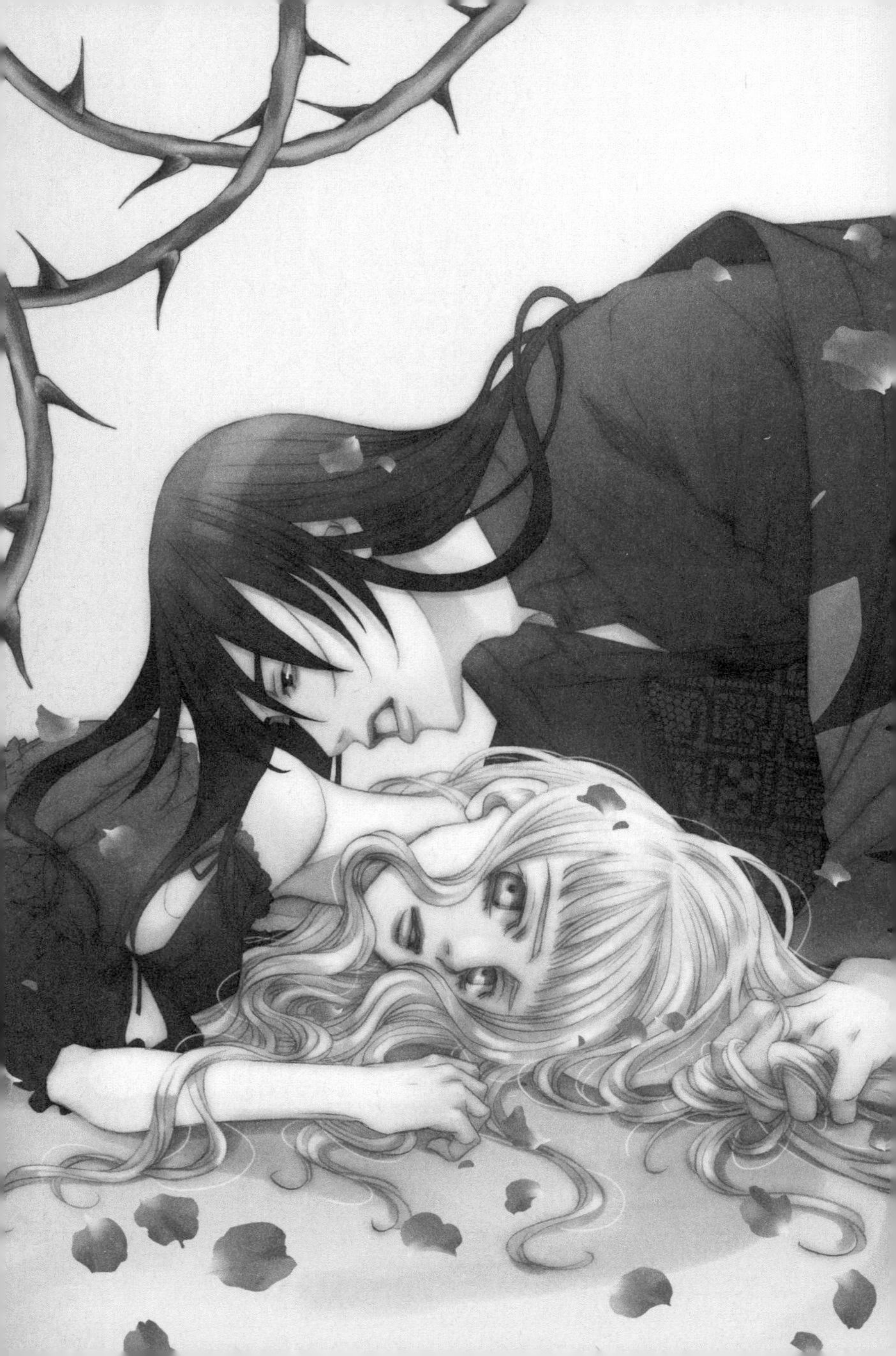

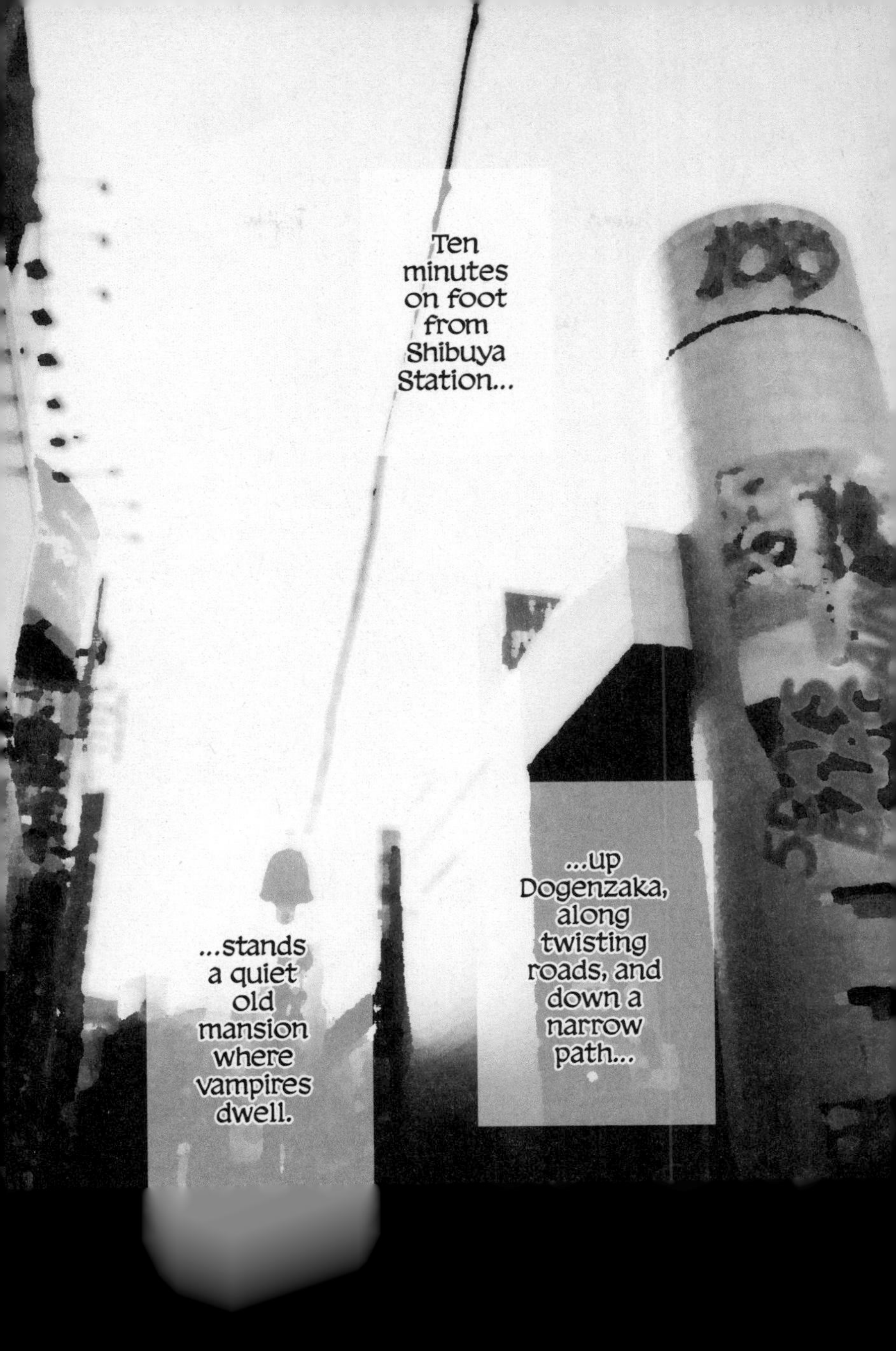
Ten minutes on foot from Shibuya Station...
...up Dogenzaka, along twisting roads, and down a narrow path...
...stands a quiet old mansion where vampires dwell.

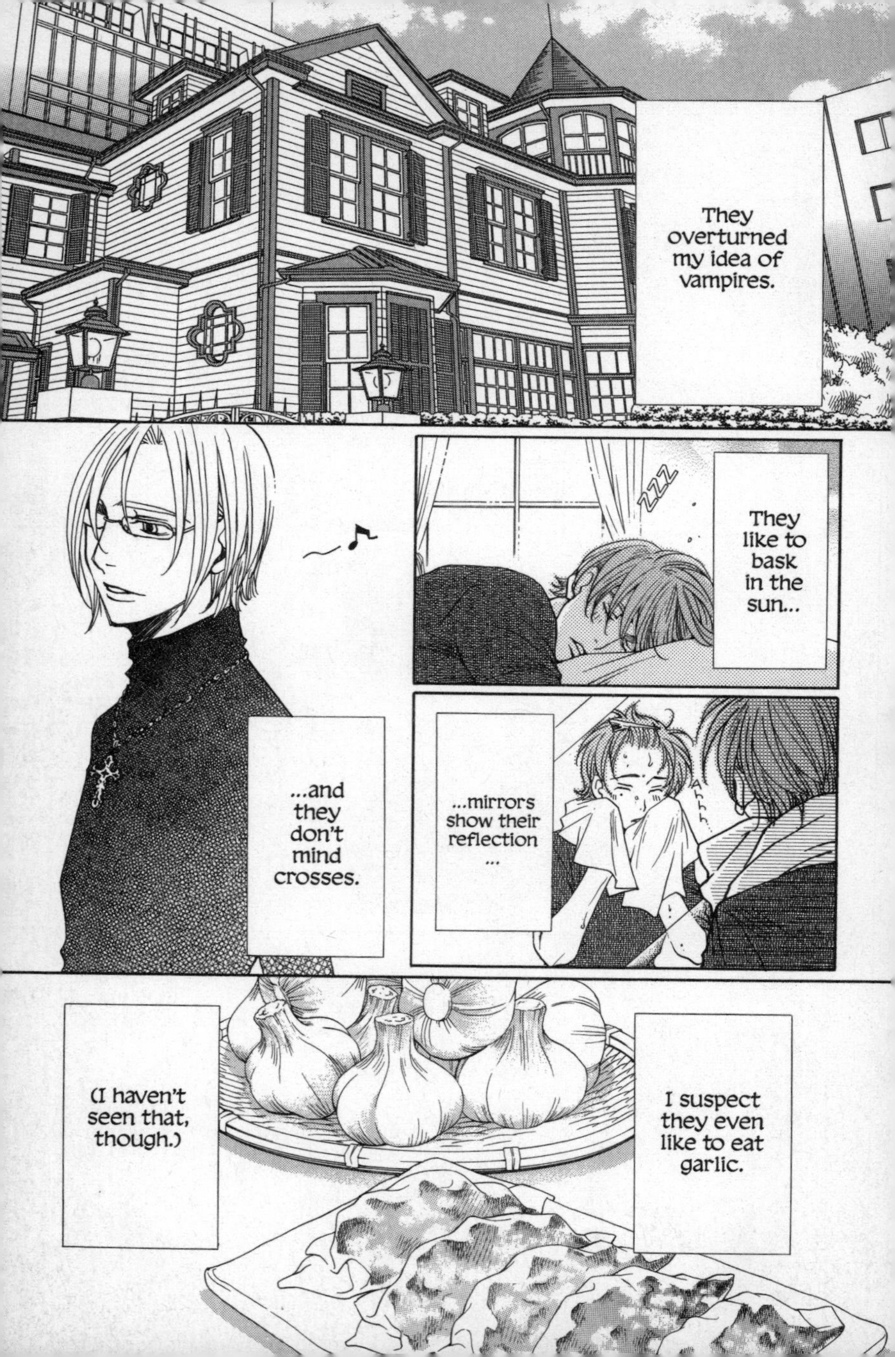
They overturned my idea of vampires.
ZZZ
They like to bask in the sun...
...mirrors show their reflection ...
...and they don't mind crosses.
I suspect they even like to eat garlic.
(I haven't seen that, though.)

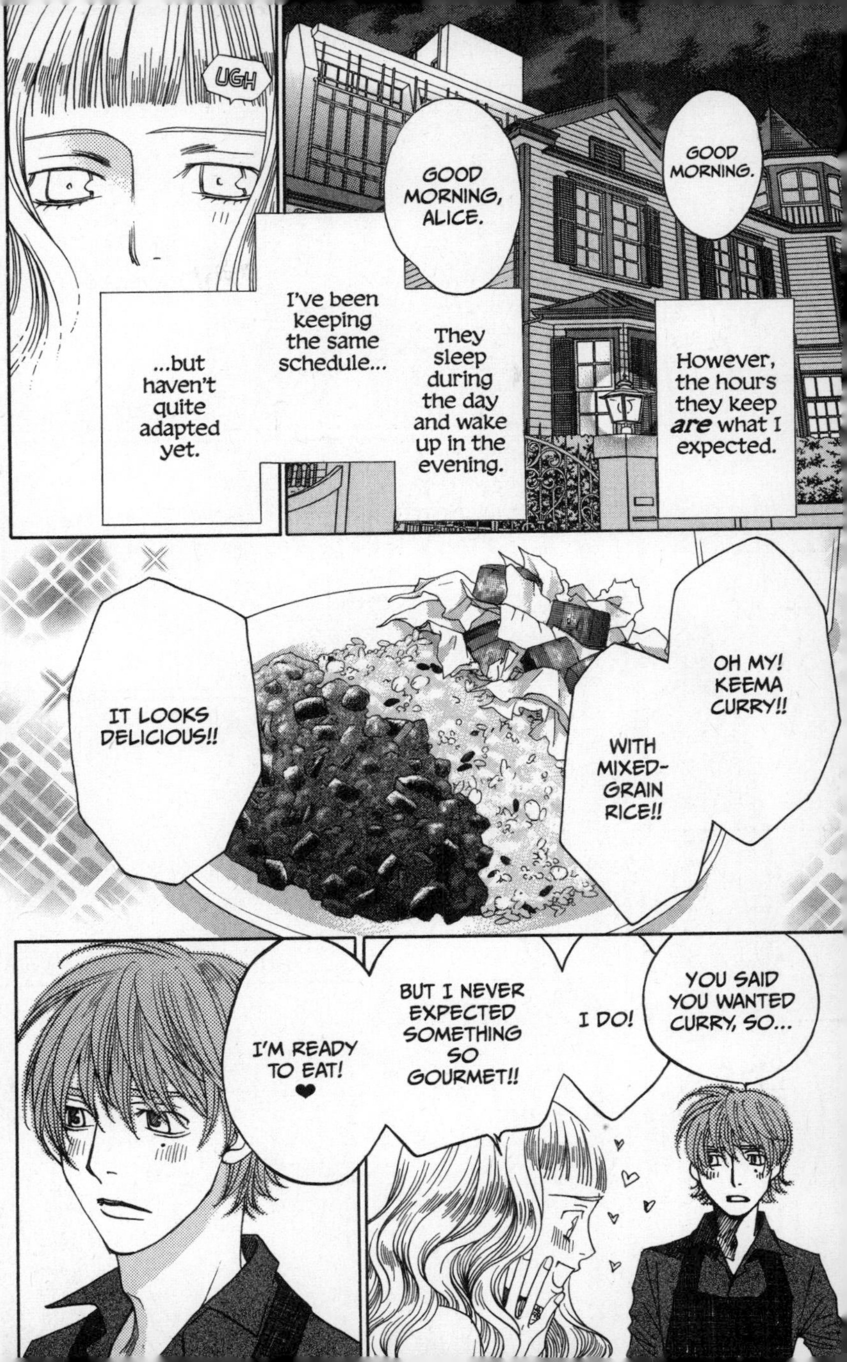
GOOD MORNING.
GOOD MORNING, ALICE.
However, the hours they keep *are* what I expected.
They sleep during the day and wake up in the evening.
I've been keeping the same schedule...
...but haven't quite adapted yet.
UGH
OH MY! KEEMA CURRY!!
WITH MIXED-GRAIN RICE!!
IT LOOKS DELICIOUS!!
YOU SAID YOU WANTED CURRY, SO...
I DO!
BUT I NEVER EXPECTED SOMETHING SO GOURMET!!
I'M READY TO EAT! ❤

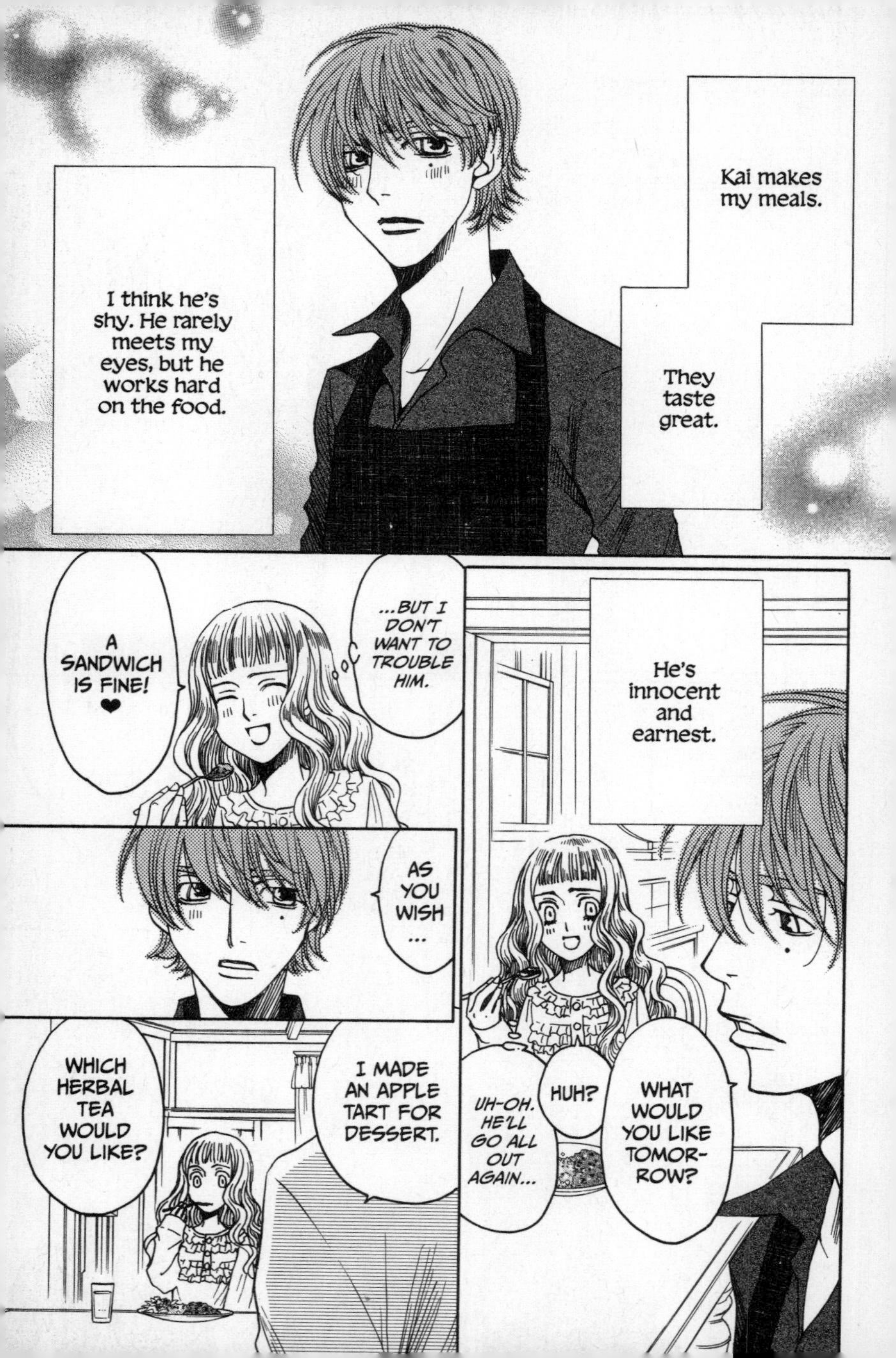
Kai makes my meals.
They taste great.
I think he's shy. He rarely meets my eyes, but he works hard on the food.
He's innocent and earnest.
WHAT WOULD YOU LIKE TOMORROW?
HUH?
UH-OH. HE'LL GO ALL OUT AGAIN...
...BUT I DON'T WANT TO TROUBLE HIM.
A SANDWICH IS FINE! ❤
AS YOU WISH...
I MADE AN APPLE TART FOR DESSERT.
WHICH HERBAL TEA WOULD YOU LIKE?

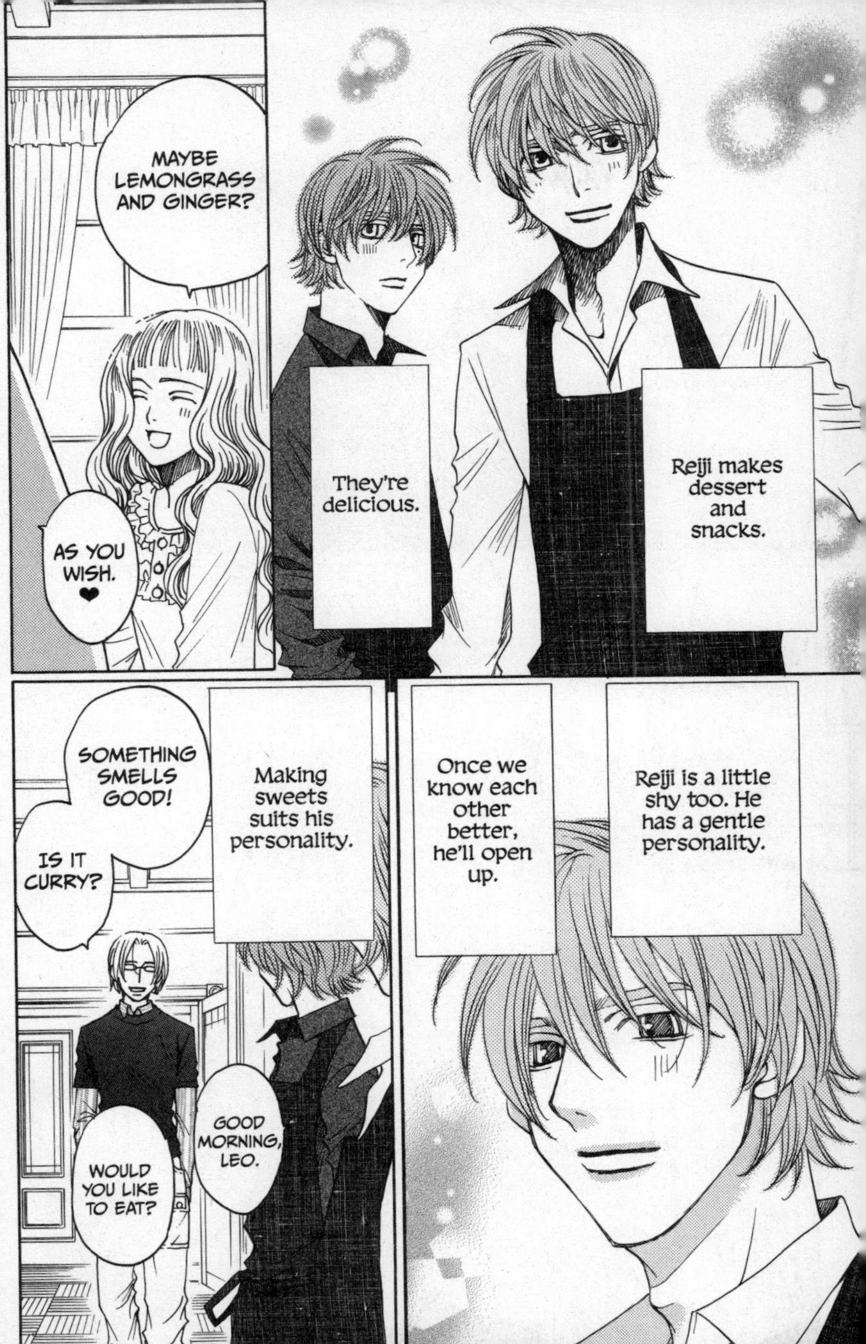
Reiji makes dessert and snacks.
They're delicious.
MAYBE LEMONGRASS AND GINGER?
AS YOU WISH. ♥
Reiji is a little shy too. He has a gentle personality.
Once we know each other better, he'll open up.
Making sweets suits his personality.
SOMETHING SMELLS GOOD!
IS IT CURRY?
GOOD MORNING, LEO.
WOULD YOU LIKE TO EAT?

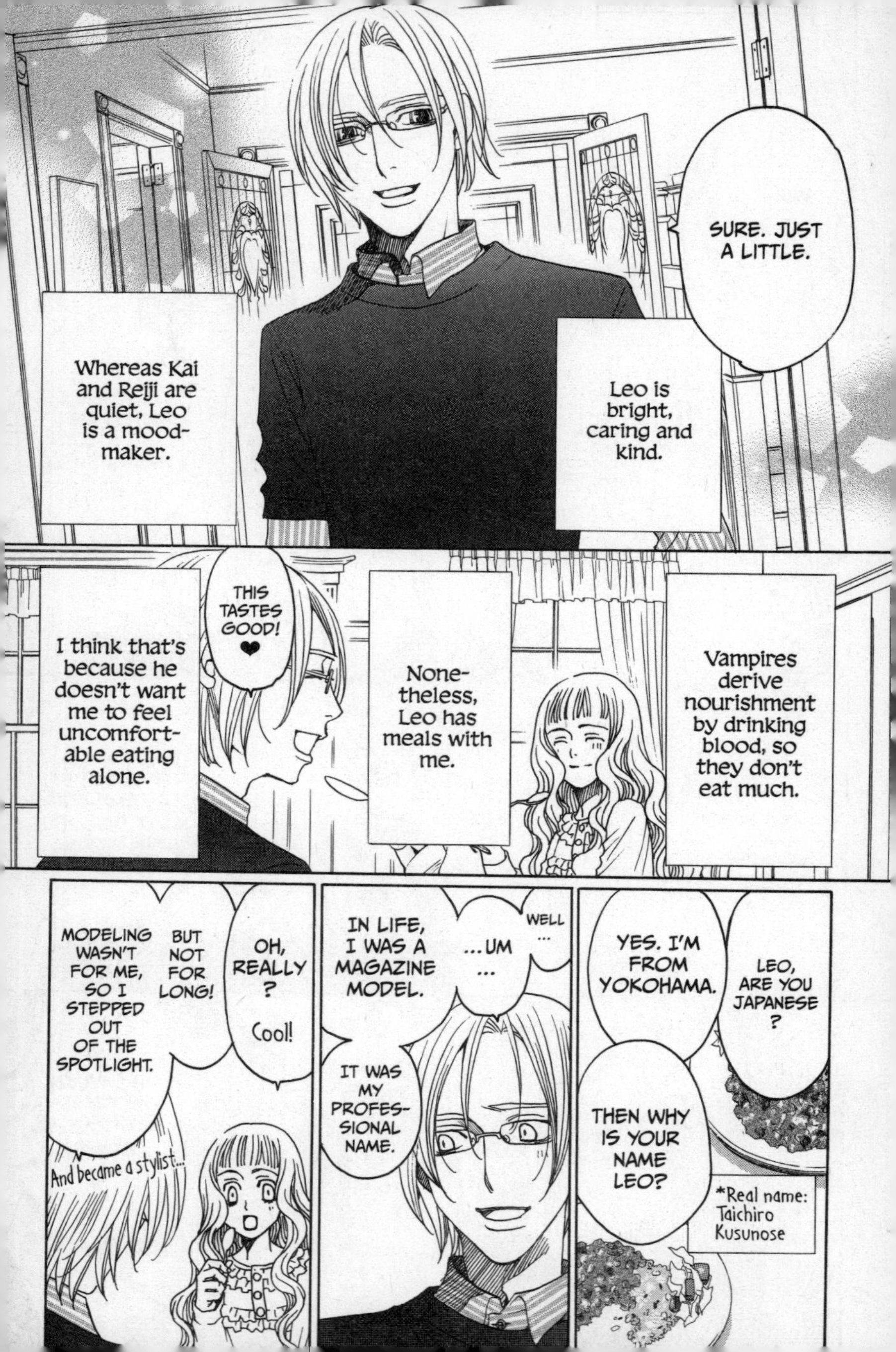
SURE. JUST A LITTLE.
Leo is bright, caring and kind.
Whereas Kai and Reiji are quiet, Leo is a mood-maker.
Vampires derive nourishment by drinking blood, so they don't eat much.
Nonetheless, Leo has meals with me.
THIS TASTES GOOD! ❤
I think that's because he doesn't want me to feel uncomfortable eating alone.
LEO, ARE YOU JAPANESE?
YES. I'M FROM YOKOHAMA.
THEN WHY IS YOUR NAME LEO?
*Real name: Taichiro Kusunose
WELL ...
...UM ...
IN LIFE, I WAS A MAGAZINE MODEL.
IT WAS MY PROFESSIONAL NAME.
OH, REALLY?
Cool!
BUT NOT FOR LONG!
MODELING WASN'T FOR ME, SO I STEPPED OUT OF THE SPOTLIGHT.
And became a stylist...

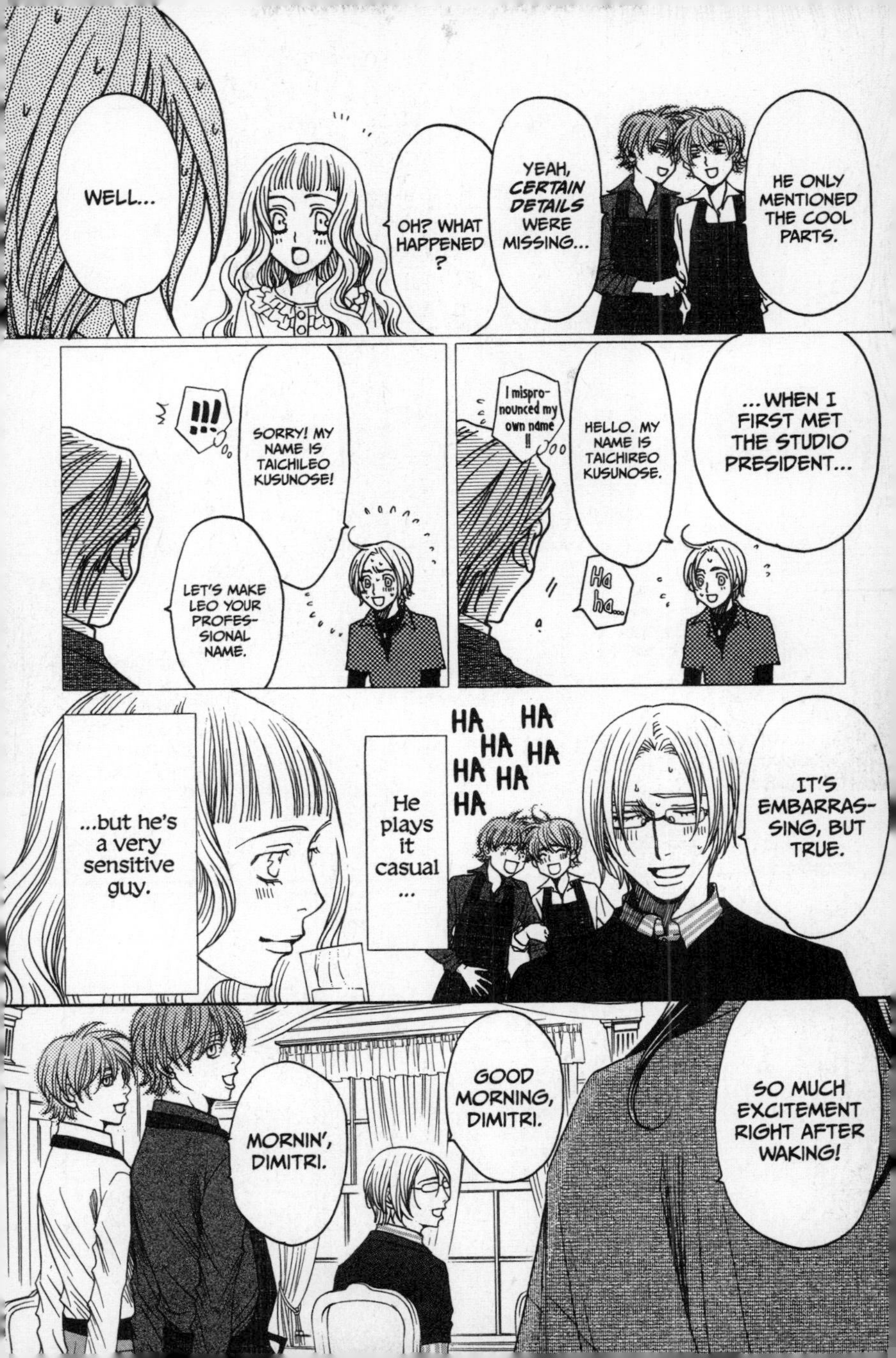
HE ONLY MENTIONED THE COOL PARTS.
YEAH, CERTAIN DETAILS WERE MISSING...
OH? WHAT HAPPENED?
WELL...
...WHEN I FIRST MET THE STUDIO PRESIDENT...
HELLO. MY NAME IS TAICHIREO KUSUNOSE.
I mispronounced my own name!!
Ha ha...
!!!
SORRY! MY NAME IS TAICHILEO KUSUNOSE!
LET'S MAKE LEO YOUR PROFESSIONAL NAME.
IT'S EMBARRASSING, BUT TRUE.
HA HA HA HA HA HA HA
He plays it casual...
...but he's a very sensitive guy.
SO MUCH EXCITEMENT RIGHT AFTER WAKING!
GOOD MORNING, DIMITRI.
MORNIN', DIMITRI.

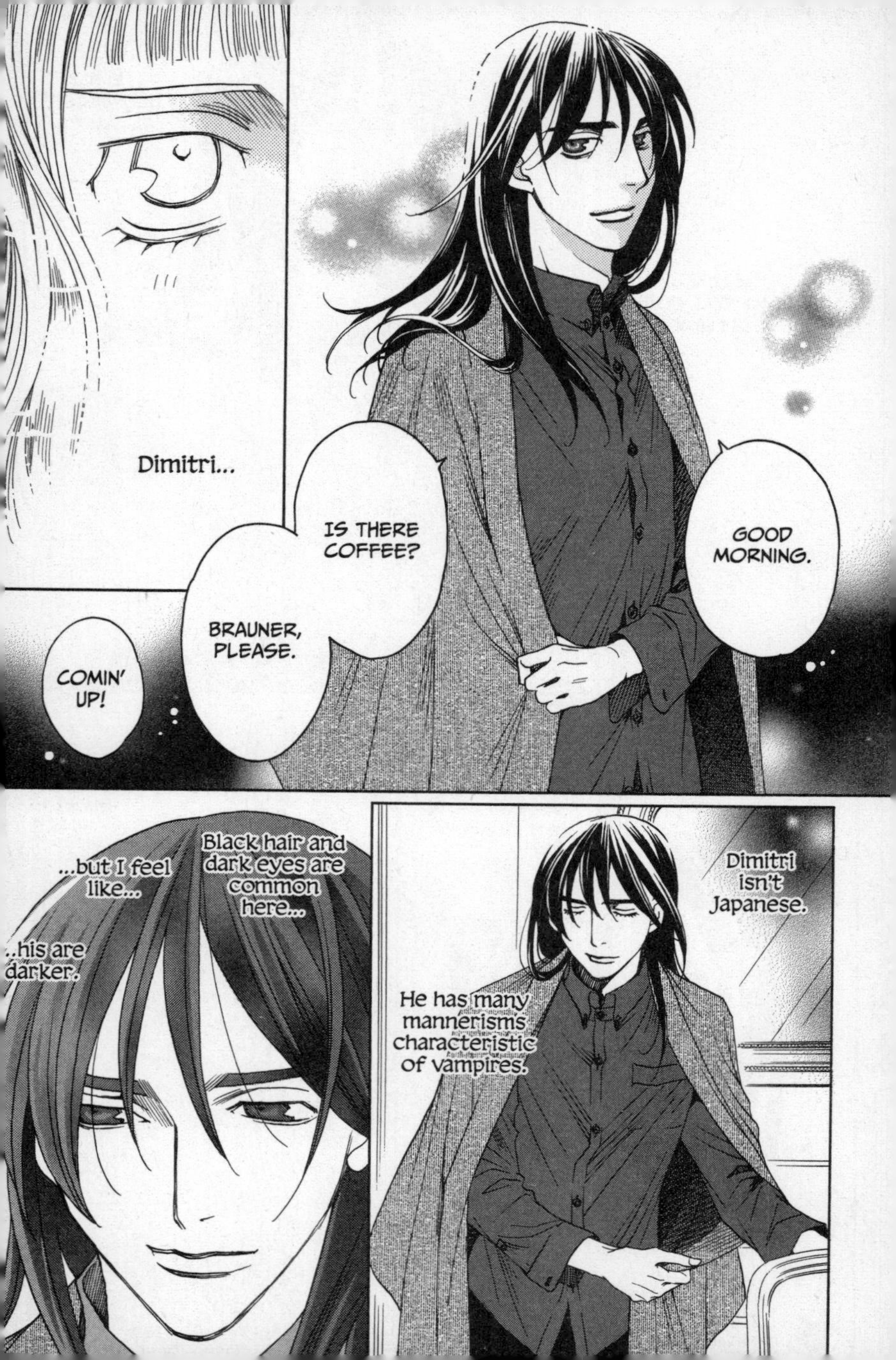
GOOD MORNING.
IS THERE COFFEE?
BRAUNER, PLEASE.
Dimitri...
COMIN' UP!
Dimitri isn't Japanese.
He has many mannerisms characteristic of vampires.
Black hair and dark eyes are common here...
...but I feel like...
...his are darker.

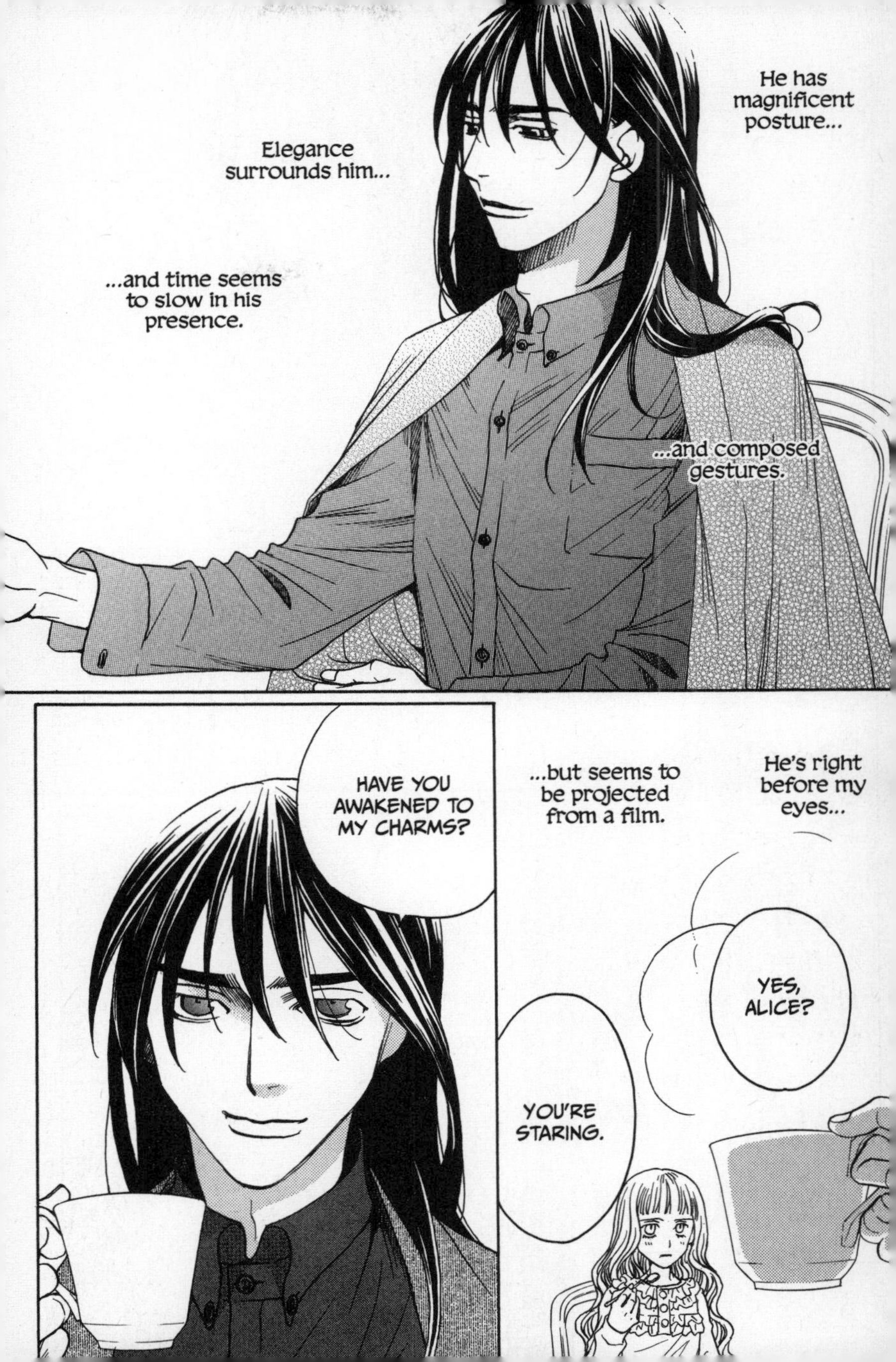
He has magnificent posture...
...and composed gestures.
Elegance surrounds him...
...and time seems to slow in his presence.
He's right before my eyes...
...but seems to be projected from a film.
YES, ALICE?
YOU'RE STARING.
HAVE YOU AWAKENED TO MY CHARMS?

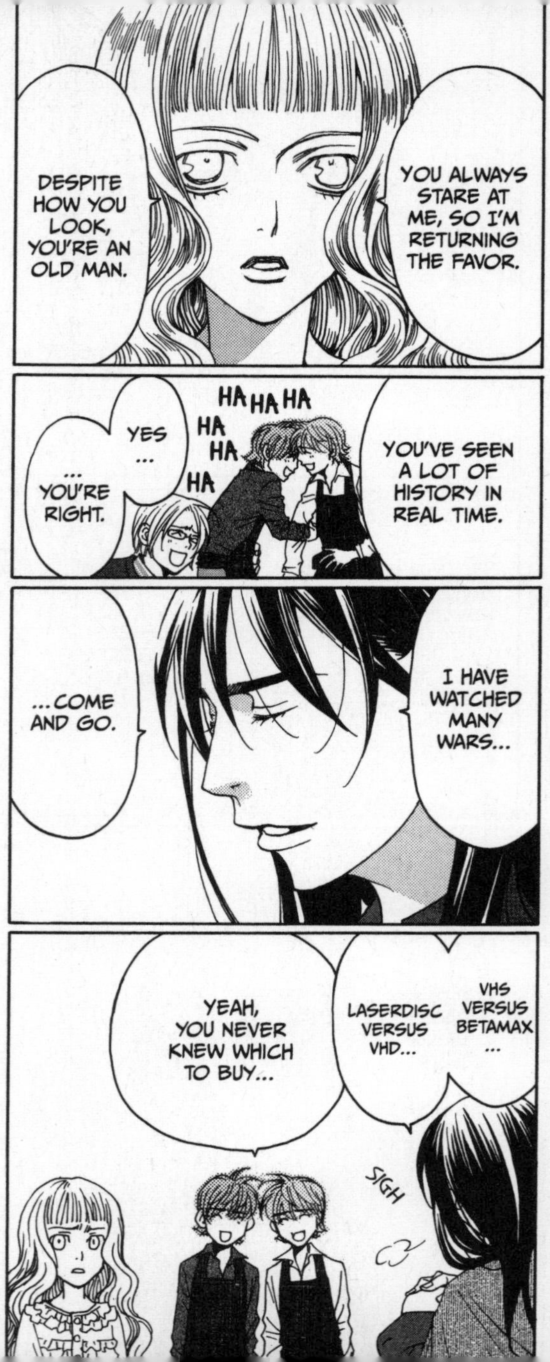
YOU ALWAYS STARE AT ME, SO I'M RETURNING THE FAVOR.
DESPITE HOW YOU LOOK, YOU'RE AN OLD MAN.
YOU'VE SEEN A LOT OF HISTORY IN REAL TIME.
HA HA HA HA HA HA
YES ...
... YOU'RE RIGHT.
I HAVE WATCHED MANY WARS...
...COME AND GO.
VHS VERSUS BETAMAX ...
LASERDISC VERSUS VHD...
YEAH, YOU NEVER KNEW WHICH TO BUY...
SIGH

<Spider>

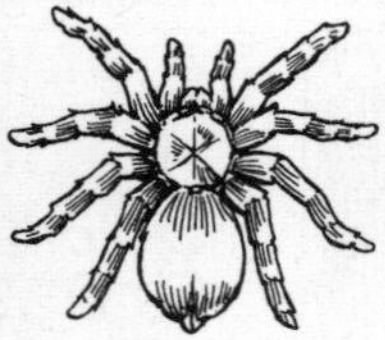

Among the many kinds of familiars, spiders have an outstanding ability to absorb and preserve enormous amounts of nutrients. They can also fix any kind of material.

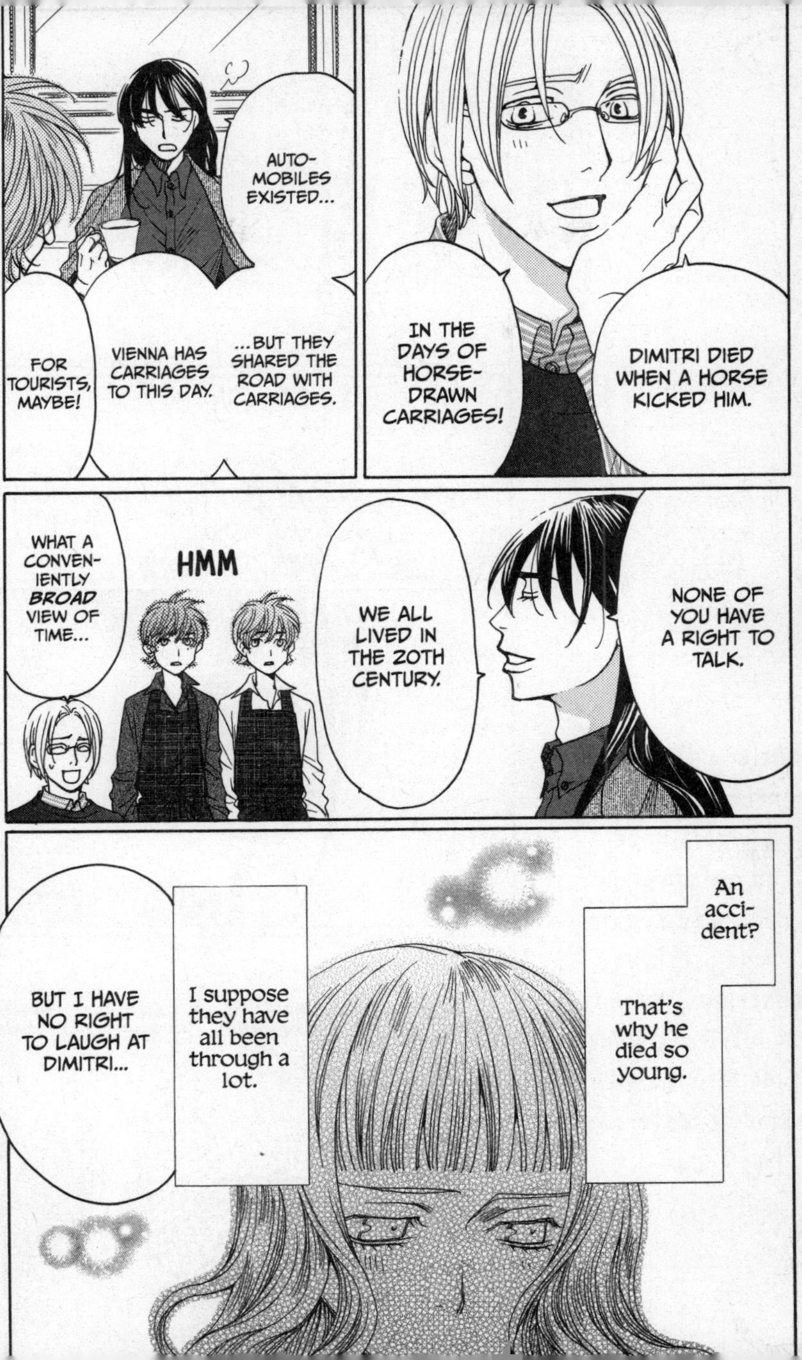
DIMITRI DIED WHEN A HORSE KICKED HIM.
IN THE DAYS OF HORSE-DRAWN CARRIAGES!
AUTO-MOBILES EXISTED...
...BUT THEY SHARED THE ROAD WITH CARRIAGES.
VIENNA HAS CARRIAGES TO THIS DAY.
FOR TOURISTS, MAYBE!
NONE OF YOU HAVE A RIGHT TO TALK.
WE ALL LIVED IN THE 20TH CENTURY.
HMM
WHAT A CONVENIENTLY *BROAD* VIEW OF TIME...
An accident?
That's why he died so young.
I suppose they have all been through a lot.
BUT I HAVE NO RIGHT TO LAUGH AT DIMITRI...

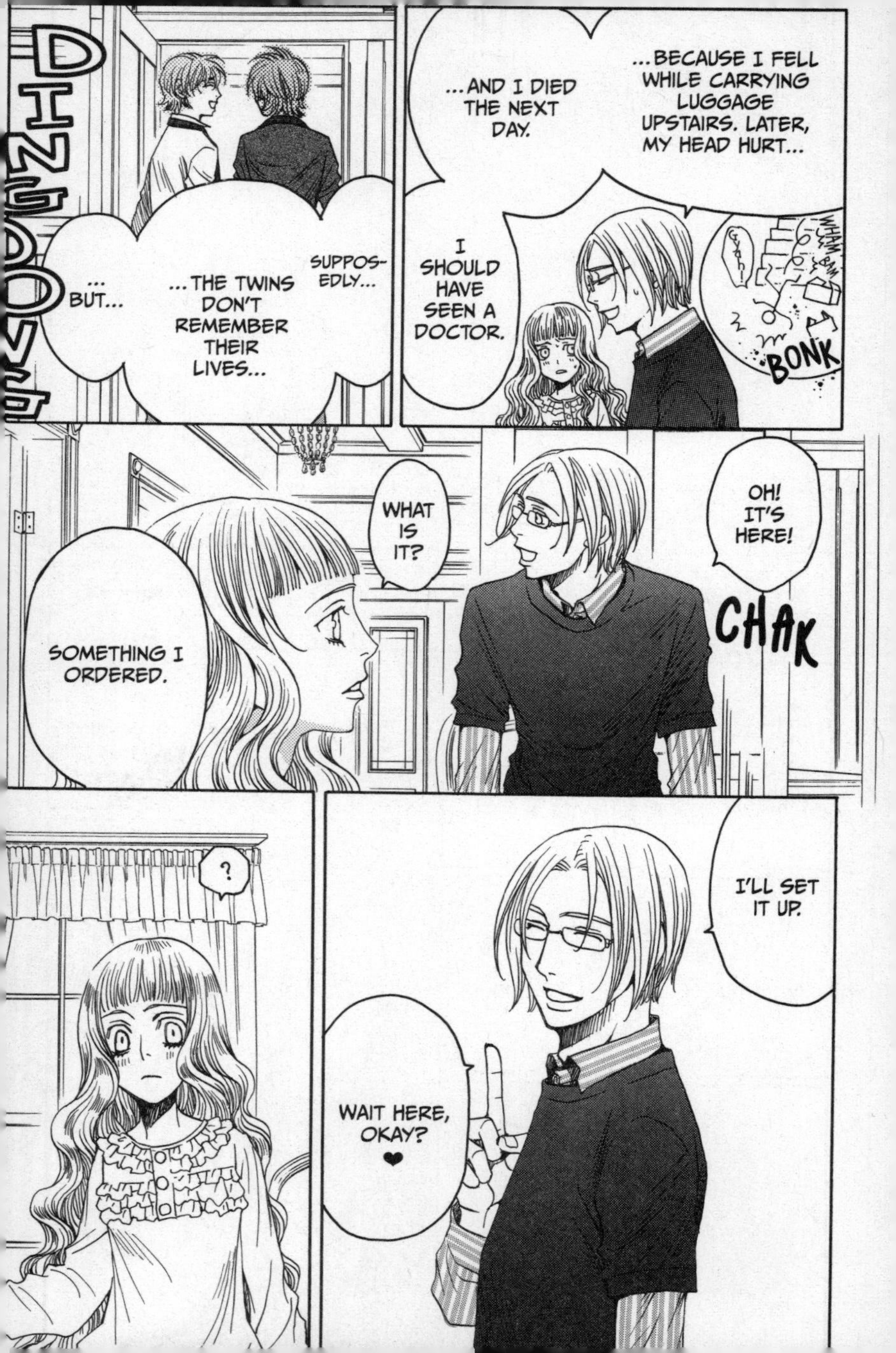
...BECAUSE I FELL WHILE CARRYING LUGGAGE UPSTAIRS. LATER, MY HEAD HURT...
WHAM BAM
BONK
...AND I DIED THE NEXT DAY.
I SHOULD HAVE SEEN A DOCTOR.
DINGDONG
SUPPOS-EDLY...
...THE TWINS DON'T REMEMBER THEIR LIVES...
... BUT...
OH! IT'S HERE!
CHAK
WHAT IS IT?
SOMETHING I ORDERED.
I'LL SET IT UP.
WAIT HERE, OKAY? ❤
?

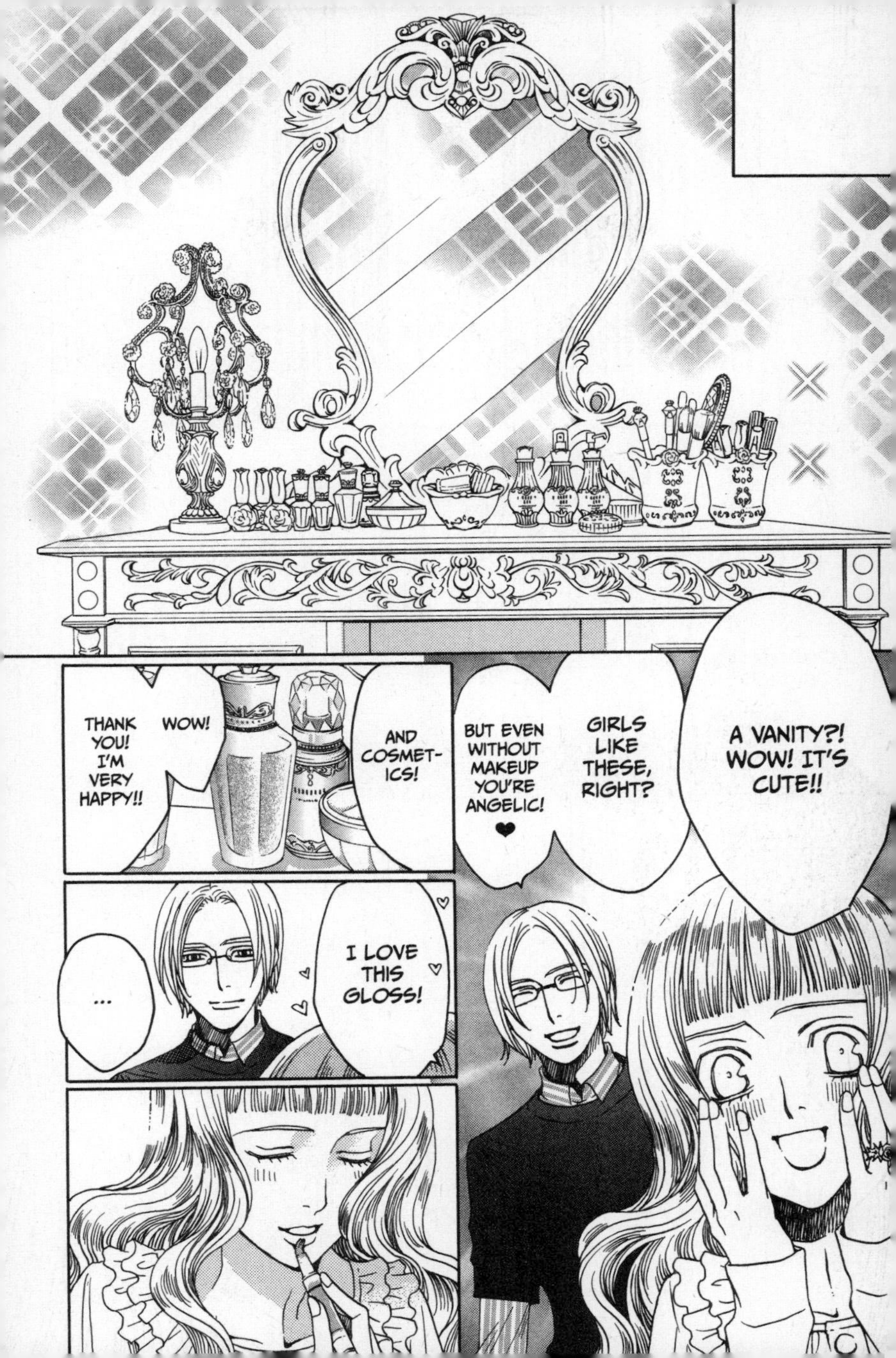
A VANITY?! WOW! IT'S CUTE!!
GIRLS LIKE THESE, RIGHT?
BUT EVEN WITHOUT MAKEUP YOU'RE ANGELIC! ❤
AND COSMET-ICS!
WOW!
THANK YOU! I'M VERY HAPPY!!
I LOVE THIS GLOSS!
...

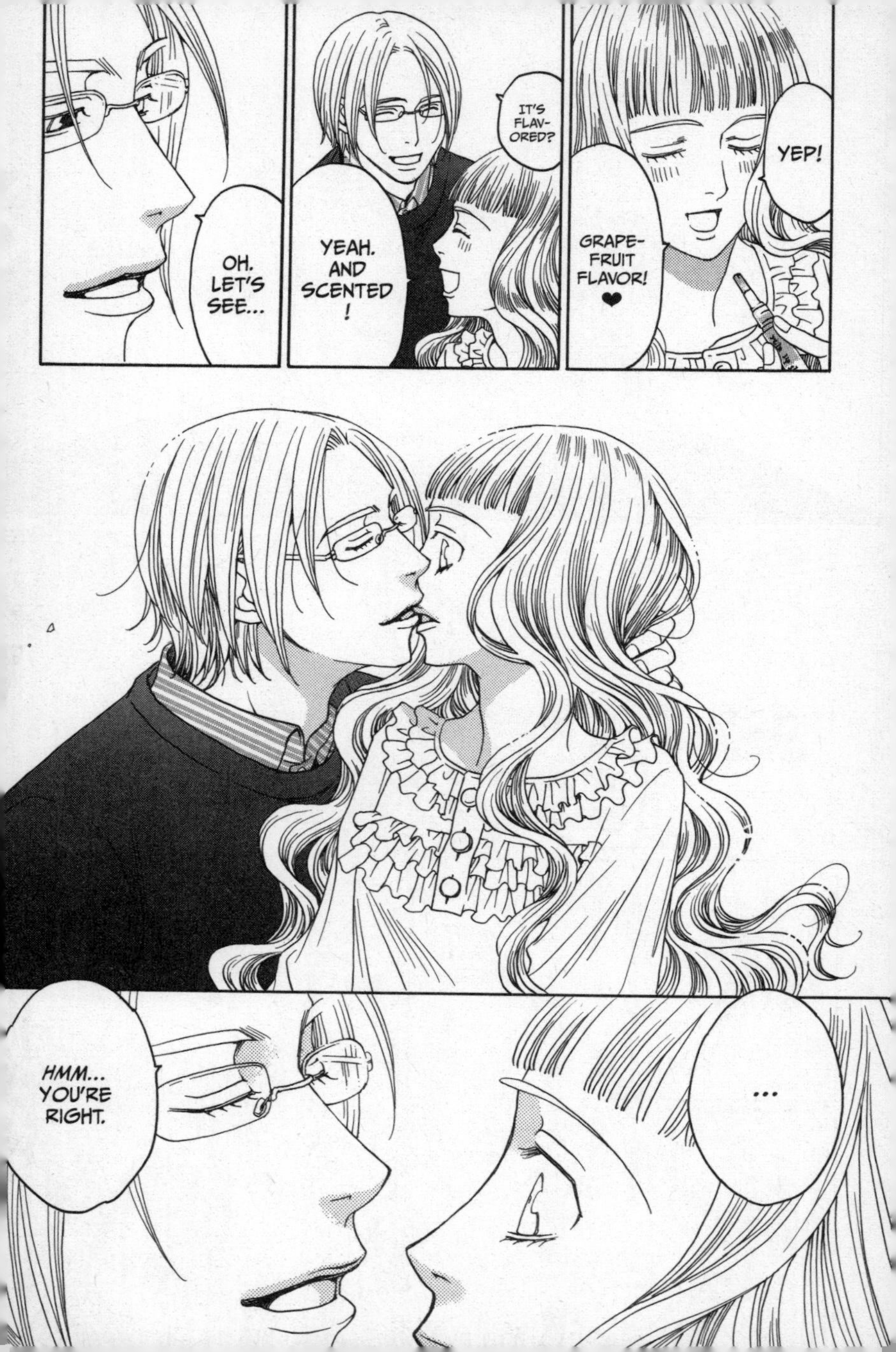
YEP!
GRAPE-FRUIT FLAVOR! ❤
IT'S FLAVORED?
YEAH. AND SCENTED!
OH. LET'S SEE...
...
HMM... YOU'RE RIGHT.

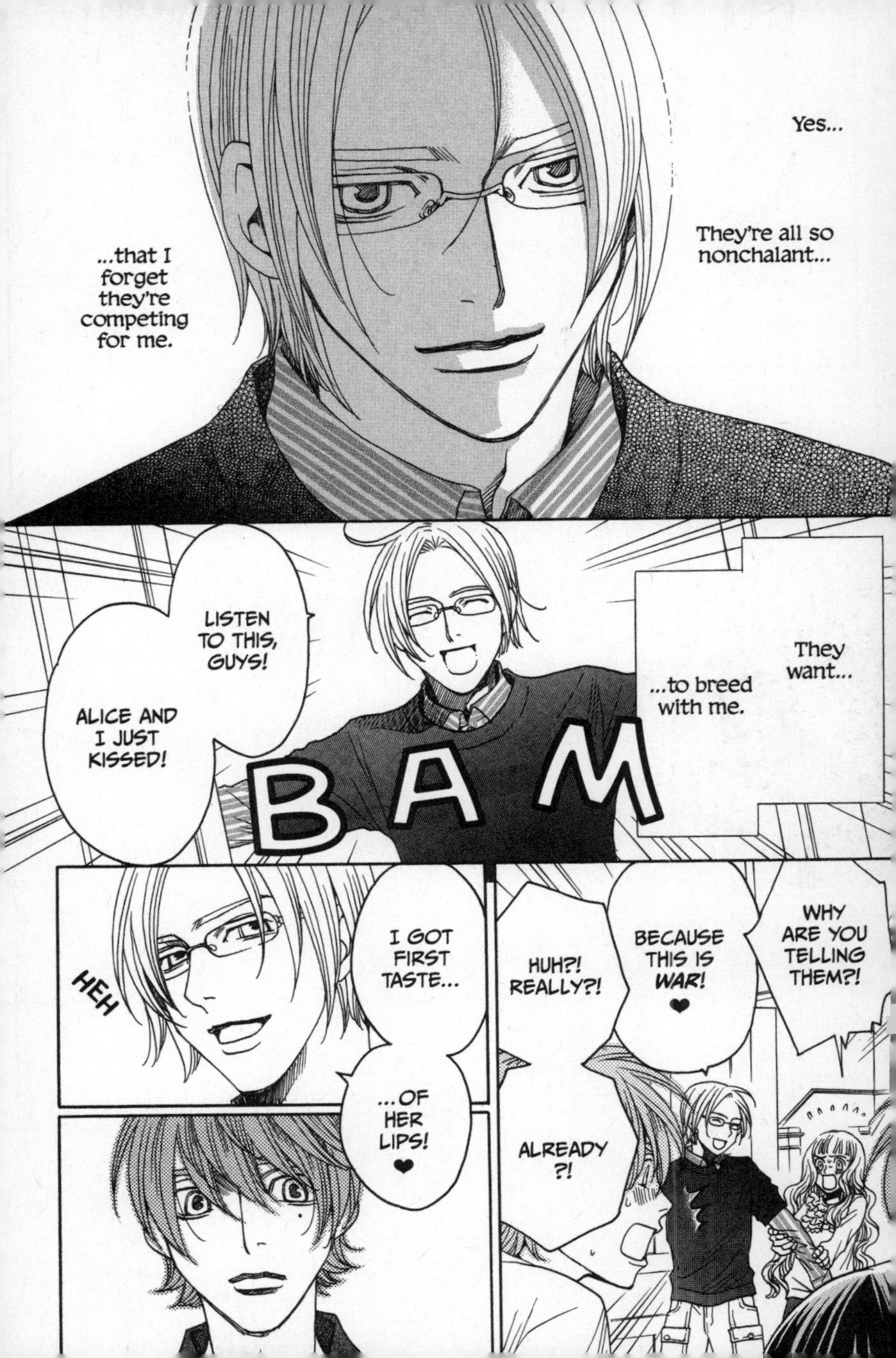
Yes...
They're all so nonchalant...
...that I forget they're competing for me.
They want...
...to breed with me.
LISTEN TO THIS, GUYS!
ALICE AND I JUST KISSED!
BAM
WHY ARE YOU TELLING THEM?!
BECAUSE THIS IS WAR! ❤
HUH?! REALLY?!
ALREADY?!
I GOT FIRST TASTE...
HEH
...OF HER LIPS! ❤

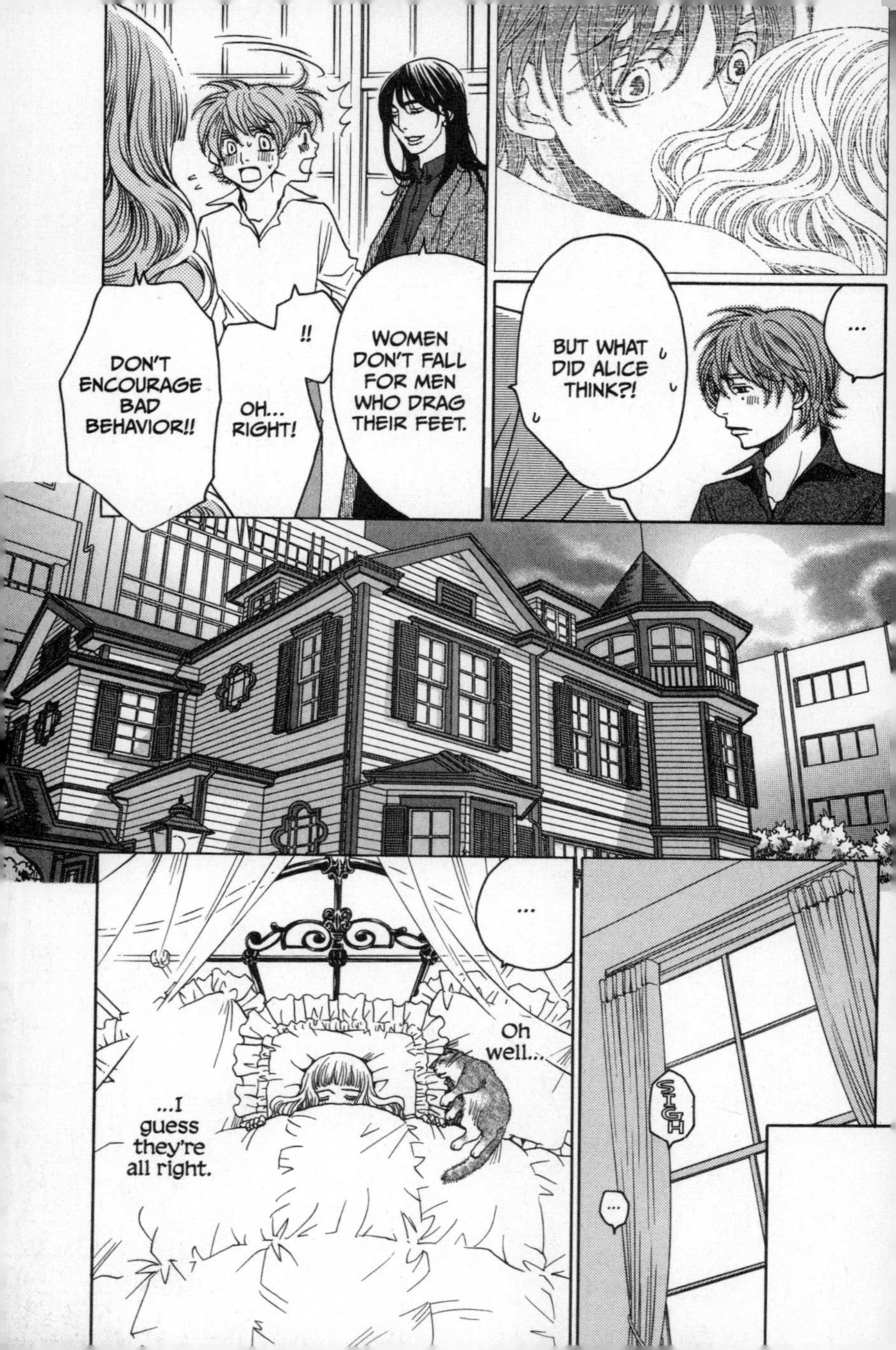
...
BUT WHAT DID ALICE THINK?!
WOMEN DON'T FALL FOR MEN WHO DRAG THEIR FEET.
!!
OH... RIGHT!
DON'T ENCOURAGE BAD BEHAVIOR!!
SIGH
...
...
Oh well...
...I guess they're all right.

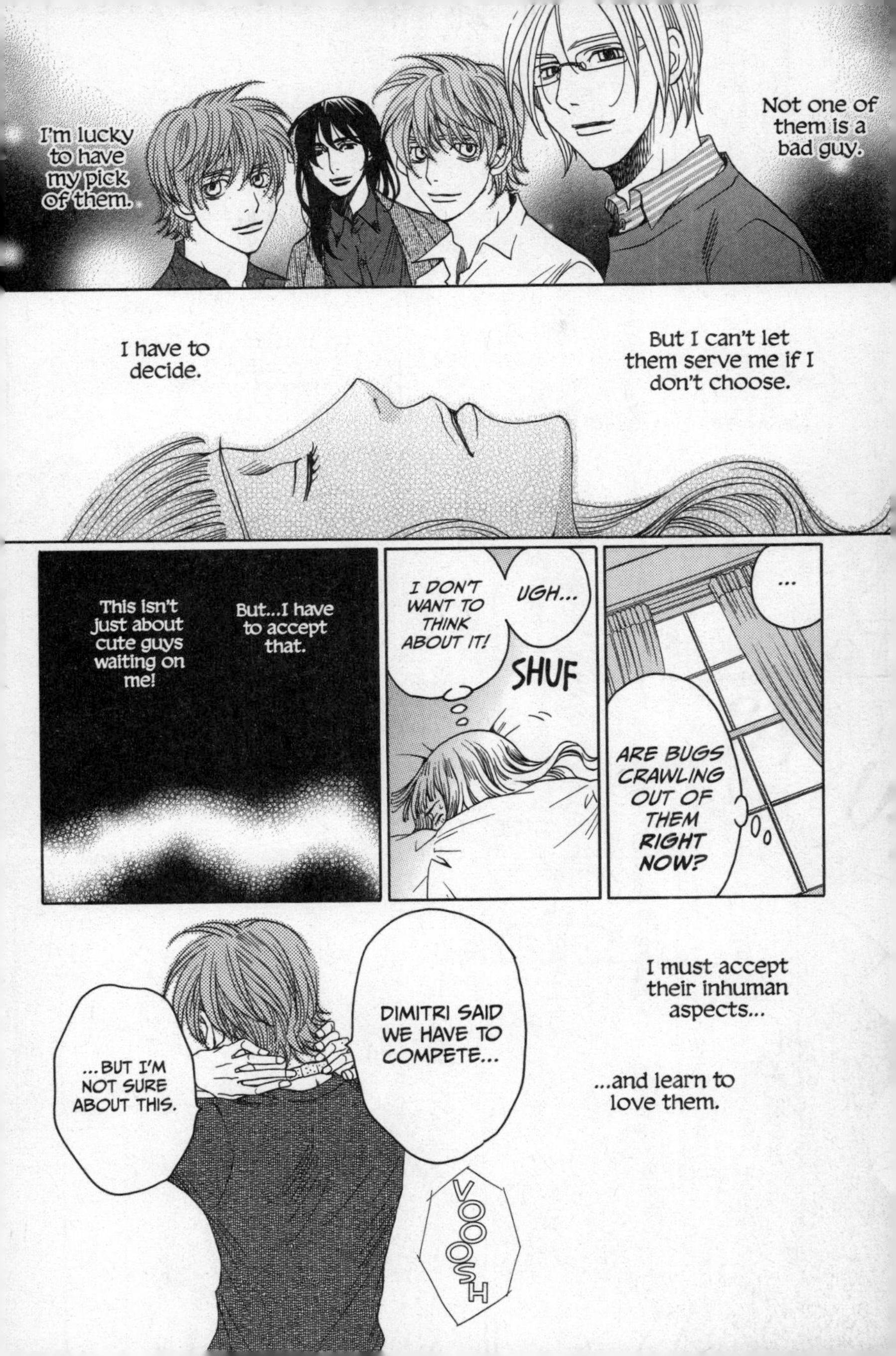
Not one of them is a bad guy.
I'm lucky to have my pick of them.
But I can't let them serve me if I don't choose.
I have to decide.
...
ARE BUGS CRAWLING OUT OF THEM RIGHT NOW?
UGH...
I DON'T WANT TO THINK ABOUT IT!
SHUF
But...I have to accept that.
This isn't just about cute guys waiting on me!
I must accept their inhuman aspects...
...and learn to love them.
DIMITRI SAID WE HAVE TO COMPETE...
...BUT I'M NOT SURE ABOUT THIS.
VOOOOSH

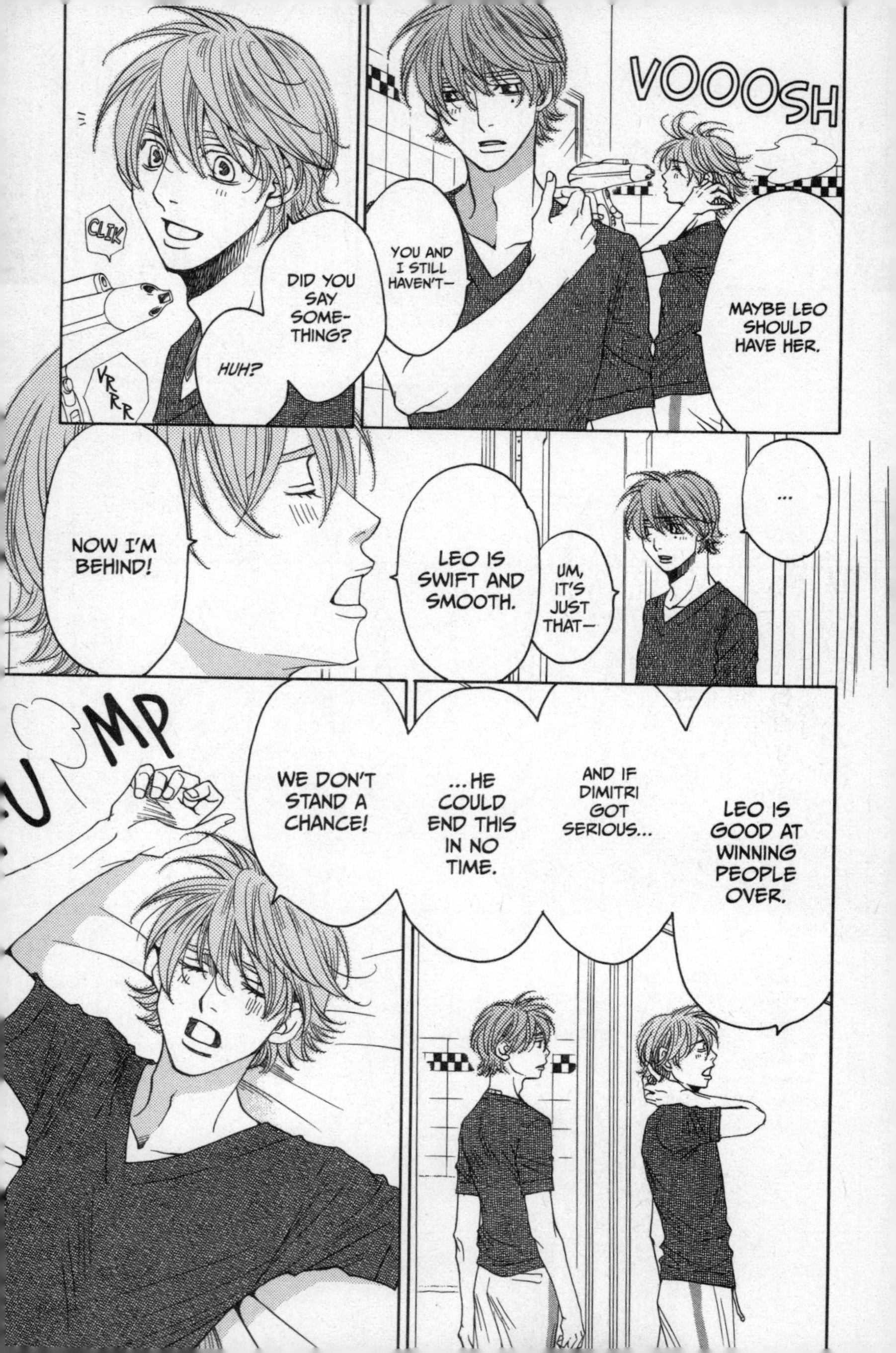
VOOOSH
MAYBE LEO SHOULD HAVE HER.
YOU AND I STILL HAVEN'T—
CLIK
DID YOU SAY SOME-THING?
HUH?
VRRR
...
UM, IT'S JUST THAT—
LEO IS SWIFT AND SMOOTH.
NOW I'M BEHIND!
LEO IS GOOD AT WINNING PEOPLE OVER.
AND IF DIMITRI GOT SERIOUS...
...HE COULD END THIS IN NO TIME.
WE DON'T STAND A CHANCE!
UMP

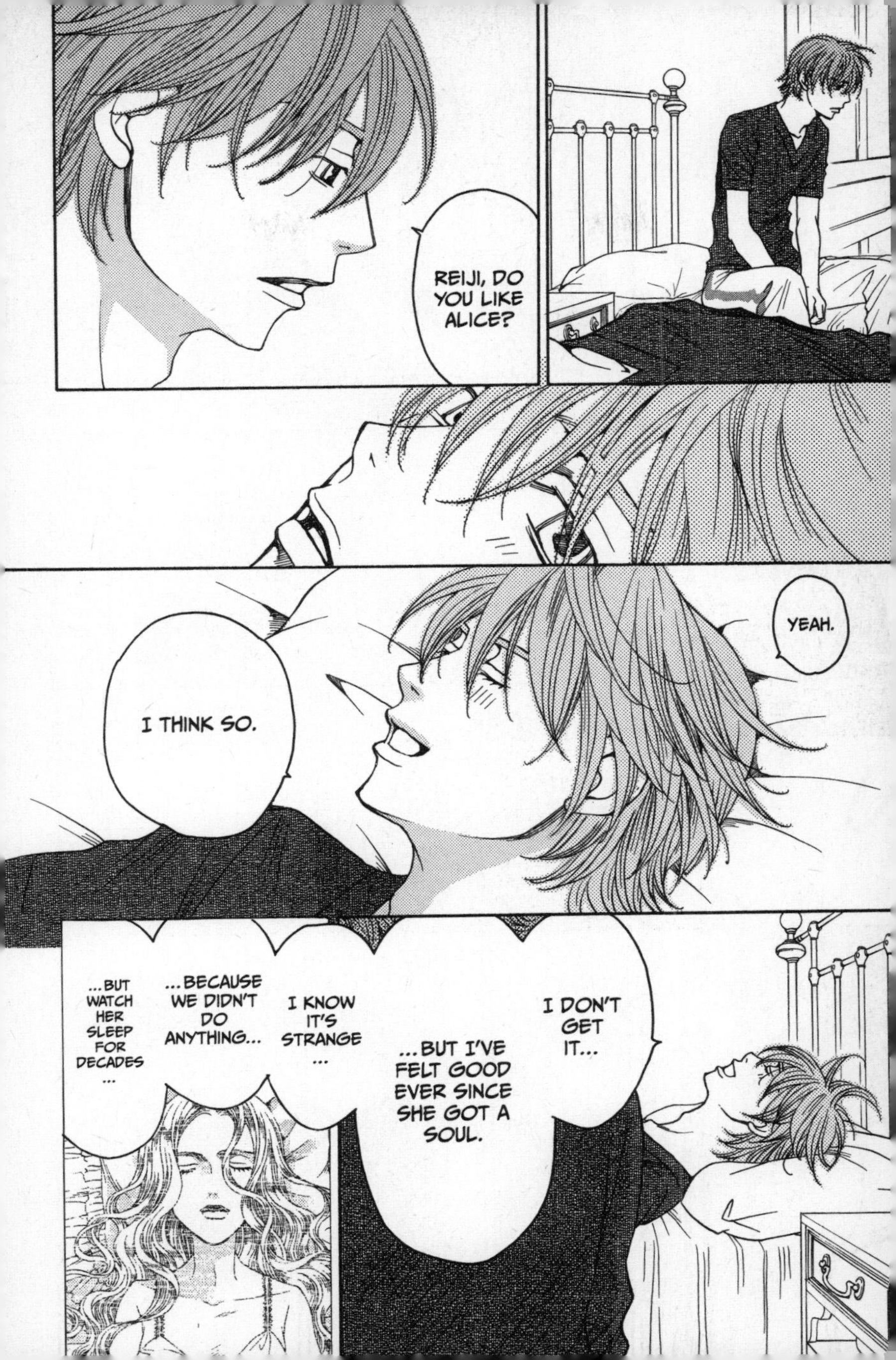
REIJI, DO YOU LIKE ALICE?
YEAH.
I THINK SO.
I DON'T GET IT...
...BUT I'VE FELT GOOD EVER SINCE SHE GOT A SOUL.
I KNOW IT'S STRANGE ...
...BECAUSE WE DIDN'T DO ANYTHING...
...BUT WATCH HER SLEEP FOR DECADES ...

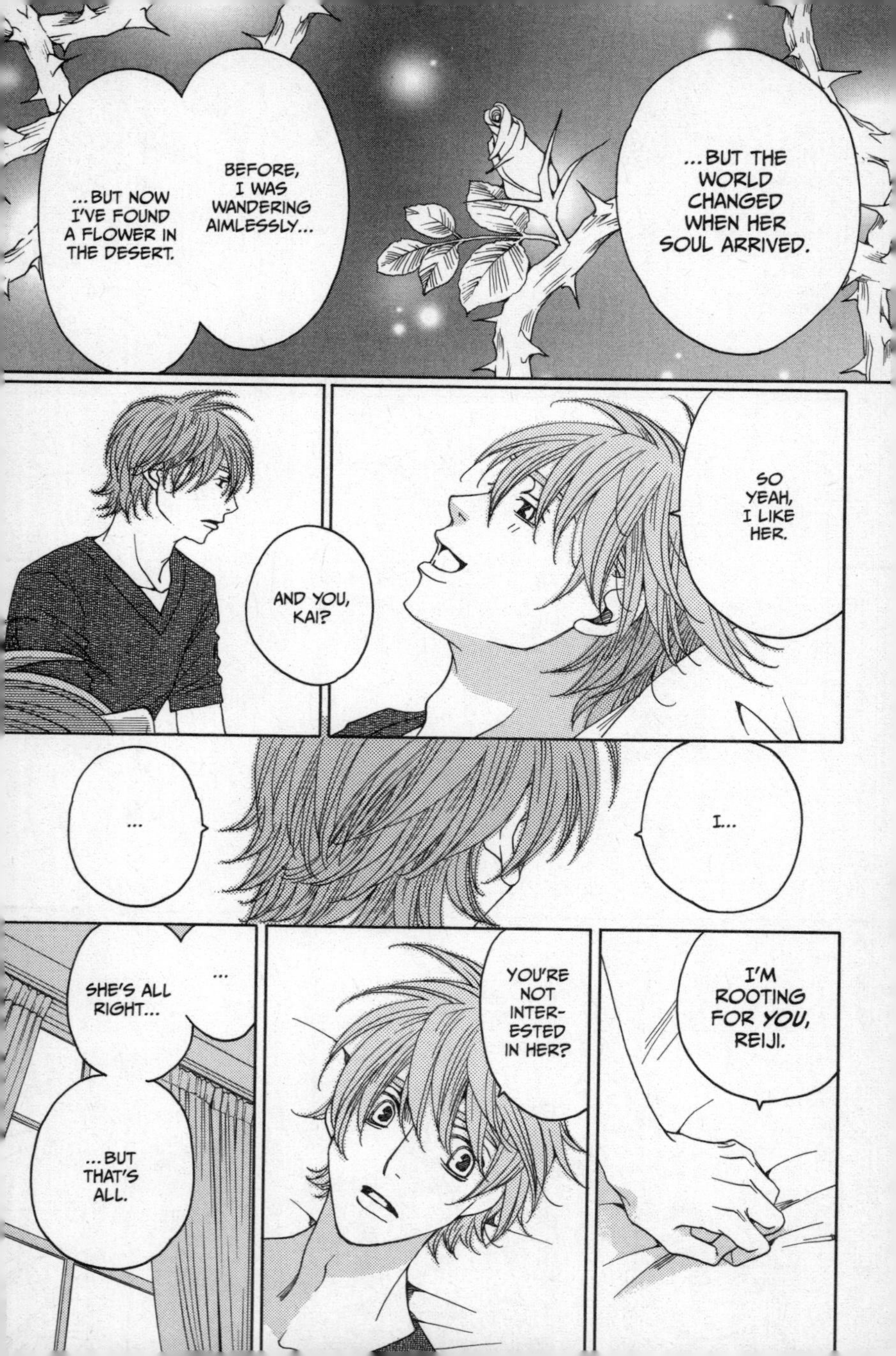
BEFORE, I WAS WANDERING AIMLESSLY...
...BUT NOW I'VE FOUND A FLOWER IN THE DESERT.
...BUT THE WORLD CHANGED WHEN HER SOUL ARRIVED.
SO YEAH, I LIKE HER.
AND YOU, KAI?
I...
...
I'M ROOTING FOR *YOU*, REIJI.
YOU'RE NOT INTER-ESTED IN HER?
...
SHE'S ALL RIGHT...
...BUT THAT'S ALL.

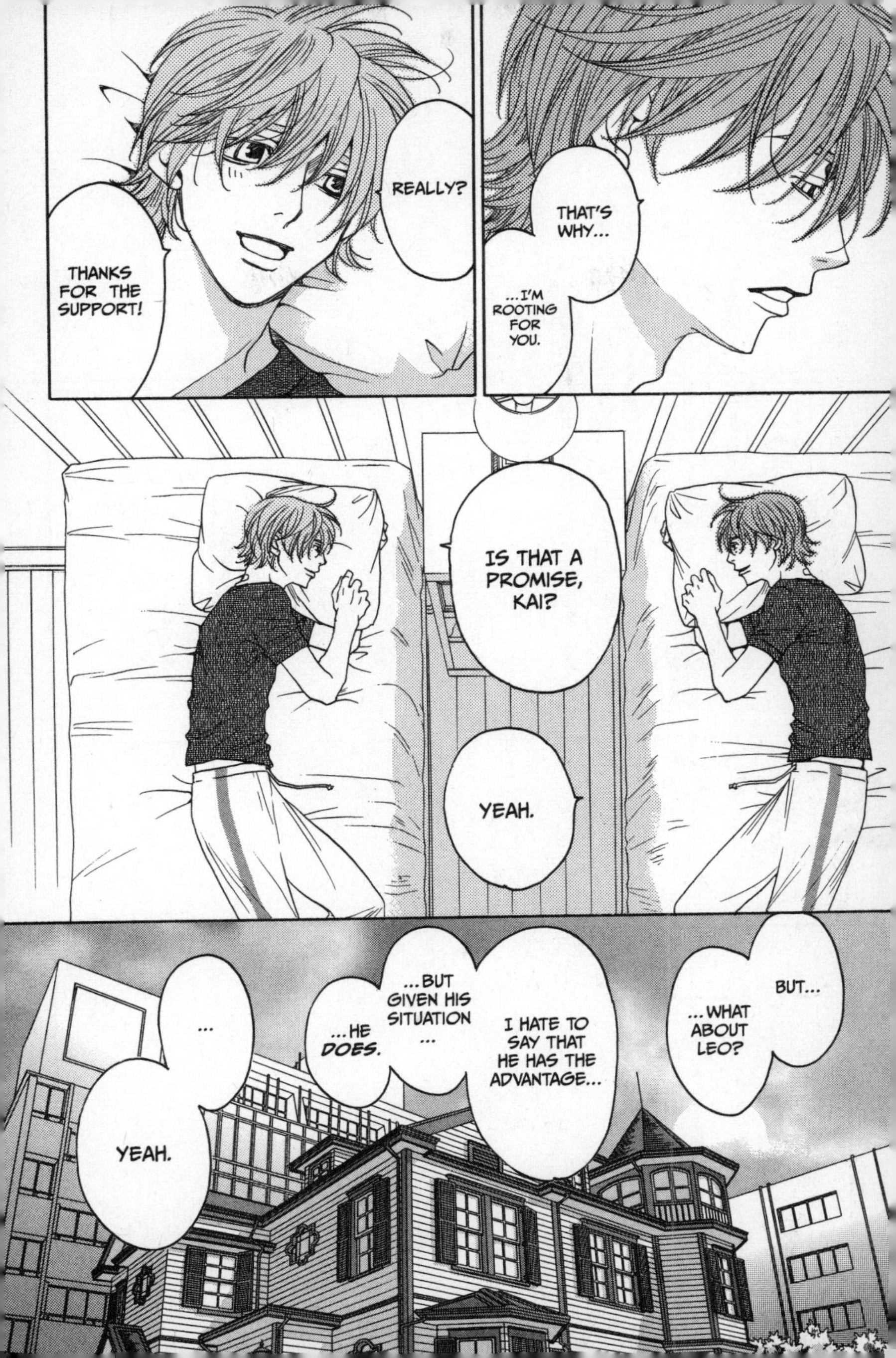
THAT'S WHY...
...I'M ROOTING FOR YOU.
REALLY?
THANKS FOR THE SUPPORT!
IS THAT A PROMISE, KAI?
YEAH.
BUT...
...WHAT ABOUT LEO?
I HATE TO SAY THAT HE HAS THE ADVANTAGE...
...BUT GIVEN HIS SITUATION ...
...HE *DOES*.
...
YEAH.

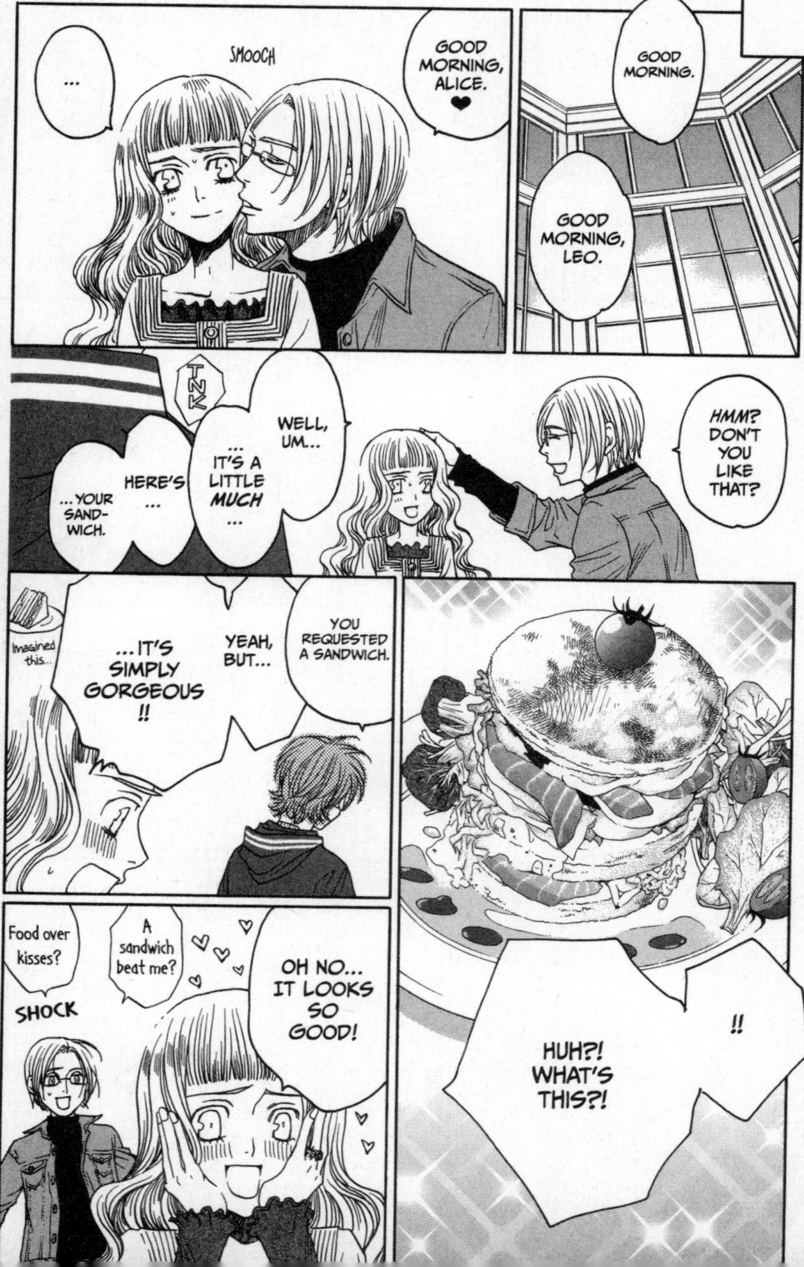

GOOD MORNING.
GOOD MORNING, LEO.
GOOD MORNING, ALICE. ❤
SMOOCH
...
HMM? DON'T YOU LIKE THAT?
WELL, UM...
... IT'S A LITTLE MUCH ...
TNK
HERE'S ...
...YOUR SANDWICH.
!!
HUH?! WHAT'S THIS?!
YOU REQUESTED A SANDWICH.
YEAH, BUT...
...IT'S SIMPLY GORGEOUS !!
Imagined this...
OH NO... IT LOOKS SO GOOD!
A sandwich beat me?
Food over kisses?
SHOCK

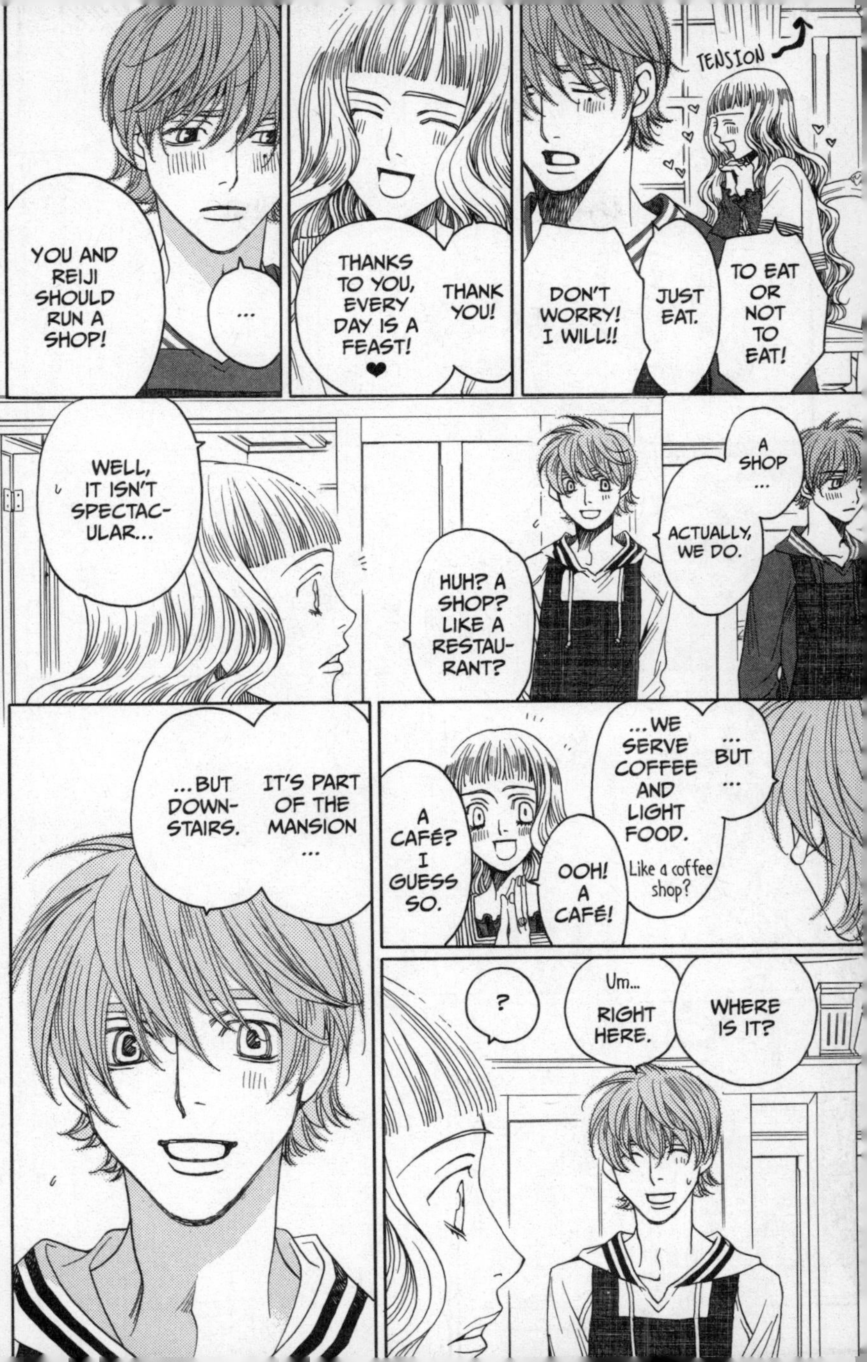
TENSION
TO EAT OR NOT TO EAT!
JUST EAT.
DON'T WORRY! I WILL!!
THANK YOU!
THANKS TO YOU, EVERY DAY IS A FEAST! ❤
YOU AND REIJI SHOULD RUN A SHOP!
...
A SHOP...
ACTUALLY, WE DO.
HUH? A SHOP? LIKE A RESTAURANT?
WELL, IT ISN'T SPECTACULAR...
...BUT...
...WE SERVE COFFEE AND LIGHT FOOD.
Like a coffee shop?
OOH! A CAFÉ!
A CAFÉ? I GUESS SO.
WHERE IS IT?
Um...
RIGHT HERE.
?
IT'S PART OF THE MANSION...
...BUT DOWNSTAIRS.

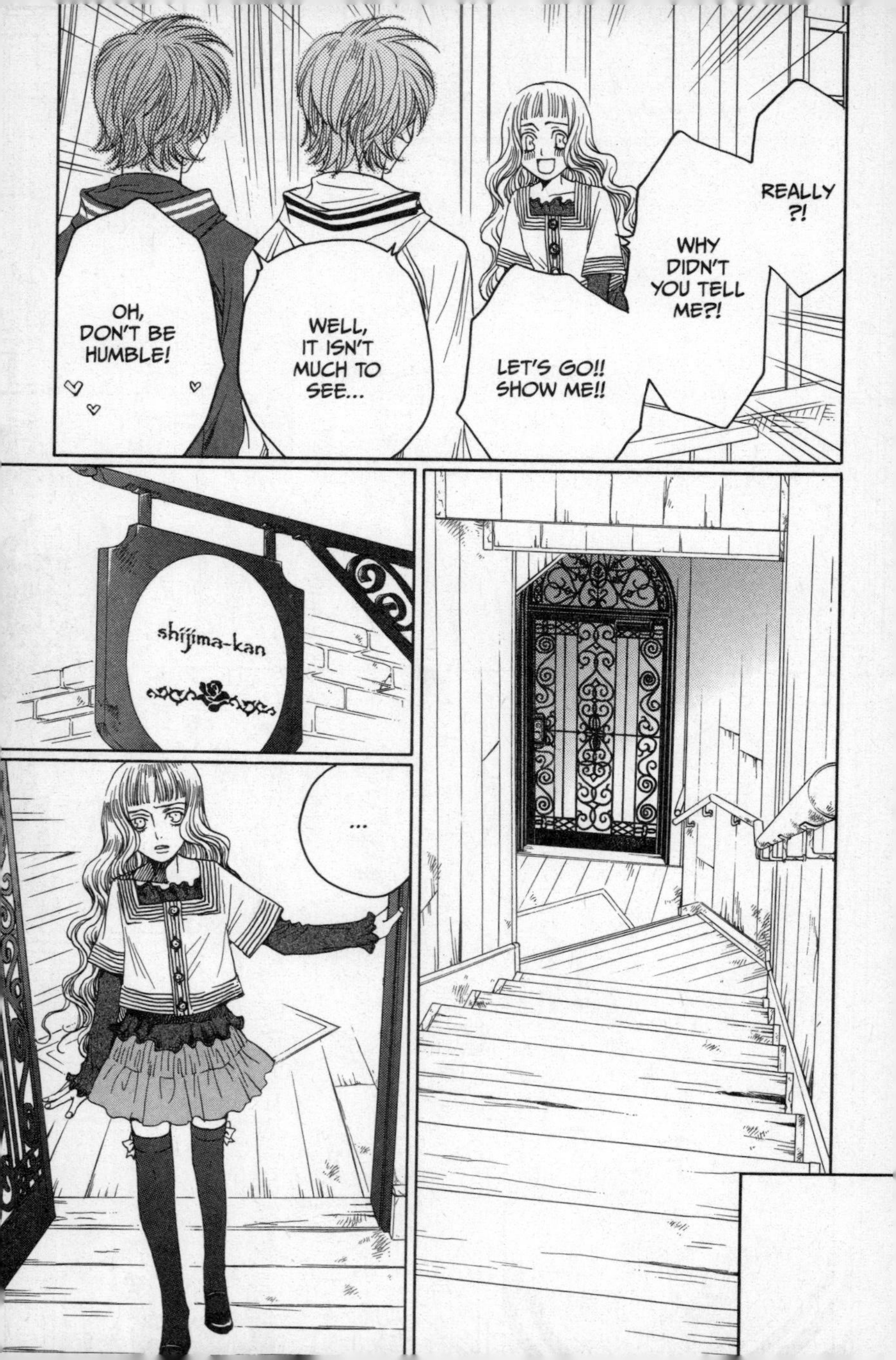
REALLY?!
WHY DIDN'T YOU TELL ME?!
LET'S GO!! SHOW ME!!
WELL, IT ISN'T MUCH TO SEE...
OH, DON'T BE HUMBLE!
shijima-kan
...

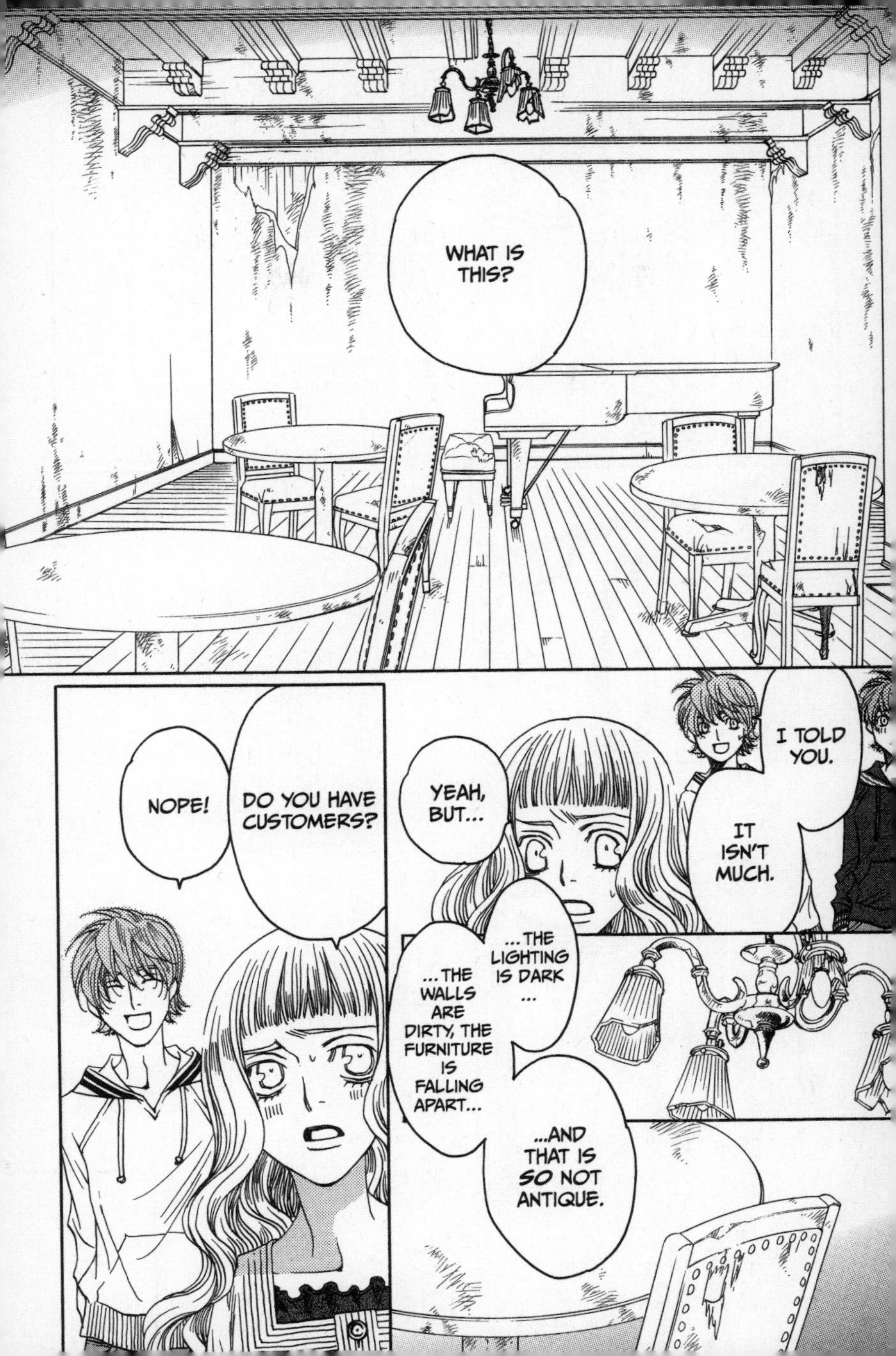
WHAT IS THIS?
I TOLD YOU.
IT ISN'T MUCH.
YEAH, BUT...
...THE LIGHTING IS DARK...
...THE WALLS ARE DIRTY, THE FURNITURE IS FALLING APART...
...AND THAT IS SO NOT ANTIQUE.
DO YOU HAVE CUSTOMERS?
NOPE!

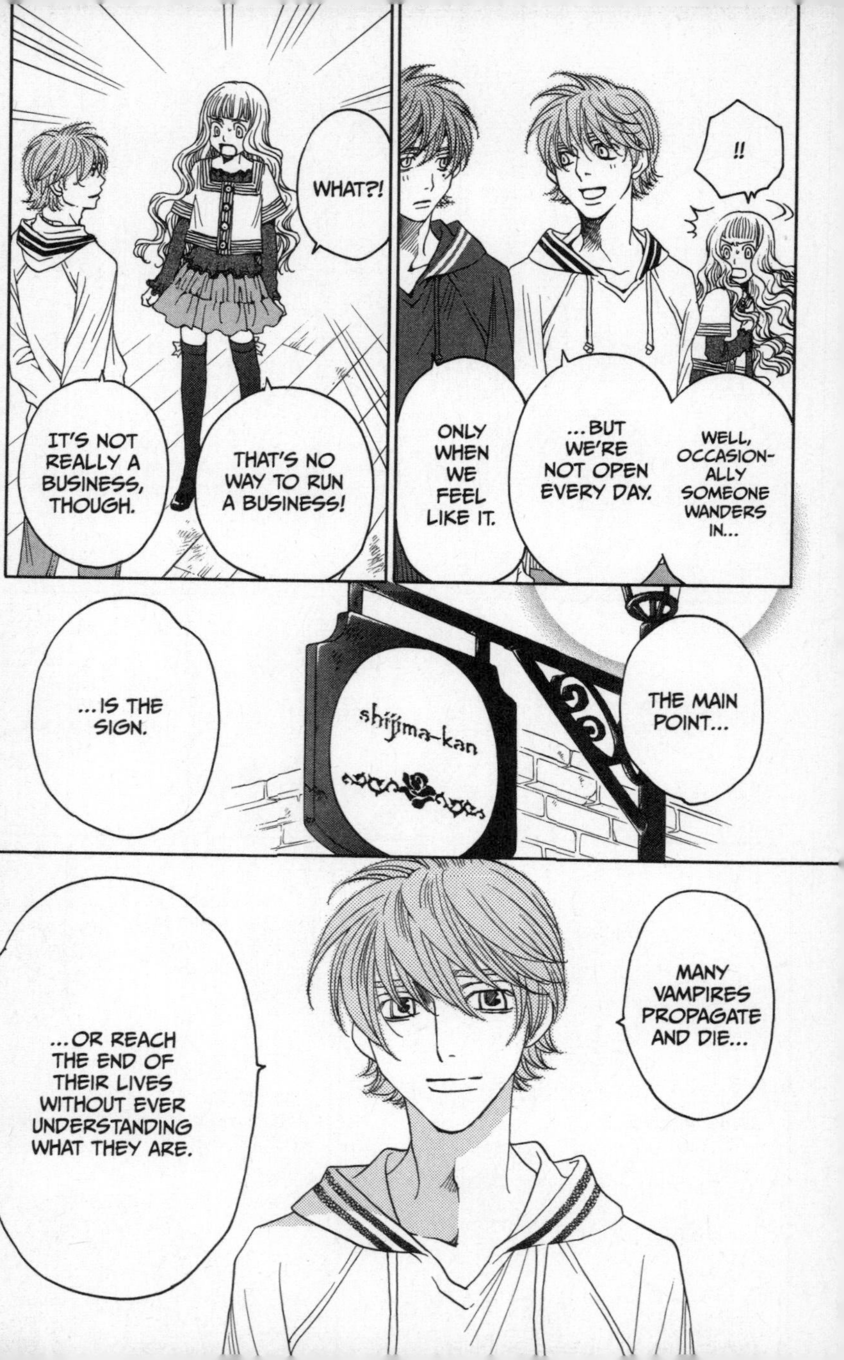
!!
WELL, OCCASION-ALLY SOMEONE WANDERS IN...
...BUT WE'RE NOT OPEN EVERY DAY.
ONLY WHEN WE FEEL LIKE IT.
WHAT?!
THAT'S NO WAY TO RUN A BUSINESS!
IT'S NOT REALLY A BUSINESS, THOUGH.
THE MAIN POINT...
shijima-kan
...IS THE SIGN.
MANY VAMPIRES PROPAGATE AND DIE...
...OR REACH THE END OF THEIR LIVES WITHOUT EVER UNDERSTANDING WHAT THEY ARE.

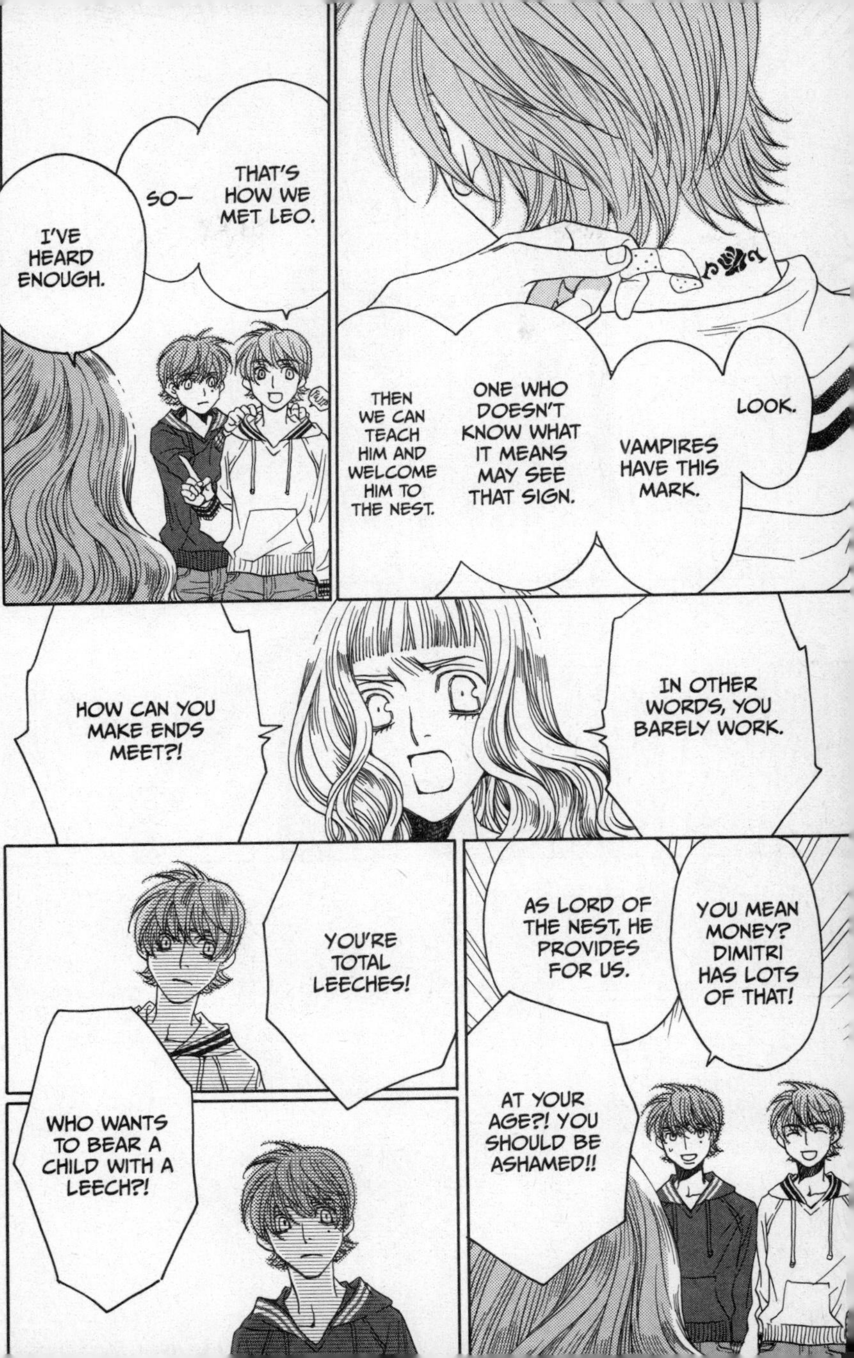
LOOK.
VAMPIRES HAVE THIS MARK.
ONE WHO DOESN'T KNOW WHAT IT MEANS MAY SEE THAT SIGN.
THEN WE CAN TEACH HIM AND WELCOME HIM TO THE NEST.
THAT'S HOW WE MET LEO.
SO—
I'VE HEARD ENOUGH.
IN OTHER WORDS, YOU BARELY WORK.
HOW CAN YOU MAKE ENDS MEET?!
YOU MEAN MONEY? DIMITRI HAS LOTS OF THAT!
AS LORD OF THE NEST, HE PROVIDES FOR US.
AT YOUR AGE?! YOU SHOULD BE ASHAMED!!
YOU'RE TOTAL LEECHES!
WHO WANTS TO BEAR A CHILD WITH A LEECH?!

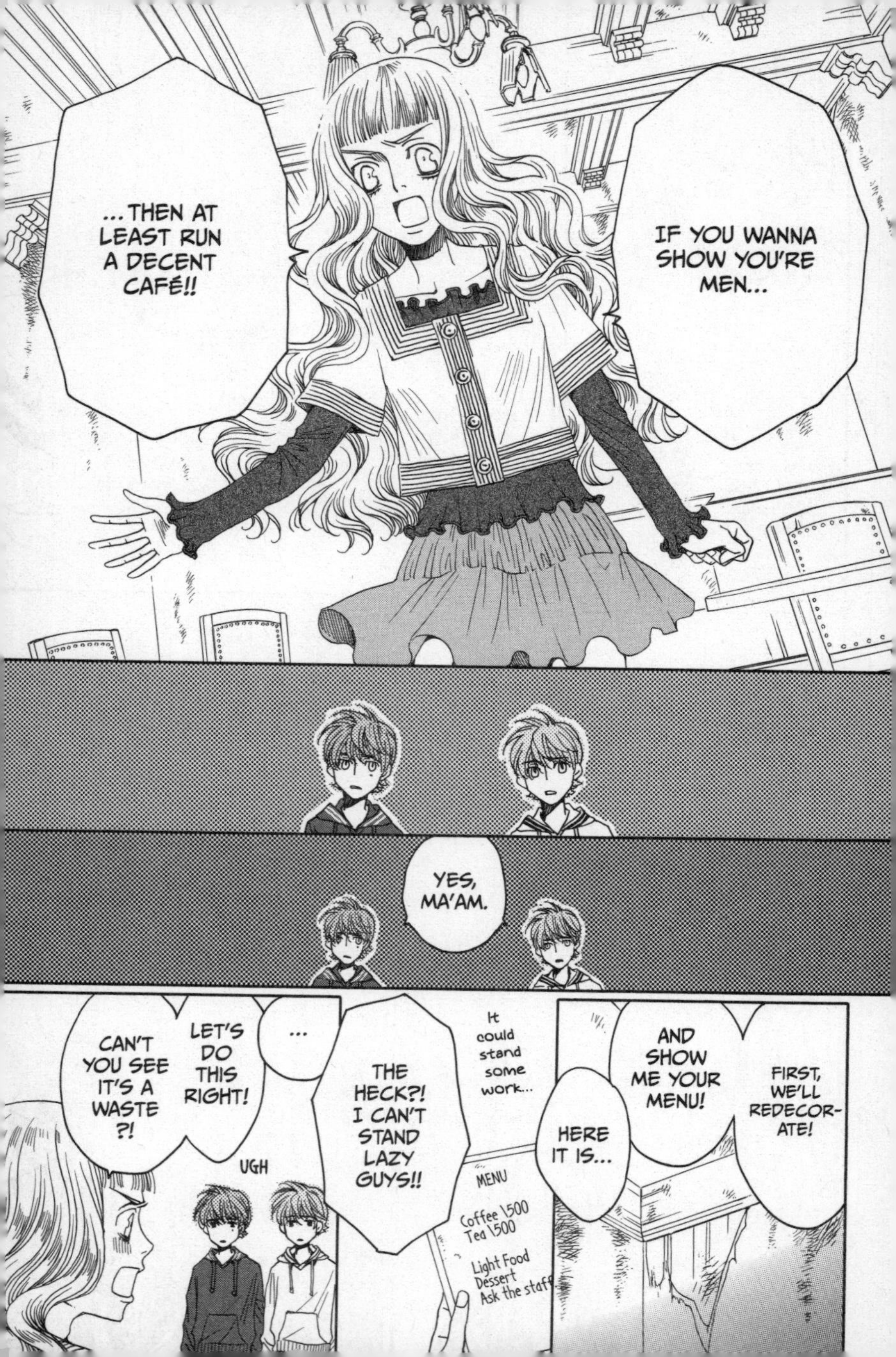
IF YOU WANNA SHOW YOU'RE MEN...
...THEN AT LEAST RUN A DECENT CAFÉ!!
YES, MA'AM.
FIRST, WE'LL REDECOR-ATE!
AND SHOW ME YOUR MENU!
HERE IT IS...
It could stand some work...
THE HECK?! I CAN'T STAND LAZY GUYS!!
MENU
Coffee ¥500
Tea ¥500
Light Food
Dessert
Ask the staff
...
LET'S DO THIS RIGHT!
CAN'T YOU SEE IT'S A WASTE?!
UGH

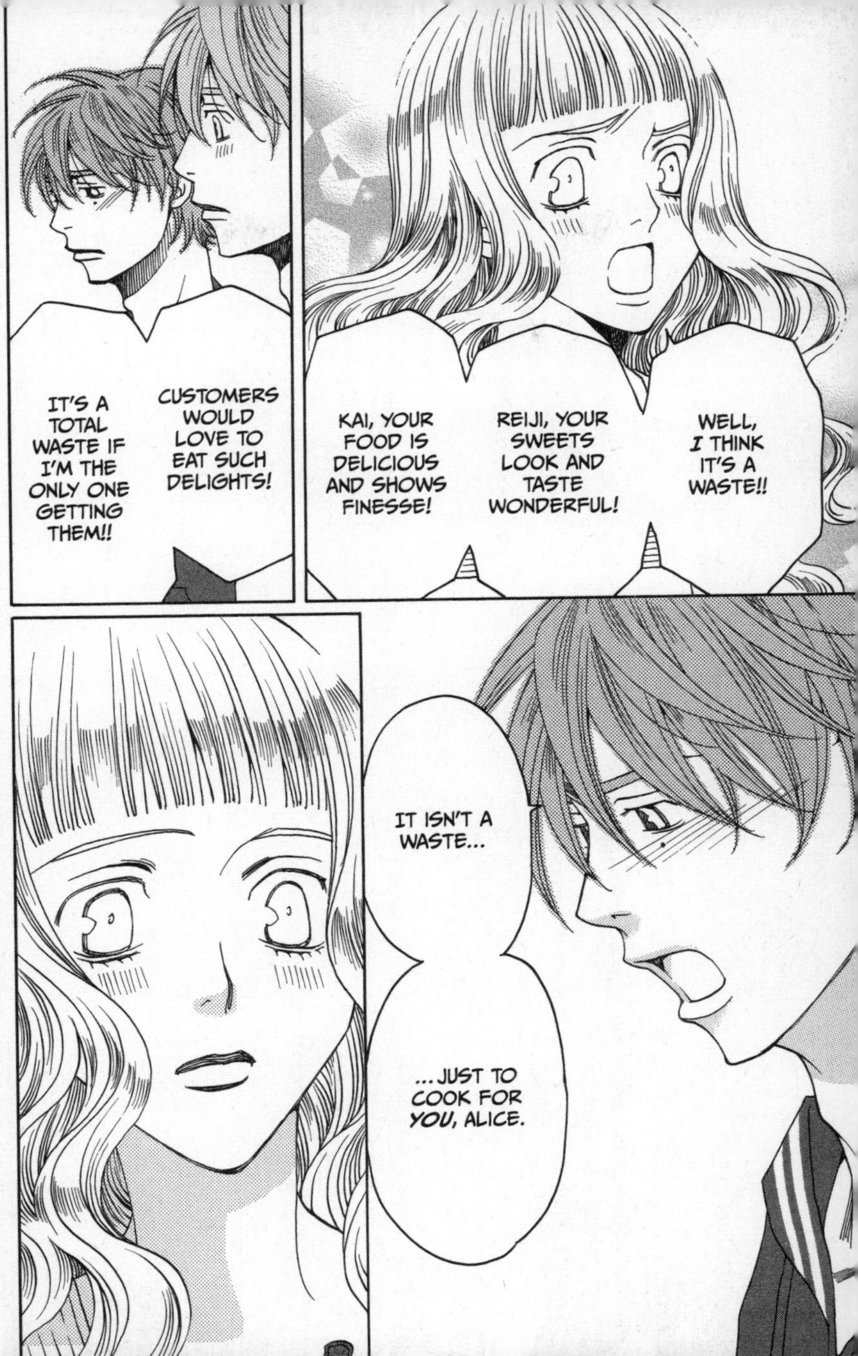
WELL, I THINK IT'S A WASTE!!
REIJI, YOUR SWEETS LOOK AND TASTE WONDERFUL!
KAI, YOUR FOOD IS DELICIOUS AND SHOWS FINESSE!
CUSTOMERS WOULD LOVE TO EAT SUCH DELIGHTS!
IT'S A TOTAL WASTE IF I'M THE ONLY ONE GETTING THEM!!
IT ISN'T A WASTE...
...JUST TO COOK FOR YOU, ALICE.

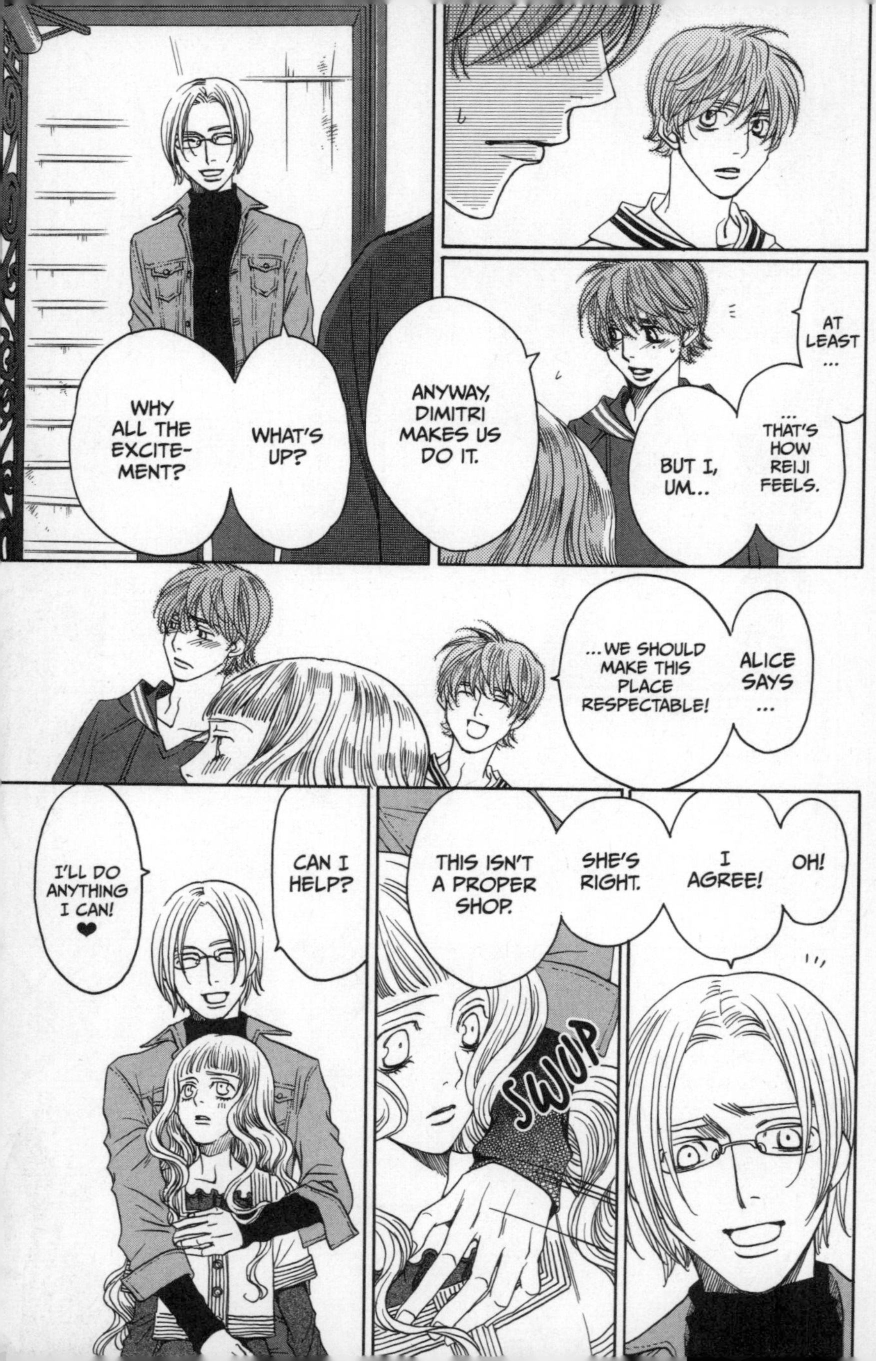
AT LEAST...
...THAT'S HOW REIJI FEELS.
BUT I, UM...
ANYWAY, DIMITRI MAKES US DO IT.
WHAT'S UP?
WHY ALL THE EXCITE-MENT?
ALICE SAYS...
...WE SHOULD MAKE THIS PLACE RESPECTABLE!
OH!
I AGREE!
SHE'S RIGHT.
THIS ISN'T A PROPER SHOP.
SWUP
CAN I HELP?
I'LL DO ANYTHING I CAN! ❤

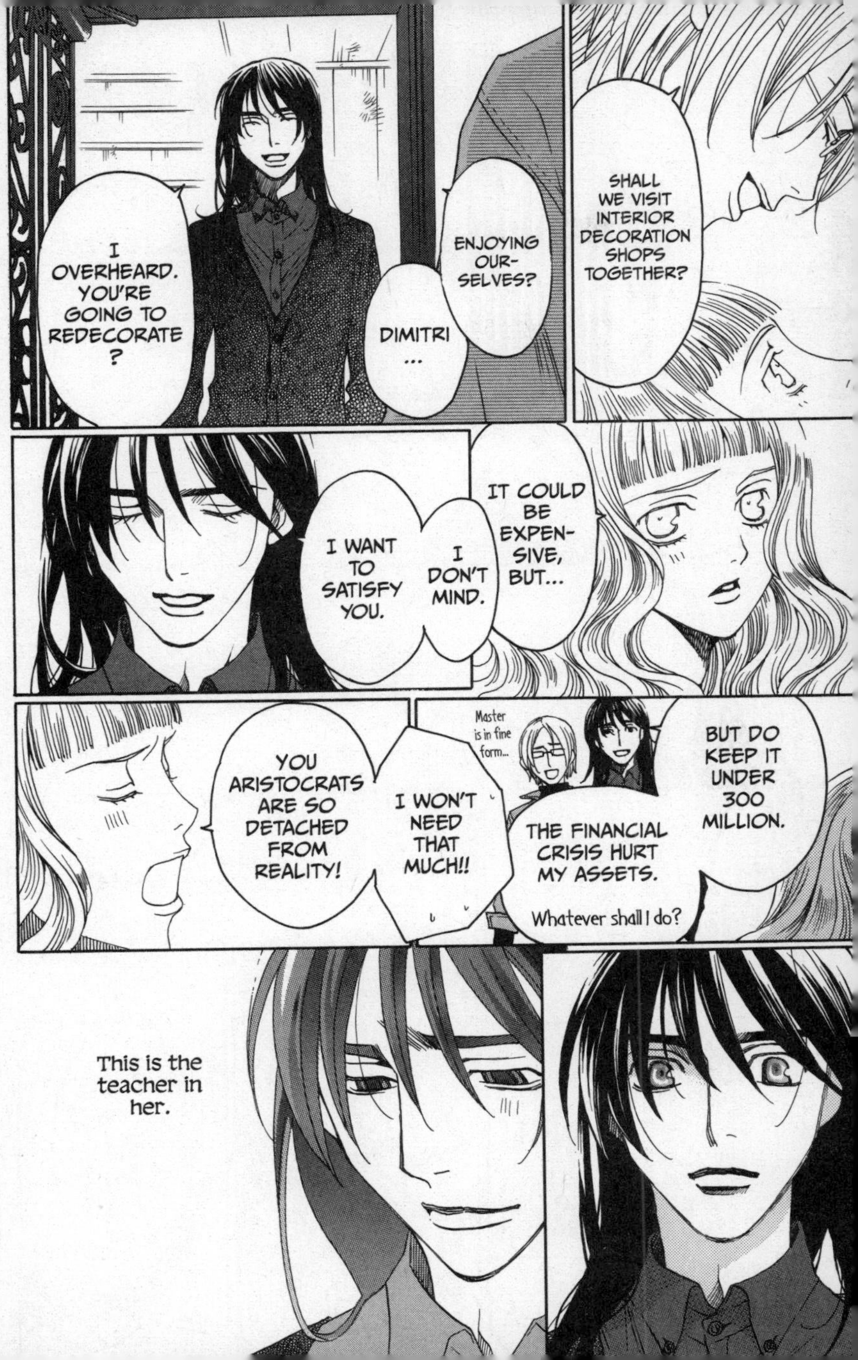
SHALL WE VISIT INTERIOR DECORATION SHOPS TOGETHER?
ENJOYING OUR-SELVES?
DIMITRI ...
I OVERHEARD. YOU'RE GOING TO REDECORATE?
IT COULD BE EXPEN-SIVE, BUT...
I DON'T MIND.
I WANT TO SATISFY YOU.
BUT DO KEEP IT UNDER 300 MILLION.
Master is in fine form...
THE FINANCIAL CRISIS HURT MY ASSETS.
Whatever shall I do?
I WON'T NEED THAT MUCH!!
YOU ARISTOCRATS ARE SO DETACHED FROM REALITY!
This is the teacher in her.

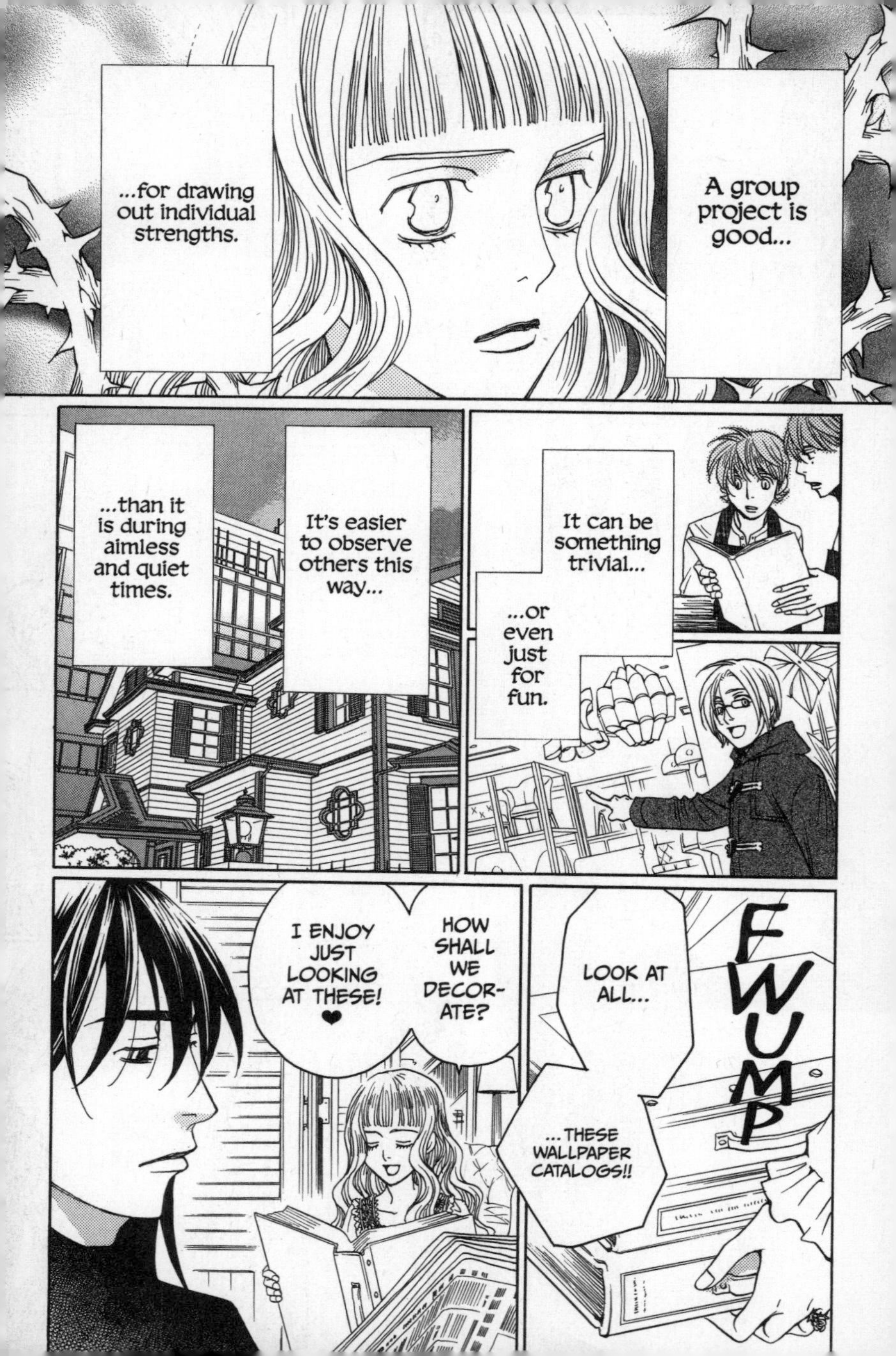
A group project is good...
...for drawing out individual strengths.
It can be something trivial...
...or even just for fun.
It's easier to observe others this way...
...than it is during aimless and quiet times.
FWUMP
LOOK AT ALL...
...THESE WALLPAPER CATALOGS!!
HOW SHALL WE DECOR-ATE?
I ENJOY JUST LOOKING AT THESE! ❤

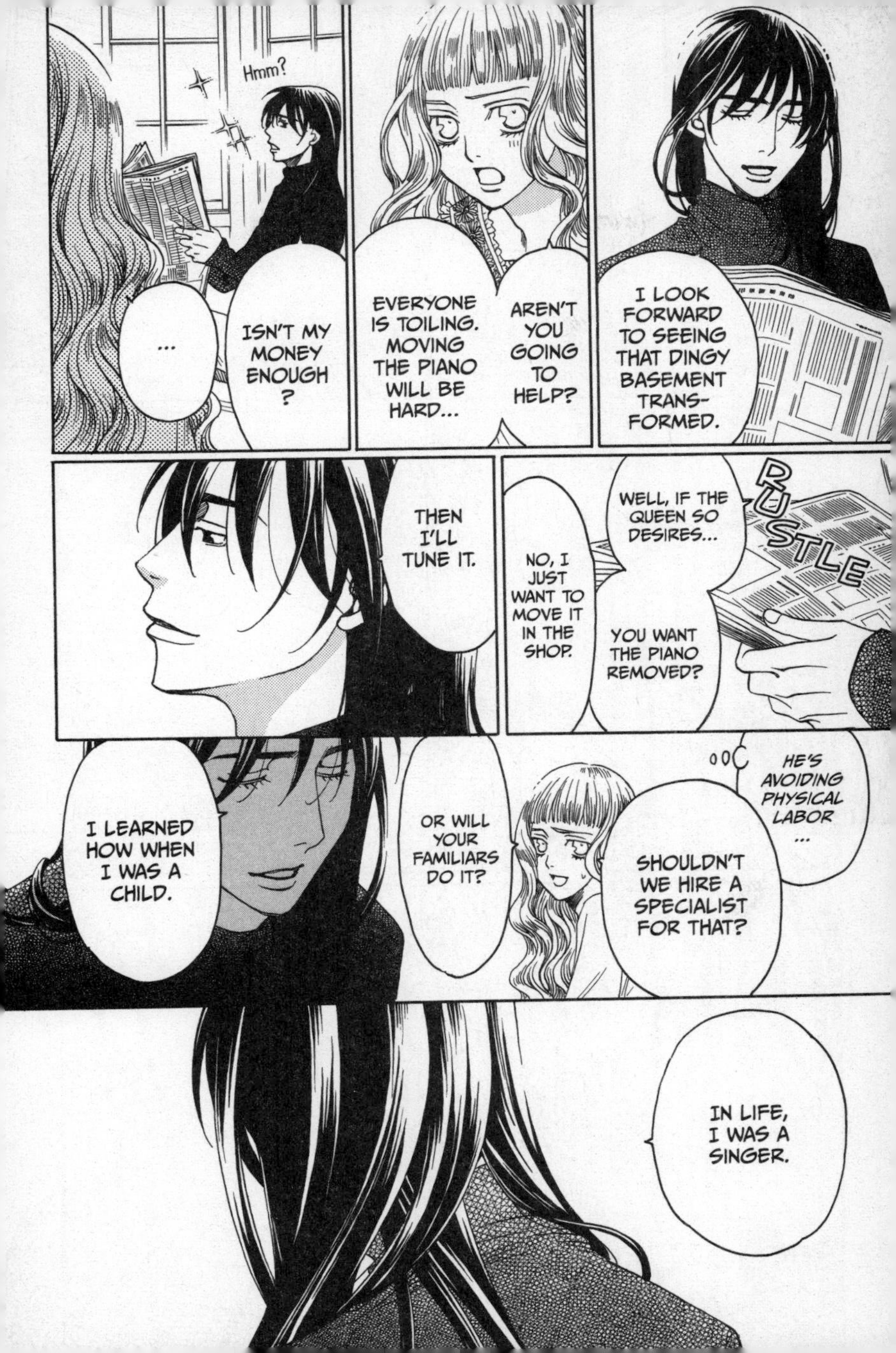
I LOOK FORWARD TO SEEING THAT DINGY BASEMENT TRANS-FORMED.
AREN'T YOU GOING TO HELP?
EVERYONE IS TOILING. MOVING THE PIANO WILL BE HARD...
Hmm?
ISN'T MY MONEY ENOUGH?
...
WELL, IF THE QUEEN SO DESIRES...
RUSTLE
YOU WANT THE PIANO REMOVED?
NO, I JUST WANT TO MOVE IT IN THE SHOP.
THEN I'LL TUNE IT.
HE'S AVOIDING PHYSICAL LABOR...
SHOULDN'T WE HIRE A SPECIALIST FOR THAT?
OR WILL YOUR FAMILIARS DO IT?
I LEARNED HOW WHEN I WAS A CHILD.
IN LIFE, I WAS A SINGER.

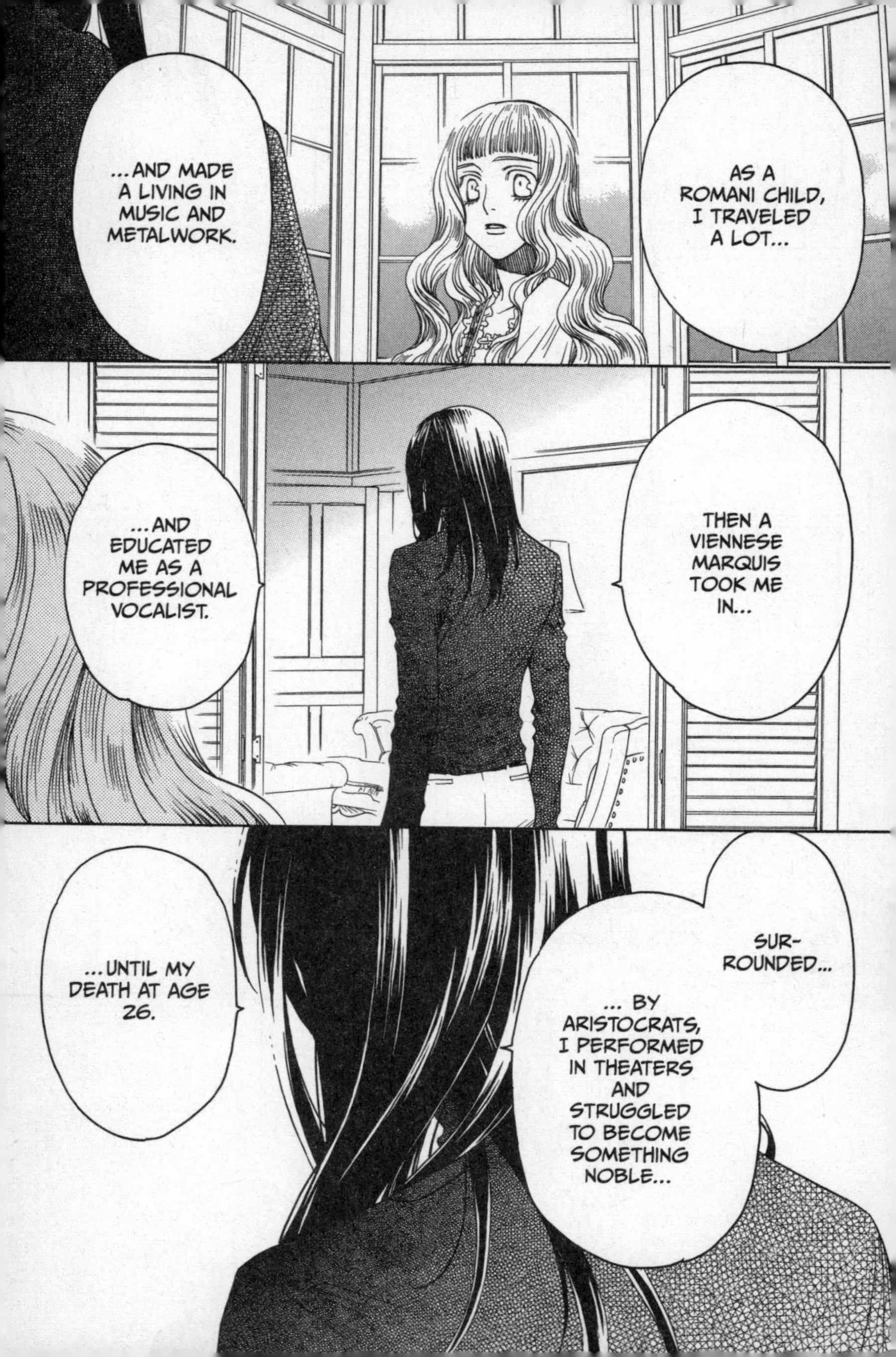
AS A ROMANI CHILD, I TRAVELED A LOT...
...AND MADE A LIVING IN MUSIC AND METALWORK.
THEN A VIENNESE MARQUIS TOOK ME IN...
...AND EDUCATED ME AS A PROFESSIONAL VOCALIST.
SUR-ROUNDED...
... BY ARISTOCRATS, I PERFORMED IN THEATERS AND STRUGGLED TO BECOME SOMETHING NOBLE...
...UNTIL MY DEATH AT AGE 26.

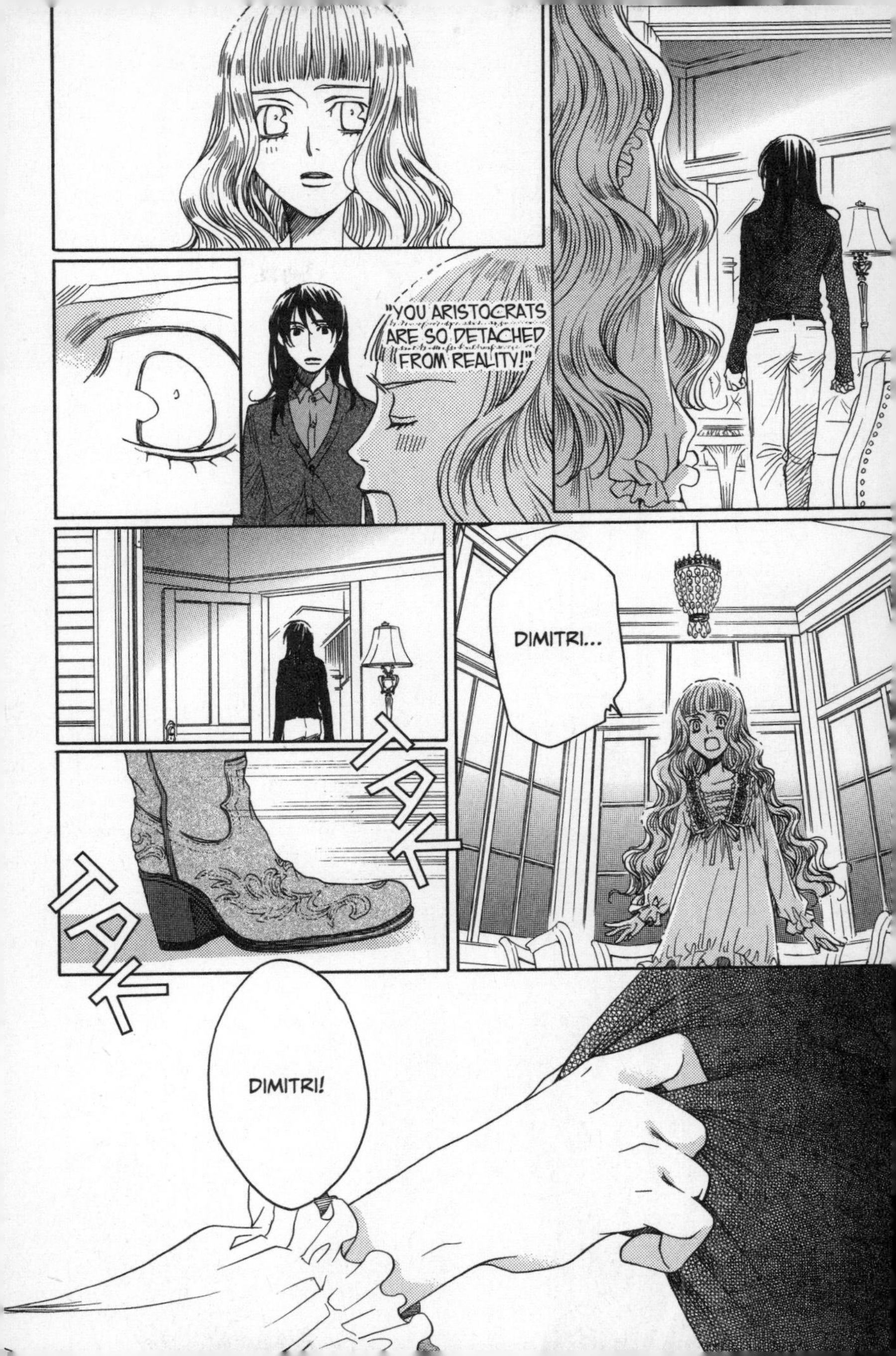
"YOU ARISTOCRATS ARE SO DETACHED FROM REALITY!"
DIMITRI...
TAK
TAK
DIMITRI!

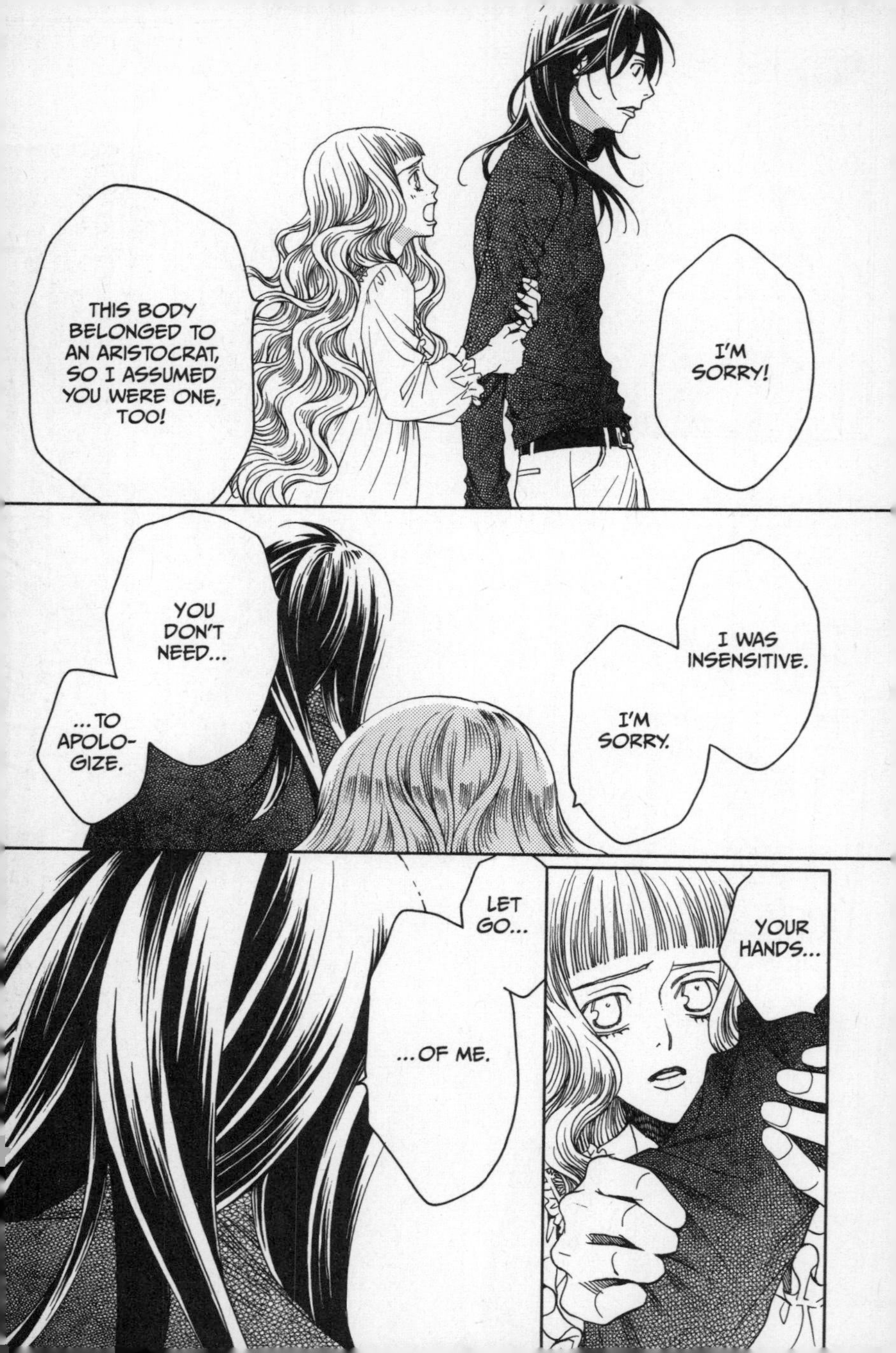
I'M SORRY!
THIS BODY BELONGED TO AN ARISTOCRAT, SO I ASSUMED YOU WERE ONE, TOO!
I WAS INSENSITIVE.
I'M SORRY.
YOU DON'T NEED...
...TO APOLO-GIZE.
YOUR HANDS...
LET GO...
...OF ME.

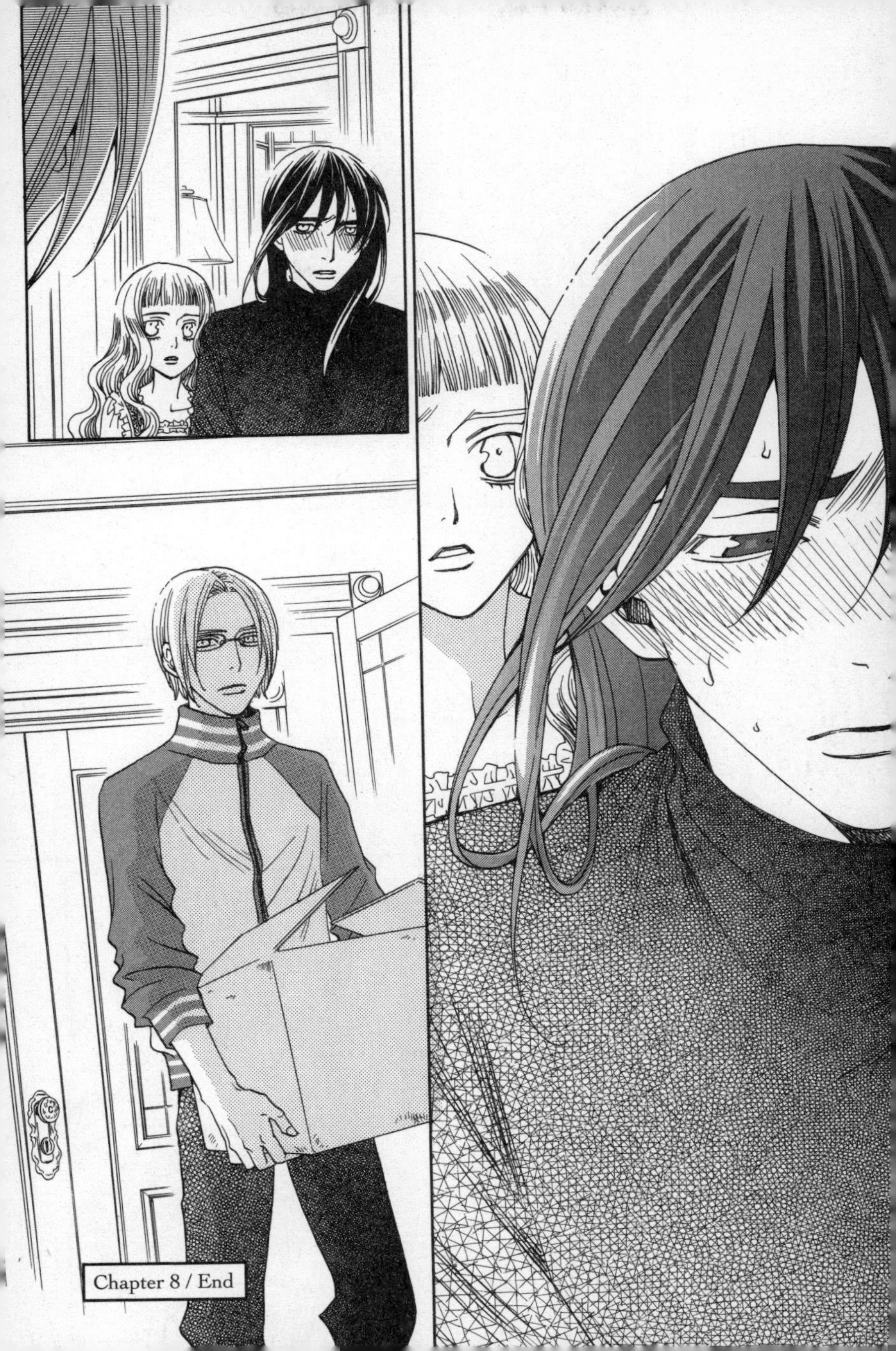
Chapter 8 / End

Black Rose ALICE

Chapter 9

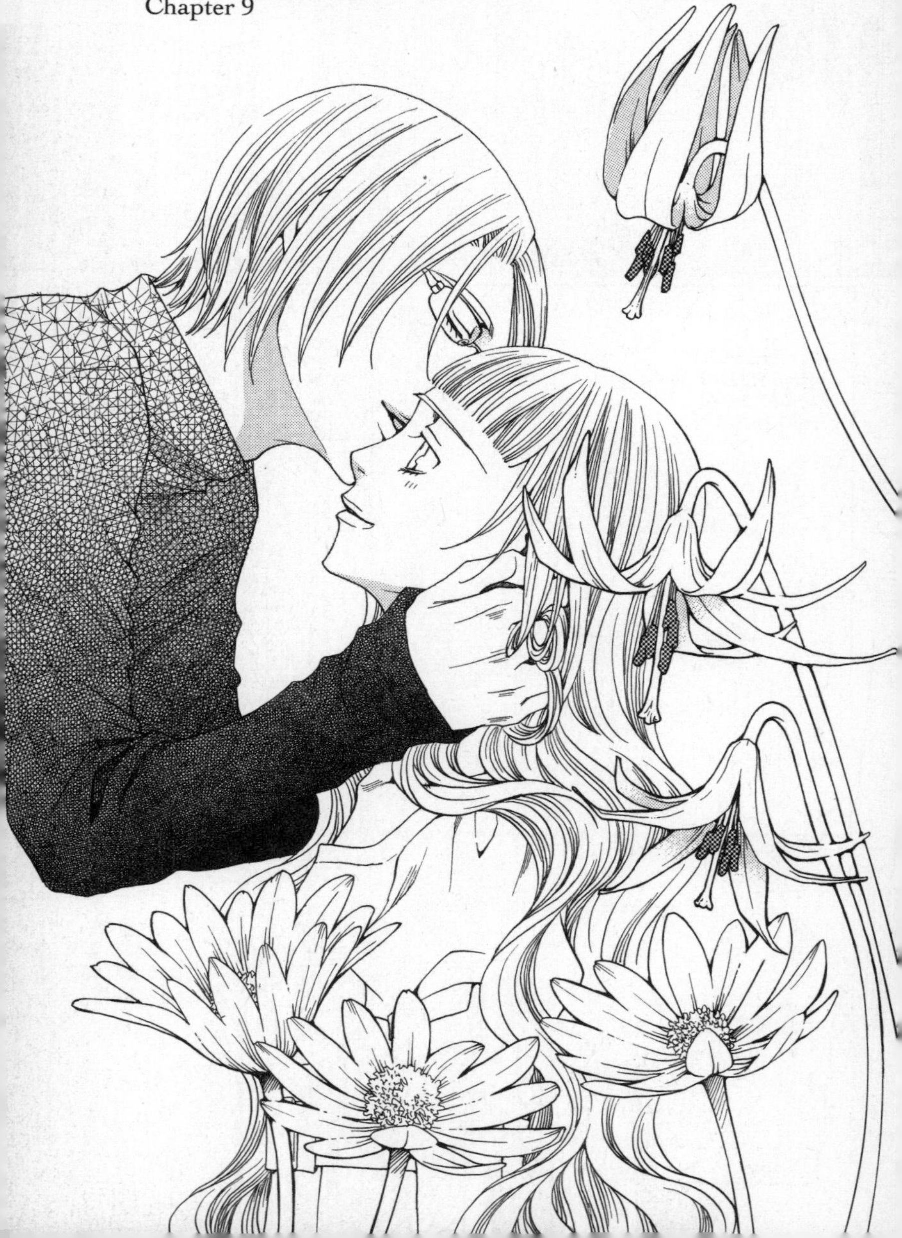

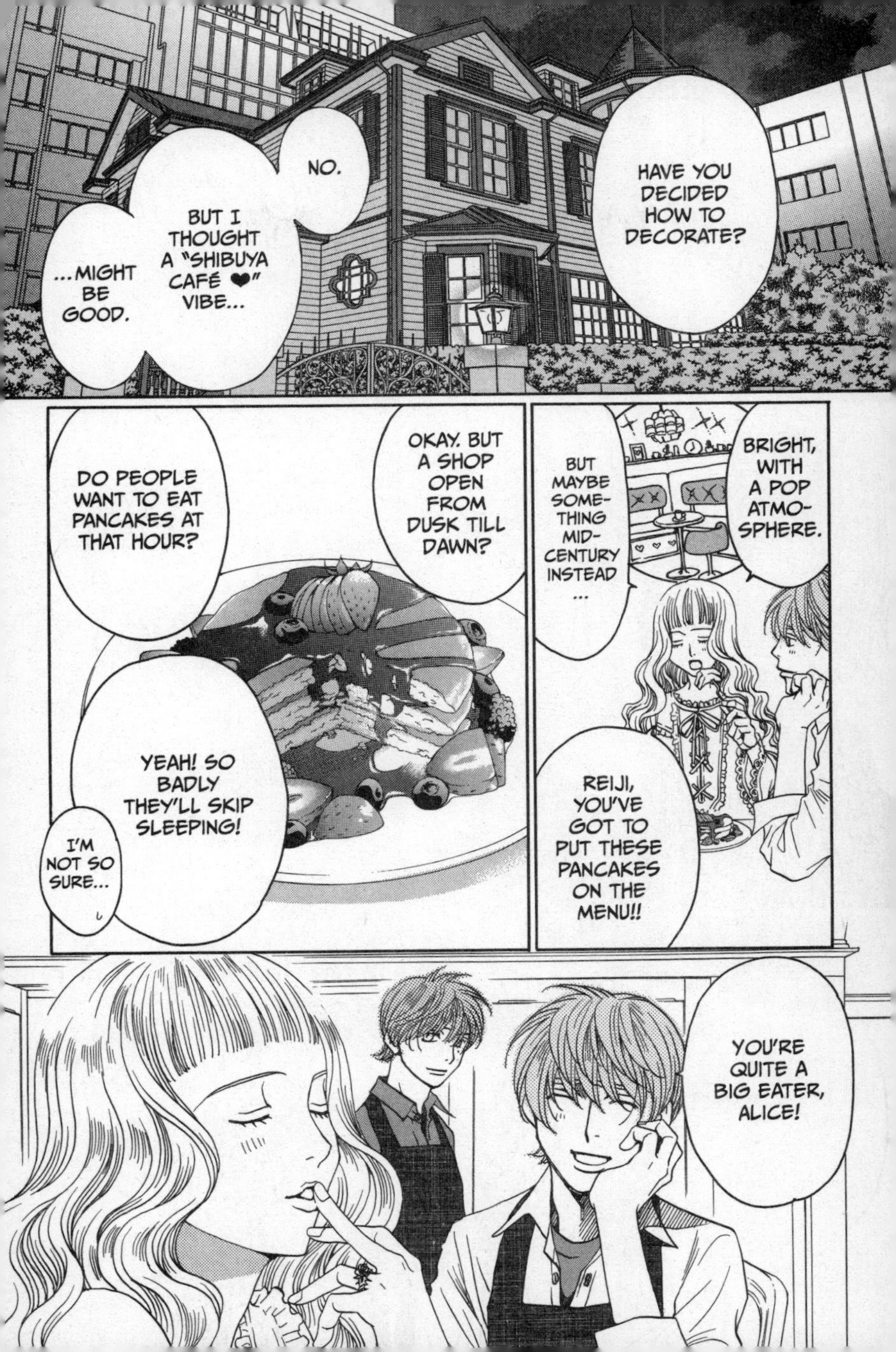
HAVE YOU DECIDED HOW TO DECORATE?
NO.
BUT I THOUGHT A "SHIBUYA CAFÉ ❤" VIBE...
...MIGHT BE GOOD.
BRIGHT, WITH A POP ATMOSPHERE.
BUT MAYBE SOMETHING MID-CENTURY INSTEAD...
REIJI, YOU'VE GOT TO PUT THESE PANCAKES ON THE MENU!!
OKAY. BUT A SHOP OPEN FROM DUSK TILL DAWN?
DO PEOPLE WANT TO EAT PANCAKES AT THAT HOUR?
YEAH! SO BADLY THEY'LL SKIP SLEEPING!
I'M NOT SO SURE...
YOU'RE QUITE A BIG EATER, ALICE!

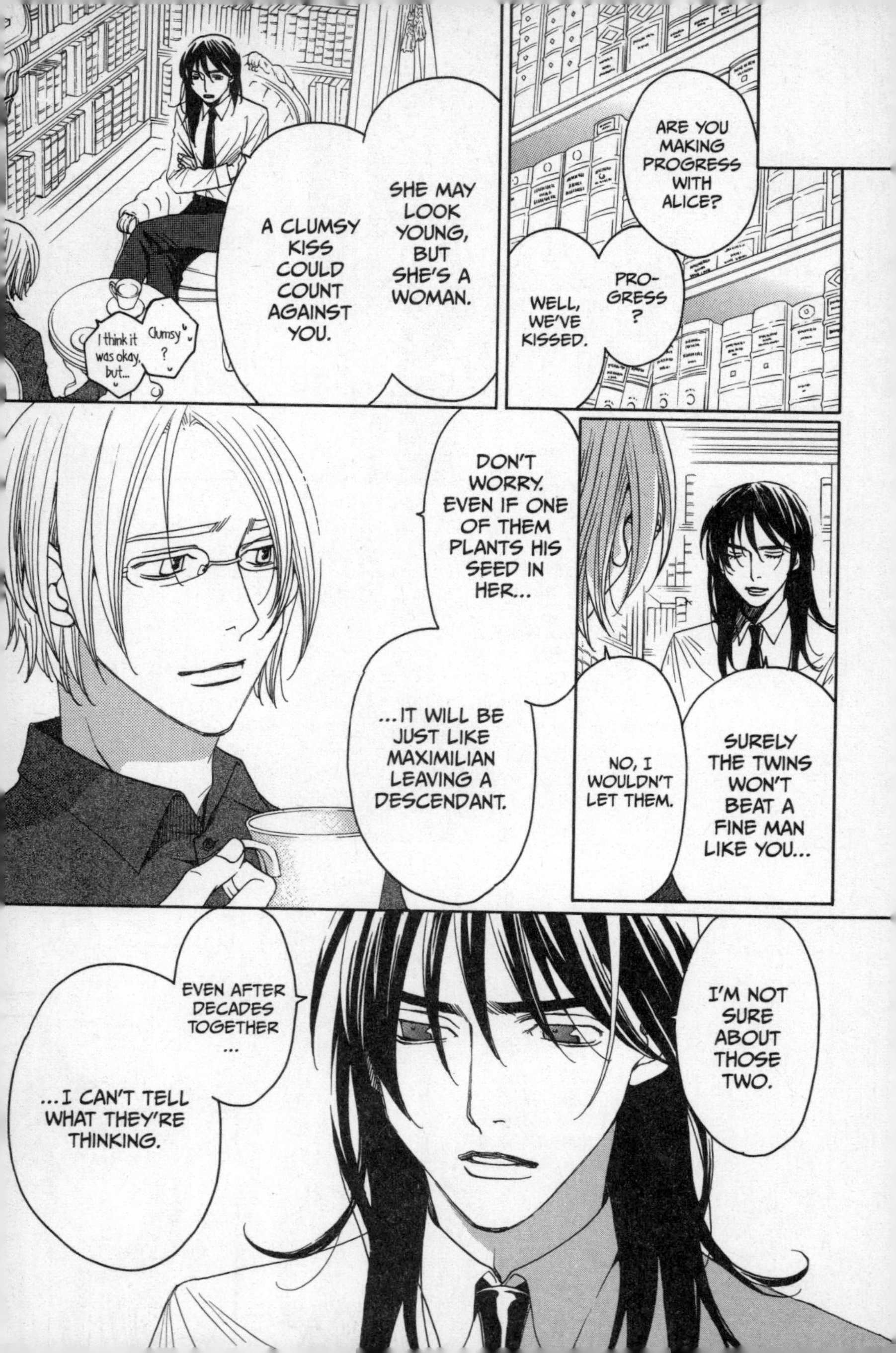
ARE YOU MAKING PROGRESS WITH ALICE?
PRO-GRESS?
WELL, WE'VE KISSED.
SHE MAY LOOK YOUNG, BUT SHE'S A WOMAN.
A CLUMSY KISS COULD COUNT AGAINST YOU.
Clumsy?
I think it was okay, but...
SURELY THE TWINS WON'T BEAT A FINE MAN LIKE YOU...
NO, I WOULDN'T LET THEM.
DON'T WORRY. EVEN IF ONE OF THEM PLANTS HIS SEED IN HER...
...IT WILL BE JUST LIKE MAXIMILIAN LEAVING A DESCENDANT.
I'M NOT SURE ABOUT THOSE TWO.
EVEN AFTER DECADES TOGETHER...
...I CAN'T TELL WHAT THEY'RE THINKING.

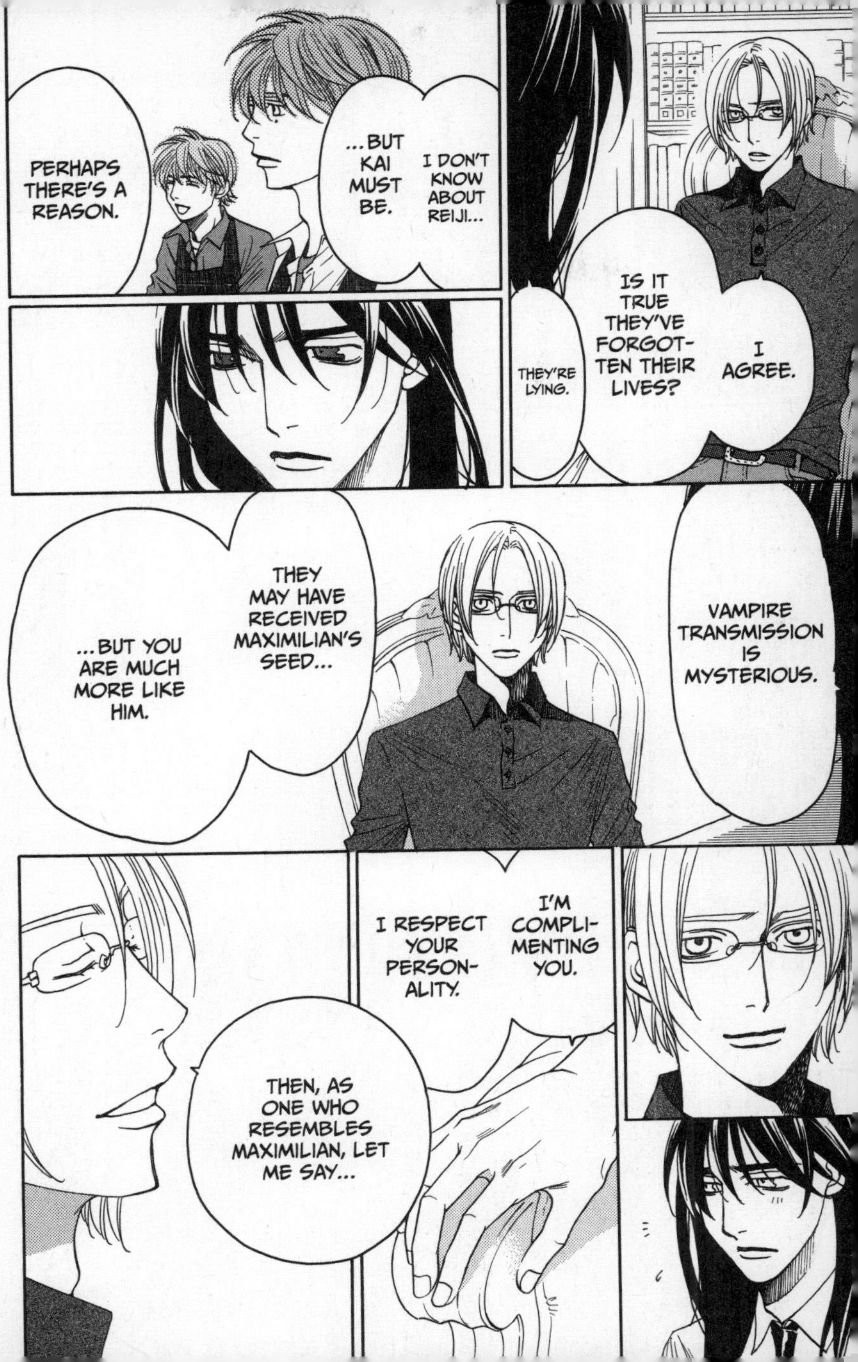
I AGREE.
IS IT TRUE THEY'VE FORGOT-TEN THEIR LIVES?
THEY'RE LYING.
I DON'T KNOW ABOUT REIJI...
...BUT KAI MUST BE.
PERHAPS THERE'S A REASON.
VAMPIRE TRANSMISSION IS MYSTERIOUS.
THEY MAY HAVE RECEIVED MAXIMILIAN'S SEED...
...BUT YOU ARE MUCH MORE LIKE HIM.
I'M COMPLI-MENTING YOU.
I RESPECT YOUR PERSON-ALITY.
THEN, AS ONE WHO RESEMBLES MAXIMILIAN, LET ME SAY...

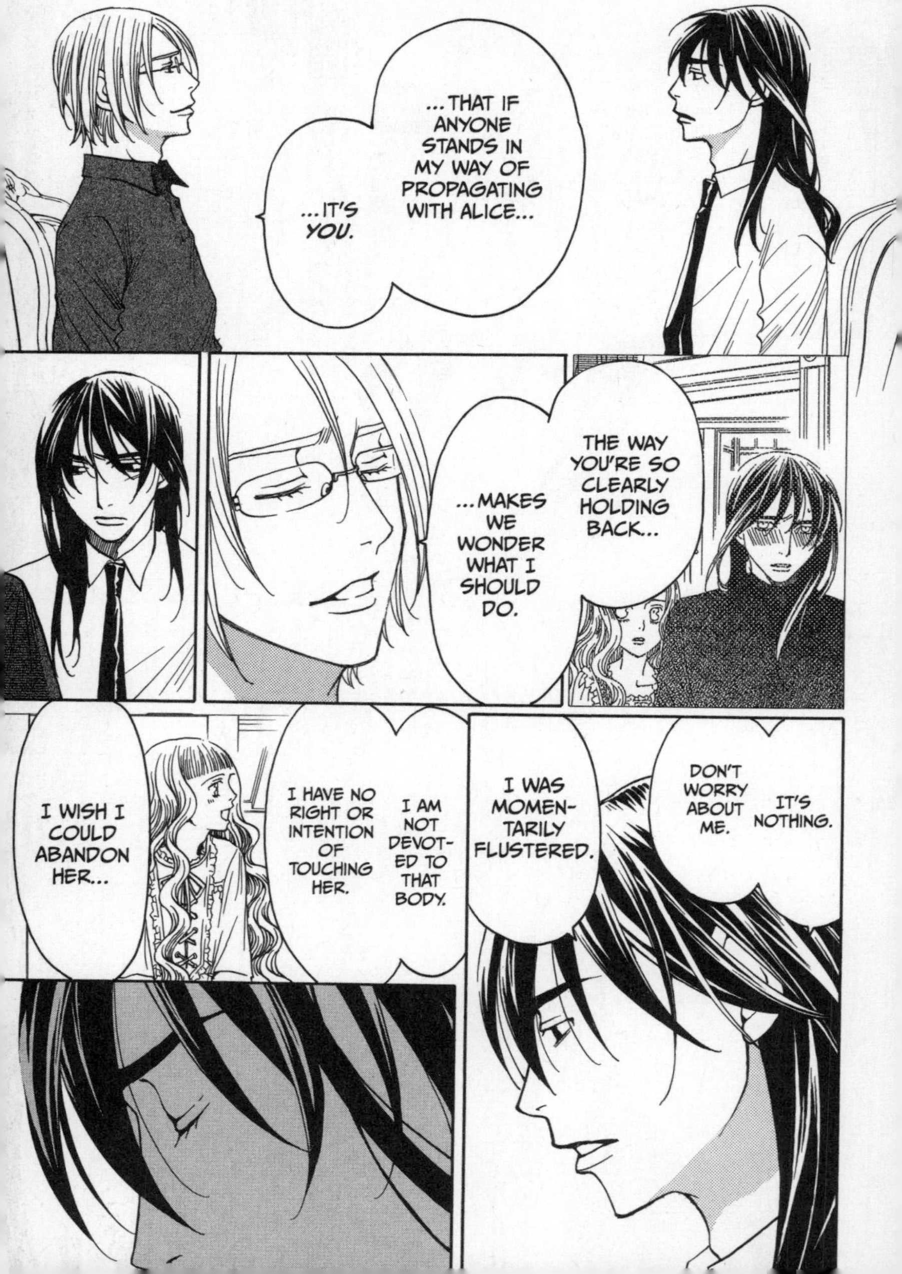
...THAT IF ANYONE STANDS IN MY WAY OF PROPAGATING WITH ALICE...
...IT'S *YOU.*
THE WAY YOU'RE SO CLEARLY HOLDING BACK...
...MAKES WE WONDER WHAT I SHOULD DO.
IT'S NOTHING.
DON'T WORRY ABOUT ME.
I WAS MOMEN-TARILY FLUSTERED.
I AM NOT DEVOT-ED TO THAT BODY.
I HAVE NO RIGHT OR INTENTION OF TOUCHING HER.
I WISH I COULD ABANDON HER...

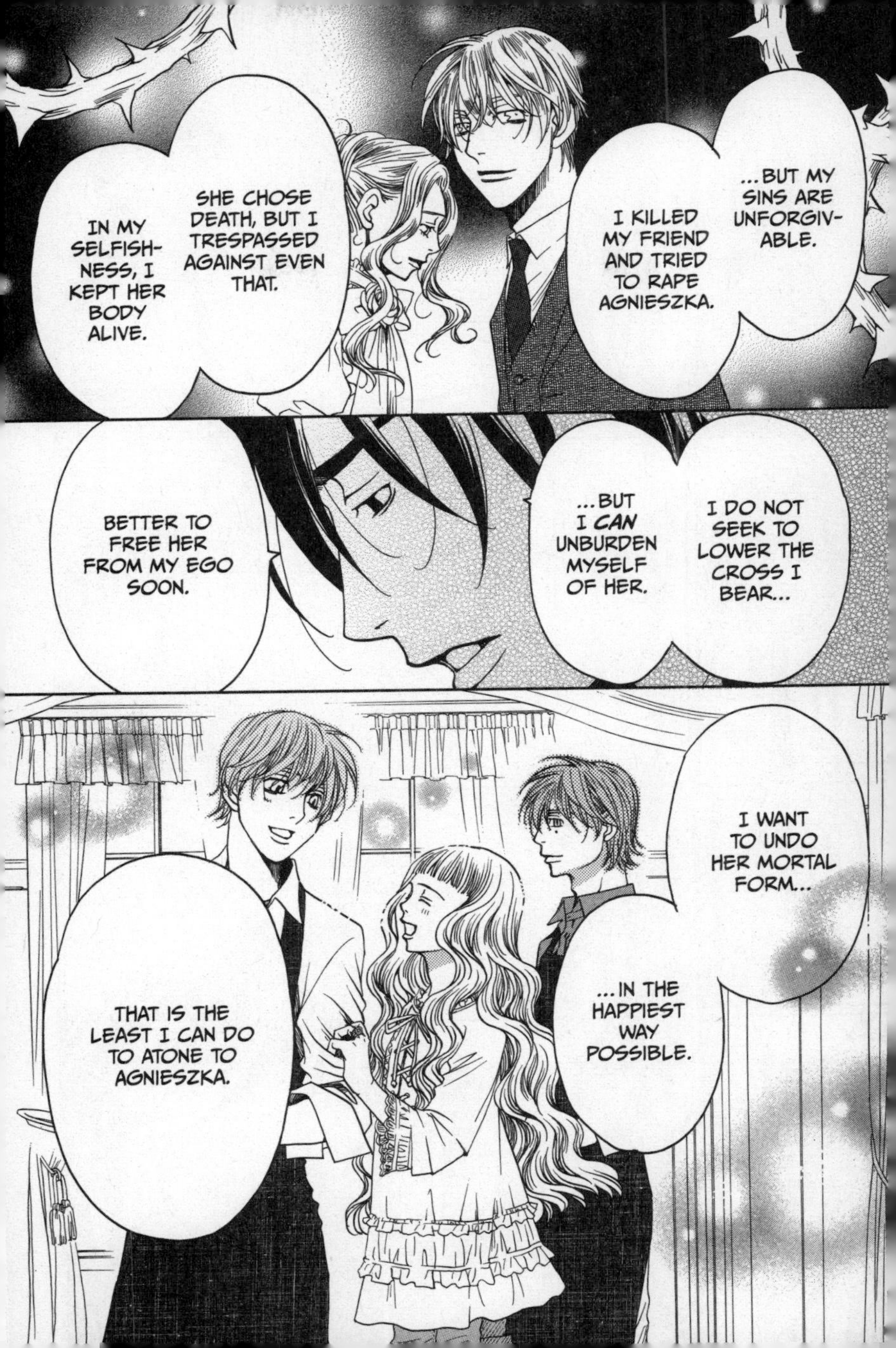
...BUT MY SINS ARE UNFORGIV-ABLE.
I KILLED MY FRIEND AND TRIED TO RAPE AGNIESZKA.
SHE CHOSE DEATH, BUT I TRESPASSED AGAINST EVEN THAT.
IN MY SELFISH-NESS, I KEPT HER BODY ALIVE.
I DO NOT SEEK TO LOWER THE CROSS I BEAR...
...BUT I *CAN* UNBURDEN MYSELF OF HER.
BETTER TO FREE HER FROM MY EGO SOON.
I WANT TO UNDO HER MORTAL FORM...
...IN THE HAPPIEST WAY POSSIBLE.
THAT IS THE LEAST I CAN DO TO ATONE TO AGNIESZKA.

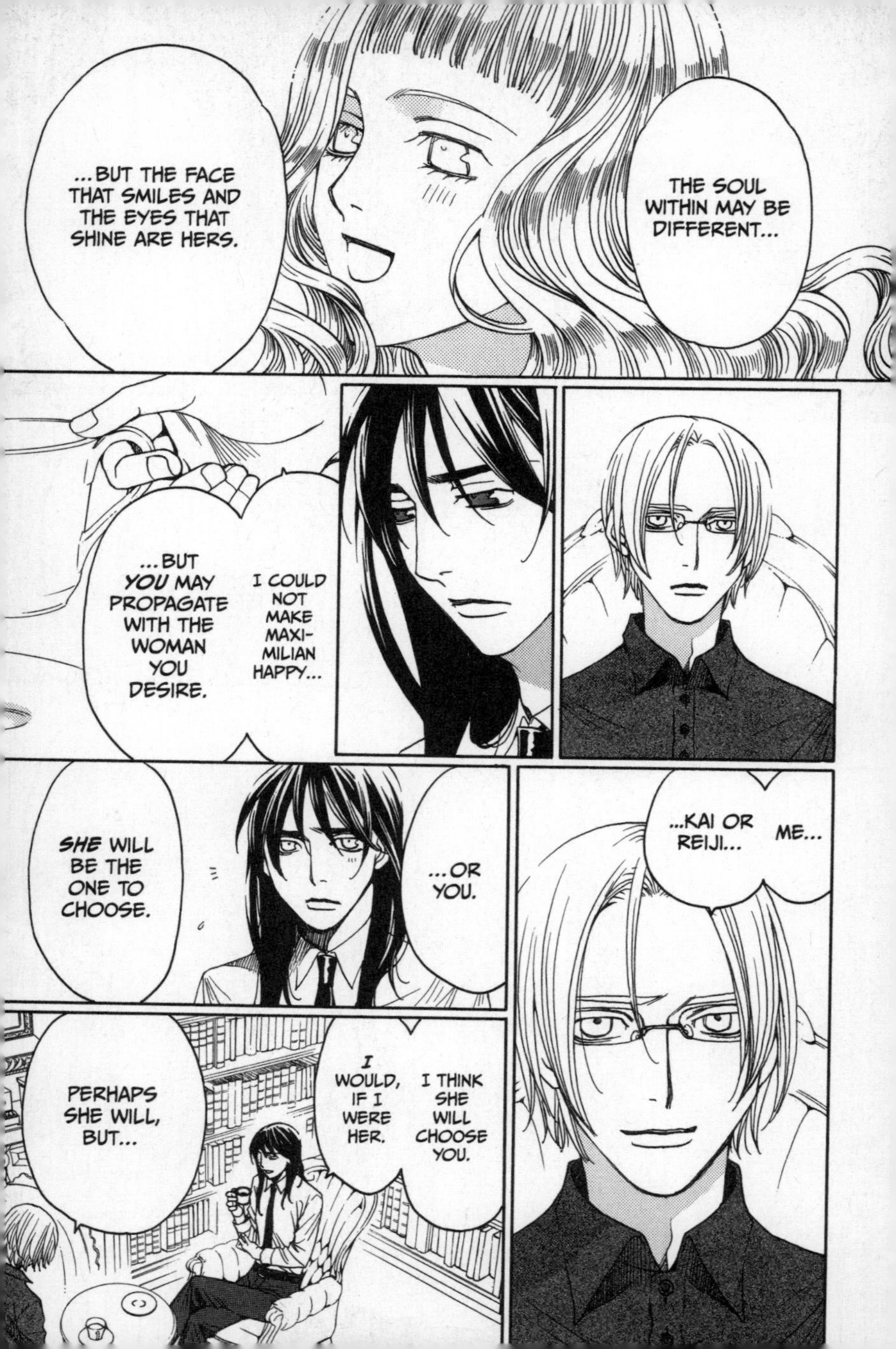
THE SOUL WITHIN MAY BE DIFFERENT...
...BUT THE FACE THAT SMILES AND THE EYES THAT SHINE ARE HERS.
I COULD NOT MAKE MAXI-MILIAN HAPPY...
...BUT *YOU* MAY PROPAGATE WITH THE WOMAN YOU DESIRE.
ME...
...KAI OR REIJI...
...OR YOU.
SHE WILL BE THE ONE TO CHOOSE.
I THINK SHE WILL CHOOSE YOU.
I WOULD, IF I WERE HER.
PERHAPS SHE WILL, BUT...

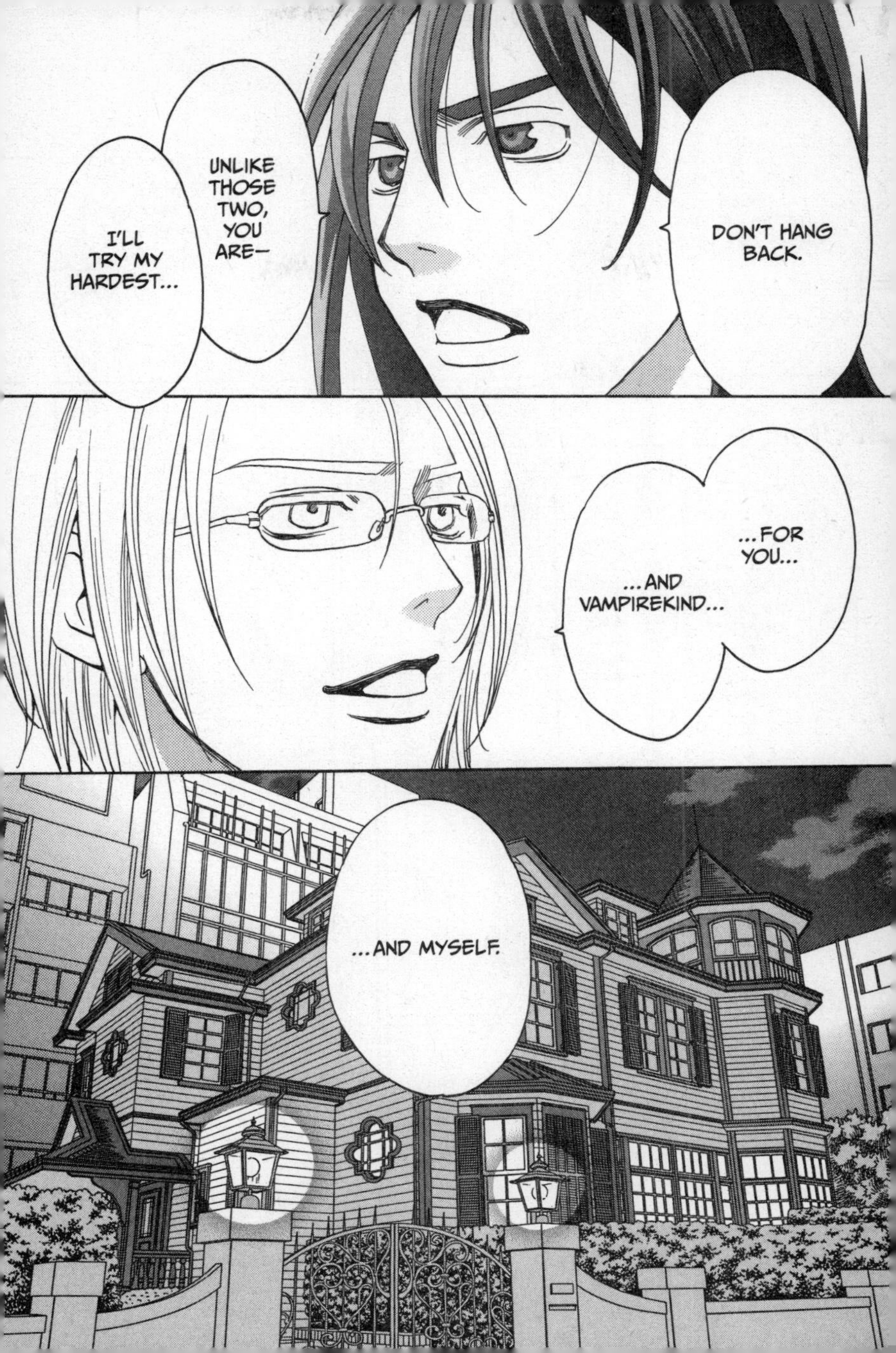
DON'T HANG BACK.
UNLIKE THOSE TWO, YOU ARE–
I'LL TRY MY HARDEST...
...FOR YOU...
...AND VAMPIREKIND...
...AND MYSELF.

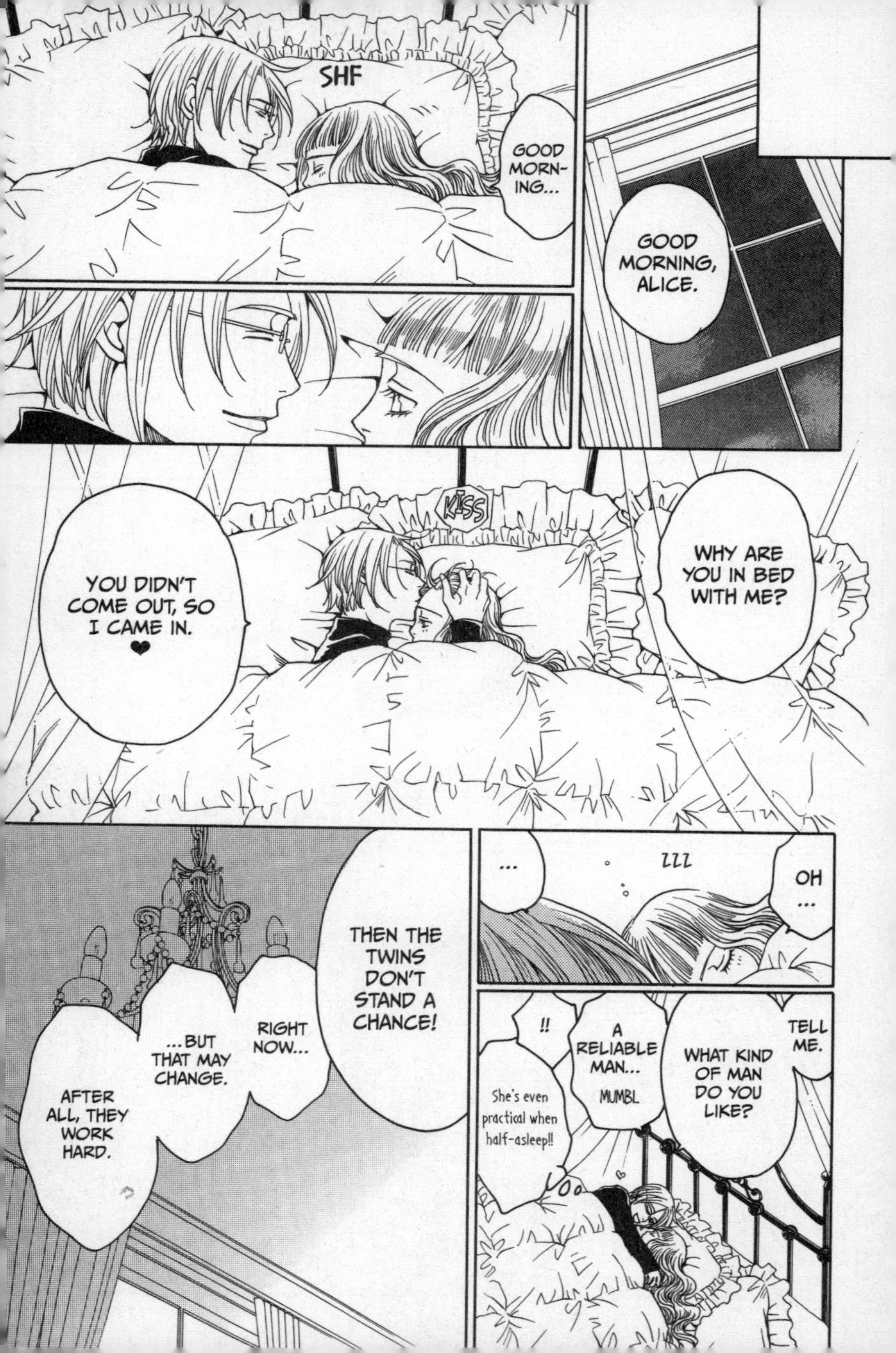
GOOD MORNING, ALICE.
SHF
GOOD MORNING...
WHY ARE YOU IN BED WITH ME?
KISS
YOU DIDN'T COME OUT, SO I CAME IN. ❤
OH ...
ZZZ
...
TELL ME.
WHAT KIND OF MAN DO YOU LIKE?
A RELIABLE MAN...
MUMBL
!!
She's even practical when half-asleep!!
THEN THE TWINS DON'T STAND A CHANCE!
RIGHT NOW...
...BUT THAT MAY CHANGE.
AFTER ALL, THEY WORK HARD.

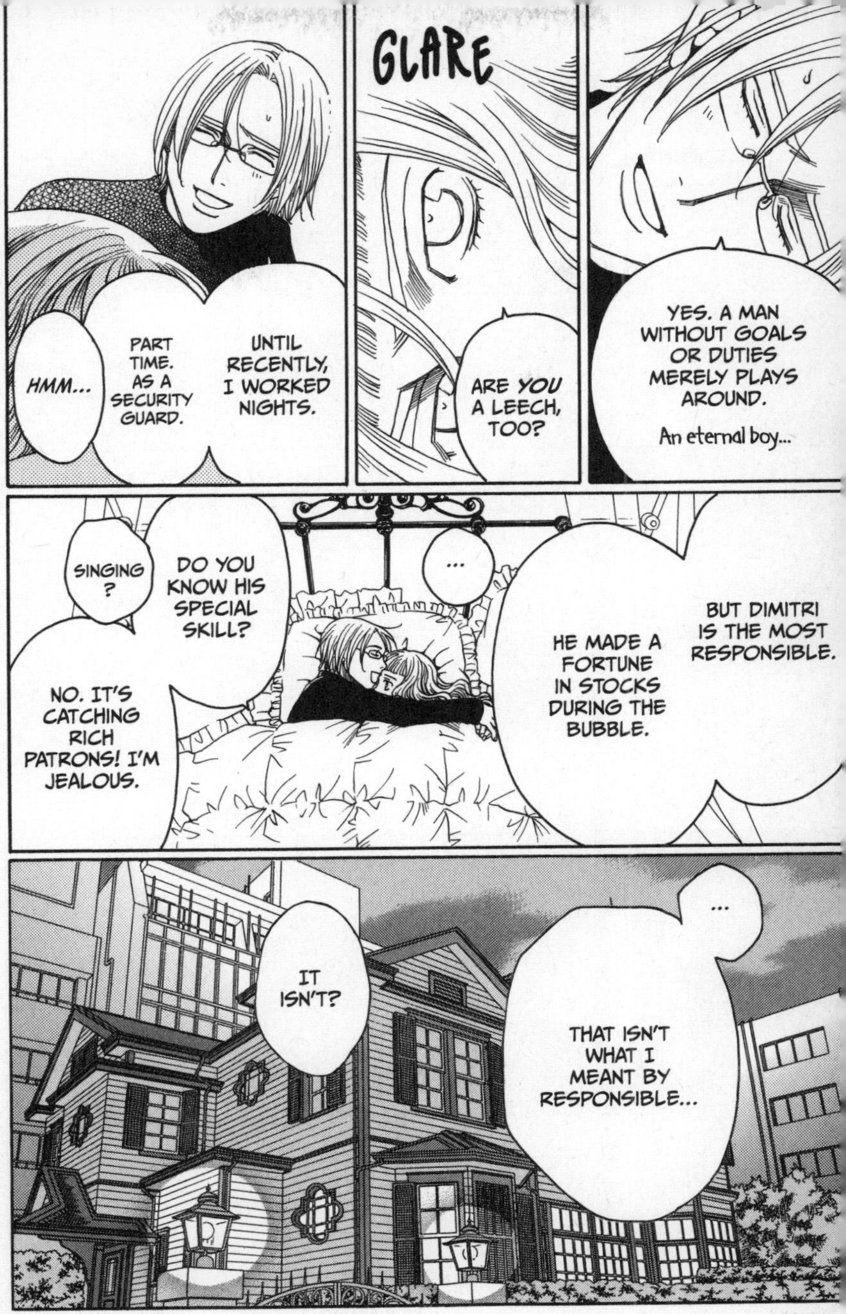
YES. A MAN WITHOUT GOALS OR DUTIES MERELY PLAYS AROUND.
An eternal boy...
GLARE
ARE *YOU* A LEECH, TOO?
UNTIL RECENTLY, I WORKED NIGHTS.
PART TIME. AS A SECURITY GUARD.
HMM...
BUT DIMITRI IS THE MOST RESPONSIBLE.
HE MADE A FORTUNE IN STOCKS DURING THE BUBBLE.
...
DO YOU KNOW HIS SPECIAL SKILL?
SINGING?
NO. IT'S CATCHING RICH PATRONS! I'M JEALOUS.
...
THAT ISN'T WHAT I MEANT BY RESPONSIBLE...
IT ISN'T?

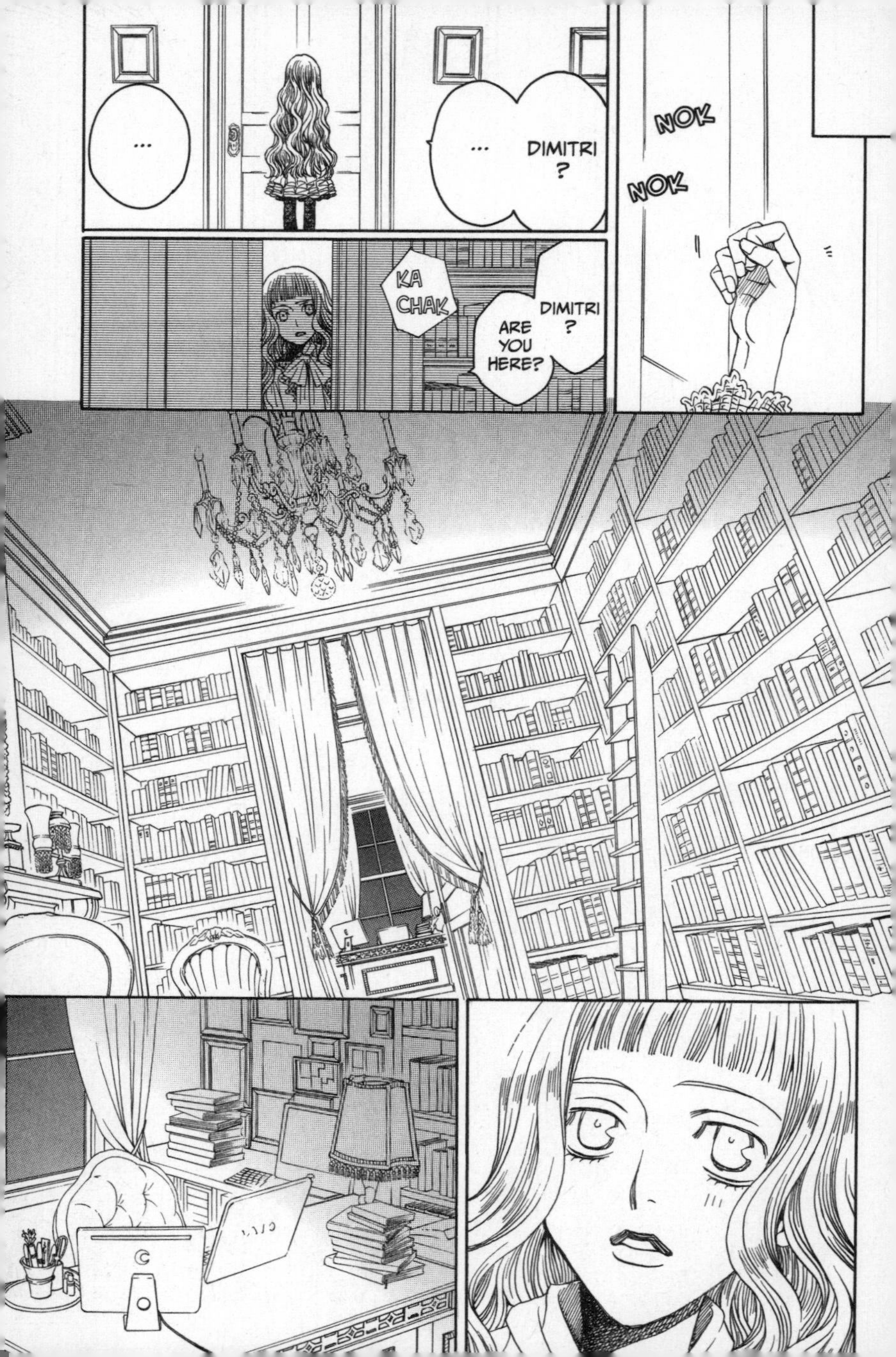
NOK
NOK
... DIMITRI ?
...
DIMITRI ?
KA CHAK
ARE YOU HERE?

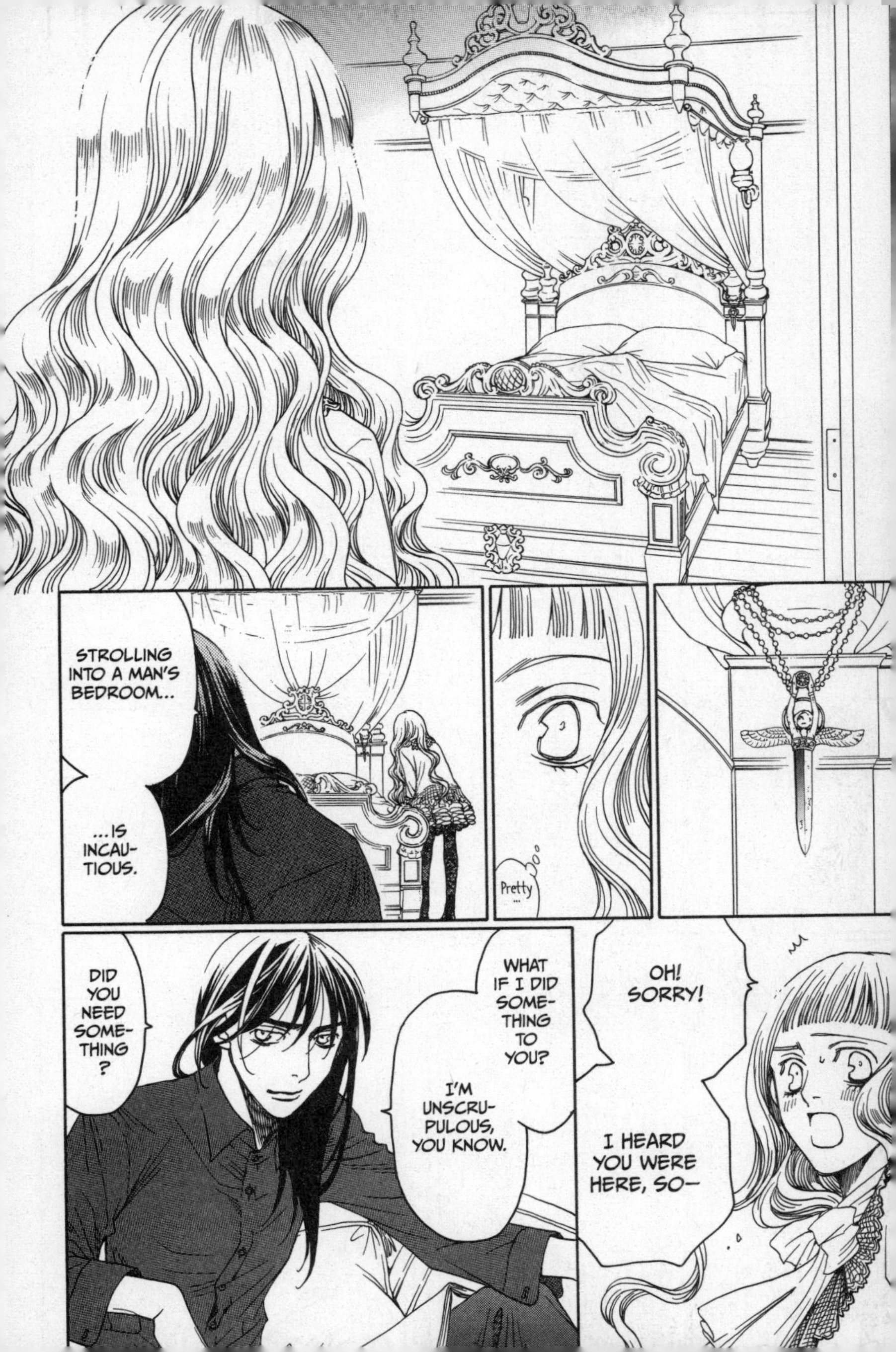
Pretty...
STROLLING INTO A MAN'S BEDROOM...
...IS INCAUTIOUS.
OH! SORRY!
I HEARD YOU WERE HERE, SO—
WHAT IF I DID SOMETHING TO YOU?
I'M UNSCRUPULOUS, YOU KNOW.
DID YOU NEED SOMETHING?

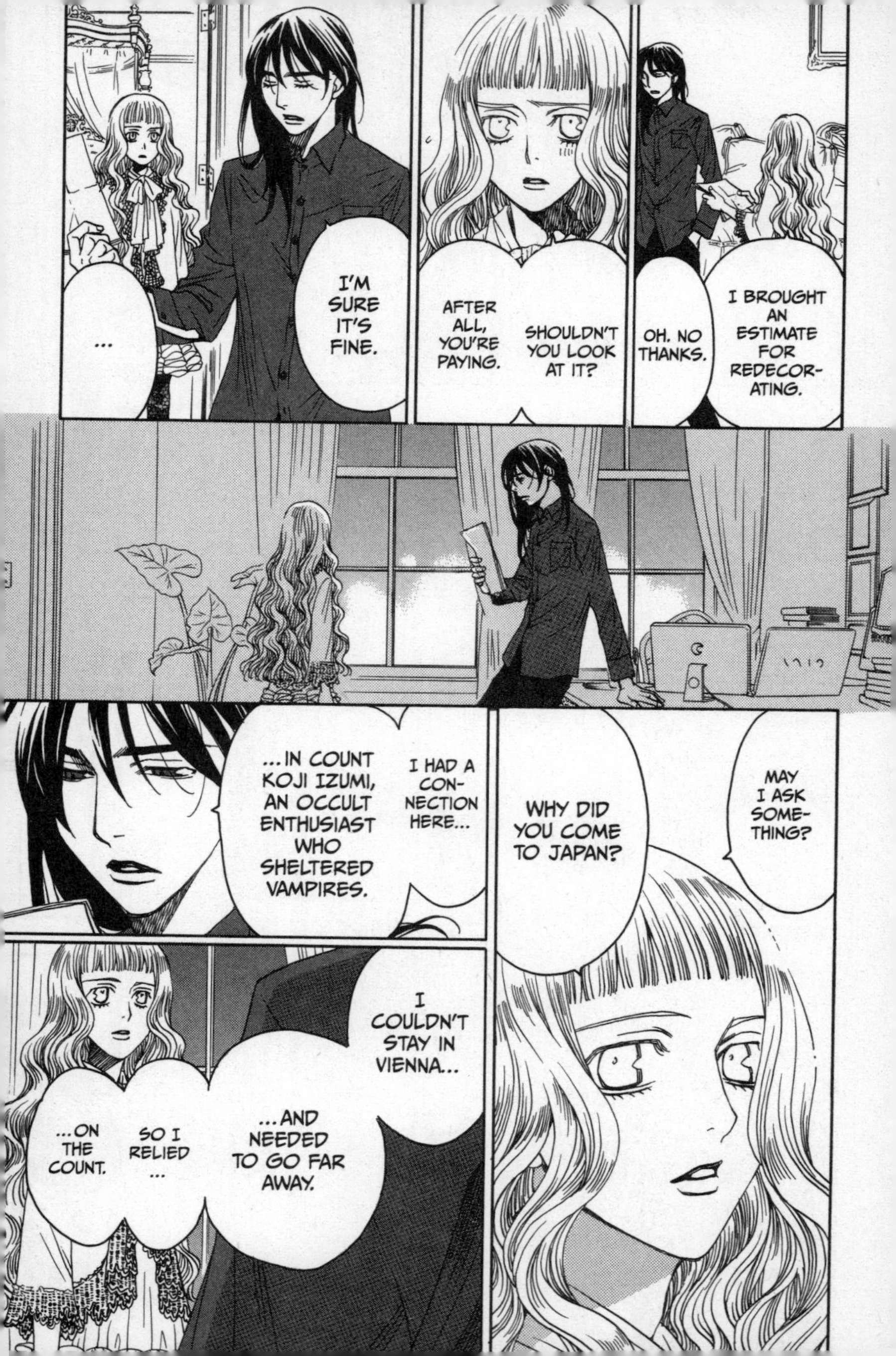
I BROUGHT AN ESTIMATE FOR REDECOR-ATING.
OH. NO THANKS.
SHOULDN'T YOU LOOK AT IT?
AFTER ALL, YOU'RE PAYING.
I'M SURE IT'S FINE.
...
MAY I ASK SOME-THING?
WHY DID YOU COME TO JAPAN?
I HAD A CON-NECTION HERE...
...IN COUNT KOJI IZUMI, AN OCCULT ENTHUSIAST WHO SHELTERED VAMPIRES.
I COULDN'T STAY IN VIENNA...
...AND NEEDED TO GO FAR AWAY.
SO I RELIED...
...ON THE COUNT.

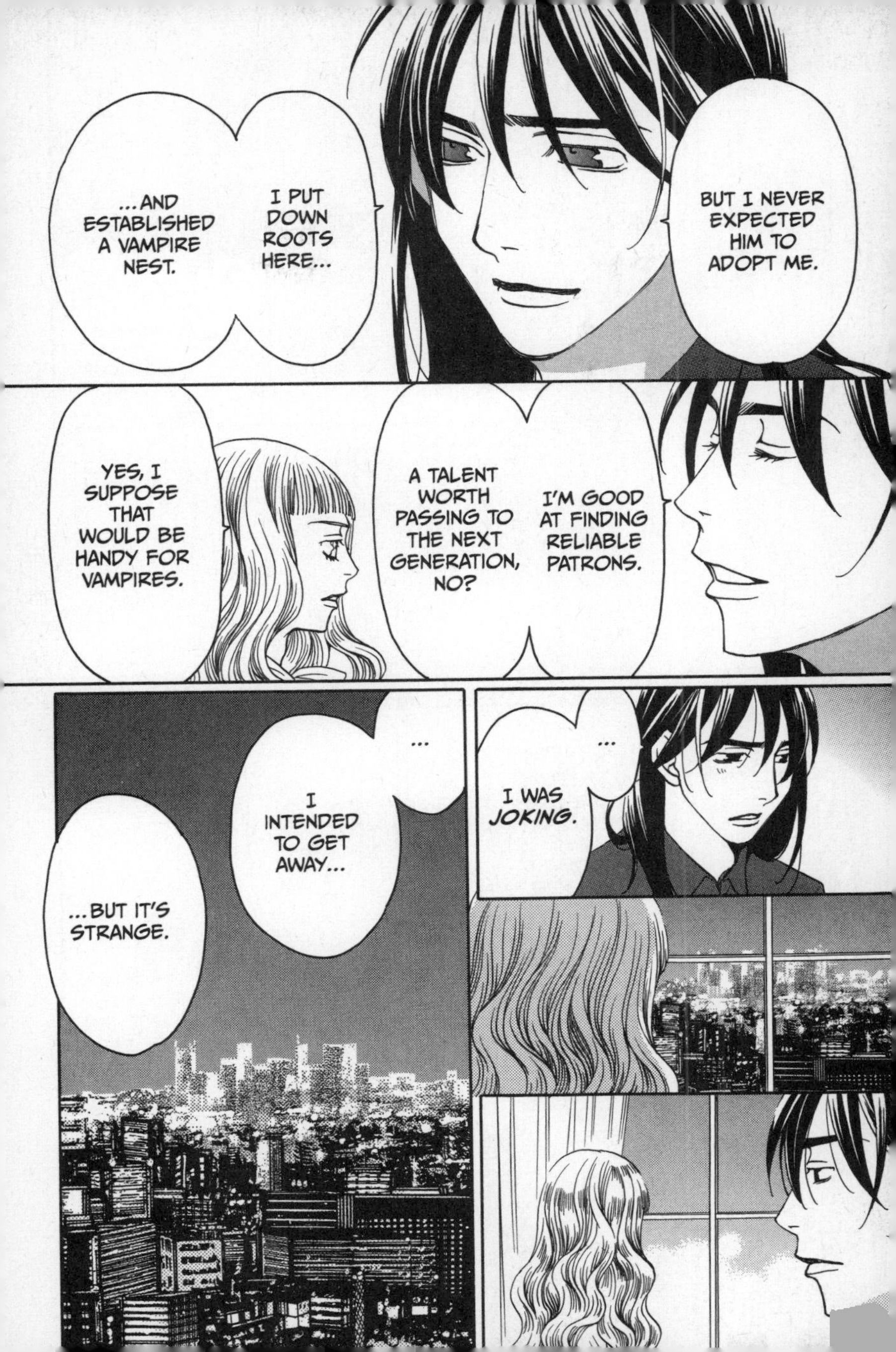
BUT I NEVER EXPECTED HIM TO ADOPT ME.
I PUT DOWN ROOTS HERE...
...AND ESTABLISHED A VAMPIRE NEST.
I'M GOOD AT FINDING RELIABLE PATRONS.
A TALENT WORTH PASSING TO THE NEXT GENERATION, NO?
YES, I SUPPOSE THAT WOULD BE HANDY FOR VAMPIRES.
... I WAS *JOKING.*
... I INTENDED TO GET AWAY...
...BUT IT'S STRANGE.

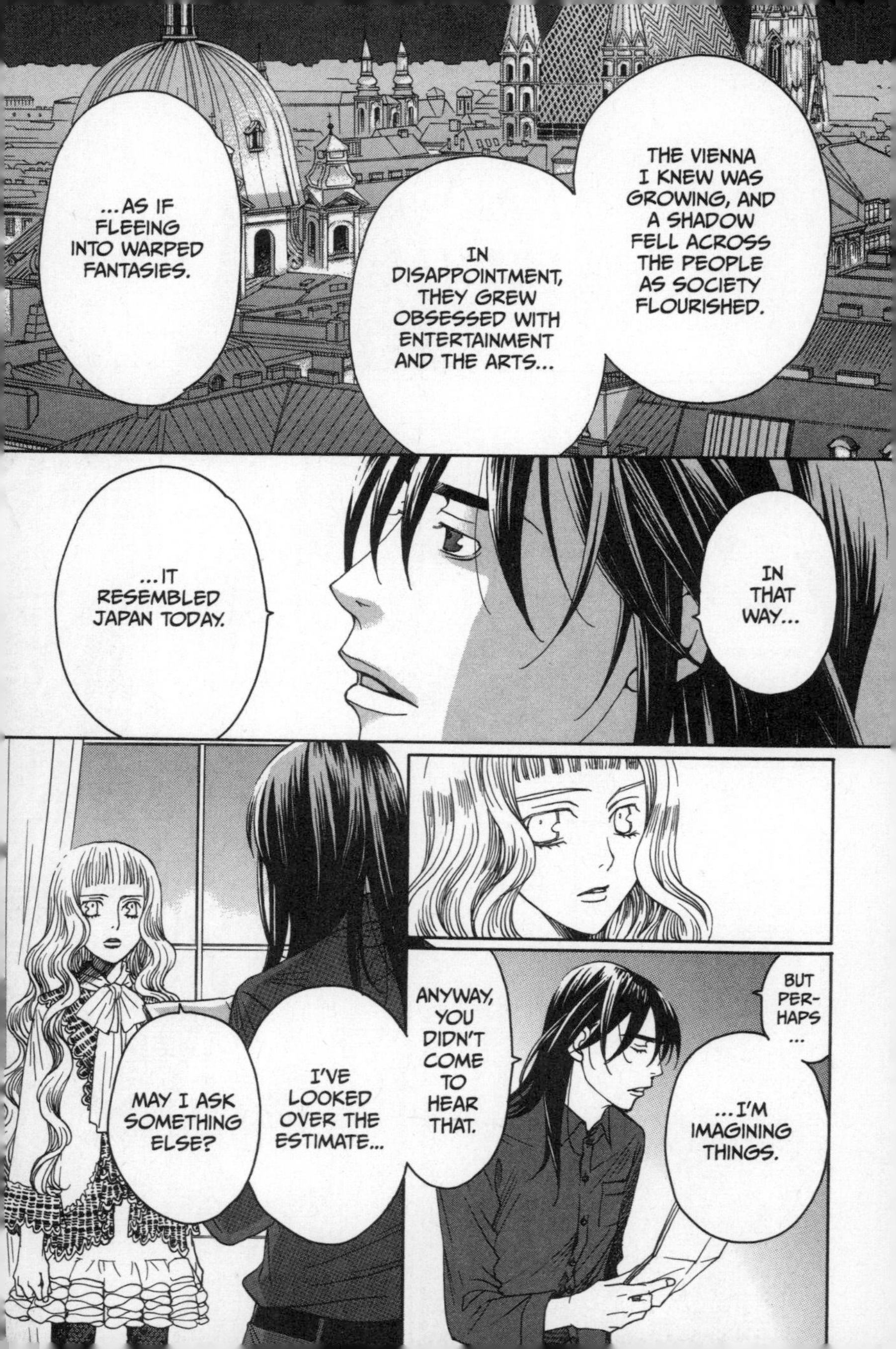
THE VIENNA I KNEW WAS GROWING, AND A SHADOW FELL ACROSS THE PEOPLE AS SOCIETY FLOURISHED.
IN DISAPPOINTMENT, THEY GREW OBSESSED WITH ENTERTAINMENT AND THE ARTS...
...AS IF FLEEING INTO WARPED FANTASIES.
IN THAT WAY...
...IT RESEMBLED JAPAN TODAY.
BUT PER-HAPS ...
...I'M IMAGINING THINGS.
ANYWAY, YOU DIDN'T COME TO HEAR THAT.
I'VE LOOKED OVER THE ESTIMATE...
MAY I ASK SOMETHING ELSE?

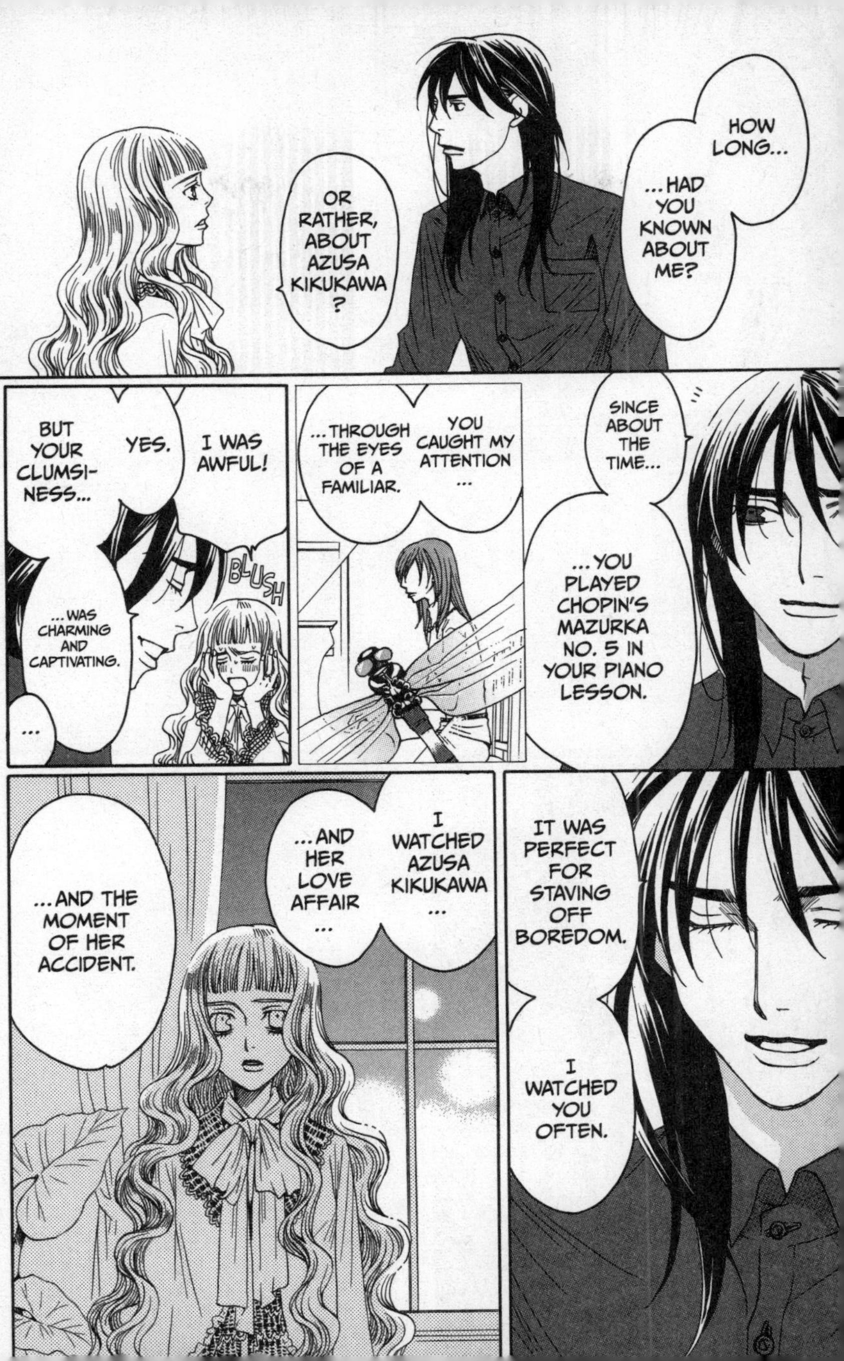
HOW LONG...
...HAD YOU KNOWN ABOUT ME?
OR RATHER, ABOUT AZUSA KIKUKAWA?
SINCE ABOUT THE TIME...
...YOU PLAYED CHOPIN'S MAZURKA NO. 5 IN YOUR PIANO LESSON.
YOU CAUGHT MY ATTENTION...
...THROUGH THE EYES OF A FAMILIAR.
I WAS AWFUL!
BLUSH
YES.
BUT YOUR CLUMSI-NESS...
...WAS CHARMING AND CAPTIVATING.
...
IT WAS PERFECT FOR STAVING OFF BOREDOM.
I WATCHED YOU OFTEN.
I WATCHED AZUSA KIKUKAWA...
...AND HER LOVE AFFAIR...
...AND THE MOMENT OF HER ACCIDENT.

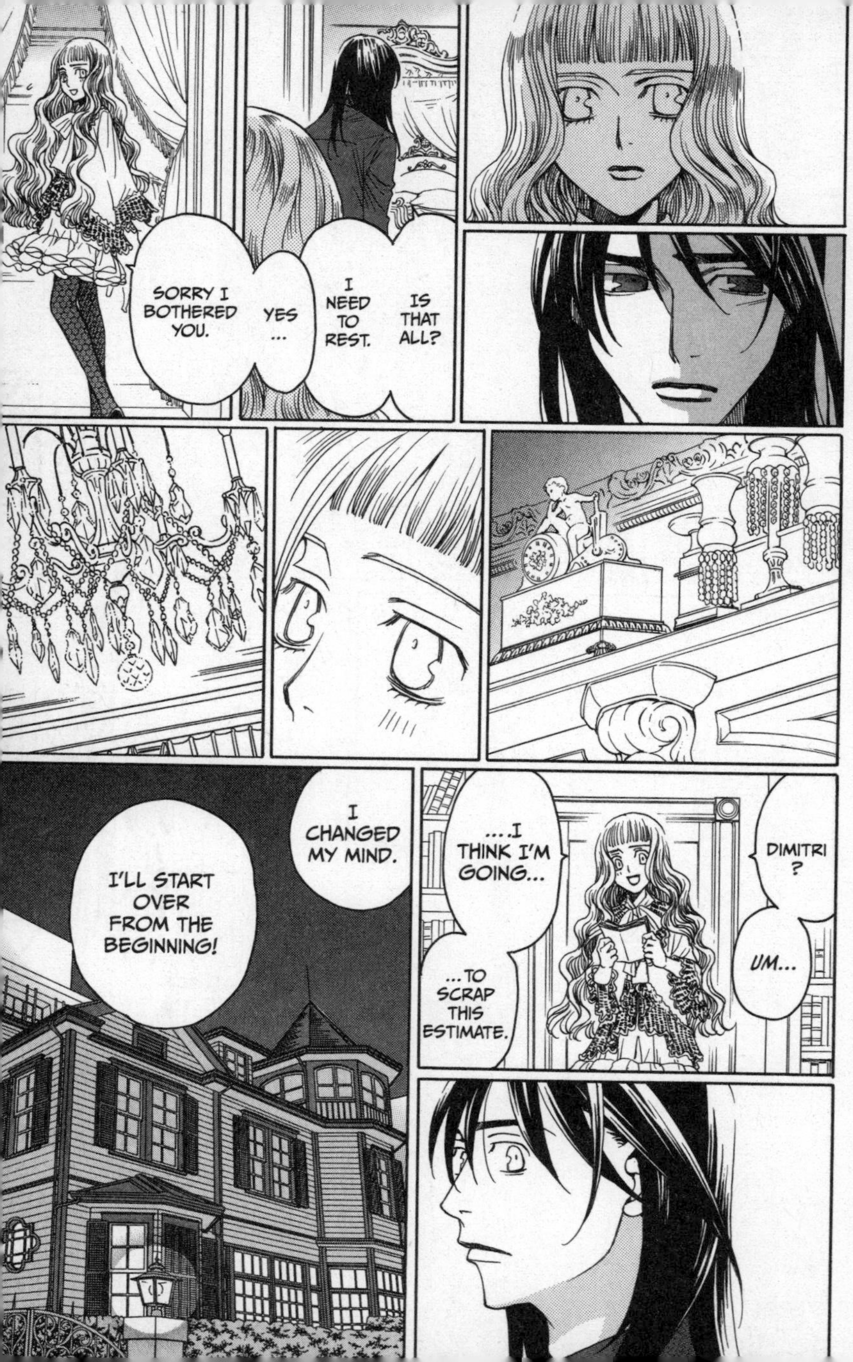
IS THAT ALL?
I NEED TO REST.
YES ...
SORRY I BOTHERED YOU.
DIMITRI?
UM...
....I THINK I'M GOING...
...TO SCRAP THIS ESTIMATE.
I CHANGED MY MIND.
I'LL START OVER FROM THE BEGINNING!

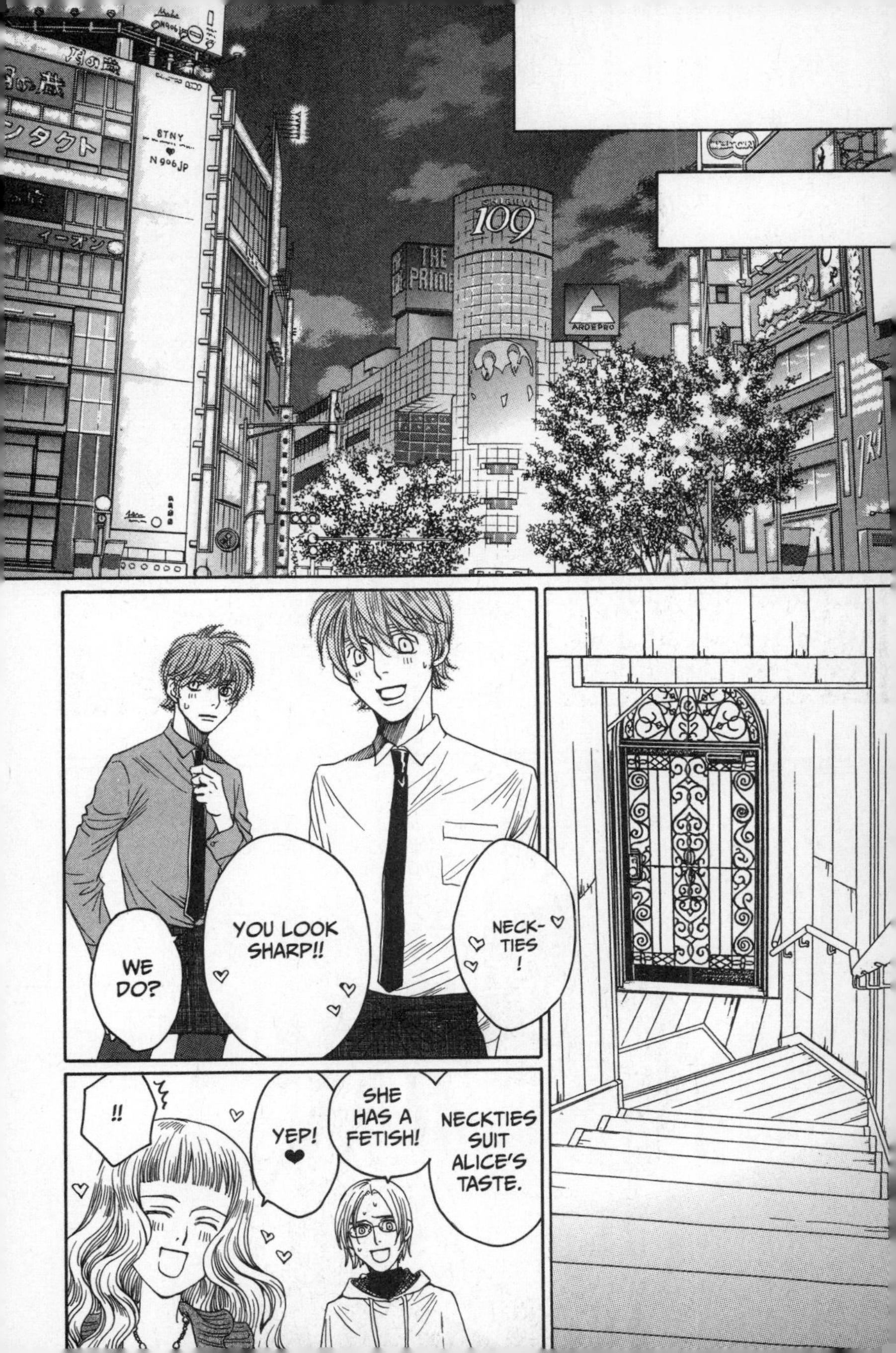
NECK-TIES!
YOU LOOK SHARP!!
WE DO?
NECKTIES SUIT ALICE'S TASTE.
SHE HAS A FETISH!
YEP!
!!

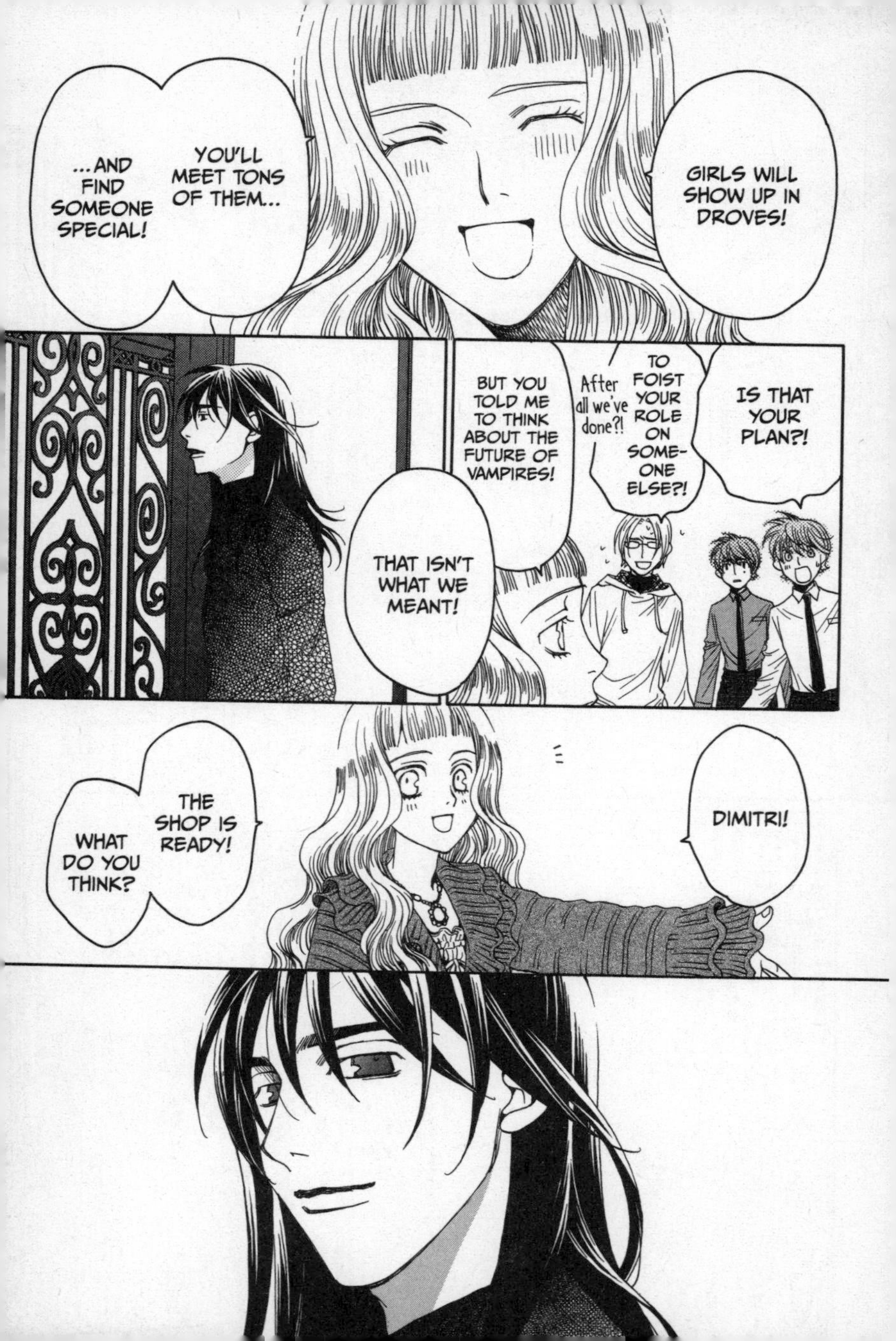
GIRLS WILL SHOW UP IN DROVES!
YOU'LL MEET TONS OF THEM...
...AND FIND SOMEONE SPECIAL!
IS THAT YOUR PLAN?!
TO FOIST YOUR ROLE ON SOME-ONE ELSE?!
After all we've done?!
BUT YOU TOLD ME TO THINK ABOUT THE FUTURE OF VAMPIRES!
THAT ISN'T WHAT WE MEANT!
DIMITRI!
THE SHOP IS READY!
WHAT DO YOU THINK?

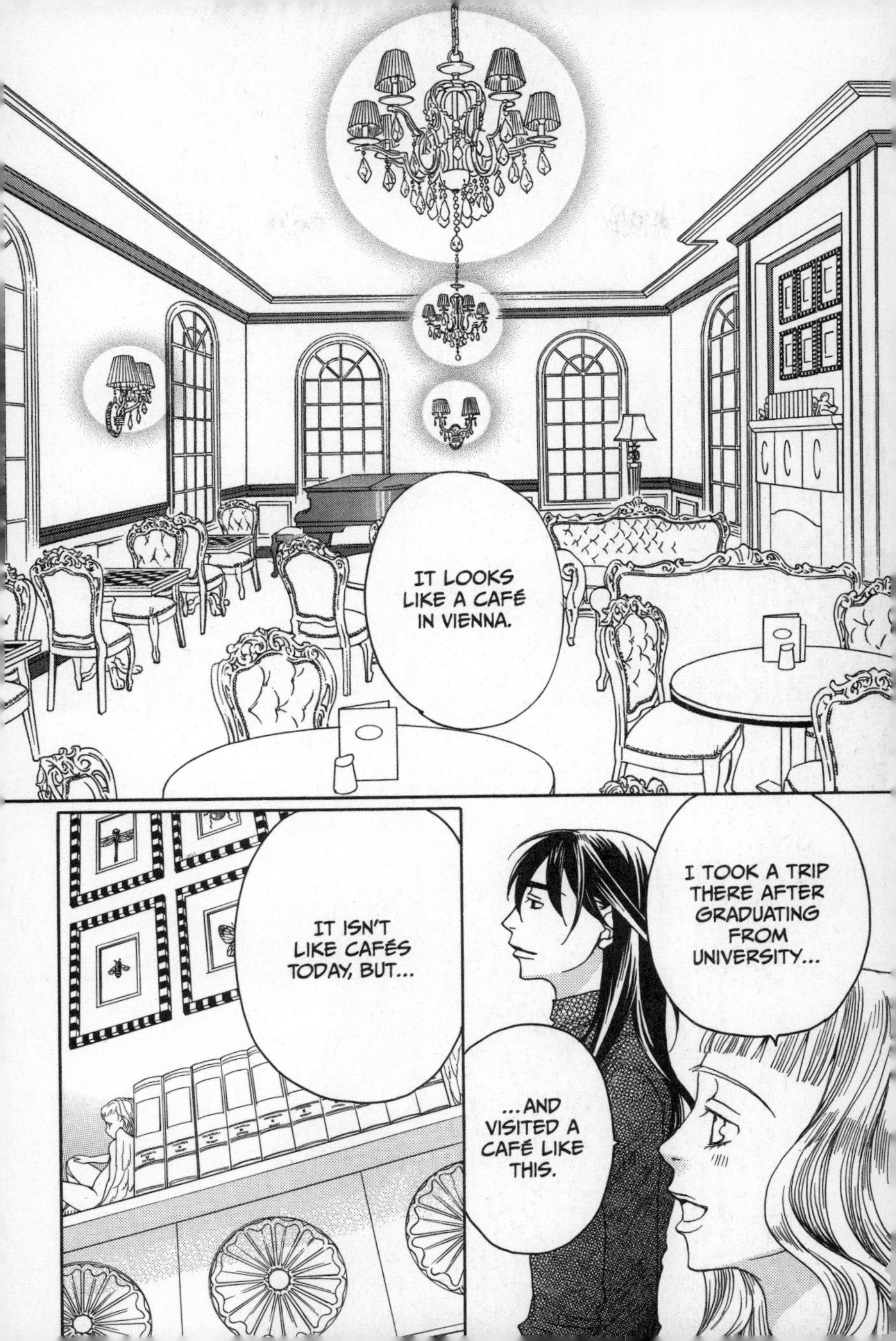
IT LOOKS LIKE A CAFÉ IN VIENNA.
I TOOK A TRIP THERE AFTER GRADUATING FROM UNIVERSITY...
...AND VISITED A CAFÉ LIKE THIS.
IT ISN'T LIKE CAFÉS TODAY, BUT...

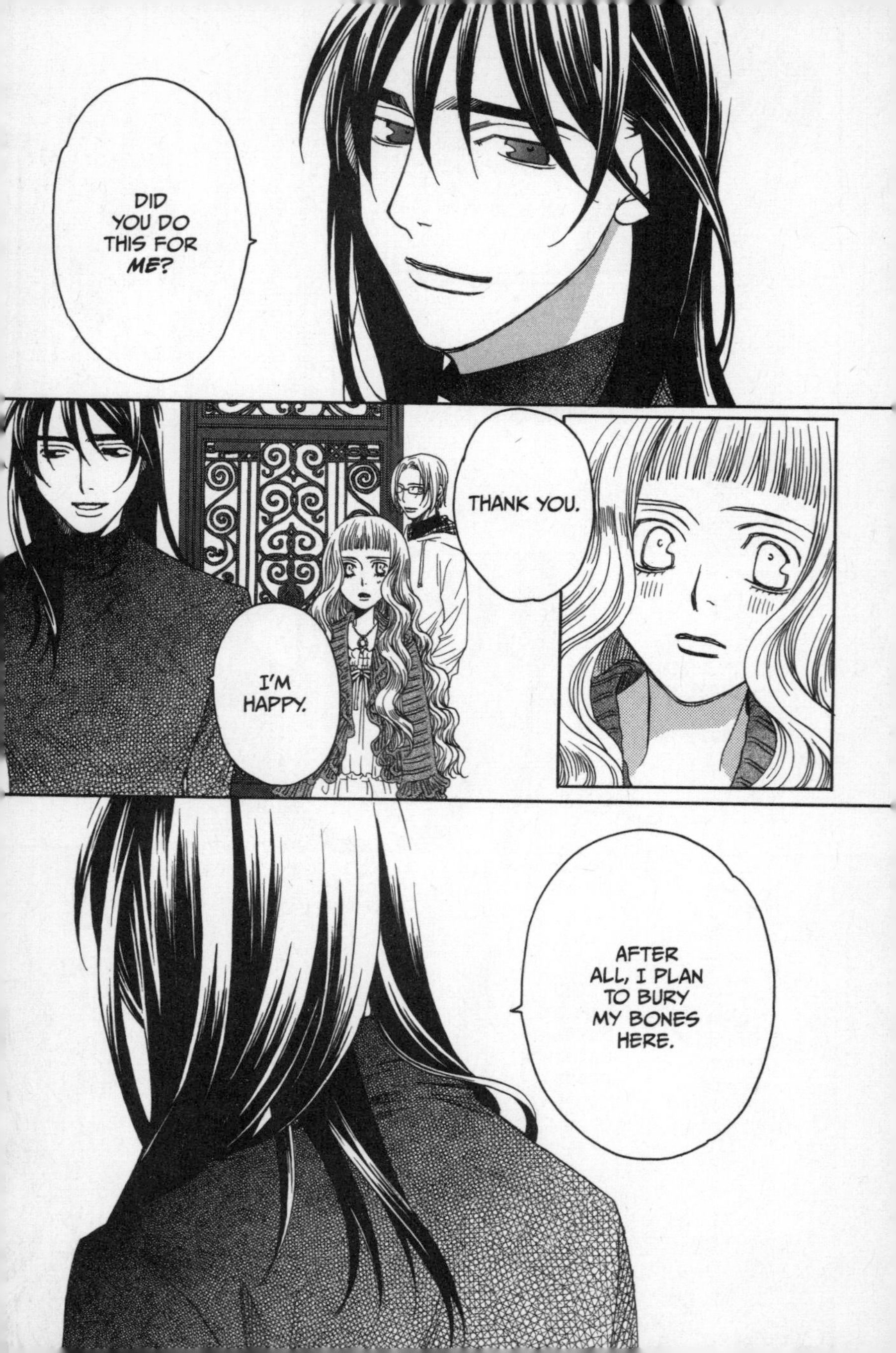
DID YOU DO THIS FOR ME?
THANK YOU.
I'M HAPPY.
AFTER ALL, I PLAN TO BURY MY BONES HERE.

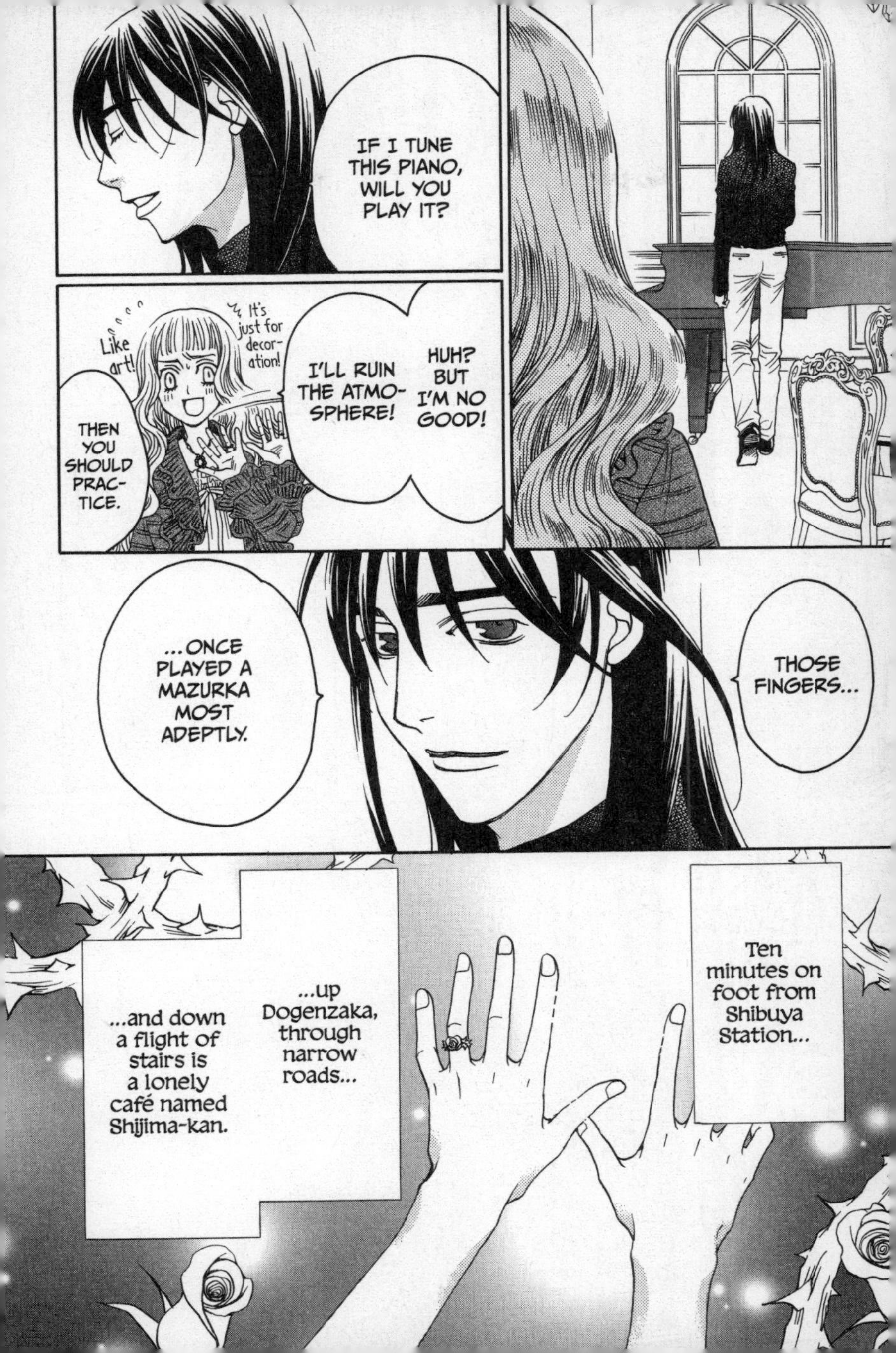
IF I TUNE THIS PIANO, WILL YOU PLAY IT?
HUH? BUT I'M NO GOOD!
I'LL RUIN THE ATMOSPHERE!
It's just for decoration!
Like art!
THEN YOU SHOULD PRACTICE.
THOSE FINGERS...
...ONCE PLAYED A MAZURKA MOST ADEPTLY.
Ten minutes on foot from Shibuya Station...
...up Dogenzaka, through narrow roads...
...and down a flight of stairs is a lonely café named Shijima-kan.

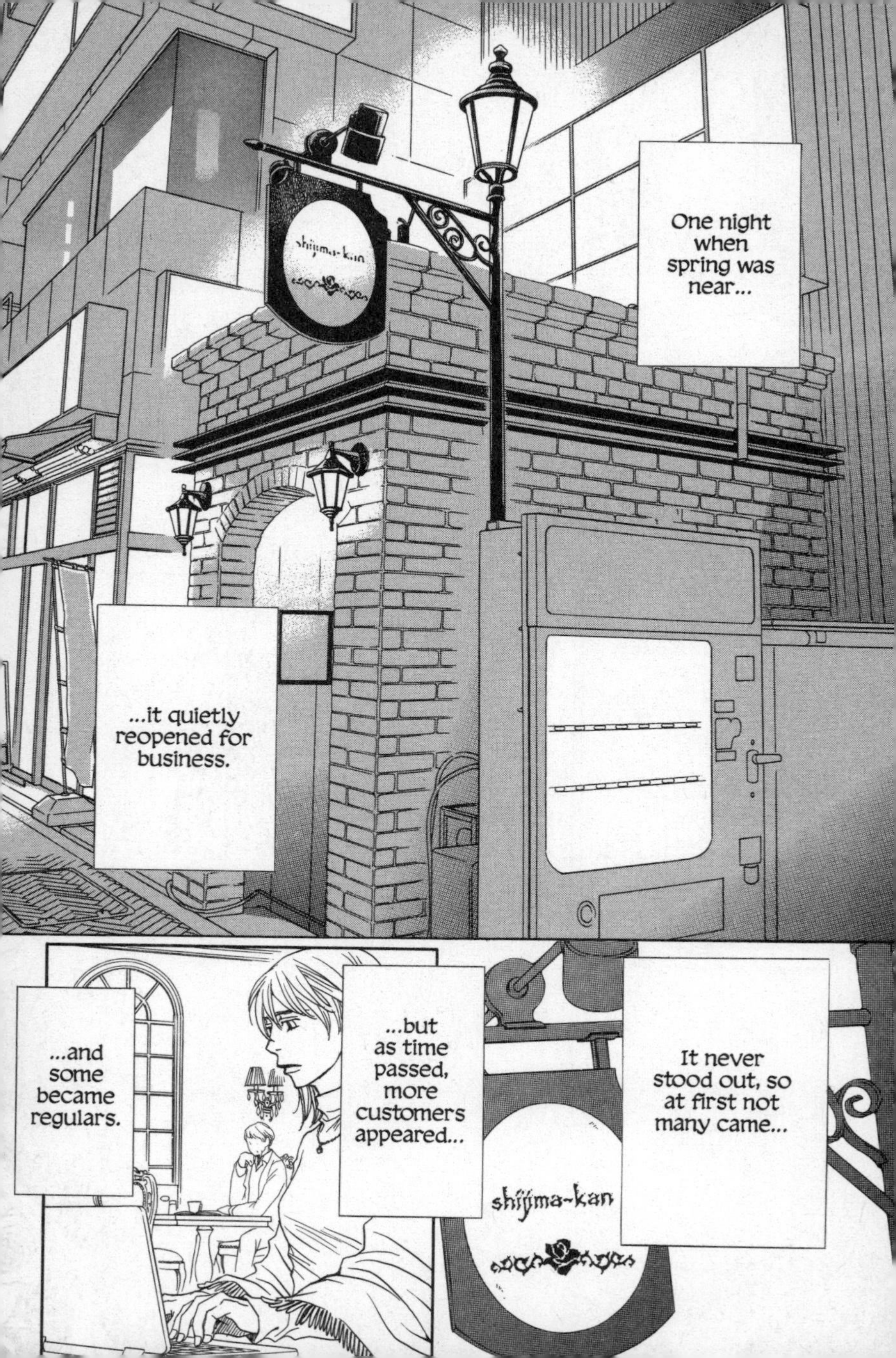
shijima-kan
One night when spring was near...
...it quietly reopened for business.
It never stood out, so at first not many came...
shijima-kan
...but as time passed, more customers appeared...
...and some became regulars.

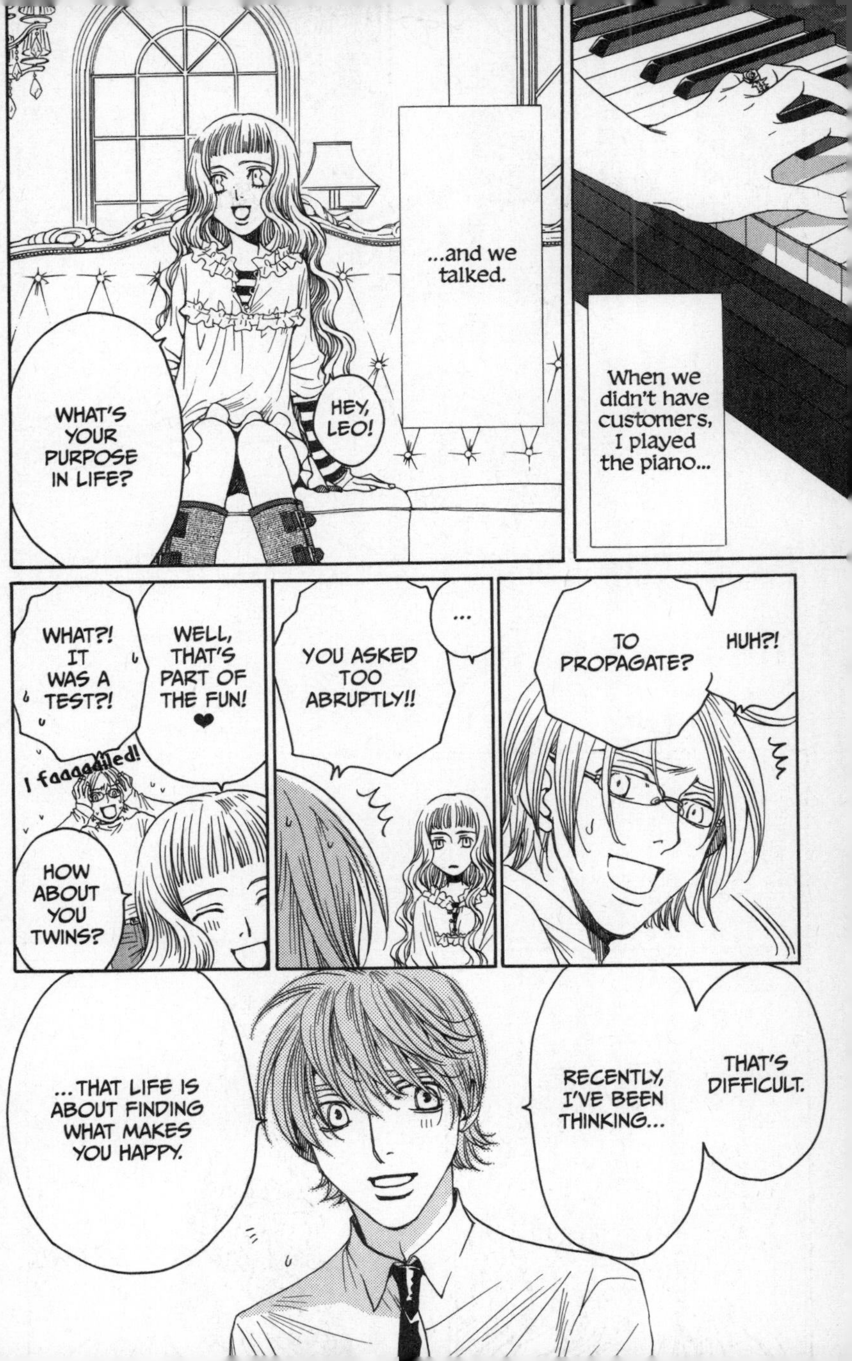
When we didn't have customers, I played the piano...
...and we talked.
HEY, LEO!
WHAT'S YOUR PURPOSE IN LIFE?
HUH?!
TO PROPAGATE?
...
YOU ASKED TOO ABRUPTLY!!
WELL, THAT'S PART OF THE FUN!
WHAT?! IT WAS A TEST?!
I faaaailed!
HOW ABOUT YOU TWINS?
THAT'S DIFFICULT.
RECENTLY, I'VE BEEN THINKING...
...THAT LIFE IS ABOUT FINDING WHAT MAKES YOU HAPPY.

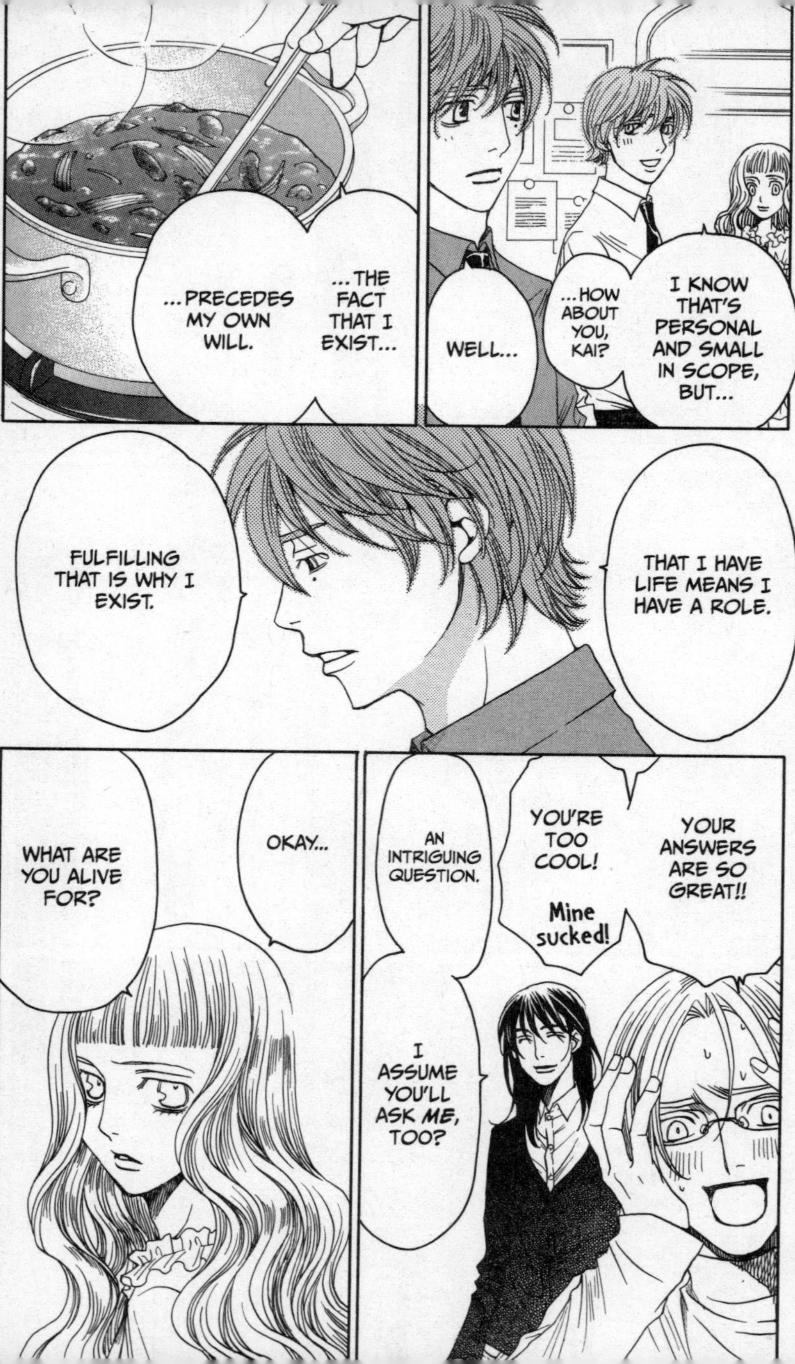
I KNOW THAT'S PERSONAL AND SMALL IN SCOPE, BUT...
...HOW ABOUT YOU, KAI?
WELL...
...THE FACT THAT I EXIST...
...PRECEDES MY OWN WILL.
THAT I HAVE LIFE MEANS I HAVE A ROLE.
FULFILLING THAT IS WHY I EXIST.
YOUR ANSWERS ARE SO GREAT!!
YOU'RE TOO COOL!
Mine sucked!
AN INTRIGUING QUESTION.
I ASSUME YOU'LL ASK *ME*, TOO?
OKAY...
WHAT ARE YOU ALIVE FOR?

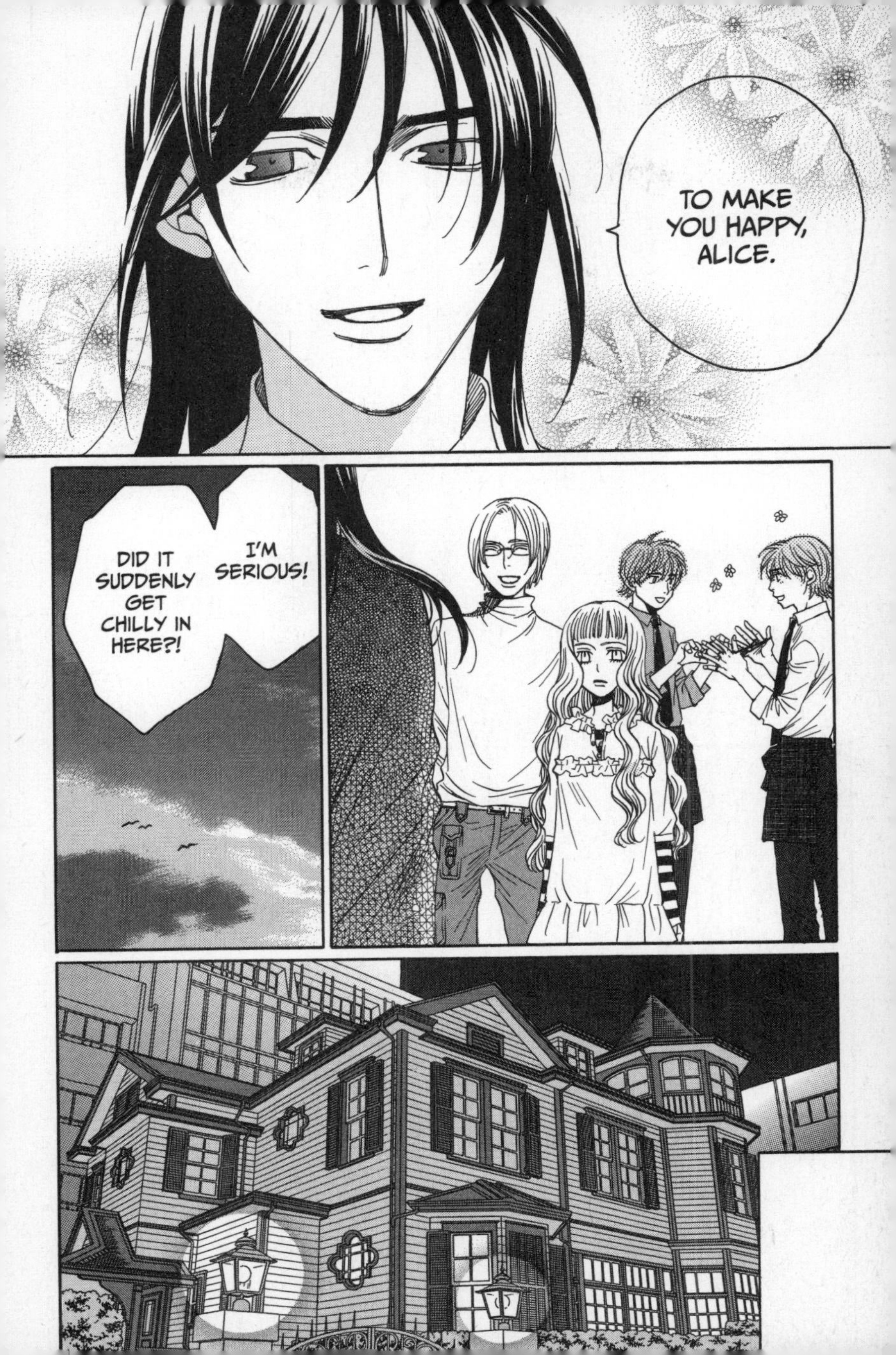
TO MAKE YOU HAPPY, ALICE.
I'M SERIOUS!
DID IT SUDDENLY GET CHILLY IN HERE?!

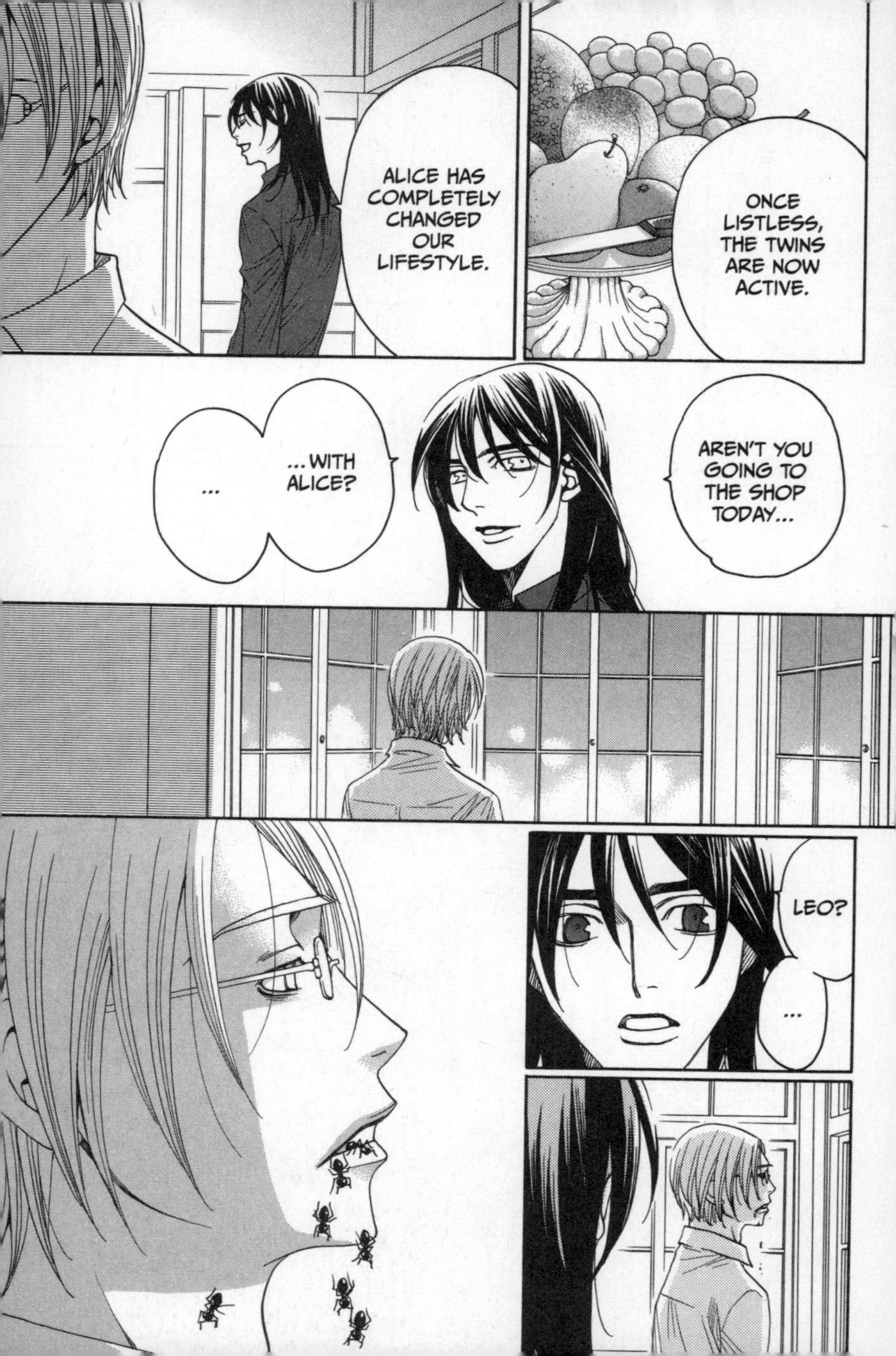
ONCE LISTLESS, THE TWINS ARE NOW ACTIVE.
ALICE HAS COMPLETELY CHANGED OUR LIFESTYLE.
AREN'T YOU GOING TO THE SHOP TODAY...
...WITH ALICE?
...
LEO?
...

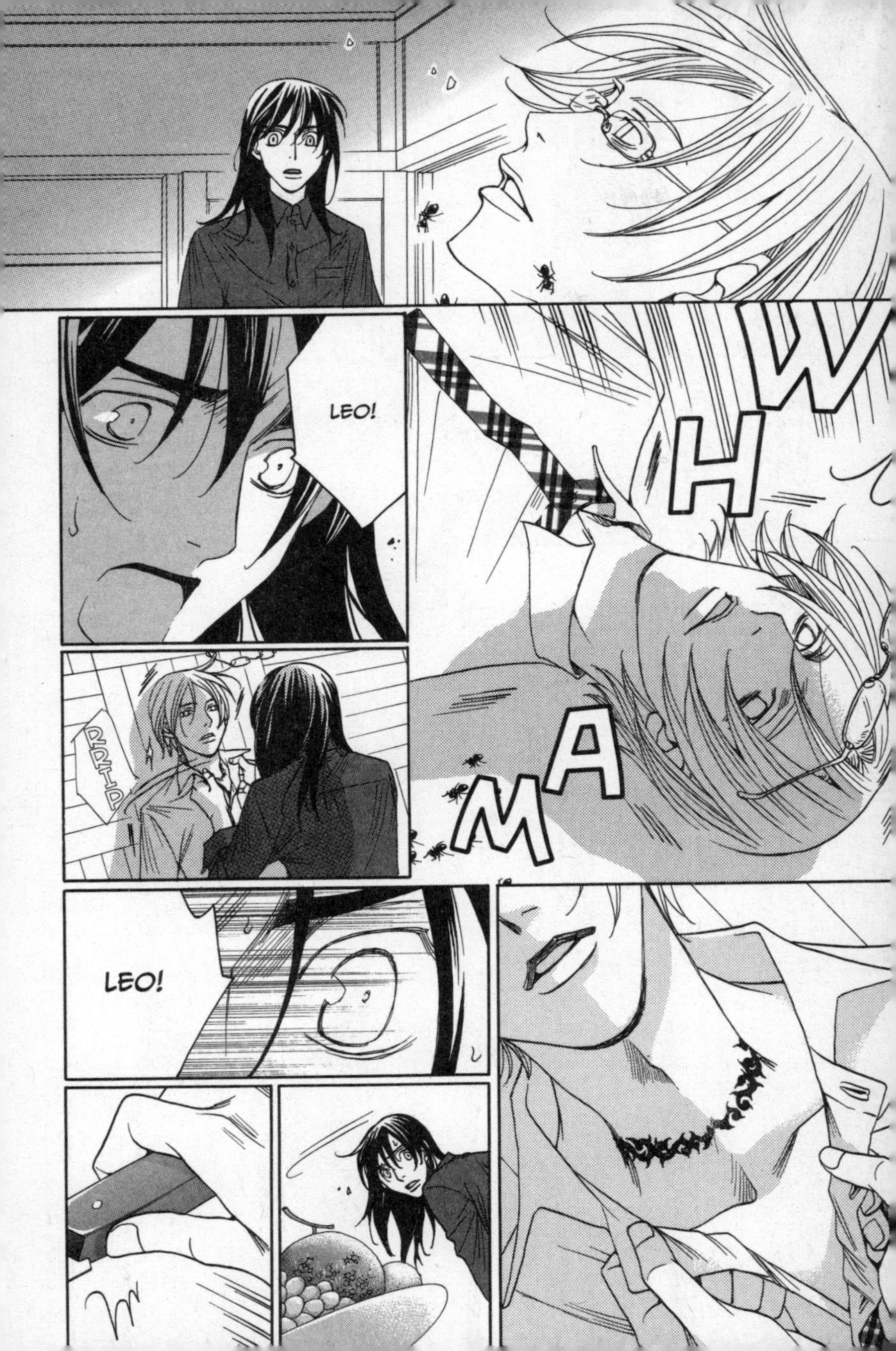
WHAM
LEO!
RRIP
LEO!

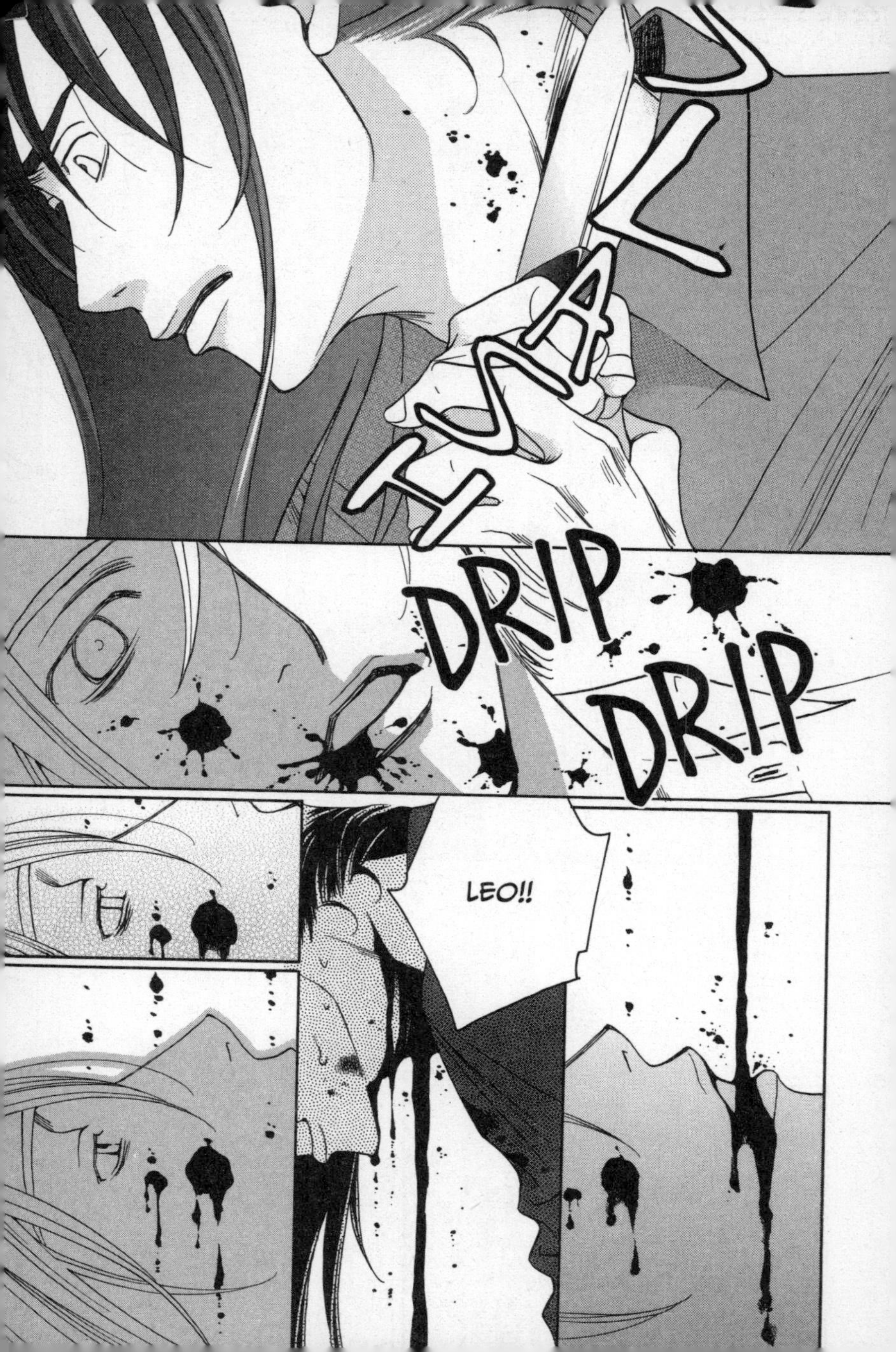
DRIP
DRIP
LEO!!

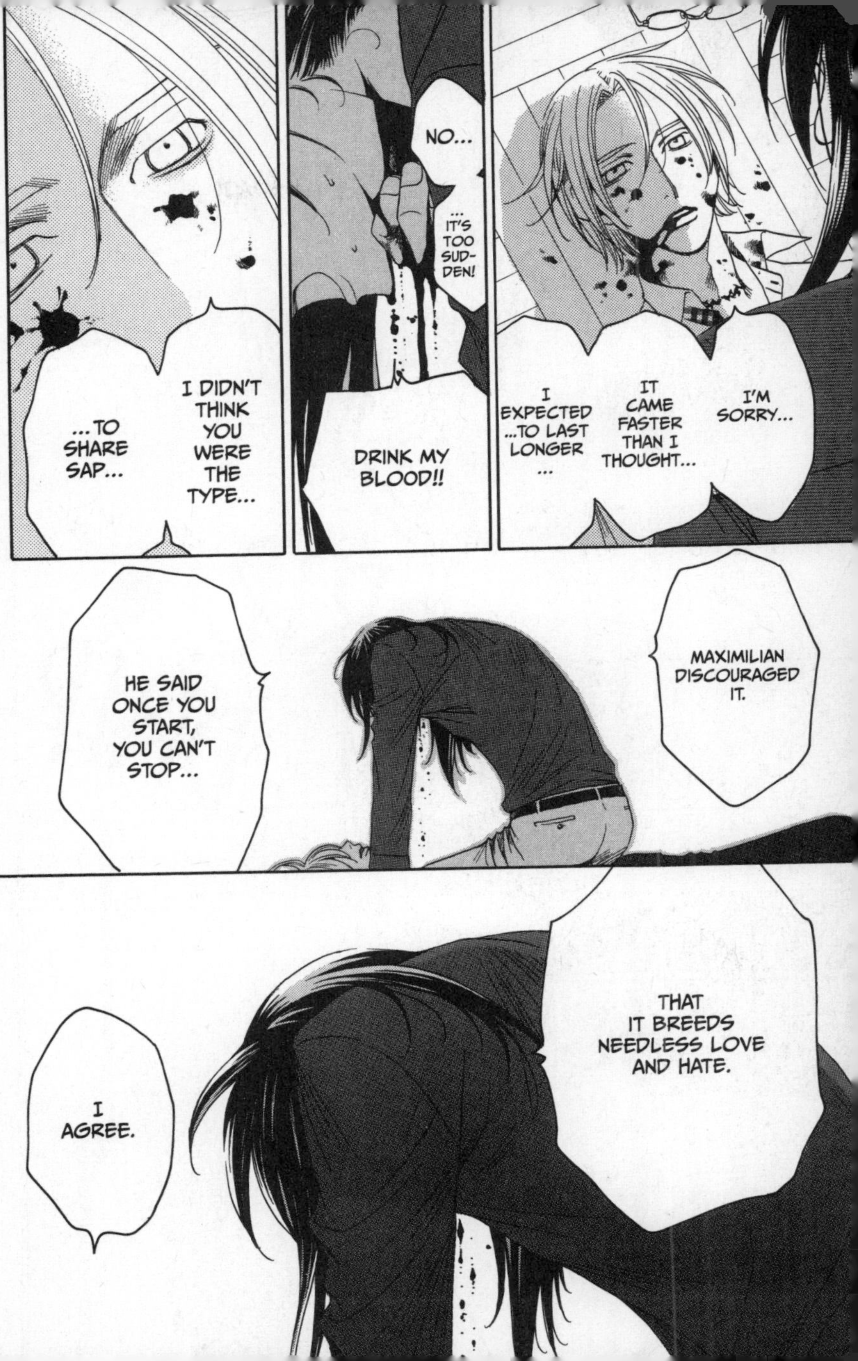
I'M SORRY...
IT CAME FASTER THAN I THOUGHT...
I EXPECTED ...TO LAST LONGER ...
NO...
...IT'S TOO SUDDEN!
DRINK MY BLOOD!!
I DIDN'T THINK YOU WERE THE TYPE...
...TO SHARE SAP...
MAXIMILIAN DISCOURAGED IT.
HE SAID ONCE YOU START, YOU CAN'T STOP...
THAT IT BREEDS NEEDLESS LOVE AND HATE.
I AGREE.

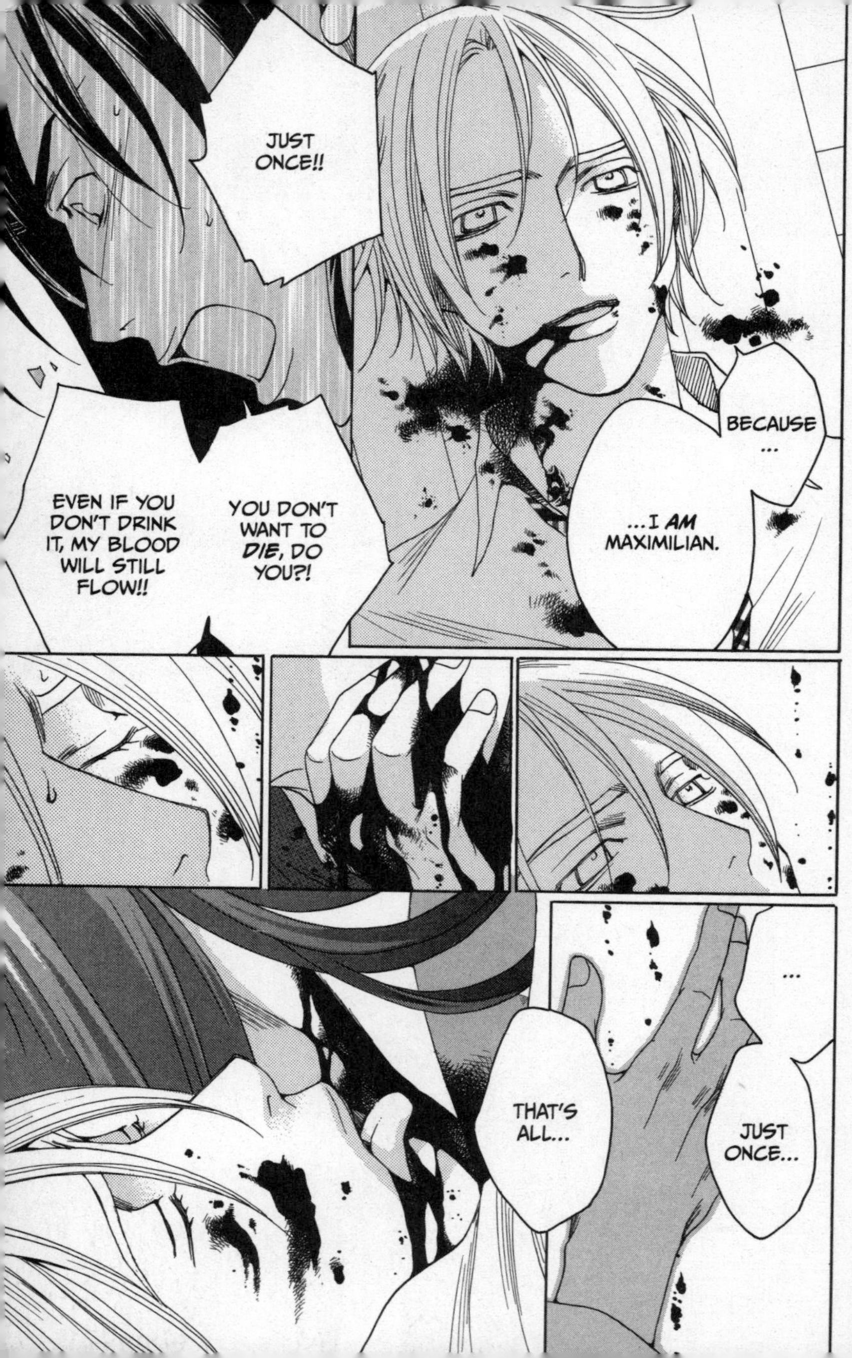

BECAUSE ...
...I *AM* MAXIMILIAN.
JUST ONCE!!
YOU DON'T WANT TO *DIE*, DO YOU?!
EVEN IF YOU DON'T DRINK IT, MY BLOOD WILL STILL FLOW!!
...
JUST ONCE...
THAT'S ALL...

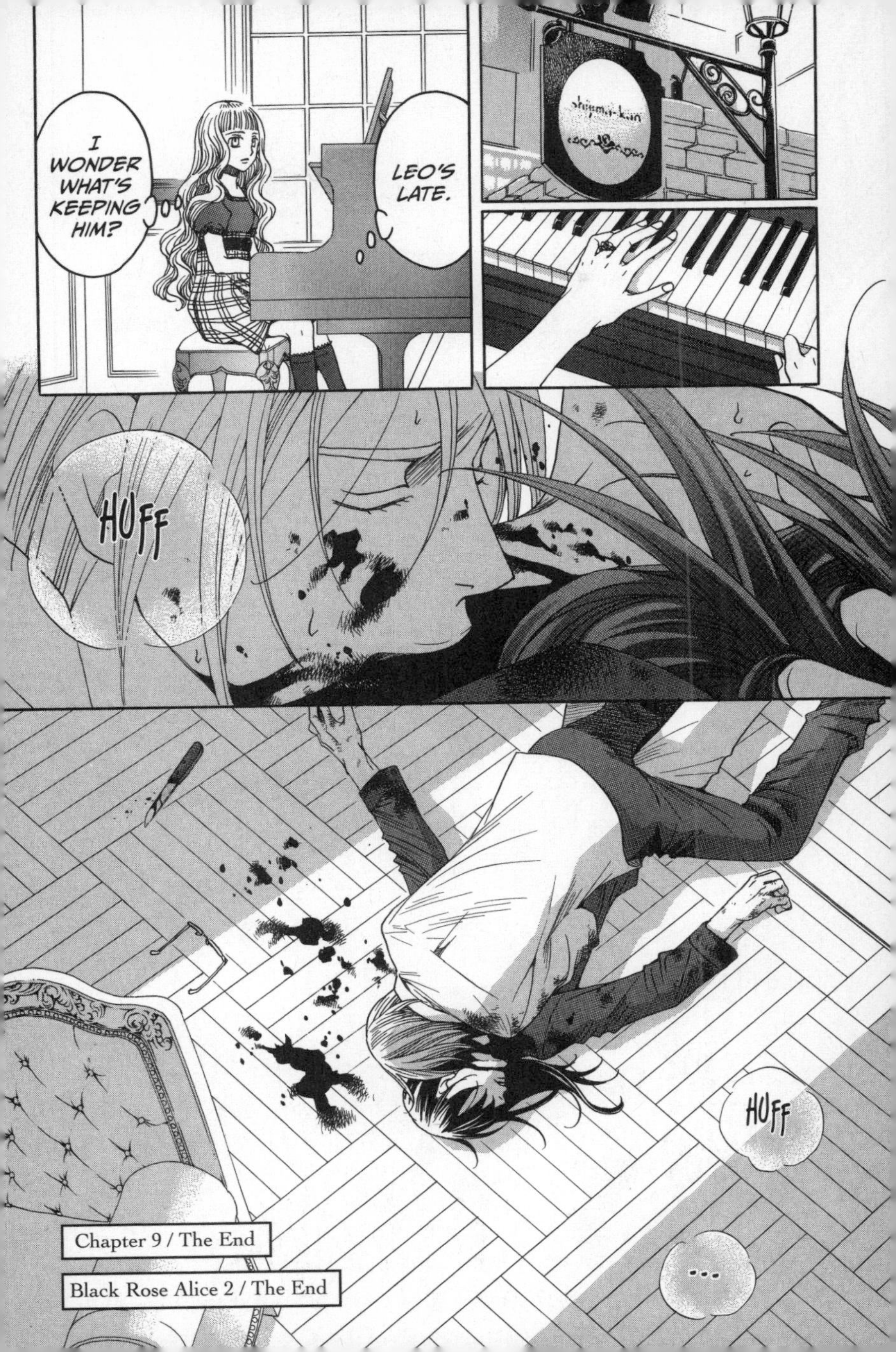
LEO'S LATE.
I WONDER WHAT'S KEEPING HIM?
HUFF
HUFF
...
Chapter 9 / The End
Black Rose Alice 2 / The End

I always wanted to draw a manga with a Lolita-style heroine.
But inside she's 28!
TOO BAD!
And her body's 116!

Visit Setona Mizushiro's official homepage: http://www.page.sannet.ne.jp/setona

Sometimes I have to draw things I don't like. In this series, it was bugs.

As I was drawing them, however, I started to enjoy it.

I like to draw plants, and I enjoy animals and birds, too. I enjoy drawing living things.

When it comes to people, I enjoy drawing them, but I also like writing their dialogue. It's exciting to write scenes of conflict in which characters cut loose and let their egos battle it out!

–Setona Mizushiro

Setona Mizushiro's professional debut was *"Fuyu ga Owarou to Shiteita"* (Winter Was Ending), and her series *After School Nightmare* was nominated for an Eisner and recognized by YALSA as a great graphic novel for teens in 2007.